HOME BASE
HIKING
EUROPE

HOME BASE
HIKING
EUROPE

An Explore-on-Foot Guide to
Unforgettable Destinations

CASSANDRA OVERBY

Foreword by RICK STEVES

**MOUNTAINEERS
BOOKS**

For Mac and June and Ginger. The three-month research trip for this book was an ambitious undertaking for our family. Thanks for hanging in there with me. Girls, I love seeing how much you took from our travels, the way you pepper everyday life with foreign phrases and ask if we can spend the weekends in Europe because you miss it. I didn't discover travel until I was an adult—it makes me so happy that you won't know life without it.

MOUNTAINEERS BOOKS is dedicated to the exploration, preservation, and enjoyment of outdoor and wilderness areas.

1001 SW Klickitat Way, Suite 201, Seattle, WA 98134
800-553-4453, www.mountaineersbooks.org

Printed in China
First edition, 2024

Design and layout: Amelia von Wolffersdorff
Cartographer: Lohnes & Wright
All photographs by the author unless credited otherwise
Cover photographs: (front, clockwise from top left) Calella de Palafrugell, Costa Brava, Spain (Destination 3); Swiss National Day celebration in Wengen (Destination 6; photo courtesy Männlichenbahn); Wengen, Jungfrau region, Switzerland (Destination 6; photo courtesy Jungfrau Region Tourismus AG); View of Berchtesgaden, Germany (Destination 9) from the Berggaststätte Kneifelspitze mountain hut; The Soleleitungsweg Ramsau (Hike 9B), in Germany's Berchtesgaden National Park; (back, from top) Dürnstein, in the Wachau Valley, Austria (Destination 10; photo courtesy Donau Niederösterreich, extremfotos.com); Savica Waterfall in Slovenia (Hike 5A); The trail from Palamós to Calella de Palafrugell (Hike 3A)
Frontispiece: Want solitude in the Alps? Head to Slovenia (Destination 5)
Photos, page 13: In Europe, you can often gondola up and hike down. (Photo courtesy Jungfrau Region Tourismus AG); page 167: Wengen's Swiss National Day celebration is a must-do if you're there on August 1; Hvar Fortress offers beautiful views of Hvar Town (Hike 8B); page 293: You can hike to Double Lake, near Lake Bohinj, on Hike 5D, Seven Lakes Valley Loop; page 312: European walking shoes are great trail—and town—shoes; page 317: Taking a wine break on trail is one of the advantages of carrying a wine bladder.

Library of Congress Cataloging-in-Publication Data is available at https://lccn.loc.gov/2024004657. The LC ebook record is available at https://lccn.loc.gov/2024004658.

Mountaineers Books titles may be purchased for corporate, educational, or other promotional sales, and our authors are available for a wide range of events. For information on special discounts or booking an author, contact our customer service at 800-553-4453 or mbooks@mountaineersbooks.org.

Printed on FSC-certified materials

ISBN (paperback): 978-1-68051-615 9
ISBN (ebook): 978-1-68051-616-6

MIX
Paper | Supporting responsible forestry
FSC
www.fsc.org   FSC® C188448

An independent nonprofit publisher since 1960

CONTENTS

FOREWORD

by Rick Steves

Imagine: You're walking high above the valleys in the Swiss Alps, tight-roping along a ridge. On one side, you've got lakes stretching all the way to Germany. On the other, it's the most glorious mountain panorama: the Eiger, Mönch and Jungfrau. And ahead of you, you hear the long legato tones of an alpenhorn announcing that the helicopter-stocked mountain hut is open... it's just around the corner... and the coffee schnapps is on. It's moments like this—merging the wonders of nature and the tasty joys of local culture—that hikers enjoy in Europe. And in this book, Cassandra Overby shares how to cobble these experiences together into a great vacation with efficiency and ease, using just the right home base as a springboard for exploration.

I first met Cass several years ago when she was a guest on my radio show, and I was immediately taken by her love of travel, her love of hiking, her love of Europe . . . and how mission-driven she is to share that love with fellow travelers. How taken was I? I flew her to France to join our TV crew as my on-camera sidekick on the long-distance Tour du Mont Blanc trail around Western Europe's highest mountain.

We had such fun faking for the camera that we were actually hiking the full 100-mile trail that I later returned to really do it. It was my first real vacation in years . . . enjoying a dimension of Europe that, after decades of travel, I'd never really appreciated: mixing European nature and culture with hikes on the Continent's venerable long-distance trails. And with Cass's savvy advice, it was a great vacation.

Cass thinks like a tour organizer and a parent combined, with a practical and spritely mix of helpful tips, on-the-trail efficiency and love. And that comes across clearly in this book. You'll hear her voice as you read it, and with her personally selected ten favorite towns for "star hiking," you'll be confident in her home base hiking suggestions.

With this book, Cass has found a travelers' need and filled it. Whether you're an older traveler with young-at-heart dreams looking for a "soft" adventure (like me) or a family eager to expose your children to the joy of hiking overseas, *Home Base Hiking Europe* provides a well-designed

Filming with Rick Steves in the French Alps and showing him my favorite way to explore Europe—on foot— was a blast.

template for enjoying your choice of hiking vacation, using ideal towns as a springboard to a series of generally easy but super-rewarding hikes. Cass recognizes the unique joy Europe offers hikers with its mix of traditional cultures (and cuisines), awe-inspiring nature and well-designed trails—while splicing in practicalities such as the advantages of loop trails and how lifts and public transportation can ensure maximum hiking rewards for your time and energy.

My world is made more fun, meaningful and accessible by the teaching and support of great tour guides. I love how guides are simply wired to educate, entertain and inspire. And with Cassandra Overby, you get a mountain guide who loves her work and knows how to write. It's her hope (and mine) that this book will help you turn your European hiking dreams into smooth and affordable reality. *Bon voyage, gute Reise,* and *buen camino!*

INTRODUCTION: START HERE

There's nothing I love more than exploring Europe on foot—breathing in the fresh alpine air, walking between charming villages, getting a hot meal and a cold beer in a mountain hut along the way. And my favorite kind of walk has always been a long trail—one with prescribed daily stages to take me to a different village or hut each night.

That changed when I decided to take my then one-year-old to Europe for her first big hiking trip. Suddenly I saw the appeal of choosing one village to home base in and hike from, which the Europeans refer to as "star hiking." To start with, it would greatly simplify our planning. We could focus on booking one place to stay, rather than a different place for each night. And once we arrived and unpacked, we'd be set for the week. That was especially important because we'd be traveling with a portable crib, a travel stroller and plenty of other kid items we normally didn't hike with. But I looked forward to it for other reasons as well. The time we'd save by not packing and unpacking our bags each day could be spent in delicious ways—savoring an extra cup of coffee on our balcony before hitting the trail, lingering in the requisite hot shower that followed every long hike and preceded dinner. We'd certainly have more time to explore. Home basing in one village would also give us options. If it poured one day, we could pivot and explore something indoors. If we were tired, we could change up our itinerary and swap in one of the shorter day hikes on our list. What sold my husband was the promise of hiking each day with a light day pack, rather than a full travel backpack.

All of those things combined made our first home base hiking trip a huge hit. But the real difference-maker was something I hadn't foreseen: **By staying in one spot for longer and living like locals, we got to know our village so much more deeply than if we had only been passing through.**

Our first night in town, we got a dinner recommendation from the farmer we were renting a room from. We loved that restaurant so much that we went back almost every night of the trip. By the end, the waiter knew us by name and the gaggle of little girls who lived above the restaurant (the owners' daughters) would watch for us out the window, scrambling down the stairs

Berchtesgaden, Germany (Destination 9), is one of my favorite towns for home base hiking Europe. (Photo courtesy Berchtesgadener Land Tourismus)

as soon as we arrived. While we ate, they played with our daughter June, holding her hand and giggling as she toddled around the restaurant. It wasn't just the people at the restaurant whom we made a connection with. It was the local butcher who advised us on the best cured meats for our trail snacks; it was the checker at the supermarket who sold us the local wine and cheese we also hiked with.

Getting to know the village and the people who lived there made the hiking part of our trip more fun and meaningful than it otherwise would've been. The hikes we did weren't just some of the best hikes in the world—they were the personal favorites of the people we'd met, to

places they were really proud of. Taking a nearby gondola up a world-famous ski area and walking around the top wasn't just an incredible alpine hiking experience, it was a way to see where people in the valley taught their kids to ski. Walking from our village to the next one over, through a picturesque valley of bright grass and colorful wildflowers, didn't just have us reaching for our cameras. It had us talking—about where our farmer's cows grazed each day and about the other farms we'd seen mentioned on restaurant menus and were now walking right past. The more we got to know our village, the more we enjoyed our hikes. The more we enjoyed our hikes, the more connected we felt to our village.

Hiking isn't just a form of exercise; it's also a better, more authentic way to travel. Here are the top five reasons why:

1 You catch a more genuine glimpse of the culture. There's something about traveling on foot that makes you more accessible to local people and thus more likely to be brought into the fold.

2 You have historical wonders all to yourself. You get to see important places that don't get visited as often, because they're not convenient to get to or are downright inaccessible by car or coach.

3 You gain a greater appreciation for the landscape. As Robert and Martha Manning, authors of *Walking Distance*, write, "The deliberate pace of walking allows us to more fully sense the world, to see its richness of detail, to touch, hear, smell and even taste it."

4 You have a better experience for less money. Your main activity each day is walking—not purchasing admission into expensive attractions or paying for spendy tours—so you don't have a lot of costs beyond gear, food and accommodations.

5 You have the restorative experience that vacation is meant to be. Exploring on foot can help you unplug, focus on your body and find your own pace.

There's so much to look forward to when it comes to exploring on foot—and there's no better place to do it than Europe. I've explored a lot of places around the world, from Central America to Southeast Asia, but I keep coming back to Europe time and time again. From world-class trails that suit every kind of interest and walker to impressive public transportation, plenty of on-trail accommodations and a variety of services that make hiking a breeze, Europe has everything it takes to be your favorite place to walk.

I knew there needed to be a guide for this kind of hiking—it was that amazing—but I couldn't find one. There are some guidebooks for day hiking Europe, but the hikes they feature are one-offs that are scattered around various countries or regions, not grouped into vacation-friendly trips. These day hiking guides focus almost exclusively on the hikes themselves, not on the greater package of a cultural hiking adventure in which local villages and their history, cuisine and other can't-miss attractions are just as important as the walking. So I did what has become my habit—I wrote the book I wanted to read.

As I started writing and talking about my new project, I was encouraged by the number of people who connected with the concept of home base hiking Europe. And it wasn't just young families like mine. The idea held especially great appeal for active older adults who are flocking to adventure travel, particularly "soft" adventure travel (think more creature comforts and less roughing it), in record numbers. Those who were new to hiking as a form of travel also found it attractive because of the simplicity of planning a home base hiking trip and the ability to choose hikes that are as easy or as challenging as desired. And even the most seasoned of travelers were intrigued by the countless combinations of very different villages and hikes to choose from in Europe.

The timing for this book couldn't be better. During the COVID-19 pandemic, so many people discovered the joys of hiking for the first time. Now we're riding an epic post-pandemic travel wave, one that has people taking their love of hiking on the road—or on the plane—more than ever before. We were pent up for so long, deprived of travel and human connection, each as essential to our souls as oxygen is to the brain. This is our chance to get both—hiking in some of the most incredible places in Europe in a more meaningful

way, one that encourages a real connection to local people and their beloved places.

I hope this book helps you feed your soul, one hike at a time.

WHAT THIS BOOK COVERS

In a matter of weeks or months, you'll be on trail in some incredible European country, having the time of your life. To get there, you and I have some work to do. In time, we'll tackle everything you need to plan your perfect trip. But first things first: You have to figure out what your perfect trip looks like. And for that, you have some dreaming to do.

Whether you prefer to do your own trip planning or would rather simply follow my recommendations, Part 1: Find Your Perfect European Home Base will help you get started. Chapter 1, Learn the Secret Sauce of Home Base Hiking, teaches you how to research and design your own trip: learn to identify villages that make ideal

A NOTE ABOUT SAFETY

Safety is an important concern in all outdoor activities. No guidebook can alert you to every hazard or anticipate the limitations of every reader. Therefore, the descriptions of roads, trails, routes and natural features in this book are not representations that a particular place or excursion will be safe for your party. When you follow any of the routes described in this book, you assume responsibility for your own safety. Under normal conditions, such excursions require the usual attention to traffic, road and trail conditions, weather, terrain, the capabilities of your party and other factors. Keeping informed on current conditions and exercising common sense are the keys to a safe, enjoyable outing.

Political conditions may add to the risks of travel in ways that this book cannot predict. When you travel, you assume this risk and should keep informed of political developments that may make safe travel difficult or impossible.

—MOUNTAINEERS BOOKS

These two kiddos have certainly made our packs heavier, but Mac and I now get the pleasure of introducing them to the kind of travel we love best.

but Part 2 breaks down your biggest considerations when it comes to planning and packing. Before you know it, you'll be ready to go.

Chapter 3, Prime Your Body, provides helpful advice about training for your time on trail and dealing with any aches and pains that come up in the process. In Chapter 4, Build Your Skills, you'll learn five key skills that can greatly improve your experience of hiking Europe. And in Chapter 5, Pack Your Bags, you'll get my top tips for trail clothes, trail shoes, day packs and day pack essentials to bring with you on your trip.

Turn to the back of the book to find Online Resources, which lists web addresses or contact information for services and attractions along the way that have a web presence (most do, but some don't). This list comes in handy for verifying that places are still open and checking their hours of operation.

– *Cass*

home bases for active adventuring and find nearby hikes that show off the best of the region.

Want to skip the research and start booking your dream trip? In Chapter 2, Get a Recommendation, I give you ten handpicked suggestions—the destinations I love more than any others for home base hiking Europe. Each destination has an in-depth guide that includes an overview of the region, why it's worth visiting and my personal recommendations on when to go, where to stay, which hikes best showcase the area and what can't-miss attractions should be on your itinerary.

Once you've made a decision on your ideal home base and the trails you'll hike, move on to Part 2: Plan and Pack for the nuts and bolts of putting together your trip. Planning a big trip can be intimidating— there are so many things to think about!—

PS: I love hearing your stories and adventures of exploring Europe on foot. Keep sending them to me at exploreonfoot@ gmail.com. You can find helpful resources, including my other books and my trip consulting service, at exploreonfoot.com.

FIND YOUR PERFECT EUROPEAN HOME BASE

1

LEARN THE SECRET SAUCE OF HOME BASE HIKING

When I put together my first home base hiking trip to Europe, I had no idea that I was embarking on a spin-off of *Explore Europe on Foot* that would revolutionize how my family and I traveled. All I knew was that I needed to find somewhere chill to hang out and hike for a couple of weeks on the heels of a week of village-to-village hiking in Germany, a trip that I was leading for extended family with my toddler, thirteen-month-old June, in tow (or rather, on my back). My head was already swimming with all of the logistics required to bring her along. Even with luggage transfer to ease the additional load of June's crib, the travel stroller and everything else she required, I knew that week in Germany was going to be challenging. But this was my first trip to Europe since becoming a mom, and darn it if I wasn't going to enjoy it and stay as long as I could. So I got online to find a couple of towns where we could stay for a week each and day hike, exploring Europe on foot without all of the logistics of switching accommodations and villages.

It was tougher than I thought. After writing *Explore Europe on Foot: Your Complete Guide to Planning a Cultural Hiking Adventure*, I was a pro at finding long trails to hike in Europe, but when I attempted to find incredible villages with equally incredible day hikes on tap, I hit a wall—or rather,

The trails along the Costa Brava, Spain (Destination 3), often lead to incredible beaches. (Photo courtesy Camí de Ronda® company)

a mountain. Everything that came up in my search results was in the Alps. Now, I love the Alps, but I *knew* other experiences existed too. So I set about figuring out how to find them. What I learned in the process of putting together that initial home base hiking trip—and the many that came after it—is that it first helps to define exactly what you're looking for in a home base. Once you do that, you can drill down to the best options with a two-pronged research approach, flesh out those options with more in-depth research and then finalize an itinerary that's perfect for you.

DEFINE THE IDEAL

There's more to the ideal home base than a nice village or region and nearby opportunities to hike. To pull off an adventure that's every bit as fulfilling as exploring an iconic village-to-village or hut-to-hut route, you need a village that's small enough to feel local but big enough to have everything a visitor needs: restaurants, accommodations, a tourist information office nearby and cultural attractions worth doing and seeing. You also need plenty of local hikes to choose from, and not just any hikes—diverse hikes that showcase the very best

World War I history is on full display in the Somme, France (Destination 2).

Where Europe doesn't shine is in marketing the amazing home base hiking opportunities it offers. But you can get good information about Europe's incredible towns and fantastic hiking if you research these topics separately. Understanding that is a game changer. All you have to do is let either the hiking or the home base take center stage in your research until you find its perfect match.

When deciding on a home base hiking trip, keep in mind that some destinations are hikeable only in certain seasons. High-elevation trails, like those in the Alps, are available only in high summer, typically from mid-June to early September, when the mountains and trails are snow-free. Mediterranean destinations like the Dalmatian Coast, in Croatia, are best in the spring and fall because summer can be prohibitively hot.

of the area, from its history to its culture to its landscape. I'm not one for seeing the same scenery twice, so if you're anything like me, that means you're also looking primarily for loop hikes or point-to-point hikes—and a robust local network of public transportation to make those point-to-point hikes possible. It seems like a tall order, and in North America it would be. Lucky for you and me, this is where Europe—with its quaint villages, walking culture and efficient public transportation—shines.

What does that look like in practice? Two great examples are Costa Brava in Spain (see Home Base 3) and the Somme in France (see Home Base 2). I found Costa Brava after searching for the best coastal trails in the Mediterranean and landing on the Camí de Ronda trail system. I knew I wanted to walk those trails, so I researched towns in the area until I found Calella de Palafrugell, which had everything I was looking for. The process was reversed with the Somme. I had read about the area's extensive World War I history and wanted to learn about it and explore the memorials in person, so I researched trails in the region and came up with several that showcased the things I wanted to see. Both spots were terrific home base hiking experiences.

Start Your Research with Trails You Want to Hike

Here are my top resources and things to keep in mind when you let the hiking take the lead in your research:

Protected land: Great hiking is typically available in protected land like national parks, natural parks and UNESCO World Heritage sites. As a bonus, sometimes park staff offer guided excursions (especially helpful for solo travelers) or family-centered activities.

Ski areas: All of those winter ski runs become summer hiking trails—often with lifts that can take you up to flat ridges or downhill hikes.

Online roundups: I'm a big fan of gathering hiking ideas from online roundups that are compiled by fellow hikers and travelers. I typically search for things like "best hikes in Europe," "best hikes in the Alps" or "best hikes in Germany" and then drill down to specific ideas from there.

Longer trails: You can break up longer village-to-village or hut-to-hut routes and day hike the most appealing individual stages. Transportation to and from these point-to-point hikes may be challenging in some locales. It's easy in a spot like the Swiss Alps, where there's great public transportation to trailheads, even ones that feel like they're in the middle of nowhere. It's a little tougher somewhere like rural Spain, where you often need a car to get around. In that case, the easiest thing to do is to park at the trailhead and have a local taxi pick you up once you're done hiking to take you back to your car.

Start Your Research with a Place You Want to Visit

You can also look for spots you want to explore in Europe and find hikes nearby. Here are my preferred resources and things to keep in mind when you let the home base take the lead in your research:

Web searches: If I know where I want to home base, I always start my hike research with an internet search for "best hikes in or around [insert destination name]."

Regional or town-focused tourism websites: Most regions and towns have tourism websites that drive people toward the best activities in that area, including the best hikes. Bonus: The local tourist information office can usually suggest a great hike for you based on your interests and abilities.

Regional hiking guidebooks: If you know the region you want to visit, regional guidebooks can help you piece together several appealing hikes.

Viator or Tripadvisor: These sites are useful for finding guided hikes by area. Hiking with a guide is an especially good idea if you want to have an active adventure that's a little more technical or demanding than what you're comfortable doing alone.

Meetup.com, volksmarching clubs and other local hiking clubs: These are great for going where the locals go—with them! When I was staying in Italy's Piedmont region, I found a hiking group that met weekly for sunset hikes and joined in, and it was one of the highlights of my time there. I gained a much better appreciation for the local people and got a lot of tips on the area from those who knew it best.

CHOOSE YOUR HIKES

Once you've landed on a home base with a handful of suitable hiking options, it's time to narrow down your routes. At a minimum, you'll need to know the following about the trails you're considering: length, approximate walking time, elevation gain and loss, what you'll see on trail, if the trail is well signed, what services are available en route and where to get paper maps and GPX tracks. (GPX tracks are similar to a GPS route you might get from Google Maps for driving directions, but they're for walking on trails; see the Learn How to Hike with the Help of GPS Data section in Chapter 4.)

While that information may be available wherever you initially found the trail, it can help to consult multiple resources, particularly when it comes to maps and GPX tracks. Local tourist information offices can often tell you whether a trail is well signed and what services, like mountain huts, are available en route. They can also help you find paper maps. Online trail databases like AllTrails and Outdooractive can be great sources of downloadable GPX tracks—and trail reviews by hikers who have done the route.

The detailed trail information you gather will help you choose the trails that best match what you want to see, how much of a physical challenge you're looking for and how long you want to

HOW DO I GET TO THE TRAILHEAD?

When researching your options for getting around your home base and to any trailheads, it can help to consult the following resources:

- **Google Maps:** I always start my transportation research with Google Maps. Its database contains quite a few buses and trains in Europe, as well as good driving and walking directions.
- **Local tourist information offices:** These are helpful for getting an overview of what public transportation is like in the area, as well as finding information on lesser-known routes. And you don't need to wait until you're there—they usually have a contact form or an email address on their website so you can get help in advance of your trip.
- **Rome2Rio:** This online aggregator gives you an overview of what transportation is available in an area, how long it takes and what it costs so you can choose between the different options and dive into specifics.
- **Bahn.de:** The German rail company's accurate and easy-to-use website is my go-to resource for train timetables throughout Europe, not just Germany.

spend walking each day. It'll also go a long way toward guaranteeing that the hikes you choose will be easily navigable, which is especially important when you hike in a foreign country, where you're already somewhat out of your comfort zone.

Speaking and/or reading the language of the place where you want to walk makes the research process a lot easier—you'll be able to quickly and easily access non-English, locals-only information. If you don't speak the local language, try copying and pasting online trail descriptions and other information into Google Translate or install a browser add-on that translates websites automatically.

PUT TOGETHER YOUR ITINERARY

Because of the long travel time required to get to Europe and the time change and jet lag you initially have to adjust to once you're there, I recommend planning a trip of at least nine days (one work week and the two weekends bookending it). Once you account for travel days and a rest day in the middle of your hikes, that leaves room for four hikes. Here's a sample itinerary:

SATURDAY: Travel day—fly to Europe

SUNDAY: Travel day—arrive in Europe (because of the time change) and travel to your home base

MONDAY: Walk day 1

TUESDAY: Walk day 2

WEDNESDAY: Rest day—explore, take a break, etc.

THURSDAY: Walk day 3

FRIDAY: Walk day 4

SATURDAY: Travel day—make your way back to the major city you flew into

SUNDAY: Travel day—fly back home

HOW FAR IN ADVANCE SHOULD I BOOK MY TRIP?

Aim to book your flights, accommodations and any guided excursions or popular museum tickets at least six months before your trip. Booking early will guarantee you the best prices and the best selection, especially when it comes to choice accommodations. You should purchase any long-distance train tickets (such as from the airport to your home base) three months before your trip, when the cheapest fares are typically released. Local point-to-point train and bus fares can be purchased on your trip as needed.

TIP: Rest days are really important. Especially if you're not used to walking multiple hours a day (and who is?), your body—particularly your legs—will likely need the break. Plan a rest day after every two to three walking days. It's a nice change of pace: You can wake up a little later, take things easy and explore something you wouldn't have made time for otherwise. By the next morning, you'll be rested up and itching to get back out on trail.

If you have two weeks to travel, your hiking time balloons from four days to ten.

It can be tough to find ten amazing (and varied) hikes in a single area, so consider chaining multiple destinations together, like I did on my initial home base hiking trip. For example, the itinerary here could be a six-hike destination and a four-hike destination, two three-hike destinations and a four-hike destination, or a three-hike destination and a seven-hike destination. Your itinerary could look more like this:

SATURDAY: Travel day—fly to Europe

SUNDAY: Travel day—arrive in Europe (because of the time change) and travel to your (first) home base

MONDAY: Walk day 1

TUESDAY: Walk day 2

WEDNESDAY: Walk day 3

THURSDAY: Rest day—explore and take a break, or travel to your next home base

FRIDAY: Walk day 4

SATURDAY: Walk day 5

SUNDAY: Walk day 6

MONDAY: Rest day—explore and take a break, or travel to your next home base

TUESDAY: Walk day 7

WEDNESDAY: Walk day 8

THURSDAY: Walk day 9

FRIDAY: Walk day 10

SATURDAY: Travel day—make your way back to the major city you flew into

SUNDAY: Travel day—fly back home

SO MANY TRAILS, SO LITTLE TIME

You may be on the hunt for one particular home base for your trip, but don't let all of the other great home bases fall by the wayside. Keep those ideas for the future. I have two separate files for trail inspiration: one is an online folder that lives in my browser; the other is a paper folder that sits on my bookshelf. Whenever I find information on a trail or home base I want to consider for the future, I add it to the appropriate file. That way, the next time I want to travel (or when I need to remember why I'm saving money or working so hard), I can page through the ideas and get inspired.

When planning which hikes to do on which days, order your trails intentionally. Longer or harder trails are best done on days when your legs are fresh, and if you have a trail that takes longer to get to, sandwich it between trails that are closer to your home base.

GET A RECOMMENDATION:

TEN HANDPICKED HOME BASES

Some people love researching and finding their own travel destinations and hikes that are off the radar. If that's you, I hope Chapter 1 gave you a better understanding of where to start when it comes to finding your own incredible home base for hiking Europe. But if you prefer personal recommendations rather than doing all of the research yourself, or if you want somewhere to start, you're in luck because I'm about to let you in on my ten favorite home bases (see Home Bases at a Glance on page 25 for a summary). I think you'll love them as well. Here's why:

They're impressive: I've done a lot of exploring on foot, so the bar I have for European villages and memorable trails is pretty darn high. These home bases and the walks they feature are the cream of the crop—they have amazing natural beauty and showcase fascinating aspects of local culture and history. They also have a wide variety of experiences on tap, from mountains to coastal areas to vineyards.

They meet my criteria: All of these home bases and their hikes meet—and exceed—my criteria for ideal home base hiking. The villages are small but not too small, with all of the services you could need and plenty of cultural attractions. The hikes (and a couple of great bike rides!) offer diverse experiences that showcase the best of the local area, are mainly point-to-point

While I love hiking in Europe, I also appreciate a good bike ride, especially if it gives me a good overview of the local area.

or loop routes so you don't have to repeat scenery and include all of the information you need to hike them—including GPX tracks (see the "Home Base GPX Tracks" sidebar in the Online Resources section at the back of the book). Nearly all of these villages and hikes have great public transportation to boot, so generally you won't have to worry about getting around. That said, I do note the areas where it's easiest to just rent a car.

They've been optimized: I stayed in all of these villages and hiked all of the trails myself, so my recommendations reflect more than just research—they reflect personal experience. In many cases, I modified the routes after hiking them to make them more interesting or accessible. For example, my routes around the memorials of the Somme (see Home Base 2) are based on routes put together by the local tourism bureau but have been modified to see even more local history and take in local cuisine.

HOW TO USE THE HOME BASE WRITE-UPS

Each of the ten handpicked home bases in this chapter includes a variety of information to introduce you to the region you'll experience, the village I recommend home basing in and the hikes I suggest. All of that should help you compare them and determine the best fit for you.

The Home Bases

The write-ups start with a high-level overview in a section titled **At a Glance**, which includes the general location of the region, the town that will serve as your home base, the local language, use of English and how family friendly the destination is on a scale of one to four, with one star being a spot you would ideally visit without kids and four stars being a spot you should absolutely seek out if you're traveling with kids. I've also included information on the relative cost of vacationing in each destination. From one to four dollar signs, the symbols represent a destination that is cheap ($), budget friendly ($$), affordable ($$$) or expensive ($$$$). There's also

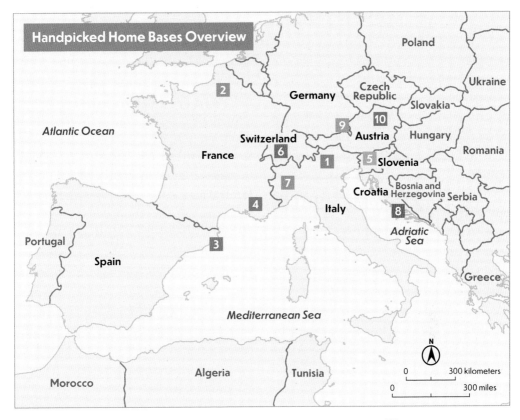

Handpicked Home Bases Overview

1 The Dolomites, Italy **2** The Somme, France **3** Costa Brava, Spain **4** Provence, France
5 Lake Bohinj, Slovenia **6** The Jungfrau, Switzerland **7** The Piedmont, Italy **8** Dalmatia,
Croatia **9** Berchtesgaden National Park, Germany **10** The Wachau Valley, Austria

information about when to go, what kind of scenery to expect and what experiences you shouldn't miss.

> In general, a walking vacation in Europe is far more kid friendly than you would expect—many of the mountain huts and villages have fun playgrounds for keeping little ones entertained on trail, and some natural parks and destinations also have kid-specific programming.

A summary follows, which tells you why I chose the region, why it's worth visiting, what to expect from the recommended village and what it's like home base hiking there. This is where you can ascertain the *essence* of each place—for me, one of the most important considerations when choosing where to go.

After the summary, I provide helpful information for planning your trip. **Getting There and Around** lists nearby airports and provides tips on how to get to your home base, as well as how to get around during your stay. Most often this will be public transportation, but I note the destinations where having a car is more convenient.

The **Where to Stay** section offers tips on booking accommodations and includes any alternate home bases I recommend for the area.

Eat and Resupply provides details on buying groceries, eating out and where to go if you need to adjust or add to your outdoor gear. This section also lists local food specialties you'll want to seek out—after all, one of the best parts of exploring Europe on foot is the amazing comfort food you can fuel your body with along the way.

I then give you tips on **What to See and Do** that highlight the best cultural attractions in the area—perfect for your rest days. And for those traveling with kids, I include my top recommendations for local activities that will be a hit with the whole family.

The Routes

Following the home base write-ups, you'll find a chart listing my recommended hikes in the area along with summary information for each route. There's also an overview map to help you determine where the trails are in relation to each other. There are four routes for each home base, the perfect number for a nine-day trip to Europe (see Put Together Your Itinerary in Chapter 1). The routes are listed in the order I suggest hiking them, but feel free to reorder them to your heart's content. Occasionally, I also include a spotlight on a local company or guide for the area.

After that, I dive into the specifics of each hike. Each route includes a descriptive summary outlining why I recommend the hike and what you'll see along the way. Then there's an information box titled **On the Trail** that contains all the stats you need to know, including the hike's duration and difficulty, which is based on a person who walks an average of 2 miles an hour

WHERE SHOULD I STAY?

Europe has a variety of accommodations, from hostels to hotels to self-catered accommodations. For home base hiking, I favor small, family-owned guesthouses and bed-and-breakfasts, where you have the opportunity to form a relationship with the owners during your stay. If you're traveling with kids, consider renting an apartment or a house so that you'll have extra room for the kids to sleep and play, laundry facilities and a kitchen—important when you don't want to eat out at every meal, especially with picky eaters. To book accommodations, I use booking.com. The local tourist information office is also a reliable source of accommodations information, especially when it comes to smaller, family-owned spots that don't want to pay the fees of the large booking websites.

HOME BASES AT A GLANCE

NO.	LOCATION	SCENERY	DON'T MISS	BEST HIKING
1	The Dolomites, Italy	Jagged Dolomites peaks, wildflower meadows, grazing cows and sheep, wooden shepherds' huts	Mountain huts, taking a lift up to high-alpine hikes, circumnavigating a mountain range, learning about South Tyrolean culture	Mid-Jun to Sept
2	The Somme, France	Peaceful river valleys, gently rolling hills, bucolic farmland, English Channel	WWI memorials and museums, British pub fare, seaside villages	Mid-Mar to Jun; Sept to Oct
3	Costa Brava, Spain	Mediterranean Sea, lighthouses, fishing villages, ancient ruins	Secluded beaches, coastal walking, fresh seafood, friendly locals	Mid-May to early Jun
4	Provence, France	Vineyards, lavender fields, hill towns, low mountains, Mediterranean Sea	Hiking village to village, French cuisine, historic abbeys, local wine	Apr to Sept
5	Lake Bohinj, Slovenia	Slovenia's highest mountain, the Julian Alps, Lake Bohinj, waterfalls	Mountain huts, taking a gondola up to high-alpine hikes, hiking in Triglav National Park	Mid-Jun to Sept
6	The Jungfrau, Switzerland	The Swiss Alps, colorful wildflowers, turquoise lakes	Mountain huts, quaint villages, Swiss comfort food, alpenhorns, *lederhosen*	Mid-Jun to Sept
7	The Piedmont, Italy	Vineyards, hazelnut orchards, hill towns	Local wine, community cantinas, Italian comfort food, *agriturismi*	May to Jun; Sept to Oct
8	Dalmatia, Croatia	Rocky Dalmatian coastline and mountains, Adriatic Sea and islands, incredible waterfalls	Secluded beaches, catamaran rides, coastal walking, warm climate	Jun; Sept
9	Berchtesgaden National Park, Germany	Berchtesgaden Alps, alpine meadows and wildflowers, Bavaria's deepest lake	Mountain huts, swimming in an alpine lake, taking a gondola up and hiking down, visiting a salt mine	Mid-Jun to Sept
10	The Wachau Valley, Austria	Extensive vineyards, the Danube River, bucolic farmland	Abbeys, castles, local wine, tiny wine-producing villages	Mar to Oct

Map Legend

☆	Recomended home base		**1**	Waypoint
→	Direction of travel		▬▬▬	Hiking trail/route
Ⓥ	Viewpoint		▬●▬	Bike route
⊕	Restroom		▪ ▪ ▪ ▪	Alternative route
⌂	Hut/restaurant/bar/hotel		⋯⋯⋯⋯	Stairs
Ⓦ	Water		▬▬▬▬	Boat route
⊟	Bus stop		———	Other trail
☷	Train station		•·•·•·•	Chairlift/gondola
🗼	Lighthouse		┝┼┼┼┤	Rail
⊿	Campground			
🏖	Beach		———	Main road
❗	Important/pay attention		———	Road
⬬	Boat/ferry		- - - - -	Dirt/gravel road
Ⓟ	Parking			
✝	Church		○	City/town/village
🎠	Playground		▲	Peak
][	Bridge		⟱	Marsh/wetland
𝝥	Table/picnic area		∥	Waterfall
⊤	Bench		～～	River/stream
•—•	Gate		⬭	Lake/ocean
▪	Point of interest		▬▬▬	Park

and can tackle a total of roughly 1,000 feet (305 m) of elevation gain. I also list distance, elevation gain and loss, the start and end of the trail and where you can eat and drink en route—helpful for when you're planning your trail snacks.

In the **Know Before You Go** section, you'll learn how well a trail is signed, if there are trail names or numbers to look out for and why the trail is rated as easy, moderate or challenging so you can better judge if the hike is a good fit for your abil-

ities. I also include essential tips for the trail in this section, such as which days are optimal for walking it based on when the attractions and services en route are open.

Alternative Routes and Activities provides tips on making the route shorter whenever possible, whether that's hiking an iconic section of it or using public transportation along the way. You'll notice that most routes don't take the full day. That's intentional, so you have part of the day to relax or explore other things (this is vacation, after all!). I give you recommendations on activities to pair with each hike, as well as ways to make the hikes themselves longer if you prefer to spend the entire day on the trail.

The **Navigating** section offers helpful tips to get to the trailhead and back to your home base once you're done hiking. This transportation information includes both public transportation, when available, and information on driving to the trailhead. This section also lists the GPS coordinates for the starting point and what services are available there, and it highlights which maps are best and where to find them.

TIP: Typically, the best spot to source your maps is also the most convenient:

the local tourist information office. In Europe, most tourist information offices are more robust than those in the US and carry a wide selection of hiking, biking and other maps.

You can download the GPX tracks that I have created for each route; see the sidebar "Home Base GPX Tracks" in the Online Resources section at the back of the book. For general information on how to navigate with GPX tracks and specific GPS coordinates, turn to the Learn How to Hike with the Help of GPS Data section in Chapter 4, where you'll also find a list of the routes from this guide where GPX tracks can be especially helpful.

For most hikes in Europe, you don't need to pack a lunch—many routes have restaurants along them, like this one on the shores of Lake Bohinj (Destination 5).

MY TOP TIPS FOR DRIVING IN EUROPE

Occasionally, it's easier and cheaper to drive in Europe than to take public transportation, especially for families. If you plan on renting a car for your trip, here are my top tips:

- Research online whether you need a vignette (like a toll sticker) to drive through the countries on your route. Some countries, like Austria and Slovenia, require them, even if you're passing through, and you can get penalized—to the tune of hundreds of euros— if you don't have one. When I was passing through Slovenia, I didn't see a single sign about needing a vignette but then got pulled over leaving the country for not having one. I was given an instant €150 fine. (They charged my credit card before allowing me to drive away.) Talk about an expensive lesson.
- Research online whether you need an International Driving Permit. Some countries like Italy and Spain require them, while in others you don't need anything beyond your regular driver's license. Although this is most important if you get pulled over, it can also be an issue when picking up your rental car.
- Even if you have a car with a navigation system, load turn-by-turn directions from Google Maps for your route. In my experience, most car navigation systems don't reroute for traffic or accidents, so Google Maps can save you a lot of time. A bonus: It will also alert you to speed zones, which most car navigation systems won't do.

One of the lengthiest sections of each hike write-up is a detailed set of directions, which are numbered to correspond to waypoints on the accompanying hike map. These walking directions include mileage (and kilometers in parentheses) to help you stay on track. Note that if you take an optional detour or walk extensively around a hut or attraction en route, your mileage will start to differ from that of the walking directions. The mileage will still be helpful, though. If, for example, you read that there's a junction at 0.4 mile (0.6 km) and a waterfall at 0.8 mile (1.3 km), even if your mileage doesn't match up (say you took an optional detour before the junction), you can still infer that the two things are 0.4 mile (0.6 km) apart, which will help you stay on track. TIP: Photocopy my walking directions so you have them with you on trail without the weight of the full book.

Occasionally, I also include a **Bonus Hike** section that lists another hike nearby, in case you have more time and would like to add another hike to your list.

The village of Santa Cristina is my favorite home base in the Dolomites. (Photo courtesy Dolomites Val Gardena—Gröden Marketing)

1 THE DOLOMITES, ITALY

Exploring the famous Dolomite Mountains of the German-speaking Italian Alps

AT A GLANCE

GENERAL LOCATION: Northern Italy

HOME BASE: Santa Cristina

LOCAL LANGUAGE: Ladin, German, Italian

USE OF ENGLISH: Widely understood and used

FAMILY FRIENDLY: ★ ★ ★ ★

COST: $$$

WHEN TO GO: Mid-Jun to Sept

SCENERY: Jagged Dolomites peaks, wildflower meadows, grazing cows and sheep, wooden shepherds' huts

DON'T MISS: Mountain huts, taking a lift up to high-alpine hikes, circumnavigating a mountain range, learning about South Tyrolean culture

When *Explore Europe on Foot* came out and I was giving book talks at libraries and bookstores to promote it, someone would invariably ask, "What about the Dolomites?" There was such curiosity about hiking these mountains of northern Italy, the "sunny side of the Alps" tucked just under Austria, that I swore I would include the Dolomites in my next book. It took a lot of research to find just the right spot. It wasn't that there was a lack of great hiking, because the Dolomites are filled with world-class hikes that could melt any seasoned traveler's heart. But I was looking for something specific, a small spot that didn't feel completely discovered, even with all of the recent interest in the area.

I was so happy to come across Val Gardena and even happier when I visited the area and found that things were better still in person than they had looked in my research. What makes Val Gardena special is that it's a valley with a collection of three little towns, all connected via frequent bus service and each with fantastic access to the mountains by gondolas and lifts. That means three times the number of home base possibilities and places to explore, each with a different flavor.

And what mountains these are! The Dolomites are so different from the other Alps. There's nothing soft or round about them. They don't lure you in with greenery and extensive forests. Instead, they put their gorgeous jagged peaks front and center. The best views of the local mountains, especially the mighty Sassolungo Group, come from my favorite home base,

the mid-valley and midsize village of Santa Cristina. If you choose your accommodations wisely, you can gaze up at the Sassolungo Group at all hours of the day, but it's especially impressive at sunrise and sunset when it takes on an ethereal glow that Italians call *l'enrosadira*.

The pale, jagged peaks and spires of the Dolomites are very different from the rest of the Alps and the other mountains of the Northern Hemisphere. That's because they're made of volcanic rock, limestone and dolomite, a rare type of limestone that contains very high levels of magnesium and was once part of the ocean floor. Due to their unique look and the rare material they're made of, the Dolomites are protected as a UNESCO World Heritage site.

The only thing better than looking at the mountains is exploring them, and that's where Val Gardena really excels. You can be in a high-alpine pasture or at the base of an impressive peak in a matter of minutes, thanks to the area's extensive selection of gondolas and lifts. The scenery rivals that of Switzerland, yet it's far cheaper, especially when you buy a multiday pass for the local transportation (see Getting There and Around).

The best time to hike the Dolomites is mid-June to September, when the mountains are snow-free and all of the hiking in the area is open and accessible. Because there are so many hiking trails in the area, you could hike all summer long and not get

When you hike in and around Santa Cristina, you can expect knockout views like this one of the Sassolungo Group.

bored—with options like a walk through Europe's largest alpine meadow or a trek to mountaintop crosses beneath the needle-like peaks of the Puez-Odle Nature Park.

Most hikes in the area pass by at least one traditional mountain hut, where you can eat and drink to your heart's content before continuing on. We're talking some of the best mountain comfort food you could ever imagine—and Austrian inspired at that, given that Val Gardena takes most of its identity from the region it's a part of, South Tyrol, rather than from its country. Historically, South Tyrol was part of the Austro-Hungarian Empire, but it was annexed to Italy in 1919, after World War I. Even today, the main language in this part of the Alps is German. Drive an hour or so east from Val Gardena, and you're back to Italian. As part of the Croda da Lago Loop (Hike 1D), you can add a day trip to Cortina in the Italian-speaking Alps, which is great for understanding the juxtaposition of the different cultures that exist in the Italian Alps.

As if dramatic mountains and rich culture weren't enough of a draw, one of the top reasons to visit Val Gardena is that the local tourist information office has made it easy to do a deep dive into both.

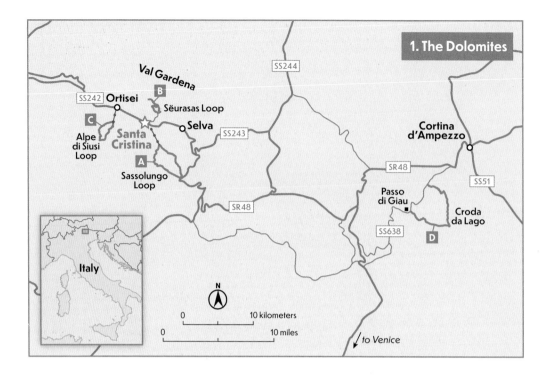

They offer extensive resources, from free maps to fun programs like cooking classes and guided hikes (see "Val Gardena Active program" in What to See and Do) that can give you the knowledge and confidence to venture farther in your explorations of the area, which is particularly valuable if you're traveling solo. Like me, you'll finally understand just why everyone is talking about the Dolomites—my new favorite Alpine destination.

Getting There and Around

While the closest airport to Val Gardena is the small one in nearby Bolzano, most people fly into one of the larger airports in the area, which are located in Innsbruck, Austria, and Venice or Milan, Italy. From the larger airports, you can take a combination of trains and buses to the town of Santa Cristina.

The best way to get around Val Gardena is by bus. The buses run frequently throughout the area, including to most trailheads, and are free with a Guest Card (see Where to Stay).

Several of my recommended hikes utilize gondolas and chairlifts. Bring the cost down by buying a Gardena Card (different from the Guest Card). This pass can be purchased for multiple days and provides unlimited rides on eighteen gondolas and lifts in Val Gardena; it can save you a lot of money. You can purchase the Gardena Card at local tourist information offices and at participating lift offices.

THE ROUTES

HIKE	ROUTE NAME	DURATION	DIFFICULTY	DISTANCE	ELEV. GAIN	ELEV. LOSS
1A	Sassolungo Loop	4.5 hours	Moderate	6 mi (9.7 km)	1,170 ft (357 m)	2,798 ft (853 m)
1B	Sëurasas Loop	3 hours	Moderate	3.8 mi (6.1 km)	1,350 ft (411 m)	1,350 ft (411 m)
1C	Alpe di Siusi Loop	2 hours	Easy	3.1 mi (5 km)	192 ft (59 m)	704 ft (215 m)
1D	Croda da Lago Loop	5 hours	Moderate	7.2 mi (11.6 km)	1,317 ft (401 m)	3,043 ft (928 m)

Where to Stay

My top choice for a home base in the Dolomites is the village of Santa Cristina, the smallest town in Val Gardena, but the nearby towns of Ortisei and Selva, on either side of Santa Cristina, could serve as alternate home bases. Ortisei is the largest town in the valley and is well known for woodcarving. Selva is the highest town in the valley.

When you book accommodations, keep in mind that most can only be booked by the week: Saturday to Saturday. Once you check in to your accommodations (as long as you're not staying in an Airbnb, which doesn't pay the local tourist tax), you'll get a Guest Card for the duration of your stay that entitles you to various discounts, including free bus rides throughout the valley.

Eat and Resupply

The village of Santa Cristina has a couple of grocery stores. It also has several restaurants and cafés. The local food reflects the

The native inhabitants of Val Gardena are the Ladins (not to be confused with the Latins), who have had a presence in the area since 5 BC. To this day, the Ladins have their own language, culture and traditions. Their language, which is spoken by about thirty thousand people in the area, is a Romance language influenced by German and Rhaetian. You'll see it on many signs in the area, along with German and Italian. The Ladin municipalities have three names. For example, the town of Ortisei (Italian) is also known as Saint Ulrich (German) and Urtijëi (Ladin).

area's regional affiliation with South Tyrol and has more in common with Austro-Hungarian cuisine than Italian cuisine. When you're out and about, be sure to track down the following local specialties:

- □ *Speck*: a cut of pork that's spiced, smoked and aged; it's typically served with *schüttelbrot*, a hard spiced bread

- *Knödel*: a version of dumplings that are flavored with cheese, pork, mushrooms, spinach or liver and often served in broth
- *Apfelstrudel*: a layered pastry filled with cooked apples, raisins and cinnamon

Both Santa Cristina and Selva have an Intersport, Europe's largest outdoor retailer, in case you need to adjust or add to your gear.

What to See and Do

VAL GARDENA ACTIVE PROGRAM

The Val Gardena Active program (see Online Resources) hosts fun summer activities for the whole family, from wine tasting to cooking classes to guided sunrise and sunset hikes. TIP: The guided sunrise *via ferrata* (a route that utilizes cables and ladders) at Grand Cir is amazing—it was the highlight of my time there. You can get a discount on Val Gardena Active program activities—or even get them for free—by staying in partner accommodations (see Online Resources).

ARTISAN MARKET

Throughout July and August, there's a weekly evening artisan market in the pedestrian area of Santa Cristina, where you can find traditional South Tyrolean handicrafts, food and music.

WOODCARVING AND LINEN SHOPS

There are many shops in Val Gardena where you can find everything from small, intricate Christmas ornaments to elaborate wooden statues—all beautifully carved—and many spots that sell handmade Italian linens. These shops are great if you want a locally made souvenir for your home. They also make for good window-shopping.

★★★★ Val Gardena gets four stars out of four for being family friendly. Kids under eight can get a multiday Gardena Card for unlimited rides on local gondolas and lifts for around €5, and for ages eight to sixteen, there's a youth card that's deeply discounted from typical adult fares.

It's a really fun spot too. Most of the huts in the area have elaborate playgrounds surrounded by tables and chairs where the rest of the family can eat and drink while the littles play. My kids especially loved the playground at Monte Pana, which also has a wooden ball drop, horse and pony rides and a kids' adventure trail called the Pana Raida.

A short walk away is Hotel Cendevaves, where kids can rent inner tubes by the hour and ride them down a track the hotel made on their steep grassy hillside. Even better: There's a magic carpet so kids can loop the track over and over again without getting tired out by the walk up.

If you'd like the kids to have some of their own activities during your time in Val Gardena—and make friends with kids from around the world—the Val Gardena Active program has drop-off camps and guided activities just for kids.

The route around the Sassolungo Group is the most iconic hike in the area. (Photo by Harald Wisthaler)

1A SASSOLUNGO LOOP

Circumnavigate the imposing Sassolungo Group

There's no more impressive view in Val Gardena than that of the Sassolungo Group, an imposing set of mountains that tower over the valley. This hike gets you close to the mountains so you can admire them in detail, leading you in a half moon around their base, then taking you up (with the help of a vintage gondola) and into their rocky core. Along the way, you'll walk through marmot-studded meadows and find several mountain huts for sustenance—and striking terrace views.

ON THE TRAIL

DURATION: 4.5 hours

DIFFICULTY: Moderate

DISTANCE: 6 miles (9.7 km)*

ELEVATION GAIN: 1,170 feet (357 m)*

ELEVATION LOSS: 2,798 feet (853 m)

START: Mont de Sëura lift station

END: Mont de Sëura lift station

EAT + DRINK: Malga Cason mountain hut, Rifugio Emilio Comici, Passo Sella Dolomiti Mountain Resort, Rifugio Toni Demetz, Rifugio Vicenza (see Online Resources)

(* See footnote next page)

Know Before You Go

Although the gondolas get you up to the level of the Sassolungo—and then into its core—there's still a decent amount of elevation gain. Also, the rocky descent through the gap can be challenging for those with stability problems or creaky knees. The route is well signed and uses Trails 526B, 528, 526 and 525.

Other notes about the route:

- This hike utilizes a total of five lifts or gondolas; it's perfect for a day when you have a Gardena Card (see Getting There and Around).
- There are several animal gates on this route—some of them electrified.

Alternative Routes and Activities

For a shorter outing, the flat section of trail between Rifugio Emilio Comici [4] and Passo Sella [6] is beautiful and has terrific views of the Sassolungo from below. Passo Sella is accessible by car and bus; the hike to Rifugio Emilio Comici and back is 3.2 miles (5.1 km) roundtrip.

Alternatively, this hike could easily take all day if you stop along the way to eat and drink. For families, Monte Pana has some impressive attractions and is a great place to explore after the hike (see What to See and Do).

Navigating

This hike starts at the top of the Mont de Sëura lift, in the remote Mont de Sëura mountain pasture at the foot of the Sassolungo. It's a short walk from the Malga Cason mountain hut, which has appetizers and desserts, as well as restrooms for customers.

STARTING POINT: **46.53892°, 11.72668°**

TRANSIT: **From Santa Cristina, take a chairlift from the valley station in town to Monte Pana, then another lift from Monte Pana to Mont de Sëura. Lift timetables can be found online (see Online Resources) or at the tourist information office in Santa Cristina.**

DRIVING: **Drive to the pay parking lot at Monte Pana and take the Mont de Sëura lift from there.** TIP: **The lot isn't large, so arrive early to get a spot—or take the lift to Monte Pana.**

MAPS: **Available at the tourist information office in Santa Cristina and tourist information offices throughout Val Gardena.**

1 From the **Mont de Sëura lift station**, exit the animal gate (beware of electrification in places, meant to keep curious cows off the lifts) into the **Mont de Sëura mountain pasture**. After taking a moment to admire the giant **Sassolungo** in front of you, head left onto wide gravel **Trail 526B**. The rustic **Malga Cason mountain hut** is on your left at 0.1 mile (0.2 km). If it's not open yet, you can always circle back to this very scenic spot after your hike and before you take the lift back down the mountain.

2 At 0.5 mile (0.8 km), go right at the junction with a trail to Tramans lift. Just

---

* This is walking distance, and it does not include the distance you travel in the Telecabin Forcella del Sassolungo. The elevation gain also reflects only the walking portion of the route. In the detailed, numbered walking directions, however, I have included the gondola ride in the mileage so people who choose to use GPX tracks don't have to remember to pause and restart them for that part of the trip.

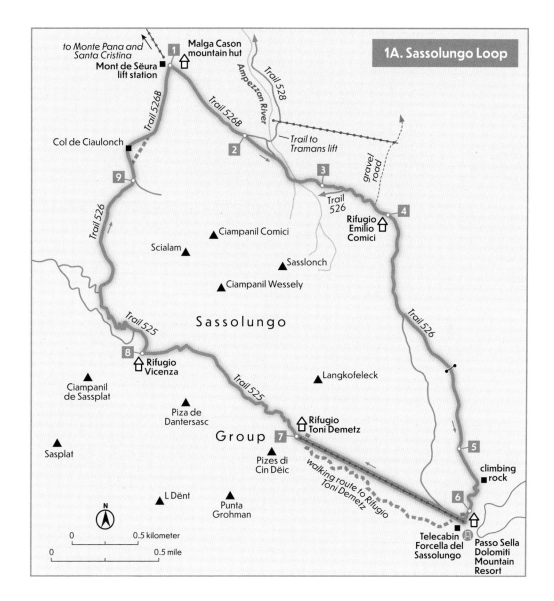

to Monte Pana and
Santa Cristina
Mont de Sëura
lift station

Malga Cason
mountain hut

1

Trail 526B

Trail 526B

Ampezzan River

Trail 528

Col de Ciaulonch

2

Trail to
Tramans lift

gravel road

3

9

Trail 526

Trail
526

Rifugio
Emilio
Comici

4

Ciampanil Comici

Scialam

Sasslonch

Ciampanil Wessely

S a s s o l u n g o

Trail 526

Trail 525

8

Rifugio
Vicenza

Langkofeleck

Ciampanil
de Sassplat

Trail 525

Piza de
Dantersasc

Rifugio
Toni Demetz

G r o u p **7**

Sasplat

Pizes di
Cin Dëic

walking route to Rifugio
Toni Demetz

5

climbing
rock

L Dënt

Punta
Grohman

6

N

0   0.5 kilometer

0   0.5 mile

Telecabin
Forcella del
Sassolungo

Passo Sella
Dolomiti
Mountain
Resort

past that, the trail passes through a pretty little forested section. You'll be above the tree line for much of this hike, so soak it in. There's another junction at 0.7 mile (1.1 km). Stay straight; **Trail 528** joins the mix, so now you're on Trail 526B/Trail 528 to Passo Sella. The trail crosses the **Ampezzan River**, more of a stream that's popular with pasturing cows, then starts to climb around boulders that have been shed by the mountain.

3 There's signage for a mountain fairy tale at 1 mile (1.6 km) that's presented in pieces. You'll see several parts of the fairy tale as you walk; unfortunately, you'll miss most of it (including the beginning)

In summer, wildflowers abound on the rocky trail circumnavigating the Sassolungo Group.

ers to enjoy—and that's before we even talk about the jaw-dropping views of the Sassolungo as you circumnavigate its base. Most of the crowds disappear at 1.9 miles (3.1 km), when you head left onto a quieter path, **Trail 526**, which stays relatively flat and has big views of the high-mountain pastures and huts to your left. At 2.3 miles (3.7 km), go through an animal gate. Just beyond that, get some knockout views of the snowy peaks ahead of you, the most imposing of which are **Gran Vernel** and **Punta Penia**—a stunning contrast to the bucolic farmland below.

5 A short, rocky section of trail starts at 2.6 miles (4.2 km). It's like you're in a rock garden, winding your way through large boulders shed by the Sassolungo amid alpine shrubs and evergreens. It's a nice, undulating path, and when the wind blows just right, the herbs underfoot smell like the Mediterranean. At 2.8 miles (4.5 km), there's a large rock that's popular for climbing classes.

6 Reach the **Passo Sella Dolomiti Mountain Resort** at 3 miles (4.8 km). The resort is accessible by car as well as foot and bike, so it's a popular destination for those wanting the big, up-close views of the Sassolungo, which you can get from the

because it doesn't exactly correspond to your route. At 1.1 miles (1.8 km), stay left at the junction with Trail 526. At 1.3 miles (2.1 km), head right on a gravel road.

4 **Rifugio Emilio Comici** is at 1.4 miles (2.3 km). Here, you'll find a restaurant, a bar, a takeaway counter and public restrooms. There are also very scenic views down to the town of **Selva** in the valley below and out to the impressive peaks of the Dolomites in the distance. TIP: For kids (or fun adults), there's a giant slide by the takeaway counter. When you're done enjoying the hut, the trail continues east along the front of it, then heads south.

From the hut, Passo Sella is signed for 40 minutes; the path between Rifugio Emilio Comici and Passo Sella is wide and busy— the busiest section you'll encounter on the route. It's not hard to see why. The trail is mainly flat and there are a lot of wildflow-

resort's large outdoor terrace, benches and lawn chairs. There's a full menu as well as a playground for kids and a little chapel you can admire. TIP: In summer, the restaurant doesn't open for food until noon, but they do serve drinks before then. When you're done at the mountain resort, walk across the grass to the **Telecabin Forcella del Sassolungo**, a vintage two-person gondola that takes you up 1,628 feet (496 m) to **Rifugio Toni Demetz**, high up in the *forcella*, or fork, of the Sassolungo. You can also walk up to the hut, which takes about an hour on the path just beneath the gondola and adds 1.3 miles (2.1 km) and 1,641 feet (500 m) of elevation gain to your hike.

7 The terrain change from down below to up top is dramatic. Gone are the lush meadows and gentle curves of the land. In their place are jagged spires of the sparkly dolomite these mountains are made of. The hut is perched on a rocky cliffside with great views down to the mountain resort and valley below. You'll likely see climbers scaling the seemingly sheer rock faces around you. There is food, as well as drinks on tap, though it can be difficult to find a table on the busy terrace. Many hikers instead choose to perch on a rock just outside the hut and eat their own snacks—or you can wait until you reach the next hut in 1 mile (1.6 km). When you're ready to continue the hike, take **Trail 525**, a rocky and sometimes steep path that travels down through the gap in the mountains. There's the occasional cable to hold on to. From here, the Mont de Sëura lift is signed for 1 hour and 40 minutes. NOTE: There are a lot of small, loose rocks on this section of trail, so take your time. Also, the trail in the gap is completely exposed and there's nowhere to tuck yourself away, so if you need to use the restroom, it's best to go at Rifugio Toni Demetz before continuing on.

8 Reach pretty **Rifugio Vicenza** at 5 miles (8 km). This makes an excellent lunch stop; it's not as busy as Rifugio Toni Demetz since there's no gondola to it, the food is very good, and it's filled with more locals. The views of the rocky gap you've been walking are lovely too. Just past the hut, at 5.2 miles (8.4 km), keep right to stay on Trail 525 and switchback down a gravel footpath in a meadow with great views across to extensive pastureland and grazing cows. At 5.6 miles (9 km), go right again, this time onto **Trail 526**, a nice ridge path that offers up more beautiful vistas of the pastures.

9 At 6.2 miles (10 km), go left for **Trail 526B**. At 6.3 miles (10.1 km), you have the opportunity to either go right to stay on Trail 526B or go left for a slightly higher-elevation side path to **Col de Ciaulonch**. The paths meet up again in 0.2 mile (0.3 km). Take the higher-elevation option for better views to the west. After that, it's all pleasant downhill walking through a marmot-studded meadow back to the lift station at 6.9 miles (11.1 km), where you started your walk, and the Malga Cason mountain hut (0.1 mile or 0.2 km from the lift station), the perfect spot for an after-hike beer.

1B SËURASAS LOOP

Hike to a scenic alpine meadow overlook above Ortisei

The hike up to the Sëurasas cross, perched high on an alpine pasture above Ortisei, is one of the most popular day hikes in the area. From the Praplan/Cristauta parking lot above Santa Cristina, walk up through a pretty pine forest to Baita Sëurasas, a traditional mountain hut with big mountain views that's run by a wood-carver. From the hut, the route passes through the scenic Sëurasas alpine pasture, past a series of old wooden cabins and views of Monte Pic, the Sella Group, the Sassolungo Group and Alpe di Siusi, to an old wooden cross and its companion bench—perfect for enjoying the stunning scenery.

ON THE TRAIL

DURATION: 3 hours

DIFFICULTY: Moderate

DISTANCE: 3.8 miles (6.1 km)

ELEVATION GAIN: 1,350 feet (411 m)

ELEVATION LOSS: 1,350 feet (411 m)

START: Praplan/Cristauta parking lot outside of Santa Cristina

END: Praplan/Cristauta parking lot outside of Santa Cristina

EAT + DRINK: Baita Sëurasas (see Online Resources)

Know Before You Go

This Sëurasas loop hike is on Trails 4, 41, 20 and 6 and is well signed. Although it's not long, the ascent from the parking lot to the cross is just that—all uphill.

Alternative Routes and Activities

For a shorter outing, walk to Baita Sëurasas, with its great views across to the Sassolungo, and back to the parking lot in approximately 2 miles (3.2 km) roundtrip.

Extend this loop hike to visit Monte Pic and the Seceda Ridgeline; Moon & Honey Travel has a helpful write-up on its website (see Online Resources). Other routes to consider:

- From the Sëurasas cross, you can walk down to Ortisei. For more information and a map of the route, inquire at any of the local tourist information offices.
- In peak season, the tourism bureau typically does a weekly guided sunset hike to Sëurasas that's really lovely. The hut even stays open later than normal to serve cocktails and snacks, which are included in the activity fee. For more information and a current schedule, check out the Val Gardena Active program (see Online Resources).
- You can also do this walk on your own as a sunset hike. If you do, Baita Sëurasas will likely be closed—it's closed in the

It's hard to imagine a more picturesque spot to watch the sunset than the bench at the Sëurasas cross. (Photo courtesy Dolomites Val Gardena–Gröden Marketing)

evenings except for the weekly tourism bureau hike. Be sure to time your walk right by looking up when the sun will set and leaving the Praplan/Cristauta parking lot with time to spare. Allow yourself at least 1 hour and 30 minutes to get to the Sëurasas cross. Pack warm layers for when the sun sinks low and it gets cold out; you'll also need a reliable headlamp for the walk down.

Navigating

This hike starts at the Praplan/Cristauta parking lot outside of Santa Cristina; no services.

STARTING POINT: **46.56645°, 11.72465°**

TRANSIT: **The parking lot is accessible from Santa Cristina via Bus 358 (direction Dantercepies), which picks up from the "Santa Cristina, Dosses" bus stop near the Conad City grocery store. Current timetables can be found at the tourist information office in Santa Cristina.**

DRIVING: **The Praplan/Cristauta parking lot is a 10-minute drive from Santa Cristina, and during the high season there's a small fee to park.**

MAPS: **Available at the tourist information office in Santa Cristina.**

1 From the **Praplan/Cristauta parking lot**, look north across the main road for a

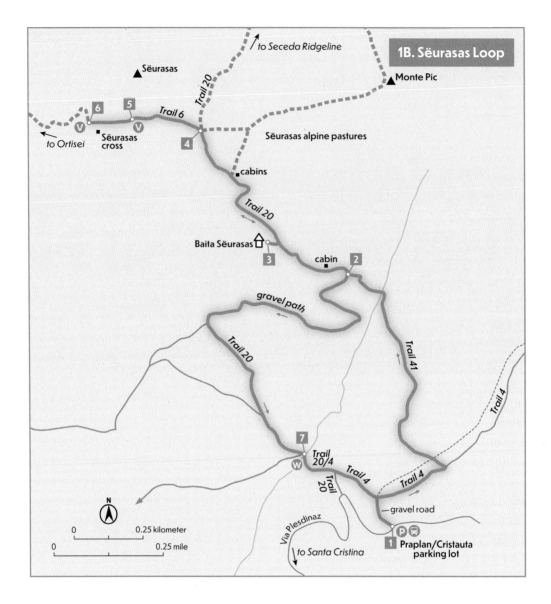

to Seceda Ridgeline

▲ Sëurasas

Monte Pic ▲

Trail 20

6 5 Trail 6

V V

to Ortisei

■ Sëurasas cross

4

Sëurasas alpine pastures

■ cabins

Trail 20

Baita Sëurasas ⌂

3 cabin ■ 2

gravel path

Trail 20

Trail 41

Trail 4

7

Trail 20/4

W

Trail 4

Trail 4

Trail 20

gravel road

N

Via Plesdinaz

1 Praplan/Cristauta parking lot

to Santa Cristina

0   0.25 kilometer

0   0.25 mile

smaller gravel road. Follow that road 0.1 mile (0.2 km) to a wooden archway with "Troi dla Schirlates," or "Trail of the Squirrels," written on it. There's a trail sign at the wooden archway, and the Sëurasas hut is signed for 50 minutes. Hike on **Trail 4** for 0.3 mile (0.5 km), then go left at a junction and continue walking uphill through the forest on **Trail 41**. You'll see many stone pines, the most important tree locally thanks to its soft wood, which is favored by Val Gardena's many wood-carvers. Interestingly, studies have shown that sniffing the needles of stone pines can slow your heart rate and help you have a good night's sleep.

2 At 0.8 mile (1.3 km), go right/uphill on a wider path, **Trail 20**. Just after that, the trail comes out of the forest. At 0.9 mile (1.4 km), pass an old wooden cabin as you start to get good views of the **Sella Group**, the **Sassolungo Group**, **Alpe di Siusi** and the **Sciliar**. To your right, as you walk, you can see **Monte Pic**.

3 Come to **Baita Sëurasas** at 1 mile (1.6 km). This small traditional mountain hut is owned by a wood-carver who has a little shop inside featuring his creations. The hut also has a full menu and perfect views across the valley to the Sassolungo Group from its welcoming terrace. If you're not hungry yet, keep working up an appetite by continuing your walk uphill to Sëurasas—you're about half an hour from the top. At 1.3 miles (2.1 km), the trail starts to level off, just before you get to two old wooden cabins. These days, because of the views they offer, such cabins sell for around 1.5 million euros.

4 At 1.5 miles (2.4 km), come to a junction in the middle of the Sëurasas alpine pastures. Here, Trail 20 continues north toward the **Seceda Ridgeline**, which you now have a nice view of. Thanks to its always-sunny, south-facing pitch, Seceda is just as popular in winter as it is in summer, and is one of the locals' very favorite spots to ski. Continue left on **Trail 6** toward the large cross.

5 At 1.6 miles (2.6 km), there's a beautiful old wooden cabin with the Sassolungo in the background. This is a great spot to stop for a photo—the cabin and mountains really sum up the Dolomites experience.

6 Get to the **summit cross of Sëurasas** and its wooden bench at 1.7 miles (2.7 km). The cross dates back to 1932, an early work by the local sculptor Vinzenz Peristi, who died in 1943 on WWII's Eastern Front. While the original is on display in the Val Gardena Heritage Museum in Ortisei to protect it from the elements, the one before you is an exact replica.

From the cross, there are picturesque views down to **Ortisei**, and you can see a trail that winds through the forests and meadows all the way to town. The cross is a beautiful spot to stop for a snack or to just take in all of the big views—no rush. When you're done, retrace your steps to [2]. Once

Like most of the huts in the area, Baita Sëurasas is family run. (Photo courtesy Cyrill Runggaldier)

you're there, continue straight on the wide gravel path rather than taking the footpath down through the forest again. At 3.1 miles (5 km), go left to stay on Trail 20.

7 At 3.5 miles (5.6 km), there's a stream with a water fountain for refilling your water bottle. Continue straight for Trail 20/ Trail 4. Just past the stream, at 3.6 miles (5.8 km), Trail 20 and Trail 4 split. Keep straight for **Trail 4** and get your last big views of the Sassolungo. Stay on Trail 4 until you reach the 0.1-mile (0.2 km) gravel road spur back to the main road and parking lot where you started.

Bonus Hike: Resciesa to the Brogles Hut

Take the lift from Ortisei to Resciesa for this out-and-back hike that leads through beautiful alpine meadows to the Brogles hut, situated picturesquely beneath the Brogles Pass and the Odle (Needle) Mountains.

DURATION: **4 hours**

DIFFICULTY: **Moderate**

DISTANCE: **6.7 miles (10.8 km) roundtrip**

ELEVATION GAIN: **1,286 feet (392 m)**

MORE INFO: **alltrails.com**

1C ALPE DI SIUSI LOOP

Wander across the largest high-altitude alpine meadow in Europe

There's nothing more peaceful than a slow wander across the Alpe di Siusi, Europe's largest high-alpine meadow, on a sunny day. It's all rolling hills, lush grass, beautiful pockets of morning fog and grazing cows. The alp is also the perfect spot to admire the surrounding mountains—the Sassolungo Group, the Sella massif and the Sciliar. This short, easy loop walk takes you to the top highlights of the Alpe di Siusi and leaves you plenty of time to enjoy the handful of traditional mountain huts that are scattered along the route—a family-friendly hut crawl with plenty of playgrounds and more mountain comfort food than you could possibly eat.

ON THE TRAIL

DURATION: **2 hours**

DIFFICULTY: **Easy**

DISTANCE: **3.1 miles (5 km)**

ELEVATION GAIN: **192 feet (59 m)**

ELEVATION LOSS: **704 feet (215 m)**

START: **Alpe di Siusi lift station (Ortisei–Alpe di Siusi line)**

END: **Alpe di Siusi lift station (Ortisei–Alpe di Siusi line)**

EAT + DRINK: **Alpe di Siusi lift station, Contrin hut, Malga Sanon hut, Sporthotel Sonne, Schgaguler Schwaige hut (see Online Resources)**

Know Before You Go

You can look forward to a mainly level hike on this well-maintained, well-signed loop that includes Trails 6A and 6B. Note that the Alpe di Siusi is also called Seiser Alm (in German) and Mont Sëuc (in Ladin).

The route utilizes a total of three lifts/gondolas; it's perfect for a day when you have a Gardena Card (see Getting There and Around). The lift from Sporthotel Sonne to the Alpe di Siusi lift station (at the end of the hike) is closed for lunch from 12:30 to 1:30 p.m. each day.

Alternative Routes and Activities

For a shorter outing, walk to the Contrin hut at 0.8 mile (1.3 km) and then back to the Alpe di Siusi lift station; this route still gets you some great views over the plateau and the experience of a traditional mountain hut (1.6 miles or 2.6 km roundtrip).

Extend the hike by walking to Compaccio or Saltria, the two settlements on the alp, or to several other mountain huts in the area. You can get more information on these and other walking routes across the Alpe di Siusi at any local tourist information office.

Other ways to extend your outing:

- Rent a horse-drawn carriage for a scenic ride across more of the alp.
- Take the opportunity to explore Ortisei, the largest village in Val Gardena.

Navigating

This hike starts at the top of the Alpe di Siusi lift, which connects Ortisei with the alp. Lift timetables can be found online

An easy walk across Alpe di Siusi is the perfect family-friendly hut crawl.

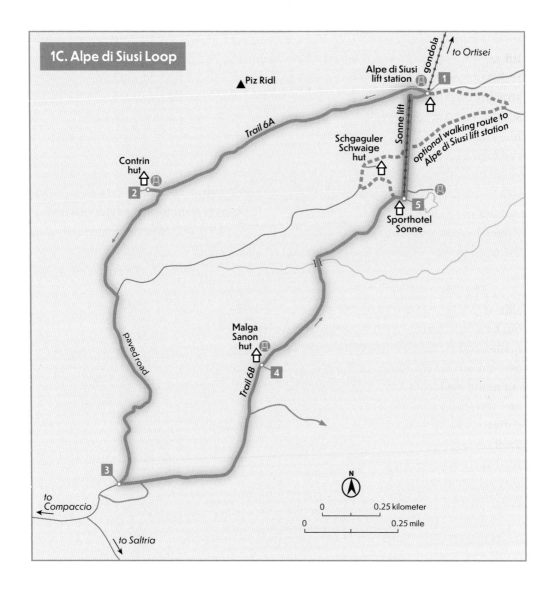

1C. Alpe di Siusi Loop

Piz Ridl

Alpe di Siusi lift station

gondola → to Ortisei

1

Sonne lift

Trail 6A

Schgaguler Schwaige hut

optional walking route to Alpe di Siusi lift station

Contrin hut

2

5

Sporthotel Sonne

Malga Sanon hut

4

paved road

Trail 6B

3

to Compaccio

to Saltria

N

0		0.25 kilometer
0		0.25 mile

(see Online Resources) or at the tourist information office in Santa Cristina. The Alpe di Siusi lift station has a restaurant (Almgasthof Mont Sëuc; see Online Resources), public restrooms and a playground.

STARTING POINT: 46.55788°, 11.66467°

TRANSIT: Take a 15-minute bus ride on Bus 350 or Bus 352 from Santa Cristina to Piazza San Antonio in Ortisei, then walk 5 minutes to the lift station. Current bus timetables can be found at the tourist information office in Santa Cristina.

DRIVING: Drive 5 minutes from Santa Cristina to the lift station in Ortisei, which has a parking garage (fee applies).

MAPS: Available at tourist information offices throughout Val Gardena.

1 From the front of the **Alpe di Siusi lift station**, go right. You'll see your first trail sign by the playground. Continue straight on **Trail 6A**. The Contrin hut is signed for 20 minutes on a slightly downhill path with great views to your left across the beautiful Alpe di Siusi—the highest-elevation views you'll have all hike.

DID YOU KNOW?

An alp is an area of green pasture on a mountainside.

---

2 The **Contrin hut** is on a grassy hillside at 0.8 mile (1.3 km). This family-run hut has a small playground for kids, homemade dishes from the area and nice views over the alp. It's also the smallest and most authentic-feeling hut on your route—a nice and welcoming spot to stop, if even for a coffee. When you're done, continue on Trail 6A until you come to a quiet paved road at 1.2 miles (1.9 km); head right. You may see a horse-drawn cart—you can rent them for tours across the alp.

3 At 1.8 miles (2.9 km), take a left on a wide walking path toward the Malga Sanon hut. At 2.2 miles (3.5 km), stay left for **Trail 6B**.

4 Come to the **Malga Sanon hut** at 2.4 miles (3.9 km). It has a play area, lawn chairs perfectly situated to admire the rolling pastures beyond and plenty of picnic tables for walkers looking to enjoy a meal. After the hut, continue northeast on the main gravel footpath. The route becomes a little more narrow, and there's a short boardwalk section across a stream

at 2.7 miles (4.3 km), right before you get to some steeper hills (you won't walk up them—you'll just walk between them). Depending on the time of year, you can see people harvesting hay by hand, an amazing feat when you consider the pitch of some of the hills.

5 Arrive at the pretty terrace of **Sporthotel Sonne** at 3 miles (4.8 km). This modern-style hotel is a good spot to enjoy a post-hike beer. There's a playground on the other side of the reservoir if you have littles needing to get out some more energy. TIP: If there's water in the reservoir and it's a sunny day, you can often get a great photo

The reflection of the mountains in the reservoir near Sporthotel Sonne is one of the most sought-after views of the Alpe di Siusi. (Photo courtesy Dolomites Val Gardena—Gröden Marketing)

of the water with the mountains towering in the background.

If you prefer traditional mountain huts over more modern spots like Sporthotel Sonne, the **Schgaguler Schwaige hut** is a 0.2-mile (0.3 km) walk uphill and has pastured animals (kids love them), an extensive playground and a full menu.

When you're done, walk the road between the buildings of Sporthotel Sonne to find the entrance to the Sonne lift, which takes you back up to the Alpe di Siusi lift station. When you exit the Sonne lift, head right. The Alpe di Siusi lift station will be on your left in 250 feet (76 m).

As an alternative to taking the Sonne lift, continue past the Schgaguler Schwaige hut to walk back to the lift station via the road; doing so will add 0.9 mile (1.4 km) and 452 feet (138 m) of elevation gain to your hike.

Bonus Hike: Seceda–Rifugio Firenze–Col Raiser

Take the lift from Ortisei to Seceda for this mainly downhill hike that has fabulous views of the surrounding mountains and visits a traditional *rifugio* along the way. From Col Raiser, you can take a cable car back to Santa Cristina—or walk.

TIP: Want the Seceda Ridgeline mainly to yourself at golden hour? (Talk about some epic photos!) Take the last cable car up and spend sunset hiking to Rifugio Firenze; spend the night there and finish the hike the next day.

DURATION: **2.5 hours**

DIFFICULTY: **Easy**

DISTANCE: **4.4 miles (7.1 km)**

ELEVATION GAIN: **531 feet (162 m)**

MORE INFO: **alltrails.com**

1D CRODA DA LAGO LOOP

Hike around the Croda da Lago mountain chain to an alpine lake and traditional mountain hut

A day trip to Cortina d'Ampezzo, Cortina for short, and its surroundings is a great opportunity to explore the Veneto region of the Dolomites—one that is proudly Italian. One of the best day hikes near Cortina is the loop around Croda da Lago, which takes you through high-alpine meadows and around the jagged Croda da Lago mountain chain to a pretty alpine lake where you can enjoy the reflection of the mountains in the water. After a nice lunch at Rifugio Croda da Lago/Gianni Palmieri, hike through the woods, past several small streams, to nice views of Cortina and Passo di Giau before taking a bus back to your starting point.

ON THE TRAIL

DURATION: 5 hours

DIFFICULTY: Moderate

DISTANCE: 7.2 miles (11.6 km)

ELEVATION GAIN: 1,317 feet (401 m)

ELEVATION LOSS: 3,043 feet (928 m)

START: Passo di Giau

END: Ponte de Ru Curto

EAT + DRINK: Berghotel Passo Giau, Rifugio Croda da Lago/Gianni Palmieri (see Online Resources)

Know Before You Go

Expect well-signed, well-maintained trails. The route includes Trails 436, 434 and 437; confidence markers are red and white stripes. There is a significant amount of elevation loss, which could be challenging for those with creaky knees.

Other notes about the route:

- If you love wildflowers, this hike is amazing in July. (Picking flowers is prohibited, though.)

- Swimming in Lago Fedèra is not allowed.
- The easiest way to do this hike is to spend the preceding night in Cortina (see Alternative Routes and Activities), which is accessible by public transportation from Santa Cristina (see Online Resources). The journey has several transfers and takes approximately 3.5 hours. If you have a rental car, you can drive from Santa Cristina to Cortina in 1 hour and 30 minutes.

The Croda da Lago mountain chain rises like a wall from the banks of Lago Fedèra.

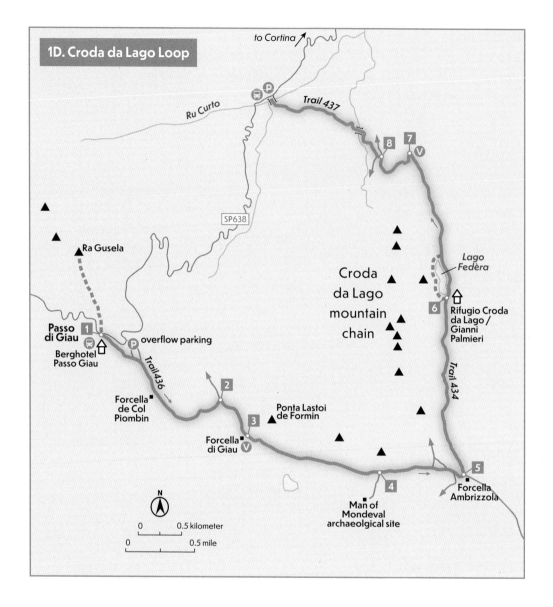

1D. Croda da Lago Loop

to Cortina

Ru Curto

Trail 437

SP638

8

7

Ra Gusela

Lago Fedèra

Croda da Lago mountain chain

6

Rifugio Croda da Lago / Gianni Palmieri

Passo di Giau

1

Berghotel Passo Giau

overflow parking

Trail 436

Trail 434

Forcella de Col Piombin

2

3

Ponta Lastoi de Formin

Forcella di Giau

V

Man of Mondeval archaeolgical site

4

5

Forcella Ambrizzola

N

0   0.5 kilometer

0   0.5 mile

Alternative Routes and Activities

For a shorter route, arrange for a jeep shuttle back to Cortina from Rifugio Croda da Lago/ Gianni Palmieri through Taxi Cortina (see Online Resources), which shaves 2.7 miles (4.3 km) off the hike.

There are a few options for extending your day:

- From Berghotel Passo Giau, take a short trail to the base of Ra Gusela for up-close-and-personal views of the impressive rock spire.
- Consider staying the night at Rifugio Croda da Lago/Gianni Palmieri, where there's a sauna for overnight guests.

- Explore the posh town of Cortina, the largest in the region, with a long history as a popular vacation destination for Italian celebrities. Walk around old town, pamper yourself with a spa experience (Grand Hotel Cristallo is wonderful; see Online Resources) and eat a nice dinner out (I recommend Ristorante Al Camin; see Online Resources).
- Visit Museo all'aperto delle 5 Torri (see Online Resources), a great open-air museum where you can combine history and hiking by walking around cannons and trenches left on the mountains from WWI. (The Dolomites were home to some of the fiercest battles of WWI because they straddled the border between the Austro-Hungarian Empire and Italy.)

Navigating

This hike starts at Passo di Giau, in front of Berghotel Passo Giau, a charming mountain hut with incredible views of the surrounding mountains, especially the peak of Ra Gusela. The hut has a full menu and restrooms for customers.

STARTING POINT: 46.48253°, 12.05373°

TRANSIT: Starting in July, Berghotel Passo Giau is accessible via a twice-daily hiking bus from Cortina, on a line run by DolomitiBus; the journey takes approximately 45 minutes. The DolomitiBus website (see Online Resources) is only in Italian, so visit the tourist information office in Cortina for more information.

DRIVING: Passo di Giau is a 30-minute drive from Cortina. There is free parking in front of Berghotel Passo Giau; if it's full, head back down the main road to the middle of the first bend and find roadside parking there.

The hike ends at Ponte de Ru Curto (the Ru Curto bridge), near a parking lot on the side of the main road up to Passo di Giau and the "Pian del Pantan (Ru Curto)" bus stop. From here, you can take the bus back up to Passo di Giau, if you need to retrieve your car, or to Cortina.

MAPS: Available at the tourist information office in Cortina, the Cooperativa di Cortina store or the Libreria Sovilla bookstore; all three are located in the town center. You can also download an overview map of hikes in the area from Cortina's tourism website (see Online Resources).

1 From **Berghotel Passo Giau**, cross the main road. You'll find the trailhead for **Trail 436** between the parking lot and the church of San Giovanni Gualberto. At 0.3 mile (0.5 km) and 0.4 mile (0.6 km), two trails from the overflow parking area join yours; stay straight on the grass track to **Forcella de Col Piombin**, which you reach at 0.6 mile (1 km). (Forcella means a fork in the path.) Once you're through the opening in the mountains, there's a beautiful wildflower-strewn valley to your right. Continue on Trail 436.

2 At 1.2 miles (1.9 km), take a right when the trail Ts. Enjoy views of another pretty valley (watch for marmots) as you walk a ridge trail that's also popular with grazing cows and then ascend in earnest to **Forcella di Giau**.

3 Forcella di Giau, at 1.5 miles (2.4 km), is worth the effort it takes to reach it. This is the highest spot on your route, and you have great views back to the valley you just skirted and to a high-alpine pasture ahead. Look up to your left to the giant rock peak of **Ponta Lastoi de Formin,** part of the Croda da Lago mountain chain, and you're likely to see climbers on its craggy walls. As you continue walking below Croda da Lago, the landscape becomes very rocky, with large boulders cleaved from the mountains above. There are views to your right of a picturesque small lake with **Monte Pelmo** behind it. Keep your eye out for sheep and goats, as well as the ever-elusive *edelweiss*—I was lucky enough to spot some when I was hiking.

Even though we think of *edelweiss* as *the plant of the Alps,* it isn't native to them. Scientists have discovered that *edelweiss* actually came from Asia—Mongolia, Tibet and the Himalaya—about one hundred thousand years ago. In the high mountains of Europe, it's typically found between about 5,000 feet (1,500 m) and 11,500 feet (3,500 m). For perspective, tree line is typically around 6,500 feet (2,000 m) in the Alps.

4 At 2.6 miles (4.2 km), pass a trail to your right for the **Man of Mondeval archaeological site.** There's not much to see there these days, but in 1987 a now famous skeleton was found under a large dolomitic rock. It was determined that the skeleton was a Cro-Magnon from approximately 6000 BC—the Stone Age. The presence of the well-preserved skeleton and its funerary items, along with other prehistoric finds in the area, confirmed that ancient people lived at high altitude in the Alps. At 3.1 miles (5 km), a couple of trails branch off the main one you are on; stay straight for the next saddle.

5 **Forcella Ambrizzola** is at 3.2 miles (5.1 km). From here, there are views of **Cortina** and its valley, as well as Rifugio Croda da Lago/Gianni Palmieri and Lago Fedèra. Head downhill on **Trail 434** to reach both the hut and the lake.

In Italy, there's a variety of mountain huts. A *baita* is a small, very local hut, while a *rifugio* is a larger, more established spot.

6 Get to **Lago Fedèra** and **Rifugio Croda da Lago/Gianni Palmieri** at 4.5 miles (7.2 km). The hut is a great spot for lunch; there's a large terrace outside with big views up to the row of mountains you just walked around. When you're done eating and enjoying the lake (you can walk around it, but you're not supposed to swim in it), continue on Trail 434 along the eastern shore of the lake and into a forested section that lasts for the remainder of the hike.

7 At 5.7 miles (9.2 km), there's a lookout with good views of Cortina, followed by a series of switchbacks and views at 5.8 miles (9.3 km) of Passo di Giau.

8 At 6.1 miles (9.8 km), head left on **Trail 437,** followed by an immediate right, toward Ponte de Ru Curto. The path travels

The climb to Forcella di Giau is worth the effort. You're rewarded with some of the best views you'll have all hike.

The green areas around Cortina—roughly 60 square miles used mainly for firewood harvesting, pasture and ski slope rentals—are collectively owned by 1,200 "historic" families who have lived in the area since around the eleventh century. The group is known as the Commons of Cortina (Regole d'Ampezzo) and meets periodically to make decisions about the land, which it feels a strong sense of duty to protect from overdevelopment.

alongside a small creek, then a larger one. At 6.3 miles (10.1 km), cross the creek on a small bridge. Cross other small bridges at 7.1 miles (11.4 km) and 7.2 miles (11.6 km)—perfect spots to soak your feet after a good, long hike. After the last bridge, there's a small switchback that takes you up to the main road, parking lot and bus stop.

World War I history is seemingly everywhere you look in the Somme.

2 THE SOMME, FRANCE

Walking World War I history through the poignant memorials of the Battle of the Somme

AT A GLANCE

GENERAL LOCATION: Northwestern France

HOME BASE: Albert

LOCAL LANGUAGE: French

USE OF ENGLISH: Widely understood and used

FAMILY FRIENDLY: ★★☆☆

COST: $$$

WHEN TO GO: Mid-Mar to Jun; Sept to Oct

SCENERY: Peaceful river valleys, gently rolling hills, bucolic farmland, English Channel

DON'T MISS: WWI memorials and museums, British pub fare, seaside villages

One of my favorite things to do as I walk is learn about history. I love exploring machine-gun emplacements and sitting inside old bunkers, gazing out and imagining what the soldiers must have seen and what their lives must have been like. For hikers who are also military history buffs, there's no better place to walk than in the now bucolic farmland of the Somme in northwestern France, where the scars of World War I remain and memorials and graves dot the landscape.

In this land, history is everywhere. Secluded farmhouses once served as billets for German and Allied soldiers; on local buildings you can still see embedded shells; each year, farmers plow up unexploded ordnance. And that's just the random spots. There are also many lovingly tended memorials and hundreds of thousands of manicured graves, all placed as closely as possible to where the actual battles occurred. Curated walks in the area take you past these memorials and graves, to placards, interactive exhibits and free guided tours of each memorial so that you can learn about the stories and men behind them.

In a broad sense, what you'll learn is that the Battle of the Somme was a key battle of WWI, and that while it ultimately gained Allied troops some ground (they advanced an average of 5 miles over the course of the four-and-a-half-month battle), it's widely considered to be a huge failure because more than one million troops from both sides were wounded or died in the process. On the first day of the battle alone, there were 57,000 British casualties, of which 19,240 were killed, making it the bloodiest day in British military history. At the site of what's now the Beaumont-Hamel Newfoundland Memorial, nearly all of the men of the island of Newfoundland were wiped out. The losses are unimaginable.

History is there to teach us lessons and to make sure we don't repeat the same mistakes. In this area, where the British Commonwealth suffered the greatest losses, the Commonwealth War Graves Commission has ensured history is well preserved. Each year, thousands of people from the British Commonwealth make the pilgrimage to the Somme to learn about their family members and see where they lie. The soldiers left their mark on the local area in more ways than memorials and graves. Although the Somme is in France, the towns and countryside are speckled with teahouses, English pubs and restaurants that serve British fare, many of which are owned by British expats. The mix of cultures is nearly as fascinating as the war history.

There's no better home base during a visit to the Somme than the small town of Albert. It is close to the hikes and has all of the services a visitor could need, from a tourist information office to museums, restaurants and grocery stores. Keeping with the theme of the area, it also has plenty of history to explore, and not just from WWI. Beneath the town are hollowed-out caverns and passageways that have been used since the Middle Ages for everything from hiding people and livestock from invaders to sheltering residents during WWII air raids. You can see one of these passageways during a visit to the Musée Somme 1916 (Somme 1916 Museum).

Although history is front and center in the Somme, there's more to the area than just that. It's home to peaceful river valleys, some of the most fertile farmland in France and charming coastal villages on the shores of the English Channel. Two of my hikes explore these facets of this area. It's such a pretty spot, it will leave you wanting to return—and always remembering those who went before you.

Getting There and Around

The closest airport to the Somme is in Paris. From there, you can take the train or drive to the town of Albert.

There isn't a lot of public transportation in the countryside of the Somme, so I recommend renting a car for the duration of your stay. Parking, especially around the memorials, is plentiful.

Where to Stay

While my top choice is the village of Albert, there are also several small rural enclaves in the area, such as Carnoy-

THE BATTLE OF THE SOMME: JULY 1–NOVEMBER 18, 1916

The first Battle of the Somme kicked off near the Somme River on July 1, 1916, and was a joint operation between British and French forces, though the British took the lead because things had heated up in the Battle of Verdun and many of the French soldiers had been diverted there. The goal of the offensive was to push back the German front line in the area—the Western Front.

The Germans had been in the Somme for quite some time and held the best positions in the area. Prior to the offensive, the British spent a week bombarding the Germans with heavy artillery meant to cut the barbed wire that guarded the German trenches and destroy the German positions. The thinking was that it would make it easier for the Allies to advance on foot from the front line and take those positions. On the morning of the offensive, a series of mines were detonated under key German positions, and at 7:30 a.m. thousands of Allies advanced across the battlefield at a walking pace. Unfortunately, the heavy artillery and the mines weren't as effective as expected and the advancing Allies suffered huge losses.

Despite the growing casualties, the deadlocked battle of attrition stretched on for four and a half long months, until November 18, 1916, when the onset of winter weather led the British to call off the offensive, at least until the following year. The most they'd pushed the Germans back during that time was 7 miles. With more than one million casualties on both sides, the Battle of the Somme has come to represent the loss and futility of war. For more information on the Battle of the Somme and the memorials in the area, see Online Resources.

You'll see many poppies—the flower of war remembrance—decorating the memorials and graves of the Somme.

Mametz, that are perfect for a French countryside getaway and where you can rent everything from a room in a charming bed-and-breakfast to a full farmhouse. A bonus: Rural accommodations can be the most economical option. For more information on them, contact the tourist information office for the Somme (see Online Resources).

Eat and Resupply

The town of Albert has several grocery stores, some of which are quite large. It also has many restaurants and cafés. Because the area is so popular with British WWI enthusiasts, much of the cuisine is British inspired or has an English bent.

When you're out and about, you'll likely see the following menu items:

- Chips: french fries
- Butty: a sandwich
- *Croque monsieur* (or *madame*): a melted ham and cheese sandwich (with a poached or fried egg on top)

Albert has an Intersport in case you need to adjust or add to your gear.

What to See and Do
GUIDED TOUR

The best way to get an understanding of WWI, the Battle of the Somme and their impact on the area is to go on a guided overview tour of the area. Having someone narrate the history, war stories and personal impacts of the war on soldiers and residents is so powerful; it will also help you appreciate the memorials you visit as you walk. Two of the memorials visited in my walks, the Thiepval Memorial to the Missing of the Somme (Hike 2A) and the Beaumont-Hamel Newfoundland Memorial (Hike 2C), have free guides on-site who are there to lead you around each memorial and give you more information on its significance and history.

LOCAL GUIDE SPOTLIGHT

If you want a guide for a battlefield tour of the Somme, I recommend Brigitte De Cuyper, an expert on local history, who took me around the Somme and gave me a great understanding of the battle (see Online Resources).

If you'd like to do a bike tour of the Somme battlefields, I recommend Carl Ooghe, an avid biker and historian whose tours can be customized to the spots you most want to visit (see Online Resources).

WWI AND WWII MUSEUMS

There are several WWI museums in Albert and the nearby town of Péronne. Two of the best are the Musée Somme 1916 (Somme 1916 Museum) in Albert and the Historial de la Grande Guerre (Museum of the Great War) in Péronne. Both of these can provide helpful context for everything you'll see on your hikes, so visit them at the beginning of your trip, after a guided tour and before you do any of the walks.

TINY TRAIN OF THE UPPER SOMME

The P'tit Train de la Haute Somme (Tiny Train of the Upper Somme; see Online Resources) is an antique train you can ride on the last remaining section of a large military railway network built during WWI to carry ammunition and transport troops. The route parallels a pretty canal of the Somme River before climbing up into the French countryside. Your admission ticket also includes a visit to the Narrow Gauge Railways Museum, which is located in the same building as the ticket office.

TIP: To guarantee yourself a seat, buy your ticket online in advance. Arrive early for the train, however, because you'll need to swap your online confirmation at the ticket booth for a physical ticket to board the train. This is a great activity to add on to Hike 2B, which is nearby.

DAY TRIP TO PARIS

You can't go all the way to France without taking some time to explore Paris. Driving into the city with a rental car can be stressful, however. Instead, leave your car at the Aulnay-sous-Bois park and ride, near the motorway and just outside Paris, where parking is cheap (it cost me less than €5 to park for the day) and plentiful. From the Aulnay-sous-Bois train station, you can easily train to the center of Paris.

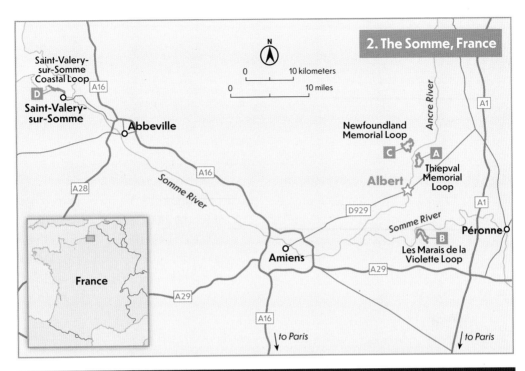

THE ROUTES

HIKE	ROUTE NAME	DURATION	DIFFICULTY	DISTANCE	ELEV. GAIN	ELEV. LOSS
2A	**Thiepval Memorial Loop**	3 hours	Easy to moderate	4.9 mi (7.9 km)	471 ft (144 m)	471 ft (144 m)
2B	**Les Marais de la Violette Loop**	2.5 hours	Easy	5.9 mi (9.5 km)	389 ft (119 m)	389 ft (119 m)
2C	**Newfoundland Memorial Loop**	3 hours	Easy	5.3 mi (8.5 km)	389 ft (119 m)	389 ft (119 m)
2D	**Saint-Valery-sur-Somme Coastal Loop**	3 hours	Easy	4.9 mi (7.9 km)	320 ft (98 m)	320 ft (98 m)

★★ The Somme gets two stars out of four for being family friendly. While playgrounds and parks are plentiful and local restaurants welcome kids, the serious nature of the subject matter—and the importance of visiting museums and taking guided tours to understand local history—makes it a tough destination for little ones, who may get scared by the depictions of war and antsy in quiet museums. While it's not great for littles, it could certainly bring history alive for older kids, especially those who are learning about WWI in school.

The Thiepval Memorial to the Missing of the Somme is the largest World War I memorial in the area. (Photo courtesy Somme Tourisme)

2A THIEPVAL MEMORIAL LOOP

Walk the highest battlefield of the Battle of the Somme

Of all of the memorials in the Somme, the Thiepval Memorial to the Missing of the Somme is the largest and the most impressive. Widely known as the most majestic British war memorial in the world, it honors 72,000 British and South African soldiers who went missing during the Battle of the Somme or died there and have no known grave. There's plenty to see and do at the memorial itself, including a free interpretive center, a museum and free guided tours from the Commonwealth War Graves Commission. But there's no better way to get a sense of the area and understand just how strategic Thiepval was during the war than by walking the area around the battlefield.

This walk takes you along the German front line from the Thiepval Memorial to quiet rural graveyards and the imposing Ulster Memorial Tower before dropping you down near the Ancre River and the base of the Thiepval Wood, from which the British—and most notably, Northern Irish—soldiers launched their offensives on the German lines. From there, you enter the small village of Authuille and have an opportunity to eat at the best-known restaurant in the region before climbing the hill back up to Thiepval—and contemplating how soldiers did it under intense machine-gun fire just over one hundred years ago.

ON THE TRAIL

DURATION: **3 hours**

DIFFICULTY: **Easy to moderate**

DISTANCE: **4.9 miles (7.9 km)**

ELEVATION GAIN: **471 feet (144 m)**

ELEVATION LOSS: **471 feet (144 m)**

START: **Thiepval Memorial Visitor Center**

END: **Thiepval Memorial Visitor Center**

EAT + DRINK: **Ulster Memorial Tower café, Auberge de la Vallée d'Ancre, Le Cottage Geneviève et Auguste tearoom (see Online Resources)**

Know Before You Go

This loop hike is a shorter, more scenic version of a longer Thiepval Memorial loop hike put together by the local tourism bureau. It overlaps in some places with their signage, which has yellow confidence markers. There's no notable elevation gain until the last 1.4 miles (2.3 km) of the hike, when you gain 253 feet (77 m) by walking from the village of Authuille up to Thiepval.

Other notes about the route:

- This trail is mostly exposed; be sure to pack extra sunscreen.
- This walk is best done Tuesday through Sunday from March 1 to November 30, when the Thiepval Museum, Ulster Memorial Tower and Auberge de la Vallée d'Ancre are all open. I recommend visiting the Thiepval Memorial and its museum after your walk, especially if the weather is warm and walking is best done earlier in the day.
- Auberge de la Vallée d'Ancre is a small—and popular—restaurant. You'll need a reservation to guarantee yourself a table, even at lunch (see Online Resources or call +33 3 22 75 15 18).

Alternative Routes and Activities

Most of the history on this route is experienced between the Thiepval Memorial and the Ulster Memorial Tower, which makes for a shorter, out-and-back walk of 1.6 miles (2.6 km).

By visiting the museums (the Ulster Memorial Tower and the Thiepval Memorial both have one) along the way, getting a guided tour of the Thiepval Memorial and stopping for lunch, this hike could easily take most of a day.

Navigating

This hike starts in front of the Thiepval Memorial Visitor Center, which has coffee and snack vending machines, as well as free public restrooms.

STARTING POINT: **50.05264°, 2.68823°**

DRIVING: **The Thiepval Memorial Visitor Center is a 15-minute drive from Albert. Parking is free.**

MAPS: **Available at the tourist information office in Albert; battlefield maps are also available at the Ulster Memorial Tower café.**

1 From the front of the **Thiepval Memorial Visitor Center**, head east through the parking lot toward the road you drove in on, Rue de l'Ancre. Head left on Rue de l'Ancre and at the junction with the D151, go right. Take a left on the D73.

THIEPVAL

Thiepval played a prominent role in the Battle of the Somme because of its high elevation. At nearly 500 feet (152 m), it was the highest village in the Somme, which allowed those who held it to see for miles in each direction—and easily defend themselves. By the time the Battle of the Somme began on July 1, 1916, the Germans had been dug in on the Thiepval Ridge for nearly two years. Their fortifications were extensive and included a series of trenches, underground buildings and nearby redoubts, all within sight—and firing range—of Thiepval. Even though it was grossly outmatched, the British-French joint offensive wanted Thiepval because of its strategic position on the German front line. Initially, military leaders hoped the hill would fall in a day, but it took until September 28, 1916, for Allied forces to beat back the Germans and successfully occupy Thiepval.

2 At 0.6 mile (1 km), come to the **Connaught Cemetery** on the left, just before and across the street from the Ulster Memorial Tower. This peaceful cemetery lies in the shadow of the **Thiepval Wood**, facing the German lines of the Schwaben Redoubt, a heavily fortified German position overlooking the **Ancre River**, where the Ulster Memorial Tower now stands. During several offensives throughout the war, Commonwealth soldiers launched attacks on the Schwaben Redoubt from the Thiepval Wood, including during the famous Ulster Division attack of July 1, 1916, when a contingent made it as far as the Germans' second line of defense at Stuff Redoubt. (By the end of the day, they were pushed back to the German front line.) Nearly 1,300 Commonwealth soldiers are buried in the Connaught Cemetery, almost half of whom are unidentified. The **Mill Road Cemetery** holds a similar number of graves and is across the street and down a dirt path.

A redoubt is a fort or temporary military shelter that usually consists of gun emplacements, trenches and dugouts. The Schwaben Redoubt was so named because the Germans occupying it mainly came from Swabia, in southwestern Germany.

3 At 0.8 mile (1.3 km), come to the **Ulster Memorial Tower**, Northern Ireland's national war memorial and one of the most striking memorials in the area—it looks like a castle. There's a small museum to explore, as well as a café. The Ulster Tower honors the men of Ulster, specifically the 36th (Ulster) Division, who gave their lives during World War I. It's a replica of a well-known Ulster landmark, Helen's Tower, which stood near the Ulster Division's training grounds at the outbreak of WWI. For many of the 36th Division, the sight of Helen's Tower was one of their last memories of home before departing for England and then the Western Front.

Just past the Ulster Memorial Tower, head right on a double track through the fields. You can see the remains of a German machine-gun emplacement at 1 mile (1.6 km). At 1.3 miles (2.1 km), when the path Ts at a bigger road, go left, and then take another left when you come to the C7/Route de Saint-Pierre Divion.

4 At 1.5 miles (2.4 km), a pretty pond makes for a scenic rest spot that's shaded.

5 Cross the D73 at 1.8 miles (2.9 km). Soon after that, the paved path you're on becomes a dirt road into the **Thiepval Wood**, just above the Ancre River, where the Ulster Division gathered before their charge on the Schwaben Redoubt. These days, it's a peaceful place with plenty of nice shade and the chance to see pheasants and grouse running through the brush.

6 At 2.7 miles (4.3 km), you're out of the forest and into the fields once again. Look left for commanding views of the Thiepval Memorial.

7 There's a small footpath to your right at 3 miles (4.8 km). Take this path as it winds closer to the river and past rural homes on its way into the village of **Authuille**. The path becomes more established as you walk; eventually it's a quiet paved road, Rue Bonnemain. When you get to Rue du Moulin at 3.4 miles (5.5 km), head right for Auberge de la Vallée d'Ancre. TIP: It's easy to miss the turnoff for the footpath at [7]. If you do miss it, you can meet up with Rue du Moulin in 0.5 mile (0.8 km), after walking a short stretch on the D151.

8 The small restaurant **Auberge de la Vallée d'Ancre** is a few hundred feet from the intersection of Rue Bonnemain and Rue du Moulin and the perfect spot for lunch. Locals describe it as the only food around worth eating; it's popular, so be sure to make a reservation well in advance. When you're done with lunch, head back the way you came, walking Rue du Moulin until you reach the busier D151 at 3.6 miles (5.8 km) from the start of the trail.

The graves at the Thiepval Memorial are lovingly tended by the Commonwealth War Graves Commission.

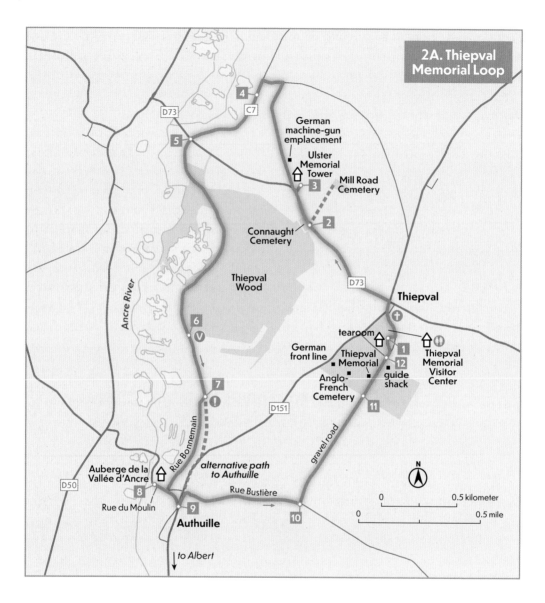

2A. Thiepval Memorial Loop

9 At this intersection, there's a **war memorial** to Authuille's WWI and WWII dead to your left and the **church of Saint-Fursy** to your right. There's a small plaque on the wall of the pretty church for the three battalions of the "**Salford Pals**," the 15th, 16th and 19th Lancashire Fusiliers (infantrymen) of the 32nd Division who held the trenches in Authuille from early 1916 and attacked the redoubts of Thiepval on July 1, 1916—losing nearly four hundred soldiers in the process. Head left on the D151 and take an almost immediate right on Rue Bustière, where you head up and into the fields once again. The elevation gain you experience on your way to the

64 | GET A RECOMMENDATION: TEN HANDPICKED HOME BASES

Thiepval Memorial helps you appreciate what a strategic position Thiepval was and gives you plenty of food for thought.

10 Take a left on a gravel road at 4.2 miles (6.8 km). This is not the typical way to access the Thiepval Memorial, but it makes an excellent shortcut for walkers.

On the Thiepval Memorial, you'll notice that occasionally a name has been cemented over. This is because the body of the person whose name was listed was discovered, identified and buried in a nearby cemetery. These names have been removed from the memorial to keep its focus on those who are missing or unidentified.

---

11 Enter the peaceful grounds of the memorial at 4.7 miles (7.6 km). It's a beautiful spot, impeccably manicured and maintained. Many consider the **Thiepval Memorial** to be the most majestic British war memorial in the world. It's certainly the largest. The red-hued brick structure looks out at the Thiepval Ridge, where so much fighting took place, and honors the 72,000 British and South African soldiers who died or went missing in the Somme between July 1915 and March 1918 and have no known grave. Below the monument is the **Anglo-French Cemetery**, which honors three hundred French soldiers on the left and three hundred Commonwealth soldiers on the right. Just beyond the white **Cross of Sacrifice** at the head of the cemetery, the ground turns rough—this was the German front line.

TIP: If you have a family member who has been honored at the Thiepval Memorial, you can look up their name in the memorial's register to find out where it's inscribed.

12 You can wander around the memorial to your heart's content. Head to the **guide shack** (straight ahead, at 4.8 miles [7.7 km]) for a free guided tour from an intern of the Commonwealth War Graves Commission—often a family member of someone who fought in the Battle of the Somme. If there's no guide in the shack, they're likely already conducting a tour and can be found walking around the memorial. Also available at the guide shack are free maps and literature about Thiepval and the Battle of the Somme.

Only seven years after the Thiepval Memorial's inauguration, WWII kicked off. During WWII, the memorial was occupied by German soldiers who used it as a spy and sniper post. They never disrespected or defaced the memorial, though several signed their names and the dates 1941–1943 on a wall beside the door leading out to the tower, which you can still see today.

When you're done exploring the memorial, there's a tearoom, **Le Cottage Geneviève et Auguste**, kitty-corner to the guide shack that serves more than just tea. Just past the tearoom, on your left, is a footpath that takes you back to the **Thiepval Memorial Visitor Center** and the **Thiepval Museum**, which is well worth a visit.

Quiet your mind with an easy walk along the pretty Somme River.

2B LES MARAIS DE LA VIOLETTE LOOP

Meander along a peaceful path among the marshes of the Somme River

The Somme River takes its name from the Celtic *samara*, which means "tranquil." And that's just how the river makes you feel when you walk along its calm, pretty shores. This is the ideal hike to let your mind wander far from the heavy things you've seen in the Somme. The nearly 6-mile (9.7 km) rural route takes you through forests, into marshes and down to the river itself, where you walk both canalized and wild portions of the most important river in the Somme.

ON THE TRAIL

DURATION: **2.5 hours**

DIFFICULTY: **Easy**

DISTANCE: **5.9 miles (9.5 km)**

ELEVATION GAIN: **389 feet (119 m)**

ELEVATION LOSS: **389 feet (119 m)**

START: **Camping Municipal La Violette**

END: **Camping Municipal La Violette**

EAT + DRINK: **N/A**

Know Before You Go

This loop trail is Route 4 of the Somme Valley's organized trail system and is relatively well signed. It is mostly flat and the trails are in great shape. Be sure to pack extra sunscreen, though, because the route is mainly exposed.

Alternative Routes and Activities

Extend your day by taking the opportunity to explore the nearby village of Bray-sur-Somme, which has a small museum detailing local history from the Celtic period to the end of World War II and several military cemeteries. (Interesting fact: Bray-sur-Somme was occupied by the Germans during WWII and was liberated by the United States Army.)

Other activities to consider:

- Ride the nearby Tiny Train of the Upper Somme (see What to See and Do) to experience a vintage train that was used to supply trenches with artillery during World War I—and get wonderful panoramic views of the area.
- Take your exploration of the river even further by getting out on the water for some fishing, canoeing or stand-up paddle

---

The peaceful nature of the Somme River belies its strategic importance over the years, and especially during WWI, when it was a key barrier to military advancement between Flanders, in Belgium, and Paris. The upper basin of the river valley saw intense fighting during the Battle of the Somme.

boarding. The website of the local tourism bureau has more information and recommendations (see Online Resources).

Navigating

This hike starts at the entrance to Camping Municipal La Violette, in the municipality of Proyart; no services. The town of Bray-sur-Somme, which does have services, is only a 6-minute drive away.

STARTING POINT: **49.90512°, 2.70216°**

DRIVING: **Proyart is a 20-minute drive from Albert. You can park in the dirt parking lot across the road (Le Chemin de Méricourt) from the entrance to Camping Municipal La Violette, where parking is free.**

MAPS: **Available at the tourist information office in Albert.**

1 From the parking lot across from the entrance to **Camping Municipal La Violette**, head north on Le Chemin de Méricourt (away from the D71). Just a few feet down the road you'll find your first trail sign for **Route 4**, Les Marais de la Violette. Follow the road as it curves to the left at 0.1 mile (0.2 km) and becomes wooded. At 0.5 mile (0.8 km), head right on the smaller Le Marais. Take the small footpath to your left at 0.7 mile (1.1 km) that leads to the marsh.

2 Once you get down to the water, the path curves right and goes across a little wooden bridge. Signs near the water depict the wildlife you can see on the route, including frogs and boars.

3 The path weaves through the pretty marshland until 1.1 miles (1.8 km), when it Ts at a wider gravel route; go left. You're

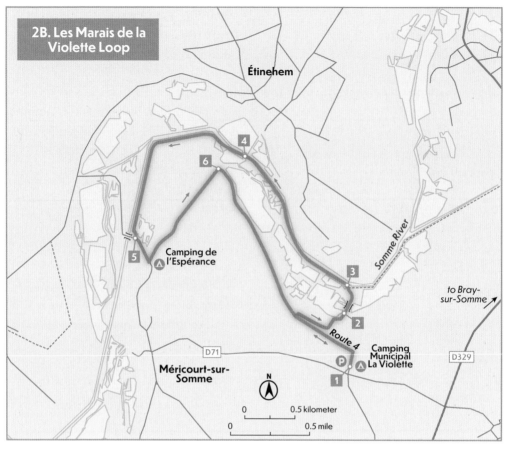

walking along a canalized portion of the **Somme River**. The water is lazy and slow, and it makes you want to take your time as well. This is a great place to meander, letting the greenery and wildflowers soothe your soul.

4 You occasionally see evidence of mechanized portions of the canal, like the old lock at 2.2 miles (3.5 km), where the water flings off the boundaries of the narrow canal and spreads itself out into a small lake, with the hamlet of **Étinehem** perched on its far shore. By 2.5 miles (4 km), the river slims down again and picks up its pace. This stretch of the river is

popular for fishing and boating, and you'll likely see people doing both.

5 At 3.4 miles (5.5 km), there's a bridge and an old building down by the water. Head left onto a paved road, then go left again near **Camping de l'Espérance** at 3.6 miles (5.8 km). Here, the route heads into fields of sheep and sugar beets—a prime example of why this area is considered the bread basket of Europe. When the paved road ends, continue straight onto a grassy path.

6 Walk over the concrete block at 4.3 miles (6.9 km) and curve right onto another grassy path, which soon turns to

double track and then a paved road. You're near the river but not right next to it, as you were during the first part of the hike. There's occasional shade from stands of trees, as well as scattered picnic benches. At 5.4 miles (8.7 km), you complete the loop portion of the walk. Continue right on the main path to retrace your route to your car.

Bonus Hike: The Machine Gun Way

Walk among more ponds and marshes of the Somme River and through the communities of Curlu, Frise, Feuillères and Hem-Monacu.

DURATION: **3 hours**

DIFFICULTY: **Easy**

DISTANCE: **6.9 miles (11.1 km) roundtrip**

ELEVATION GAIN: **424 feet (129 m)**

MORE INFO: **visit-somme.com**

The bright colors of the flora along the shores of the Somme River will have you reaching for your camera.

2C NEWFOUNDLAND MEMORIAL LOOP

Visit the largest preserved battlefield in the Somme and a touching memorial to Newfoundland soldiers

Of all of the memorials in the Somme, the Beaumont-Hamel Newfoundland Memorial is perhaps the most touching. World War I wiped out most of the young men from the island of Newfoundland, and they died on the very land you walk through. It's the largest preserved battlefield in the Somme and was purchased by their mothers and widows so they would never be forgotten.

This walk starts in the nearby town of Auchonvillers and takes you through fields of poppies on your way to the memorial, which has free guided tours. It then passes through the town of Beaumont-Hamel, Redan Ridge Cemetery No. 2, Sunken Lane and the Hawthorn Ridge Crater, created by the explosion that signaled the start of the Battle of the Somme. Celebrate your hike with lunch at a historic tearoom that serves British fare and a visit to a small museum of WWI and WWII artifacts from the area.

ON THE TRAIL

DURATION: 3 hours

DIFFICULTY: Easy

DISTANCE: 5.3 miles (8.5 km)

ELEVATION GAIN: 389 feet (119 m)

ELEVATION LOSS: 389 feet (119 m)

START: Church of Saint-Vincent in Auchonvillers

END: Church of Saint-Vincent in Auchonvillers

EAT + DRINK: Avril Williams "Ocean Villas" Guesthouse and Tea Room (see Online Resources)

Know Before You Go

This loop hike mostly corresponds with a trail put together by the local tourism bureau called *Le Circuit du Caribou* (the Caribou Circuit), though I have rerouted the walk in a couple of places to cut out some uninteresting parts near the town of Beaumont-Hamel and to visit the Hawthorn Ridge Crater. You'll see the Caribou Circuit's signs and yellow confidence markers along the route, but follow the steps outlined here for the reroutes.

Other notes about the route:

- Enjoy gently rolling hills and well-maintained paths.
- The route is mainly exposed and can be windy (you'll see plenty of wind farms in the distance); pack sunscreen and a sweater.
- This hike is best done Tuesday–Sunday, when the visitor center at the Beaumont-Hamel Newfoundland Memorial has extended hours.

Alternative Routes and Activities

For a shorter outing, walk to the New-foundland Memorial and then have lunch at the Avril Williams "Ocean Villas" Guest-house and Tea Room in Auchonvillers on your way back to your car—a roundtrip walk of 2.8 miles (4.5 km).

You can also extend your outing with the following activities:

- The Avril Williams "Ocean Villas" Guest-house and Tea Room makes for a charming (and very historic) lunch stop after your walk.
- Visit the largest and most famous of the WWI craters in the area, the Lochnagar Crater, whose mine was placed beneath a German stronghold called Schwaben Höhe.

Navigating

This loop hike starts at the Church of Saint-Vincent in Auchonvillers (3 Rue Dufour). There's not much in this mainly residential part of Auchonvillers besides the Avril Williams "Ocean Villas" Guest-house and Tea Room.

STARTING POINT: 50.08174°, 2.62964°

DRIVING: Auchonvillers is a 15-minute drive from Albert. There's free parking in a circular neighborhood pullout just beyond the church.

This statue of a caribou, a symbol of Newfoundland and Canada, overlooks the Newfoundland Memorial. (Photo courtesy Somme Tourisme)

MAPS: **Available at the tourist information office in Albert.**

1 From the **Church of Saint-Vincent** in Auchonvillers, where you see your first trail sign, walk south on Rue Dufour. Continue straight through the first intersection, with the D174/Rue d'en Bas, and pass a war memorial for local soldiers on your left, as well as the **Avril Williams "Ocean Villas" Guesthouse and Tea Room** soon after on your right. It's a delightfully quirky spot—there are a lot of chickens running around, and if you sit outside, they'll come over to your table, hoping for a few crumbs.

It's also a very historic spot. At the back of the guesthouse is a restored WWI trench that you can visit. The artifacts found in the trench are on display in the guesthouse. At the front of the property, in a small indentation near the main road, is a cellar that was used as a dressing station during WWI. James Crozier, a sixteen-year-old British soldier who was famously executed for desertion during WWI, is believed to have been kept prisoner in this cellar before his execution.

Across the street is a museum that Avril Williams helped establish, which has memorabilia from WWI and WWII. After the guesthouse, the area becomes more rural, with farms and cows. Follow the road as it curves right (don't continue straight on the busier D73).

2 At 0.3 mile (0.5 km), take a left on a signed double track through fields laced with bright red poppies in summer, sticking up bravely from the dirt and swaying

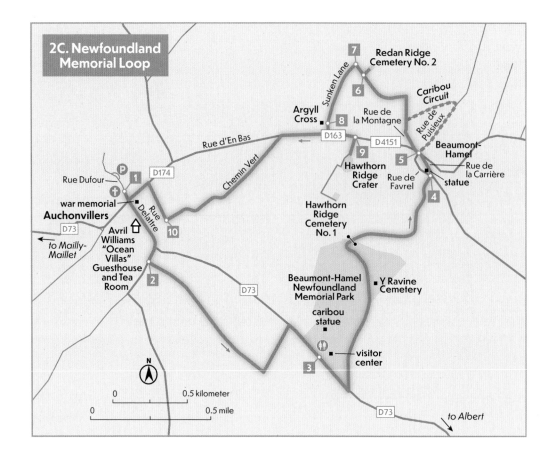

2C. Newfoundland Memorial Loop

in the breeze. Poppies are associated with war because they're the first flowers to come back after the land is ripped apart by battle. They can be dormant for eighty years and need freshly tilled (or torn-apart) soil to bloom. They're the color of fresh blood, and soldiers like to say they're the land's way of pushing the blood of the dead and wounded back up and out. They also like to say that poppies don't last long, just like soldiers. As you walk through the fields, don't be surprised if you flush a pheasant—I did while I was walking. At 1 mile (1.6 km), the path takes a sharp left toward the **Newfoundland**

Memorial. Take a right on the D73 at 1.2 miles (1.9 km).

3 The entrance to the memorial is at 1.4 miles (2.3 km), where you will see a guide shack for the student guides from Veterans Affairs Canada who are there to take you around the site (for free) and share its history. They also have maps and literature about the memorial, though you'll find more extensive information at the memorial's visitor center. Several paths meander around the memorial, and there is plenty to see, from an imposing caribou statue (the symbol of Newfoundland and Canada) to cemeteries and several smaller memorials. You can also walk inside a trench that has been restored. Stay on the marked paths to avoid any danger of unexploded ordnance.

This is the largest battalion memorial on the Western Front and the largest area of the Somme battlefield that has been preserved. The land was purchased in 1921 by the widows and mothers of Newfoundland to honor their dead from WWI, and it encompasses the area where these men fought and died.

At 8:45 a.m. on July 1, 1916 (the first day of the Battle of the Somme), the Newfoundland Regiment (consisting of most of the young men from the island), along with a British regiment, was ordered to advance toward the German line. The communications trench that they were supposed to travel in was clogged with dead bodies, so they had to run on the battlefield itself—out in the open. Within 15 minutes of leaving their starting trench, 80 percent of the 780 men from the Newfoundland battalion were dead or wounded. The only unit to suffer greater casualties during the Battle of the Somme was the 10th Battalion of the West Yorkshire Regiment, which fought near Fricourt.

When you're done exploring the memorial, head back to the guide shack at the entrance. The walking route continues southeast on the D73. At 1.6 miles (2.6 km), take the footpath on your left, which skirts the memorial before entering it near the **Y Ravine Cemetery**. At 2.2 miles (3.5 km), go right on a footpath that leaves the memorial through a back gate and heads into the fields before passing some farms and becoming a quiet paved road.

4 At 2.7 miles (4.3 km), come to the D4151/Rue de Favrel. Go right, then head left on Rue de la Carrière after the statue of a woman and a fallen soldier, a memorial to the dead soldiers of Beaumont.

5 Come to an intersection in the heart of **Beaumont-Hamel** at 2.9 miles (4.7 km). Instead of following the Caribou Circuit by taking a right on Rue de Puisieux, briefly continue straight before veering right on Rue de la Montagne. The Caribou Circuit soon joins the trail again. At 3.1 miles (5 km), go left on a country path that's signed for the **Redan Ridge Cemetery No. 2**.

6 At 3.3 miles (5.3 km) there's a turnoff for the raised grass path to the cemetery, the second of three cemeteries on the ridge named for the Redan, a group of British frontline trenches from 1916. The cemetery holds more than 250 war casualties, 100 of whom are unidentified, from the 4th, 29th and 2nd Divisions.

In the Somme, you'll see many small cemeteries—they're scattered everywhere, it seems. This is because the British have traditionally believed in burying soldiers as close as possible to where they fell. After WWI, few soldiers' remains were repatriated to their home countries, in part because of the risk of disease. Most of the repatriated remains were American.

While exploring WWI memorials, it's especially touching to see delicate poppies blowing in the wind.

the Lancashire Fusiliers advancing for his famous film *The Battle of the Somme*. You can find the hour-long silent film, which was a huge hit in its time, on YouTube.

FILM AND WORLD WAR I

During WWI, soldiers weren't allowed to take pictures, but armies could and did engage photographers and cameramen to document the war and write war histories. In part, the information was also used as propaganda. Geoffrey Malins's film (a new medium at the time), *The Battle of the Somme*, was commissioned by the British government to show that everything was going fine on the Western Front—except it wasn't.

7 Just past the cemetery, at 3.5 miles (5.6 km), take a left on a peaceful path that soon gives you your first shade of the hike. It's a beautiful spot, the road a bucolic depression between trees and thick bushes that feels like a leafy tunnel, but it has a bloody past. This small road is called **Sunken Lane** and it's where the 1st Battalion of the Lancashire Fusiliers advanced toward the German front lines on July 1, 1916, after the explosion of the Hawthorn Ridge mine. The battalion lost 163 men in the process, with 312 more wounded and 11 missing. Sunken Lane is also where war journalist **Geoffrey Malins** set up his camera and captured footage of the Hawthorn Ridge mine being detonated and

8 At 3.7 miles (6 km), come to the Celtic-looking **Argyll Cross**, which honors the Argyll and Sutherland Highlanders who finally took Beaumont-Hamel on November 13, 1916. Just a few feet later is a junction with the D163. Here, the Caribou Circuit heads right, and you will too—after you visit the **Hawthorn Ridge Crater**. To get to the crater, take a left on the D163.

9 At 3.9 miles (6.3 km) from the start of the trail, come to a smaller road on the right that leads to the crater. This is where one of the seventeen mines that were exploded by the British on July 1, 1916, to signal the start of the Somme offensive went off, and it is one of the few remaining craters. Strangely, the mine detonated 8 minutes before the other sixteen, which alerted the

Germans that something big was coming and contributed to the bungled offensive. The crater is 40 feet deep and 300 feet wide. TIP: If you walk past the crater, you can also visit the Hawthorn Ridge Cemetery No. 1. After viewing the crater, retrace your steps to the D163 and head left. At 4.3 miles (6.9 km), go left on a smaller country road (Chemin Vert) through the fields.

🔟 At 5 miles (8 km), go right down a shaded, grassy tunnel of leaves and skirt a farm. At the end of the pretty country lane, meet up with the paved D174 and head left. When you get to an intersection at 5.2 miles (8.4 km), go left for lunch at the Avril Williams "Ocean Villas" Guesthouse and Tea Room or right to end the hike at the church where you started at 5.3 miles (8.5 km).

2D SAINT-VALERY-SUR-SOMME COASTAL LOOP

Discover a beautiful seaside town and ancient ruins of the Bay of the Somme along a scenic coastal path

The Somme is best known for two things: World War I history and its beautiful bay. This walk takes you along the banks of the Somme River and through the charming seaside town of Saint-Valery-sur-Somme to great views of the saltwater marshes and mudflats of the Bay of the Somme on the shores of the English Channel. Along the way, you'll discover ancient ruins that were once explored by Joan of Arc and William the Conquerer, as well as beautiful checkerboard churches, a weekly market chock-full of local delicacies, several fun beach bars and even a sandy beach to sun yourself on.

ON THE TRAIL

DURATION: 3 hours

DIFFICULTY: Easy

DISTANCE: 4.9 miles (7.9 km)

ELEVATION GAIN: 320 feet (98 m)

ELEVATION LOSS: 320 feet (98m)

START: Office of Tourism of Saint-Valery-sur-Somme

END: Office of Tourism of Saint-Valery-sur-Somme

EAT + DRINK: Saint-Valery-sur-Somme

Know Before You Go

This loop route makes use of parts of the Sentier du Littoral Baie de Somme (Bay of the Somme Coastal Path) and the Saint-Valery-sur-Somme Heritage Trail. You can look forward to wide, well-maintained paths. The only notable elevation gain on the route is from the beachside path up to Chapelle des Marins de Saint-Valery.

From Saint-Valery-sur-Somme, there are good views across the water to the town of Le Crotoy. (Photo courtesy Somme Tourisme)

Other details to keep in mind:
- This hike is best done on a Sunday, which is market day in Saint-Valery-sur-Somme. The weekly market starts at Place des Pilotes and extends along the promenade. It's one of the best markets in the area, full of fresh fruits and vegetables, buttery pastries and hot prepared food. (You can also find home goods and many nonfood items.) TIP: Don't miss the *gâteau battu,* a local brioche-type delicacy traditionally given to friends and family on special occasions.
- The pretty herbarium on the route [9] closes for lunch on the weekends from 12:30 to 3:00 p.m.

Alternative Routes and Activities

The shorter 4.3-mile (7 km) Heritage Trail makes for a nice, alternative walk through town. A map of the route is available at the Office of Tourism.

Or extend your outing with one of these options:
- Saint-Valery-sur-Somme is a wonderful little seaside town; you could easily spend several hours exploring its markets, cafés and beach bars or getting out on the water in a rental kayak. This would also make a great overnight.
- At low tide, you can walk across the Bay of the Somme to the town of Le Crotoy. The walk takes about 3 hours and can be tricky because of slippery mud and tides, so join a guided group. More information is available from the Office of Tourism in Saint-Valery-sur-Somme (see Online Resources).
- Get more views of the Bay of the Somme and the ocean from nearby Pointe du Hourdel, a little fishing village, and the resort town of Cayeux-sur-Mer. Things to look forward to include a lighthouse, a huge sandy beach at low tide, the

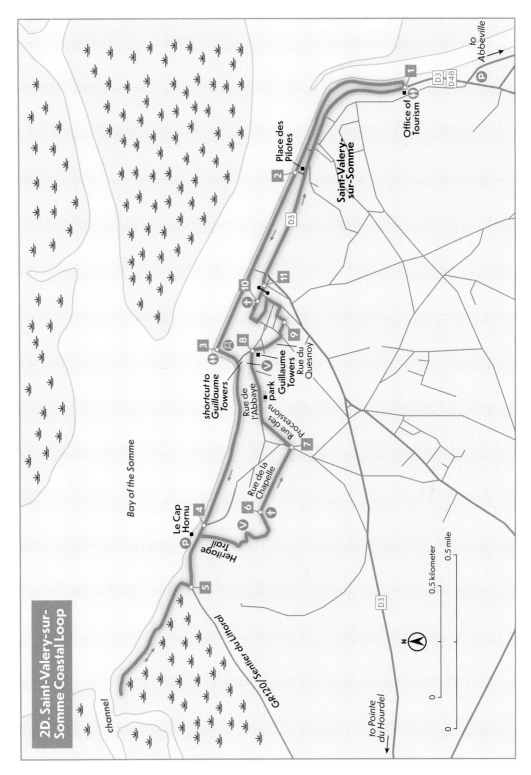

2D. Saint-Valery-sur-Somme Coastal Loop

channel

Bay of the Somme

GR120/Sentier du Littoral

to Pointe
du Hourdel

N

0   0.5 kilometer

0   0.5 mile

D3

to
Abbeville

D3 D48

P

1 Office of Tourism

D3 D48

2 Place des
Pilotes

Saint-Valery-sur-Somme

D3

11

10

3 shortcut to Guillaume Towers

8

V

Rue de l'Abbaye

park

Guillaume Towers

9

Rue du Quesnoy

Rue des Processions

7

Rue de la Chapelle

V

6

4 Le Cap Hornu

P

Heritage Trail

5

D3

largest colony of harbor seals in France, trails through the dunes and the longest boardwalk in France. TIP: You can walk the Sentier du Littoral from Saint-Valery-sur-Somme to Pointe du Hourdel for an approximately 6-mile (10 km) hike and then taxi back.

Navigating

This loop hike is in Saint-Valery-sur-Somme, which is on France's Atlantic coast where the Somme River drains into the English Channel. The hike starts from the Office of Tourism, which is located across the street from Quai Lejoille, part of the Somme River. The Office of Tourism has public restrooms and is a short walk away from many cafés and restaurants.

STARTING POINT: 50.18240°, 1.64370°

DRIVING: Saint-Valery-sur-Somme is a 1-hour-and-15-minute drive from Albert. There are a couple of paid parking lots as well as paid street parking along the D3/D48 as you approach the Office of Tourism. Parking is at a premium on Sunday, which is market day, so plan to arrive early.

MAPS: Available at the Office of Tourism of Saint-Valery-sur-Somme.

1 From the **Office of Tourism**, cross the main road to walk north on the boardwalk that runs alongside a canal of the Somme River. The Heritage Trail and Sentier du Littoral overlap here, and the route heads farther into town, passing many cafés, restaurants and shops, as well as numerous benches for those wanting to relax on the promenade and enjoy the water views.

2 **Place des Pilotes**, where the Sunday market is held, is at 0.4 mile (0.6 km). This is a great spot to stock up on provisions for your hike, especially if you plan to stop at the locals' favorite picnic spot [6]. After the busy market, the vibe of the promenade relaxes. The buildings become more spread out, peppered with mini-golf courses, ice cream stands and chill bars, all with views of the water and the town of **Le Crotoy** across the river. Keep your eye out for sheep. In the summer, it's common to see hundreds of sheep frolicking in the marshes of the Somme River. They move like schools of fish or swarms of bees—all liquid motion, all at once. They're a special breed, called *agneau de pré-salé*, that grazes on halophyte grasses, which are high in saline and iodine and cause their meat to have a distinct taste that's considered a local delicacy. Also likely on display: seals, oystercatchers and avocets.

3 At 1 mile (1.6 km), just past a spot where you can rent kayaks, the promenade rounds a sharp bend. Just beyond that are free public restrooms on the left and a path down to a large playground. On your right, find a large sandy beach. There's a beach bar here that's hopping in the afternoons, as well as a restaurant; this is a place you may want to return to after your hike. It's easily accessible via a staircase from the Guillaume Towers [8], the watchtowers you see above you. As you continue on the promenade, the trail turns to more of a nature path, with big trees on your left and beach grass—and beach—on your right. As you head farther away from the heart of town, you gain solitude.

4 Pass a trail that branches off to your left at 1.6 miles (2.6 km) and a couple hundred feet beyond that reach a second trail heading left. You'll come back to this spot in a bit and ascend to Chapelle des Marins de Saint-Valery via the second one, the continuation of the Heritage Trail. For now, continue straight on the **Grand Randonée (GR) 120/Sentier du Littoral**. You'll pass a parking lot for **Le Cap Hornu** at 1.7 miles (2.7 km).

5 Just after that, at 1.8 miles (2.9 km), a footpath branches off on the right and heads into the marsh. (The Sentier du Littoral continues to run southwest; don't follow it.) Follow this pretty path through mudflats for 0.4 mile (0.6 km), taking in the cool ocean breeze, seabirds and tall marsh grass, until you dead-end in front of a channel of the river. After taking in the views, retrace your steps past the parking lot and turn right onto the Heritage Trail [4]. Ascend the hill with great views of Le Cap Hornu and the **Bay of the Somme**.

6 Reach the locals' favorite picnic spot,

Chapelle des Marins de Saint-Valery, at 3.1 miles (5 km). This is where local families historically came to pray for the safe return of their fishermen and boats. The neo-Gothic church that stands today was built in 1878 to replace a much older Romanesque one. Its picturesque checkerboard walls were constructed by alternating limestone and flint. When you're done exploring the church, head right on Rue de la Chapelle to head back into town through a nice residential section of homes with colorful shutters.

7 At 3.3 miles (5.3 km) from the start of the trail, where the road Ts, take a left on Rue des Processions, which runs into Rue de l'Abbaye at 3.4 miles (5.5 km) and passes a pleasant little park at 3.5 miles (5.6 km).

8 There's a nice viewpoint of the **Beach of Saint-Valery-sur-Somme** to the left at 3.6 miles (5.8 km), just before you walk

The ancient, flower-bedecked ramparts of Saint-Valery-sur-Somme are a delight. (Photo courtesy Somme Tourisme)

between the **Guillaume Towers**. From the viewpoint, a staircase descends to the playground and beach below. To continue the hike, walk through the Guillaume Towers and the upper gate, or **Joan of Arc Gate**, in memory of her stay in 1430. The towers date back to the eleventh century, when William the Conqueror's fleet was forced to stop here, and originally also included underground passages, a prison and a drawbridge. In the summer, the tower walls are home to a variety of pink carnations known as crusade carnations. After going through the gate, take your second right onto Rue du Quesnoy and walk along beautiful flower-bedecked ramparts. When the road Ts, go left on Rue de Ponthieu and take an immediate right on Rue Brandt.

9 Come to the **Herbarium Fruticetum Baie de Somme** (see Online Resources) at 3.8 miles (6.1 km), an ancient garden nestled within the town's medieval ramparts that makes a nice, quiet detour. You can wander the paths within to enjoy more than one thousand plants. After the herbarium, the road cuts hard left. Take a right on Rue du Comté Robert, a left on Rue du Puits Salé and another left on Rue Questive. When the road Ts, go right on Rue de Ponthieu and right into Place Saint-Martin.

10 There's another checkerboard church, the large **Église Saint-Martin**, at 4 miles (6.4 km). Although the original church dates back to the twelfth century, it was burned to the ground in 1475 by order of King Louis XI, to prevent it from falling into the hands of the British. The church that stands today, which was consecrated in 1500, suffered some damage during the French Revolution when pictures and the reliquary were burned and the church bells were melted down. You can step inside to get a view of the church, including the noteworthy seaman's nave. Just beyond the church, exit the medieval part of town through the lower gate, also called the **Nevers Gate**. There are several cafés below the church. Go left on Rue de la Porte de Nevers and continue on the D3 (also called Quai du Romerel) after the curve in the road.

11 Along the D3/D48, there are many shops, restaurants and cafés with outdoor seating. You also pass by Place des Pilotes, home of the Sunday market. If you'd like to end your hike with water views, crossing Place des Pilotes takes you back to the promenade you started the walk on. Otherwise, continue on the D3 until you reach the **Office of Tourism** once again at 4.9 miles (7.9 km).

Bonus Hike: Saint-Valery-sur-Somme–Pointe du Hourdel Loop

Walk the GR 120/Sentier du Littoral from Le Cap Hornu to Pointe du Hourdel with great views of the bay and its salt meadows, then loop back on a more inland path.

DURATION: **5 hours**

DIFFICULTY: **Easy**

DISTANCE: **12.9 miles (20.8 km)**

ELEVATION GAIN: **115 feet (35 m)**

MORE INFO: **wikiloc.com**

The sandy beaches and turquoise water of Costa Brava make it an ideal place to not just hike but vacation.

3 COSTA BRAVA, SPAIN

Coastal walking on the shores of the Spanish Mediterranean

AT A GLANCE

GENERAL LOCATION: **Northeastern Spain**

HOME BASE: **Calella de Palafrugell**

LOCAL LANGUAGE: **Catalan, Spanish**

USE OF ENGLISH: **Widely understood and used**

FAMILY FRIENDLY: **★ ★ ★ ☆**

COST: **$$**

WHEN TO GO: **Mid-May to early Jun**

SCENERY: **Mediterranean Sea, lighthouses, fishing villages, ancient ruins**

DON'T MISS: **Secluded beaches, coastal walking, fresh seafood, friendly locals**

During my research and hiking for this book, there was one place that surprised me more than any other—Costa Brava, in the Catalonia region on the northeastern coast of Spain, about an hour north of Barcelona and tucked just below France. There are some places you go and immediately feel at home, and for me, that happened here. Everything about Costa Brava felt *right*, from hanging out in the friendly small towns on the water to hiking some of the most gorgeous coastal scenery I've ever experienced. What made it even more special was that the other hikers and vacationers I met were all Spanish—it was a local, not a global, hot spot, and that made me love it even more. Although you can hike Costa Brava year-round because of its mild climate, the very best season for coastal walking in the area is mid-May to early June, when the beach bars are open for the summer season and it's warm enough to swim but the high heat hasn't set in yet.

The coastal walking in Costa Brava is excellent because you get to see and experience so much, from small towns that were originally fishing villages to lookout points of the water from high, rocky lighthouse promontories. Along the way, there are secluded beaches to stop and swim at, beach bars where you can grab a drink and some food, and history—a lot of history—including ruins that predate the Romans and a house that belonged to the famous artist Salvador Dalí. When you hike in Costa Brava, expect it to take all day, not because the trails are that long but because there is so much to stop and savor. Pack your swimsuit and towel so that you can swim at one of the beaches along the way; book a tour of the Dalí house; toast your hike with a traditional vermouth from a weather-beaten lighthouse.

The hiking is so wonderful, you won't want to stop, except that spending time in town is just as enjoyable. Of the many villages along Costa Brava, my favorite home base is Calella de Palafrugell, which is smaller and less well known than many of the others. *Calella* means "small cove," so the name means "small cove of Palafrugell," Palafrugell being a larger town that's slightly more inland than this former fishing village affectionately known just as Calella. It's directly on the water, and if you plan your accommodations right, you can get sea views from your balcony and have a sub-5-minute walk to the beach. The beach is where everyone wants to be, along with the beachside promenade that's home to many of the area's restaurants, cafés and ice cream shops. There's more to do than just sunbathe. You can also rent kayaks and stand-up paddle boards to explore the peaceful little bays and rock arches of

CAMÍ DE RONDA

A couple of the recommended Costa Brava routes are on the Camí de Ronda, a network of coastal paths between the villages of Blanes and Portbou that have ancient roots but are best known for their use in the nineteenth and twentieth centuries by local policemen and Spanish military guards doing *la ronda*, or "the rounds," against fraudsters and smugglers that approached by sea. Smugglers were particularly active from 1940 to 1958, in the aftermath of the Spanish Civil War, when Spain was hit with international embargoes and sanctions that crippled its economy.

the coast. When you're ready to head back home for a siesta, shower off at one of the free showers on the beach so you don't bring sand back with you.

Most of the people who visit Calella are from Barcelona. They have second homes in town and use it as a weekend getaway throughout the year. A lot of them tend to eat in at lunch, but come dinner, they all make their way to the beachside promenade, and the town comes alive. Music plays from little restaurants, families mingle on the promenade and the delicious smell of food—mainly fresh-caught seafood—mixes with the salty brine of the water in an intoxicating way that will make you want to enjoy a two-to-three-hour dinner like the locals do. Dine to your heart's content— after all, come morning, you'll walk it all off.

Getting There and Around
The largest airport in the area is in Barcelona. From there, the easiest way to get to Calella de Palafrugell is to drive or use a taxi. It'll take around 1 hour and 45 minutes. Buses run from the Barcelona airport and Barcelona city center to Palafrugell with Sarfa company (see Online Resources).

Public transportation options are limited in Costa Brava; the best way to get around (especially to the two farther-out hikes) is to drive. TIP: Spain requires drivers to have an International Driving Permit.

Where to Stay
My top choice for a home base is Calella de Palafrugell, but several other towns along Costa Brava could also serve as good home

Well-maintained paths connect the seaside villages of Costa Brava. (Photo courtesy Fons IPEP)

bases: Palamós, to the south, is larger than Calella and has more cultural offerings on tap, like museums. Tamariu, to the north, is smaller than Calella but still has a nice beach and beachside promenade. Wherever you stay, I recommend getting as close to the beach as possible.

Note that there are more apartments for rent in this area than hotel rooms. A

Getting out on the water gives you a different perspective of the local landscape—and the Mediterranean Sea. (Photo courtesy Fons IPEP)

useful resource for local rentals is Corredor Mató Villas (see Online Resources).

Eat and Resupply

Calella has a couple of small Spar grocery stores, the largest of which is the Spar on the west side of town (Carrer Lladó, 40). If you'd like to stock up, head into Palafrugell for much larger grocery stores.

Calella has a wide selection of lively restaurants and cafés, many of which serve the local specialty—fresh seafood. The restaurants in Calella tend to fill up at dinner, so make reservations in advance. When you're out and about, be sure to track down the following local dishes:

- *Pa amb tomàquet*: a starter of bread or toast topped with tomato, salt and olive oil
- *Dorada*: gilt-head sea bream (fish) that's grilled or baked in salt
- *Gambas de Palamós*: famous sweet red prawns from Palamós

TIP: Paella and sangria are Spanish specialties, not Catalan ones, so while you will see them on the menu at many restaurants, they're not traditionally of the area.

If you need to procure anything, from a SIM card to a water bottle, Palafrugell is the place to get it. There's also an Intersport in Palafrugell for outdoor gear.

If you want to order fish in Costa Brava, you'll likely be presented with a wheeled cart containing multiple fish of the day. Once you pick your fish (most are large enough to split with another person), they will weigh it and charge you for the full fish, then cook it and fillet it for you. It's typically served with olive oil and sea salt, as well as a side.

What to See and Do

BIKE THE COUNTRYSIDE

You get to see some of the beautiful inland Costa Brava on the Pals to La Bisbal d'Empordà hike (Hike 3C), but if you have extra time, consider doing a bike tour of the area. To rent a bike near Calella de Palafrugell, I recommend Gran Fondo in Palafrugell, which rents bikes (and can deliver them to your accommodations), offers cycling classes and weekly group rides that anyone can join, and even has a café.

Renting a bike could also be combined with a day trip to Girona (see the "Day Trip to Girona" sidebar). More details on self-guided (and guided) bike tours of the pretty farmland around Girona are available from Cycle Tours Catalonia (see Online Resources).

KAYAK THE SEA

Getting out onto the calm water surrounding Calella is a must. Most of the small boat rentals are found on the beach in Llafranc, a bedroom community of Calella, and from there you can embark on either a self-guided or guided kayak tour of the

shoreline, which has a variety of rock formations to explore. A bonus: Some of the best views of whitewashed Calella are from the water, so bring your camera (and a waterproof case). A local mother-and-son company that runs excellent kayak tours of the area—and offers rentals—is Tourist Service (see Online Resources).

EXPLORE PALAFRUGELL

The closest main town to Calella is Palafrugell, which is a 5-minute drive away. Palafrugell has a bountiful farmers' market in its old town (near Plaça Nova) from Tuesday to Sunday, 8 a.m. to 1 p.m. (the Sunday market is the best). There's also a covered seafood market next to the fresh market, as well as several bakeries and cafés where you can enjoy a pastry and an espresso as you take in the action.

DAY TRIP TO GIRONA

While Barcelona is an obvious choice for a day trip, smaller Girona is close by and also well worth a visit. Girona is the capital of the region, a cultural hot spot that boasts several museums and cathedrals, but my favorite feature of the town is the extensive ramparts of the old fortress that you can walk around.

★★★ Costa Brava gets three stars out of four for being family friendly. It's relatively affordable compared to many other spots in Europe, and there are many parks and playgrounds for kids to explore. Their favorite feature will definitely be the

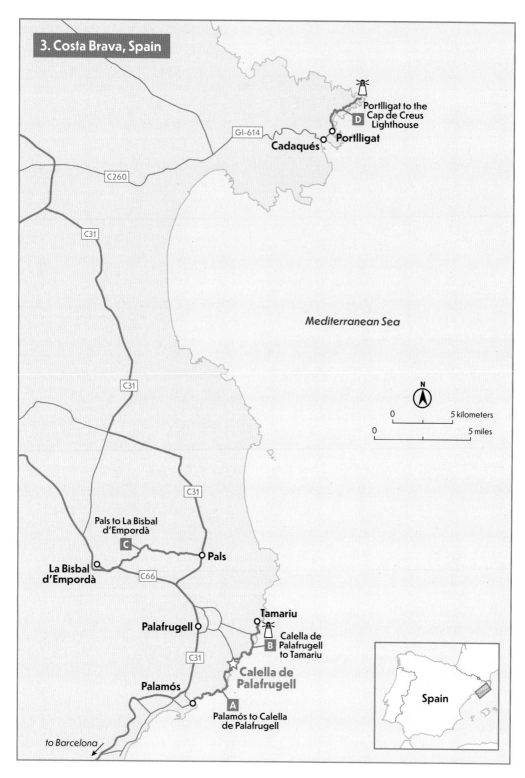

3. Costa Brava, Spain

Portlligat to the
Cap de Creus
Lighthouse

D

GI-614

Cadaqués   **Portlligat**

C260

C31

C31

Mediterranean Sea

N

0   5 kilometers

0   5 miles

C31

Pals to La Bisbal
d'Empordà

C

**La Bisbal
d'Empordà**   **Pals**

C66

Tamariu

Calella de
Palafrugell
to Tamariu

B

Palafrugell

C31

**Calella de
Palafrugell**

Palamós

A

Palamós to Calella
de Palafrugell

to Barcelona

Spain

beach—my kids spent hours and hours playing in shallow little coves, paddling around in a rented kayak and searching for tiny crabs under the rocks. Restaurants are well equipped with high chairs, and you'll see many local families walking along the beachside promenade together, especially on the weekends.

LOCAL HIKING COMPANY SPOTLIGHT

While hiking routes in Spain are public property and anyone can access them freely, a local company named after the trail network, the Camí de Ronda® company, has cultivated this trail system and offers several products to make it easier to walk, from maps and GPX tracks to luggage transfer and even guided hikes. You can find out more about their routes and products at their website (see Online Resources). They provide more information for the hikes featured here—the path from Palamós to Calella de Palafrugell, which is on their linear route, and the Pals to La Bisbal d'Empordà trail, which is part of their circular route. TIP: **You can purchase maps from the Camí de Ronda® website. If you do, let them know that you have my book and they will send you the corresponding GPX tracks for free. You can also buy a welcome pack that includes a Camí de Ronda map, GPX tracks and samples of a variety of local products. The company will email you the GPX tracks and can either mail the maps to you or deliver them to your Costa Brava accommodations so they're waiting for you when you arrive. The local product samples are delivered to your accommodations.**

THE ROUTES

HIKE	ROUTE NAME	DURATION	DIFFICULTY	DISTANCE	ELEV. GAIN	ELEV. LOSS
3A	**Palamós to Calella de Palafrugell**	3 hours	Moderate	5.1 mi (8.2 km)	962 ft (293 m)	922 ft (281 m)
3B	**Calella de Palafrugell to Tamariu**	3.5 hours	Moderate	4.2 mi (6.8 km)	859 ft (262 m)	882 ft (269 m)
3C	**Pals to La Bisbal d'Empordà**	3 hours	Easy	6.9 mi (11.1 km)	616 ft (188 m)	531 ft (162 m)
3D	**Portlligat to the Cap de Creus Lighthouse**	3 hours	Moderate	3.6 mi (5.8 km)	723 ft (223 m)	483 ft (147 m)

3A PALAMÓS TO CALELLA DE PALAFRUGELL

Experience Costa Brava through the ages on a gorgeous village-to-village route

One of the most beautiful walks in all of Costa Brava is the route from Palamós to Calella de Palafrugell. From amazing coastal views to secluded coves to vibrant flowers, this trail has it all. What's even better is that there's so much history along the trail. Just a sampling: you can see ruins that predate Christ, small seaside settlements that became a large part of local culture during the Industrial Revolution, and the house where Truman Capote wrote *In Cold Blood*.

ON THE TRAIL

DURATION: 3 hours

DIFFICULTY: Moderate

DISTANCE: 5.1 miles (8.2 km)

ELEVATION GAIN: 962 feet (293 m)

ELEVATION LOSS: 922 feet (281 m)

START: Platja de Sant Esteve de la Fosca in Palamós

END: Punta dels Burricaires in Calella de Palafrugell

EAT + DRINK: Platja de Sant Esteve de la Fosca, Platja de Castell, Calella de Palafrugell (see Online Resources)

Know Before You Go

This walk is on the Camí de Ronda and the Grand Randonée (GR) 92, which sometimes overlap, and is not well signed. There are also many unsigned boot paths along the way. I recommend purchasing GPX tracks from the Camí de Ronda® company (see the "Local Hiking Company Spotlight" sidebar) to accompany the step-by-step directions outlined here.

Other notes about the route:

- While the trail has almost 1,000 feet (305 m) of elevation gain, there are really only two noticeable climbs. The other sections are very much rolling. Walking across the occasional sandy beach adds to the challenge of the hike.

- You can do the hike in the opposite direction, from Calella de Palafrugell to Palamós, but the views are much better when hiking northbound.

- This hike is best done from mid-May to early June. During this time, the beach bars en route are open (they're open from mid-May to mid-September) and the weather isn't too hot. You can also do this hike in July or August, but be aware that it can get very hot.

Alternative Routes and Activities

For a shorter walk, call a taxi at the Cap Roig Botanical Gardens outside of Calella de Palafrugell to shave 1.3 miles (2.1 km) off the hike. There's also an open-top tourist

Along the route from Palamós to Calella de Palafrugell, there are numerous coves and beaches for swimming. (Photo by Daniel Punseti)

bus that runs from the botanical gardens to Calella de Palafrugell, but the bus operates only from mid-July to the end of September (see Online Resources).

Or you can extend your outing in a number of ways:

- By stopping to swim, eat and drink, you can easily spend a full day on this hike.
- There's an optional detour at 3.8 miles (6.1 km) for the Cap Roig Botanical Gardens.
- Fishing has historically been of tremendous importance to Costa Brava. Visit Museu de la Pesca, or the Fishing Museum (see Online Resources), in Palamós to learn more about how fishing has shaped—and continues to define— the region.
- A stop by the fish market that's attached to the Fishing Museum is a must. The

market opens in the evening, once the fishermen have returned to port with their catches from the day. For hours and more information, check out the museum's website. I recommend doing the hike in the morning, when it's not so hot, and then doubling back to Palamós in the late afternoon for the museum and market; this works best if you have to pick up your rental car from Platja de Sant Esteve de la Fosca anyway.

- Palamós is larger than Calella de Palafrugell and is a great spot to have dinner and explore.

Navigating

The route begins at La Fosca, a popular sand beach in Palamós that's divided into two halves—Platja de la Fosca and Platja de Sant Esteve de la Fosca—by a big black rock that gives the beach its name, "the beach of the dark rock." Your starting point is the "Platja de la Fosca" sign near that dark rock, on the stone walkway in front of the little bars and restaurants just inside the Sant Esteve de la Fosca section—a good stop for when you want another cup of coffee before hitting the trail.

STARTING POINT: **41.85905°, 3.14470°**

DRIVING: **There's no public transportation between Calella de Palafrugell and La Fosca, so your best options for getting to the start are driving (approximately 20 minutes) or hiring a taxi. If you drive, there's free street parking on Carrer de Garbí, which runs parallel to the beach, behind the restaurants.**

The hike ends on the promenade in front of Punta dels Burricaires in Calella de Palafrugell. If you left your car at La Fosca, a quick taxi ride is the best way to retrieve it.

MAPS: **Available at tourist information offices in Palafrugell and Calella de Palafrugell. An overview map of this route can also be purchased from the Camí de Ronda® company—it's part of their linear route from Blanes to Portbou. That said, the Camí de Ronda® map doesn't have sufficient detail to help you with turn-by-turn navigation on trail. The company's GPX tracks for the route are more helpful and can be purchased online (see the "Local Hiking Company Spotlight" sidebar).**

1 When facing the water and the **"Platja de la Fosca" sign**, head left on the stone walkway, past the cafés and restaurants that line the beach. At the end of the

beach, you'll see your first official trail sign for the **GR 92**.

2 A short climb takes you to the ruins of the medieval **Castell de Sant Esteve de Mar** at 0.2 mile (0.3 km), which was built in the twelfth century as a display of wealth and power by a Spanish royal who wanted control of the Palamós area and the bay you just walked past.

SPOT IT ON TRAIL

- ☐ Succulents
- ☐ Wildflowers
- ☐ Pine trees
- ☐ Tamarisk trees
- ☐ Fig trees
- ☐ Anise

3 At 0.6 mile (1 km), come to a series of whitewashed buildings with brightly colored doors. This settlement is called **S'Alguer** and is mistakenly assumed by many to be a former fishing village. In fact, outposts like these have their roots in the Industrial Revolution. When workers won the right to a day off work each week, they discovered nature and built these huts together with friends and coworkers for day trips. They'd walk to them, trapping and fishing along the way, and then have a big cookout and daylong picnic with their buddies. Many local recipes have their roots in the dishes that were created in these outposts. The buildings have been passed down over generations, and although they are private, you can walk

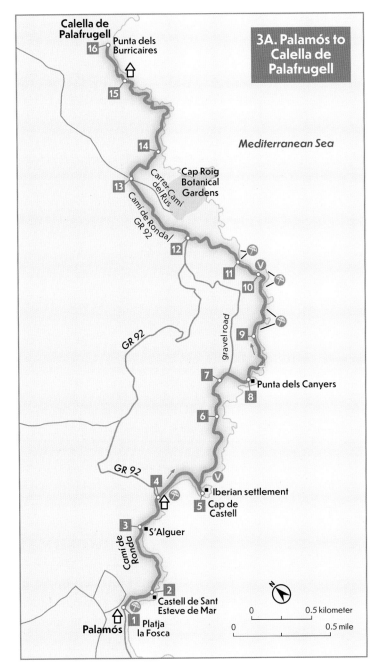

Calella de
Palafrugell
16
Punta dels
Burricaires

15

14

Mediterranean Sea

13
Carrer Camí
del Rus

Cap Roig
Botanical
Gardens

Camí de Ronda/
GR 92

12

11

10

GR 92

9

gravel road

7

Punta dels Canyers
8

6

GR 92

4
V

Iberian settlement
5 Cap de
Castell

3
S'Alguer

Camí de
Ronda

2
Castell de Sant
Esteve de Mar

Palamós
1 Platja
la Fosca

0   0.5 kilometer
0   0.5 mile

4 The **Camí de Ronda** and the GR 92 deviate at 0.8 mile (1.3 km). While the GR 92 heads inland, stay right for the Camí de Ronda, which continues to hug the coast. Almost immediately you come to **Platja de Castell** (Castle Beach), which has a *chiringuito*, or beach bar, that's open from mid-May until mid-September. This is also the start of the **Castell–Cap Roig Protected Natural Area**, which doesn't have any physical borders or entry fees. Walk across the beach, then climb briefly to the ruins of an Iberian settlement.

5 Reach the ruins at 1.1 miles (1.8 km). The Iberians predated the Romans, and this settlement was built more than two centuries before Christ. Some of the ruins are closed due to landslide risk, but from the viewing area, you can see what remains of two towers that guarded the entrance to the settlement. As you continue your

through the two-part enclave—the walkway is public. You may even spot a modern-day owner enjoying a day at the beach.

The walk back into Calella has several beautiful stone tunnels.

walk, you'll get a better view of the rest of the settlement from across a natural harbor that was part of it. Another good lookout of the ruins—and of La Fosca, where you started—comes at 1.3 miles (2.1 km).

6 Keep your eye out at 1.6 miles (2.6 km) for a prehistoric tomb on your left and a large white house ahead. This is where Truman Capote wrote several chapters of *In Cold Blood*. Capote loved to vacation in Costa Brava with his boyfriend, who was friends with Marilyn Monroe. The couple was staying at that white house when they got the call that Monroe had died. They flew back to the United States for her funeral and never returned because they then associated the area with her death.

7 At 1.9 miles (3.1 km), the trail comes out on a gravel road. You only walk the gravel road for 30 seconds or so before taking a right on a dirt footpath. NOTE: It's easy to miss this turn. Eventually the routes converge again, but not until [12], and those who take the gravel road miss many of the best sights of the Camí de Ronda.

8 The Camí de Ronda heads toward the Mediterranean, coming out to a beautiful panorama of the sea at **Punta dels Canyers** at 2.1 miles (3.4 km) before skirting the small cove of **Cala Corbs**.

Along the trail, you'll see several places where gorgeous flowers cascade down slopes from the houses above. Many aren't native varieties but are escape artists, spread by the wind from the homes' private gardens.

9 At 2.4 miles (3.9 km), come to a traditional fishermen's house where fishermen used to wait out the changing winds because they had only sails, no motors. If the winds were blowing in the wrong direction and they couldn't make it home, they'd stop here for a day or two until the winds changed direction and allowed them to sail home. The fishermen's house marks the beginning of a series of four sandy beaches you'll walk across—ideal for swimming on a hot day. NOTE: These beaches are nude beaches, so don't be surprised if you see whole families sunbathing sans clothes— it's part of the culture in Costa Brava.

You're not required to be nude on the beach, so carry on in your hiking clothes unless you feel otherwise inclined.

10 At the end of the final beach, at 2.8 miles (4.5 km), there's a rock outcropping and panorama point that marks the border between Palamós and Calella de Palafrugell. This is where you get your first views of Calella and Llafranc.

11 Two infamous spots at 2.9 miles (4.7 km) and 3 miles (4.8 km)—**Cala de la Font Morisca** (Islamic Fountain Beach) and **Cala del Crit** (Cry Beach)—are connected by a large rock with a "window" that you'll walk through. Islamic Fountain Beach is so named because it was frequented by pirates from North Africa and Turkey searching for fresh water. (Cane is a sign of fresh water—keep your eye out for it and suddenly you'll see it growing everywhere.) The pirates would stop in this cove for water and then go up the hill to pillage local farms. And that's where Cry Beach comes in. Local lore has it that one day the pirates went to a farm and raped a woman, then carried her down the hill to take her to their ship and sell her into slavery. The stories diverge here. Some say she bit the pirate and he cried out so loudly that everyone around could hear. Others say the pirate slit the woman's throat and her cry was so loud it echoed.

In the middle of Cry Beach, there's a staircase that you'll ascend. This starts the most challenging part of the hike where you'll gain 354 feet (108 m) in 0.5 mile (0.8 km) over about 15 minutes. At the top of your climb is a pine forest that smells wonderful and offers great shade. It can also be brushy and the paths are a bit overgrown.

12 At 3.4 miles (5.5 km), go right on the **GR 92**, a wider dirt path than the one you've been walking on for a while. Once you take this right, don't miss the cork trees growing around you. Costa Brava's famous cork forests are used for some of the best wines in the world. What's interesting is that cork is self-renewing; harvesting doesn't kill the tree. Only the bark is harvested and it grows back in nine years, at which time it can be harvested again. When wine is bottled, the cork allows the wine to breathe and change over time.

13 There's an optional detour to the **Cap Roig Botanical Gardens** at 3.8 miles (6.1 km). The garden is accessed by taking a right on Carrer Camí del Rus, a quiet road. If you enjoy local plants, it's a worthy stop. To continue the walk from the intersection of the GR 92 and Carrer Camí del Rus, continue straight on **Avinguda Costa Brava**. After 0.1 mile (0.2 km), descend the staircase to your right, then take a left on Carrer Cant dels Ocells to continue. Stay right when the road splits.

14 Descend another staircase at 4.2 miles (6.8 km). This starts one of the most spectacular sections of the hike. The walk back into Calella is full of beautiful tunnels, rock-lined paths, lookouts over the ocean and, eventually, views of the town itself. Walk slowly and soak it in. Take the staircase to your right at 4.7 miles (7.6 km) to stay close to the water.

15 At 4.8 miles (7.7 km), come out at **Hotel Sant Roc**, which has a nice terrace with good views of the ocean. Stay on the path that passes in front of the terrace as it runs high above two small beaches and eventually becomes Carrer del Canyers. Continue right when Carrer del Canyers is joined by another path on the left.

16 Your walk ends at 5.1 miles (8.2 km), at the intersection of the promenade—in the south end of the town center—and the path down to the flag at **Punta dels Burricaires**.

Bonus Hike: Sant Feliu de Guíxols to Palamós

Explore the village of Sant Feliu de Guíxols, walk past several beaches and through a river estuary and snake your way along cliffs with views of the ocean below.

DURATION: **4.5 hours**

DIFFICULTY: **Moderate**

DISTANCE: **10.8 miles (17.4 km)**

ELEVATION GAIN: **745 feet (227 m)**

MORE INFO: **camideronda.com**

3B CALELLA DE PALAFRUGELL TO TAMARIU

Hike to a lighthouse with superb views of Costa Brava and to two small villages and a secluded beach

There's a lot to love about this hike from Calella de Palafrugell to Tamariu, from peaceful seaside walking to some of the biggest views of the Mediterranean you'll experience in this area. The route starts at Canadell Beach in Calella de Palafrugell and passes through the small town of Llafranc before climbing to the Sant Sebastià Lighthouse, the eastern-most lighthouse on the Catalan coast, as well as a watchtower that you can climb and the remains of an ancient Iberian settlement that you can explore. The route continues down windswept cliffside paths to a pretty agricultural hamlet before descending to the secluded rocky beach of Cala Pedrosa, where you can swim and sunbathe to your heart's content. From Cala Pedrosa, walk through a pine forest and across a rocky beach with tide pools and lizards on your way to the old fishing village of Tamariu.

ON THE TRAIL

DURATION: **3.5 hours**

DIFFICULTY: **Moderate**

DISTANCE: **4.2 miles (6.8 km)**

ELEVATION GAIN: **859 feet (262 m)**

ELEVATION LOSS: **882 feet (269 m)**

START: **Restaurant Puerto Limón in Calella de Palafrugell**

END: **The beachside promenade in Tamariu**

EAT + DRINK: **Calella de Palafrugell, Llafranc, Far NOMO, El Far Hotel-Restaurant (see Online Resources), Tamariu**

From the Sant Sebastià Lighthouse complex, you have big views back to Llafranc, Calella and Palamós. (Photo courtesy Fons IPEP)

Know Before You Go

This well-signed route on the GR 92 has almost 900 feet (274 m) of elevation gain, most of which you tackle on the ascent to the lighthouse. Between the lighthouse and Tamariu, several sections of trail are steep and skirt big drop-offs without any barriers; take your time if you have balance issues or are scared of heights, and keep small children close. Confidence markers are red and white stripes.

Alternative Routes and Activities

For a shorter walk, shave 1.7 miles (2.7 km) off the hike—and eliminate most of the elevation gain—by taking a taxi to the Sant Sebastià Lighthouse and walking to Tamariu from there.

Alternatively, you could easily spend a full day on this hike by stopping to swim, eat and drink. You can also rent kayaks and stand-up paddle boards to explore the sea in Llafranc and Tamariu.

Navigating

This walk starts in front of Restaurant Puerto Limón, which is located at the intersection of Carrer de Villaamil and Passeig Canadell in Calella de Palafrugell, on the walkway above Canadell Beach and easily walkable from the rest of town. Nearby are several other restaurants and cafés, as well as a Spar grocery store (the smaller, east-side one).

STARTING POINT: **41.88867°, 3.18666°**

RETURN: **The walk ends on the beachside promenade in Tamariu. From there, you can call a taxi or—better yet—have your waiter call one for you when you celebrate the end of your hike with a drink or a meal. The ride back to Calella de Palafrugell takes about 15 minutes.**

MAPS: Available at tourist information offices in Palafrugell and Calella de Palafrugell. An overview map of this route can also be purchased from the Camí de Ronda® company—it's part of their linear route from Blanes to

Portbou. NOTE: The company's highlighted Camí de Ronda route does not always match your route on the GR 92.

1 From **Restaurant Puerto Limón**, walk east along the wide pedestrian walkway. At the end of the promenade, you'll see a footpath on your right. Take this footpath and continue skirting the beach on a path close to the water. Ascend the stairs at 0.2 mile (0.3 km) and take an immediate right. You'll see a trail sign for the **GR 92**, with Llafranc signed for 15 minutes and the Sant Sebastià Lighthouse signed for 55 minutes. Around the next curve, get your first views of the town of Llafranc, with its pretty whitewashed buildings and single cove.

2 At 0.4 mile (0.6 km), stay right on the main path (another route branches off on the left), continuing along **Passeig de Xavier Miserachs**. Come to a memorial for Miserachs, one of Catalonia's leading photographers, who had a house in Esclanyà (next to Palafrugell) and took many pictures in the area. He died in 1998.

3 There's a nice bench to enjoy the views of Llafranc at 0.6 mile (1 km), along with a camera holder so you can get a selfie with the scenic town in the background. Soon after, you'll take a right to descend a large staircase into Llafranc. At the base of the stairs, the lighthouse is signed for 40 minutes and Tamariu for 1 hour and 55 minutes.

4 **Llafranc**, at 0.7 mile (1.1 km), is more of an extension of Calella de Palafrugell than a completely separate town. It's built around a single cove and has a lot of restaurants, cafés and shops. Everything is on display as you walk the beachside promenade to the opposite side of the cove, from kayak and stand-up paddle board rentals on the sandy beach to the small port where most of the dive boats in the area leave from.

5 At 1 mile (1.6 km), near the start of the red pavement of the port, take the stairs to your left. Over the next 0.7 mile (1.1 km), from here to the lighthouse complex, you'll be walking up, up, up (and gaining 515 feet, or 157 m, of elevation), first on stairs and then, after you take a right at the top of the stairs, on quiet residential streets with spectacular seaside homes. Several benches in picturesque spots offer opportunities to rest, including one at the top of the stairs. Go left at the Y at 1.1 miles (1.8 km) and straight at the Y at 1.6 miles (2.6 km).

6 Reach the **Sant Sebastià Lighthouse complex** at 1.7 miles (2.7 km). The lighthouse, built in 1857, presides over the sea from its vantage point 574 feet (175 m) above it and is the lighthouse with the greatest reach along the Catalan coast. As you approach the complex, there's a large lookout on your left with benches and beautiful views back to Llafranc and Calella de Palafrugell. Once you've had your fill of the scenery (and you've caught your breath from the walk up), take the stairs that are located near the postcard shop to access the lighthouse, Far NOMO (the restaurant within the lighthouse), the watchtower, and the Iberian settlement.

At the top of the stairs, stay right. Just below El Far Hotel-Restaurant—a great spot to sample the vermouth that's popular in the region—find free public restrooms and impressive 180-degree views of the Mediterranean Sea. Across from the restrooms, there's a short panoramic trail that leads to the best views of the lighthouse.

7 At 1.8 miles (2.9 km), come to the entrance of the **Sant Sebastià watchtower**, which was built in the sixteenth and seventeenth centuries to watch over the coast and protect it from invasion by pirates and privateers. You can pay a small fee to climb the tower and enjoy the sweeping ocean views.

Just beyond the watchtower are the remains of the Iberian village of Sant Sebastià de la Guarda, which dates back to the sixth century BC. The settlement was discovered

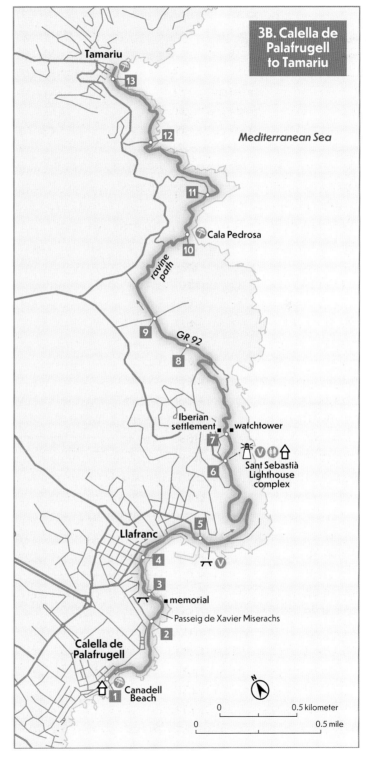

3B. Calella de Palafrugell to Tamariu

Tamariu

Mediterranean Sea

Cala Pedrosa

ravine path

GR 92

Iberian settlement — watchtower

Sant Sebastià Lighthouse complex

Llafranc

memorial

Passeig de Xavier Miserachs

Calella de Palafrugell

Canadell Beach

0   0.5 kilometer

0   0.5 mile

in the late 1950s, and you can walk around the excavated area for free; there's signage about the Iberians and what was discovered here.

Once you're done exploring the lighthouse complex, take the paved path that skirts the Iberian settlement and heads north. The path soon turns to dirt and there's a trail sign for the GR 92. Just past the sign, head to your right on a steep downhill path with large rocks that you'll need to climb down. Don't worry—the path soon gets easier to walk as you come to stairs and the trail flattens out a bit. This is one of the wildest sections of the route, and it's so beautiful, with bright wildflowers, cacti, flowering pines and tamarisk trees all around; the air smells like rosemary, and the ocean seems endless.

At 2.1 miles (3.4 km), stay left at a junction. There's another junction at 2.2 miles (3.5 km); this time, stay right. Just beyond that, you'll see several smaller paths branching off the main one; stay on the main path. At 2.3 miles (3.7 km), a smaller trail continues straight but you want to curve left.

8 The path brings you away from the rocky coast and into agricultural fields at 2.4 miles (3.9 km). The farmland, giant rolls of hay and country homes offer a different look at local life. Given the beautiful surroundings, it's not hard to imagine why rural tourism (staying on a farm) is popular in this area.

9 At 2.6 miles (4.2 km), come to a junction with a quiet road. Stay straight, enjoying the farmland, peaceful olive groves and bright red poppies until you head downhill (right) at 2.7 miles (4.3 km) on the lush ravine path to Cala Pedrosa. This part of the trail has excellent shade and is particularly beautiful thanks to the many wildflowers and their bright purples, yellows, and pinks that surround you. At 2.9 miles (4.7 km), pass a staircase on your left and continue straight.

10 The small, rocky beach of **Cala Pedrosa** is at 3.1 miles (5 km). This is a great place to sunbathe or take a dip if you're hot. It's also a relaxing spot to read a book or stare out at the sea while the waves rhythmically crash against the shore. When you're ready for some shade, there's a large canopy over an open shelter that makes for a pleasant picnic spot. When you're done enjoying the beach, take the steep, narrow staircase up the cliff on the north side of

CHRISTOPHER COLUMBUS

Scientists have recently concluded that Christopher Columbus, previously thought to be Italian or Spanish, came from the Kingdom of Aragon, which included the area now known as Costa Brava, and was a native speaker of Catalan. His discovery of America in 1492 had a profound, unexpected effect on this area—it ultimately led to a shift in the center of world trade from the Mediterranean to the Atlantic, not the best development for the local economy.

the beach. The stairs look intimidating but they don't last long; once you get to the top of the cliff, the trail is flat and wide again.

⓫ At 3.3 miles (5.3 km), stay right when the trail splits. Walk out on a cape through a beautiful pine forest that has peek-a-boo views back to Cala Pedrosa. Several small boot paths run through this forest; stick to the outside of the cape (hug the water) for the best views. Once you round the cape, you have your first views of Tamariu. The path hugs the shore as you get closer to town.

⓬ Stay right at the junction at 3.8 miles (6.1 km). Just beyond, the trail descends to a rocky expanse where you can explore tide pools and watch lizards scampering around. When you get to the building at the end of the rocks, cross the boat ramp and go up the stairs on the other side of it. Stick close to the rock wall; the path will take you around an inlet and up and over more rocks as it draws closer to Tamariu.

⓭ At 4.1 miles (6.6 km), reach the first sandy beach of **Tamariu**. You can walk across the sand or take the stairs and path above to the main beach. Skirt the main beach until you come to the whitewashed

The stairs leading out of Cala Pedrosa look intimidating but don't last long. A bonus: they give you great views of the sea.

buildings of town at 4.2 miles (6.8 km). There's a promenade along the beach with cafés, restaurants and services. When you're done exploring, taxi back to Calella.

3C PALS TO LA BISBAL D'EMPORDÀ

Walk thousand-year-old inland trade routes to four ancient villages

Most of the hikes I recommend for Costa Brava are on the water; this is the big exception. This inland walk allows you to see a completely different side of the region, one that's just as captivating as the coast, yet so different—beautiful fields, ancient trade routes and a collection of small, stone medieval villages. The route starts in Pals, where you can walk cobblestone streets, climb ancient towers and walk old ramparts before heading out on a footpath that's more than one thousand years old. From there, you stroll past olive groves and old vineyards to the town of Peratallada where you can lunch in the main square, pop into cave-like shops and see ruts in the stone roads that were made when chariots were a popular mode of transportation. Walk more fields and farms past the hamlet of Vulpellac to the largest town on the route, La Bisbal d'Empordà, a former Roman settlement that's now famous for pottery and its weekly market.

ON THE TRAIL

DURATION: 3 hours

DIFFICULTY: Easy

DISTANCE: 6.9 miles (11.1 km)

ELEVATION GAIN: 616 feet (188 m)

ELEVATION LOSS: 531 feet (162 m)

START: Parking lot adjacent to the "Pals, Marquesina" bus stop in Pals

END: Square in front of the Church of Santa Maria de la Bisbal d'Empordà in La Bisbal d'Empordà

EAT + DRINK: Pals, Restaurant Bonay (see Online Resources) and others in Peratallada, La Bisbal d'Empordà

Know Before You Go

This relatively flat route on the Camí de Ronda is on easy-to-walk paved roads and dirt footpaths. It is not well signed, though. Carefully follow the steps outlined here; I also recommend purchasing GPX tracks from the Camí de Ronda® company, which has curated the route (see the "Local Hiking Company Spotlight" sidebar).

Alternative Routes and Activities

Enjoy a shorter walk on the most scenic section, from Pals to Peratallada, which is a one-way hike of 3.3 miles (5.3 km).

Or extend your outing with one of these activities:

- Begur, near Pals, is a fun town to explore. It is much higher in elevation than the other coastal spots I feature, perched on a cliff above the ocean. The town boasts many charming cafés and restaurants and a castle you can walk up to that offers views of the coast and inland Costa Brava, where you'll walk. In Begur, you'll see a lot of homes in the Cuban style, looking like little palaces. Catalonia—and Begur in particular—has a big connection to Cuba. In the nineteenth century, many Catalonians immigrated to Cuba and eventually returned back home, bringing with them Cuban architecture and customs. It's common to see spots like Bar Restaurant Havana and plays on the name Che Guevara, and the Catalonian independence flag is often confused for the similar-looking Cuban flag. TIP: You can walk from Begur to Pals, the official start of this hike, which adds 4.3 (downhill) miles (6.9 km).

This walk through ancient inland trade routes will have you feeling like you've gone back in time. (Photo courtesy Pals Tourism)

- There's also plenty to see at the end of the hike in La Bisbal d'Empordà, including a pottery museum that showcases one of the most important facets of local culture and a weekly Friday market with more than 150 stalls (open from 9 a.m. to 1 p.m.).

Navigating

This walk starts in the parking lot adjacent to the "Pals, Marquesina" bus stop, which is a short walk from several cafés and restaurants, as well as the heart of old town.

STARTING POINT: 41.96994°, 3.14635°

DRIVING: Pals is a 20-minute drive north from Calella de Palafrugell. The parking lot is easily found on Google Maps (search "Pals, Marquesina bus stop") and is free and has no maximum stay from September 16 through the end of May. From June 1 to September 15, the parking lot charges a nominal fee and has a time limit of 3 hours. During that summertime period, a good alternative parking lot that's free and has no limit is on Carrer Camí Fondo (at 41.971324°, 3.146396°), a short walk away.

The walk ends in La Bisbal d'Empordà, in front of the Church of Santa Maria de la Bisbal d'Empordà. From there, you can call a taxi for the 15-minute ride back to Pals.

MAPS: Available at the tourist information office in Pals. An overview map of this route can also be purchased from the Camí de Ronda® company—it's part of their circular route. That said, the Camí de Ronda® map doesn't have sufficient detail to help you with turn-by-turn navigation on trail. The

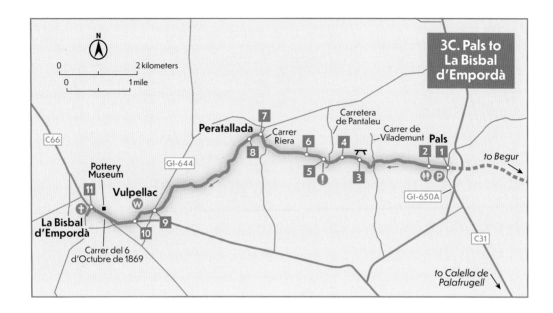

company's GPX tracks for the route are more helpful and can be purchased online (see the "Local Hiking Company Spotlight" sidebar).

1 From the parking lot, walk west along Avinguda Paul Companyó. Stay straight through the roundabout; just past it, there's a private parking lot for residents on your left that has free public restrooms. Just beyond the parking lot, take a left on a small lane, Carrer de la Mina. When Carrer de la Mina splits, take a left and then an immediate right on an unnamed lane that leads out to the fields.

TIP: If you want to explore beautiful medieval Pals before starting your walk, go right on Carrer de la Creu instead of left on Carrer de la Mina just past the private parking lot. Stay on this road until you get to Plaça Major, the main square, where you'll find town hall and

the Office of Tourism, which has maps and more information about Pals. Places that should be on your list of things to see: Carrer Major, a main street that shows off the stone walls and stone buildings of Pals to picture-postcard perfection; Torre de les Hores, the ninth-century master tower of what once was the Pals Castle; the countryside lookout of Mirador de Josep Pla; and the walkable ramparts of the once-fortified village.

2 At 0.2 mile (0.3 km), the path becomes a double track through fields—an old trade route to Peratallada that's more than one thousand years old. The landscape is stunning—golden wheat, giant hay bales, chamomile, poppies, fennel, rosemary, wild roses. As you walk, you'll see many olive trees, including a special variety called Argudell that's grown only in this region and demands a very high price due to its exquisite quality. At 1.1 miles (1.8

km), cross a main road (Carrer de Vilademunt) to continue on the footpath.

3 Come to a picnic table and garbage can at 1.5 miles (2.4 km). While there aren't any views here, it's a good place to stretch if you're still warming up your muscles.

4 You'll start to see evidence of old walls and vineyards that time has forgotten—old vines hanging from trees and cascading down stones—at 1.8 miles (2.9 km). They speak to the long history of wine production in this region, which goes back more than two thousand years. While the Romans made wine in Costa Brava from grapes, they also made wine from local wild roses, which you'll still see all around—their blooms look like those of a wild strawberry. At 2 miles (3.2 km), cross another main road (Carretera de Pantaleu) to continue on the footpath through the fields.

5 At 2.1 miles (3.4 km), come to an important junction that many people miss—in large part because it's not signed. It's a small path to your left that crosses an old, dry stream bed and initially appears to dead-end at a fence. Once you reach the fence, head right and skirt it for approximately 80 feet (25 m), until you come out into the fields once more.

These fields on the way to Peratallada are owned by individual farmers, who may own fifteen or so separate plots in different locations. All of the farmers in the region sell to a single cooperative, which represents their interests and keeps the money made from agriculture local.

6 The footpath comes out onto a road with views of Peratallada at 2.4 miles (3.9 km). At 3.1 miles (5 km), it joins a larger road, **Carrer Riera**. Cross the stream before heading right on Carrer Riera to walk past pretty, jasmine-bedecked homes on the outskirts of town.

7 At 3.3 miles (5.3 km), come to the entrance of **Peratallada**. Head into town by taking a left on Plaça de les Voltes, which leads you to the main square, Plaça Major. TIP: Restaurant Bonay, at Plaça Major, is an excellent place to enjoy a traditional Catalan meal.

Peratallada is a gem—my favorite town on the route. The medieval village is smaller and quieter than Pals, though it still has a tower (also named **Torre de les Hores**) that you can climb for views of the surrounding countryside, as well as a moat. *Peratallada* means "cut stone" and refers to the large natural stone in the middle of town that the buildings and streets were

Costa Brava is a land of contrasts, and not just between the coast and the fields. Mixed in with the locals are also many people from Barcelona, and all over the world, with money—big money. For professionals from Barcelona, the coast is their version of the Hamptons. The billionaires, however, prefer inland Costa Brava, where they can go relatively unnoticed and live in peace. Same with others who are recognized internationally. As you walk, you'll pass by several homes owned by top models and businessmen, but they don't look like anything special—they're meant to blend in.

Pals and Peratallada are both beautiful stone villages. (Photo courtesy Pals Tourism)

made from. (Look down as you walk—in places, you can see ruts in the stone from iron chariot wheels.) The mazelike streets of town are wonderful to wander, filled with cafés, *vinotecas* (wine bars) and shops built into caves.

Once you're done exploring, continue west on Plaça de les Voltes from Plaça Major. When the road Ts, take a left. Soon after, at 3.4 miles (5.5 km), pass a small market on your left and take a left on Carrer d'en Vas. When it Ts, take a right on Carrer Mas Bou, which will lead you to a forest path at 3.5 miles (5.6 km).

8 From the start of the forest path, it's about an hour's walk to La Bisbal d'Empordà. This is another old trade route. Initially, the path through the trees is on

bedrock (granite), and in places you can see indentations from chariot wheels. Eventually the path turns to dirt, then country roads, as you walk near farms on the outskirts of another medieval village, Vulpellac.

9 At 5.7 miles (9.2 km), cross the busy GI-644 road and continue west on Carrer Nou to skirt **Vulpellac**, which doesn't have any services for visitors aside from a water fountain to refill your water bottle just down a village street off Carrer Nou at 5.9 miles (9.5 km). Just beyond that, the road splits. Go left on Carrer del Llorer.

10 Carrer del Llorer joins the C66, a main road heading toward **La Bisbal d'Empordà**, at 6.1 miles (9.8 km). Continue right (west); there's a sidewalk for you to walk on. You'll be on this busy road and, after the roundabout, Carrer del 6 d'Octubre de 1869, for only 10 minutes or so as you pass through the new part of the city on your way to old town. At 6.5 miles (10.5 km), you'll see the **Terracotta Museu**, or Pottery Museum, which is worth a visit if you have the time; La Bisbal d'Empordà is famous for its pottery and antiques.

11 At 6.8 miles (10.9 km), take a left onto Carrer Ample, then a right just a few feet later on Carrer Germans Sitjar. This small alley takes you alongside the **Church of Santa Maria de la Bisbal d'Empordà**, which dates back to the tenth century. The route ends in front of the church, near the main square.

There's a lot of history in La Bisbal d'Empordà. It's built on the site of an old Roman settlement, though the modern town has roots back to the year 901, when the Church of Santa Maria de la Bisbal d'Empordà was consecrated. The name La Bisbal is derived from the Catalan word for bishop, because it was owned for a time by the bishops from Girona. It became popular as a new home for French immigrants after the French Revolution. These days, the local economy relies heavily on pottery and agriculture. Since 1332, there's been a weekly market held at the main square every Friday. The old town is worth exploring; there's a palace to check out, as well as many cafés and restaurants. When you're done, a taxi can take you back to Pals.

3D PORTLLIGAT TO THE CAP DE CREUS LIGHTHOUSE

Experience Salvador Dalí's favorite landscape, from Portlligat to the Cap de Creus Lighthouse

Discover the landscape that famous local artist Salvador Dalí loved more than any other on this walk from the town of Portlligat and through the wilds of the Cap de Creus Natural Park to the Cap de Creus Lighthouse, the easternmost lighthouse on the Iberian Peninsula. Along the way, there are many secluded beaches to swim at. You can also pair your walk with a guided visit to the Salvador Dalí House in Portlligat.

ON THE TRAIL

DURATION: **3 hours**

DIFFICULTY: **Moderate**

DISTANCE: **3.6 miles (5.8 km)**

ELEVATION GAIN: **723 feet (223 m)**

ELEVATION LOSS: **483 feet (147 m)**

START: **Parking Portlligat in Portlligat**

END: **Cap de Creus Lighthouse**

EAT + DRINK: **Portlligat, Restaurant Cap de Creus, Restaurant Bar Sa Freu (see Online Resources)**

The sea views from Restaurant Cap de Creus are stunning.

Know Before You Go

Although there's not a ton of elevation gain over the length of the trail, expect a couple of steep climbs, especially if you choose to visit some of the secluded beaches along the way. Because it's exposed, this can be a challenging hike in the heat. It's typically too hot to do this hike in July or August. Better times are May, June and September. Be sure to pack plenty of water (at least 2 liters per person); there's nowhere to refill your water bottle en route.

This walk is on the Grand Randonée (GR) 11/Camí de Ronda/Camí Antic de Cap de Creus and is relatively well signed once you get to the footpath at 1 mile (1.6 km). Confidence markers are green and red stripes in the beginning of the hike and red and white stripes near the end, once the trail joins the GR 11.

Other notes about the route:

- Sometimes, for the safety of visitors, the natural park and its trails must close. This happens mainly during the hot summer months (June–September). There's a website that updates daily to let you know whether the park is closed (see Online Resources); check it before you hike. The park is located in the Alt Empordà area; when this area is red or black on the website, hiker access to the park is closed.
- It's best to do this walk on the weekend, when the shuttle from the Cap de Creus Lighthouse to Portlligat Beach is most likely to be running.
- To avoid walking in the heat of the day, hike in the morning and visit the Salvador Dalí House in the late afternoon. Be sure to allow yourself plenty of time to

shuttle or taxi back to Portlligat Beach for your timed admission to the Dalí House. If you get back early, you can always relax on the beach or enjoy a cocktail at the little beach bar while you wait. And though the lighthouse makes a fantastic end point, you could do the hike in the opposite direction, from the lighthouse to the Salvador Dalí House, if preferred.

- Car traffic in the natural park is limited to people with reservations at one of the restaurants on-site (verify at the time of reservation), taxis and the shuttle bus, so don't plan on leaving a car there.

- Because this is a protected area, it's important to stay on official hiking paths. You can see the different routes available on the natural park's map (see Navigating).

Alternative Routes and Activities

If you prefer a shorter route, you could call a taxi and have them meet you along the natural park's road; the trail crosses the road several times.

Or extend your outing with one of the following activities:

- This is a great opportunity to visit the Salvador Dalí House (see Online Resources), where the famous Spanish surrealist lived and worked from 1930 to 1982. You can tour the house and the grounds with a guide to learn about the artist and his work. It's a very quirky spot. Among other things, you can see the mirror Dalí had specially placed to beam the first light of the sunrise to his bed and the tiny cricket cage on his bedroom wall—perfect for listening to the sound of the crickets as he fell asleep. TIP: Tickets to the Salvador Dalí House go quickly; buy them as soon as you book your trip. Also, you must pick up your tickets at least 20 minutes before your tour or they will resell them. Backpacks aren't allowed in the house since they may bump against the relics, but lockers are available for rent across from the ticket office—you'll need €1 coins to use them.

- There are many coves you can walk down to on the route; you could easily lengthen this hike by swimming at several of them.

- From the lighthouse, you can make a loop walk by taking a different part of the GR 11 and the road back to Portlligat Beach (consult a local map).

- The nearby seaside town of Cadaqués is a picturesque place to have dinner and walk around. It's also a fun overnight destination.

Navigating

This walk starts at Parking Portlligat, a pay lot near Portlligat Beach and the Salvador Dalí House in the town of Portlligat, with several cafés and a beach bar nearby.
STARTING POINT: 42.29545°, 3.28679°
DRIVING: From Calella de Palafrugell, Portlligat is a 1-hour-and-30-minute drive north. The last half hour or so of the route is narrow and curvy and the road is popular with bicyclists; it can take longer to drive than expected.

The walk ends at the Cap de Creus Lighthouse. From there, depending on the season, there is occasional shuttle service

The short climb at the end of Hike 3D, up to the Cap de Creus Lighthouse, has a great payoff—two restaurants where you can celebrate your walk in style.

back to Portlligat. The shuttle picks up near the main restaurant at the lighthouse complex and drops off at a parking lot that's a short walk from the one you started in; there's a small trail in the southeast corner of the shuttle parking lot that connects the two. For current shuttle times, call the Moventis Sarfa shuttle company (+34 902 302 025) or visit the information center at the lighthouse. Alternatively, you can hire a local taxi for the 15-minute drive back to Portlligat Beach; the waitstaff at the lighthouse complex can call one for you.

MAPS: Available at the tourist information office in Cadaqués. The route also appears on the Camí de Ronda® company's linear

route from Blanes to Portbou, though it doesn't always correspond to their high-lighted Camí de Ronda route. Or you can download a map of the trails in the natural park (see Online Resources).

1 From **Parking Portlligat**, head south on the access road and toward the water. TIP: You may see a wild boar or two walking around the parking lot looking for food. They typically don't bother anyone, but keep your distance. When you hit the beach, with its fun beach bar and kayak rentals, continue straight on the road you've been walking. It will turn into a larger road with recreational vehicles parked alongside it.

Continue walking on the road as it curves and heads into a quiet residential area. Take the opportunity to pause at one of the several panoramas and benches along the way. You'll pass an olive grove and a vineyard as the road becomes even quieter, as well as a couple of secluded coves. Keep walking; the ones on the more remote part of the trail are even better.

2 Leave the road at 0.8 mile (1.3 km), where you see a trail sign that points you down a rocky double track to the right. (If you were to continue down the main road for another few feet, you'd come to a junction with the natural park road.) Even though you're somewhat close to the road, it's easy to forget it exists, especially because hardly any cars are allowed on it. Walk along a remote-feeling terraced hill-side bursting with flowering cacti and bird-song. At 0.9 mile (1.4 km), a trail descends

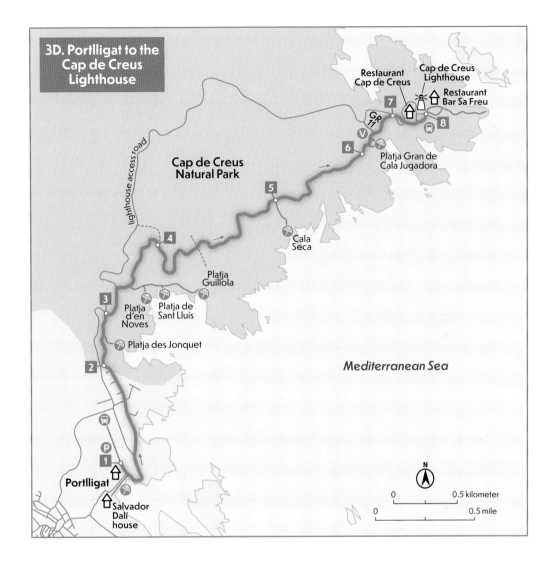

on the right to remote **Platja des Jonquet**. At 1 mile (1.6 km), stay right and walk through a beautiful olive grove that's also home to many butterflies.

3 At 1.1 miles (1.8 km), the trail comes out on the natural park road. Go right and continue for a short distance. The quiet road is lined with stone walls and olive trees. At 1.2 miles (1.9 km), the trail leaves the road on a dirt footpath to your right.

Enjoy views out to the ocean and the sound of waves crashing onto the rocks below. At 1.3 miles (2.1 km), stay left when a trail branches off to the right for the coves of **Platja d'en Noves**, **Platja de Sant Lluís** and **Platja Guillola**.

4 At 1.6 miles (2.6 km), go right on a dirt road. This is the halfway point of your hike, and a trail sign here has the lighthouse signed for 1 hour and 10 minutes.

Walk along this road, with its smattering of rural houses, for 0.4 mile (0.6 km), until the footpath deviates from the dirt road once more and you enter the most remote and enchanting part of the hike, one dotted with old stone walls, sharp thistles and tall rosemary.

5 Catch your first glimpse of the **Cap de Creus Lighthouse complex** from the top of a rise at 2.5 miles (4 km). There's also a trail here that branches off to the right for **Cala Seca**, a secluded cove below. You'll soon start to have great peek-a-boo views of the sea.

6 At 3.1 miles (5 km), pass the first of two trails to **Platja Gran de Cala Jugadora**, the most beautiful and most popular of the coves on the route. From above, the water is several gorgeous shades of blue. There's a nice spot to enjoy the views at 3.2 miles (5.1 km)—the best panorama of the hike, with views of the lighthouse above and the idyllic beach below.

A few feet beyond that, there's a trail sign for the **GR 11**. The lighthouse is signed for 15 minutes. From here on out, the trail will be signed with both green and red stripes and white and red stripes.

7 The trail ascends steeply to the natural park road at 3.4 miles (5.5 km). Once you're on the road, cross it and look for a painted rock, where the footpath continues. You'll cross the road once more at 3.5 miles (5.6 km), then head up a steep, rocky footpath for the final flourish. Although this last part of the route is challenging, it only lasts 0.1 mile (0.2 km).

8 At the top, you've got plenty to explore. Head right for the **Cap de Creus Lighthouse**, the easternmost lighthouse on the Iberian Peninsula. It was built in 1853 on a spot previously occupied by a watchtower to guard against pirate attacks.

Check out the beautiful views of the Mediterranean to the east of the lighthouse and the quiet **Restaurant Bar Sa Freu** to the south that sells drinks and tapas in a relaxed atmosphere. TIP: I recommend the café's sangria, which is made daily with fresh fruit. A couple of small trails lead out onto the rocks and are worth exploring—one heads to a cave.

On the west side of the lighthouse complex (to the left when the trail Ts at the top), the larger **Restaurant Cap de Creus** has a full gourmet menu.

When you're done exploring, take the shuttle back to Portlligat or hire a taxi to drive you back (see Driving at the start of the Navigating section for more information).

Bonus Hike: Santa Helena–Monasterio de San Pedro de Roda Loop

This hike within the Cap de Creus Natural Park, near the town of **La Vall de Santa Creu**, takes you on a circular route with incredible views of the Girona countryside, mountains and coastline—and to a monastery that you can visit.

DURATION: **2 hours**

DIFFICULTY: **Moderate**

DISTANCE: **2.6 miles (4.2 km) roundtrip**

ELEVATION GAIN: **643 feet (196 m)**

MORE INFO: **alltrails.com**

The stone village of Gordes cascades down a hillside. (Photo courtesy Destination Luberon/kos-crea)

4 PROVENCE, FRANCE

Into the lavender fields and ancient abbeys of France's most idyllic region

AT A GLANCE

GENERAL LOCATION: Southeastern France

HOME BASE: Gordes

LOCAL LANGUAGE: French

USE OF ENGLISH: Widely understood and used

FAMILY FRIENDLY: ★★☆☆

COST: $$$

WHEN TO GO: Apr to Sept

SCENERY: Vineyards, lavender fields, hill towns, low mountains, Mediterranean Sea

DON'T MISS: Hiking village to village, French cuisine, historic abbeys, local wine

At the weekly market in Gordes, you can pick up provisions for your hikes. (Photo courtesy Destination Luberon/want2becity)

As soon as I saw a picture of the village of Gordes, in the southern French region of Provence, I knew I needed to visit. There was something about the stoic-looking stone city perched atop a hill and cascading down it, overlooking the verdant green of agricultural fields and the vivid purple of blooming lavender, that just called to me. I had visions of walking its winding streets and cobblestone paths to a good viewpoint at sunset, wineglass in hand, as the stone turned ochre. I could just picture myself with my market basket, buying fresh bread, olive oil, hard salami and soft cheese for my hikes.

The reality of Gordes didn't—and doesn't—disappoint. There's a reason the village has been voted one of the Most Beautiful Villages in France (an official designation), and the most beautiful hilltop town in Provence—it really is stunning. Part of its beauty comes from the old stone buildings that give the town its unique character. Although some of these buildings, like the castle that dominates the center of the village, date back to the tenth century, the history of Gordes goes back much further, to Gallo-Roman times when it was a fortified settlement for the main city of Cavaillon. Over time and as its rulers changed, Gordes held on to its identity as a fortification and a refuge for surrounding inhabitants. Some of that history is on display at Les Caves du Palais Saint-Firmin (see Online Resources), which gives you a glimpse into the underworld that was part of the town's defenses. Other parts of the town's long and interesting history come alive with one of the tourism bureau's curated self-guided walking tours of Gordes (see Bonus Hike), where you can see ramparts and other sections of the old fortification.

These days, the town doesn't keep people out, it welcomes them in, with market days, quaint shops where you can buy picnic supplies and local artwork, and ancient-feeling accommodations. (I stayed in a tall, winding house built into the rock that was originally a tannery in the Middle Ages.) Gordes also makes a great launching point for other adventures in the area, such as visiting the famous Abbaye Notre-

Dame de Sénanque and Le Village des Bories, a collection of restored huts from the 1600s (for a hike that visits both, see Hike 4B). With a short drive, you can be in the "Venice of Provence," the riverside town of L'Isle-sur-la-Sorgue, which has a completely different feel from that of the arid countryside. Drive a little farther and reach the Mediterranean coast, one of my favorite spots in Provence, where you can enjoy fresh seafood, bury your toes in the hot sand and swim at secluded beaches that are only accessible on foot (see Hike 4D, Calanques National Park).

From Gordes, you can also walk and bike village to village, savoring Provence the way it should be savored—slowly—while seeing a host of other beautiful places that most people usually drive to, take some pictures of, and move on from. What those people don't realize is that the landscape of Provence—its fertile valleys, low mountains and rocky gorges—is just as worthy of attention as the hilltop towns that have made it famous. When hiking and biking the area, you'll typically have the trails and back roads of the area mostly to yourself. As a reward, enjoy views that most people never see from viewpoints that are hidden from the road.

The lavender fields bloom in early summer, typically around mid-June to mid-July, so aim to visit in late June if you want to see the lavender in bloom. But if you do, be prepared to adventure in the heat—you'll need plenty of sunscreen and water. And check to make sure local trails are open—they often close in high summer, when it's hot and the risk of fire is high. Alternatively, plan to visit in spring or fall, when the weather is more pleasant.

With picture-postcard natural beauty, a ton of history and more scenic diversity than most people realize, Provence isn't just an ideal place to visit—it's an ideal place to walk.

THE LUBERON

The area of Provence that you'll spend most of your time in for this home base hiking trip is the Luberon, which is dominated by the Luberon Regional Natural Park. This is a park without physical borders and there's no pass or permit required to visit it. The park comprises the Luberon mountain range to the south, the Vaucluse mountain range to the north and the Calavon Valley in between. Gordes is in the park's northwest corner.

Getting There and Around

The largest airport in Provence is in the coastal town of Marseilles. From there, it's a 1-hour drive to Gordes.

There isn't good public transportation in and around Gordes, and it's difficult to get to Gordes—and to the day hike in Cassis (see Hike 4D, Calanques National Park)—without a car, so you'll want to rent one for your trip to Provence. Having your own vehicle will also allow you to explore farther afield and stock up on groceries at the cheaper, larger grocery store in Coustellet.

Where to Stay

While my top choice for a home base in Provence is the village of Gordes, nearby Roussillon, which is visited on the Gordes–Joucas–Roussillon hike (Hike 4C), is another great choice. The rural bed-and-breakfasts in the valley beneath Gordes can also make for very scenic stays. If

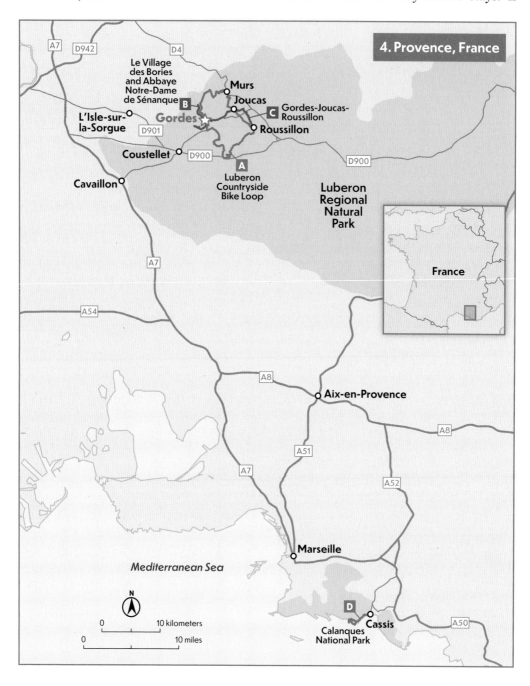

THE ROUTES

HIKE	ROUTE NAME	DURATION	DIFFICULTY	DISTANCE	ELEV. GAIN	ELEV. LOSS
4A	Luberon Countryside Bike Loop	4 hours	Moderate	26.8 mi (43.1 km)	3,222 ft (982 m)	3,222 ft (982 m)
4B	Le Village des Bories and Abbaye Notre-Dame de Sénanque	4.5 hours	Moderate	7.5 mi (12.1 km)	1,257 ft (383 m)	1,257 ft (383 m)
4C	Gordes–Joucas–Roussillon	5 hours	Moderate	8.4 mi (13.5 km)	1,098 ft (335 m)	1,214 ft (370 m)
4D	Calanques National Park	5 hours	Moderate to challenging	6.4 mi (10.3 km)	1,820 ft (555 m)	1,820 ft (555 m)

you plan your trip in summer to catch the blooming of the lavender, try to find a place with a pool so you have somewhere to cool off from the heat.

And keep in mind that Gordes flows down the front of a big hill. If you don't want to hike up and down the hill each day (the main part of town is at the top of the hill), look for accommodations in the very center of the village.

Eat and Resupply

The town of Gordes has a small Spar grocery store, but it's expensive and doesn't have a wide selection. Instead, drive 12 minutes to Coustellet, where there's a larger Super U and an Aldi.

Gordes has quite a few dining options, most of which are located at the top of the hill. When you're out and about, be sure to track down the following Provençal specialties:

- *Ratatouille*: a colorful vegetable stew dreamed up in the eighteenth century by farmers looking to use up their annual harvest of summer vegetables
- *Bouillabaisse*: a fish stew in a saffron-infused broth, a specialty of Marseilles that's served family style
- *Nougat*: a confection with the consistency of fudge, made of sugar or honey and egg whites and embedded with pistachios and almonds
- *Herbes de Provence*: a mixture of dried herbs now sold internationally that are typical of Provence—often marjoram, oregano, rosemary, savory and thyme

There's an Intersport in Cavaillon and a Sport 2000 in L'Isle-sur-la-Sorgue in case you need to adjust or add to your hiking gear.

What to See and Do
GORDES MARKET

Every Tuesday morning, there's a fresh market in Gordes, with stalls set around Place Genty Pantaly in the center of the

In Provence, local produce and artisan products take center stage in the cuisine. (Photo courtesy Destination Luberon)

L'ISLE-SUR-LA-SORGUE

One of the most charming and distinctive towns in Provence—and my favorite day trip in the area—is L'Isle-sur-la-Sorgue, an island town built on the Sorgue River that feels like a smaller Venice. Aside from being exceptionally photogenic—think flowing water, water wheels and cascades of flowers everywhere—the town is known for its antique shops and weekly markets. It's also a great place to grab lunch on the river.

village. While the emphasis is on local products like lavender and soap, this is also a convenient place to grab picnic supplies—wine, olive oil and fresh bread.

DONKEY TREKKING

Take a slow, relaxing walk on quiet countryside roads and through the charming village of Maubec in the company of a donkey, which will carry your pack for you. Young kids can ride on the donkeys. For more information, contact Les Oreilles du Luberon (see Online Resources).

★★ Provence, specifically Gordes, gets two stars out of four for being family friendly. There's not a ton for kids to do in the area, and you'll likely hear some complaining about climbing up and down the hill each day if your accommodations aren't in the very center. (Or you'll have to give a lot of piggyback rides.) This said, my then four-year-old's favorite activity of our whole three-month research trip for this book was the donkey ride with Les Oreilles du Luberon (see What to See and Do)—she still talks about it.

4A LUBERON COUNTRYSIDE BIKE LOOP

Bike through the Luberon Regional Natural Park to seven beautiful villages

Occasionally I find a bike ride in a spot where I normally hike that's ideal for providing a high-level overview of the area. This countryside ride, which travels through seven villages and the vineyards, cherry orchards and meadows that connect them, is just that kind of a ride. It starts in Gordes before descending to the floor of the Calavon Valley to visit the towns of Saint-Pantaléon and Lumières, then climbs gently to Goult and

Roussillon. After descending to the valley floor once more and crossing to the other side, it leads you up the base of the Vaucluse Mountains to Joucas and the highest town on the route, Murs, before taking you back to Gordes via a pretty pass with views of Abbaye Notre-Dame de Sénanque.

ON THE TRAIL

DURATION: **4 hours**

DIFFICULTY: **Moderate**

DISTANCE: **26.8 miles (43.1 km)**

ELEVATION GAIN: **3,222 feet (982 m)**

ELEVATION LOSS: **3,222 feet (982 m)**

START: **Place Genty Pantaly in Gordes**

END: **Place Genty Pantaly in Gordes**

EAT + DRINK: **Gordes, Lumières, Goult, Roussillon, Joucas, Murs**

Know Before You Go

The route is an established local ride but is not well signed. Follow the steps outlined here or use my GPX tracks to stay on track; these will also help with staying on the larger routes (the D roads, for example), which are composed of multiple smaller roads.

Other notes about the route:

- Unless you love the workout of road biking, use an e-bike, which takes the sting out of the uphill climbs, especially the section from Joucas up to Murs. (Without an e-bike, this is a challenging ride.) Remember to turn off the electric assist when you don't need it so that you have enough juice for the climbs.
- Electric Move (see Online Resources) is a shop that rents bikes and related gear, including e-bikes, helmets and even bike seats and trailers for kids. They can deliver the bikes to your accommodations, too, so you don't have to worry about transporting them.
- Pack a bike lock so you can confidently leave your bike as you explore, and use a

handlebar-mounted cell-phone holder if you want to follow my GPX tracks.

- This route includes a couple of towns you'll explore in greater depth when you hike them (Joucas and Roussillon). To prioritize your time and make the most of your ride, stop in the other villages that you won't visit again, especially Goult and Murs, which are my favorite spots on the route.

Alternative Routes and Activities

There are several shorter bike rides in the area, including a loop around Gordes that visits just Gordes, Joucas and Murs. For help planning a shorter route, see the local tourist information office in Gordes.

Or you can extend your outing:

- By stopping to explore the villages en route, this bike ride can easily take most of a day.
- The network of bike routes in the area makes it easy to extend the loop by adding in other nearby villages like Cabrières d'Avignon or Coustellet.

The Luberon Countryside Bike Loop is on quiet country roads that skirt beautiful lavender fields. (Photo courtesy Destination Luberon)

Navigating

This bike ride starts and ends near the fountain at Place Genty Pantaly (Genty Pantaly Square) in Gordes, an easy ride from the rest of town and close to several restaurants, cafés and a grocery store.

STARTING POINT: **43.91089°, 5.20012°**

MAPS: Available at the tourist information office in Gordes (conveniently located at Place Genty Pantaly) and at local bike shops.

1 From the fountain at **Place Genty Pantaly**, head east on Rue Baptistin Picca, which becomes Route Neuve. Take a right at 0.1 mile (0.2 km) on Chemin de Lourdanaud as you descend through the village. At 0.3 mile (0.5 km), take another right on Chemin de la Calade, then a left on Rue de la Font Basse, which you follow down to the D2. Go right on the D2, then left at 0.9 mile (1.4 km) onto Chemin de Fontourin. Take that until the road Ts, where you'll go left on Chemin de Saint-Chafret. At 1.9 miles (3.1 km), go right on the D104.

2 At 4 miles (6.4 km), the D104 curves around the hamlet of **Saint-Pantaléon**. There aren't any visitor services in town—it's mainly just a few houses scattered around a town hall, though the village does have a twelfth-century Roman chapel. At 5.3 miles (8.5 km), take a right on Chemin de la Bounotte, then a right on the D60 at 5.8 miles (9.3 km).

3 Take a left on the D105 at 6.6 miles (10.6 km). If you'd first like to explore the tiny enclave of **Lumières**, which has a couple of cafés and a bakery, stay straight

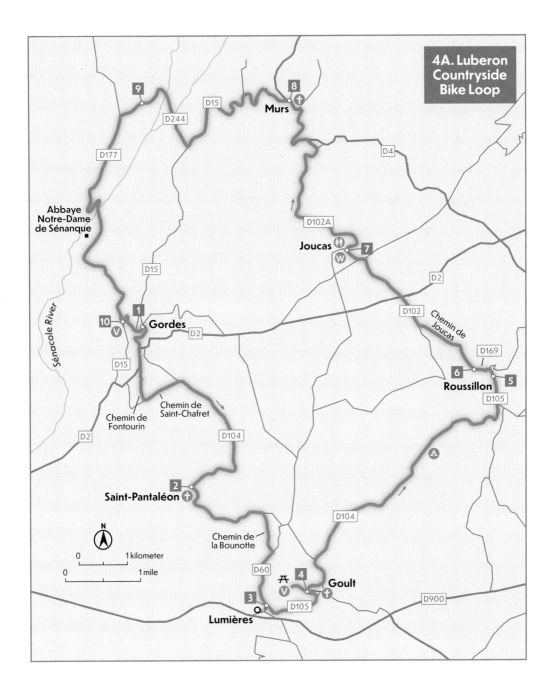

Abbaye Notre-Dame de Sénanque

Sénacole River

Gordes

D177

D244

D15

D15

D15

D2

D2

Chemin de Fontourin

Chemin de Saint-Chafret

D104

Saint-Pantaléon

Chemin de la Bounotte

D60

Lumières

D105

Goult

Murs

D4

D102A

Joucas

D2

D102

Chemin de Joucas

D169

Roussillon

D105

D104

D900

N

0   1 kilometer

0   1 mile

instead, which will take you in short order to the main street through town.

4 At 7.6 miles (12.2 km), find yourself at Église Saint-Sébastien, in the relatively large (for the area) and charming town of **Goult**. Like Gordes and Roussillon, this is a hill town, but it's off most tourists' radar. Continue cycling up the main street and you'll find cute cafés, markets and shops. This is the perfect place to stop for a cup of coffee or lunch or just to explore.

For good views, turn left on Rue du Jeu de Paume at 7.9 miles (12.7 km), which takes you to a circular parking area. To the south, there's an old windmill, the **Moulin de Jérusalem**, and a short trail with panoramic views back to the wooded green slope of Goult. To the north, there's a network of footpaths to picnic benches and a lookout over the surrounding countryside.

When you're done exploring Goult, head back to [4] and turn left to get back on the D105. At 8.7 miles (14 km), take a right at the roundabout onto the D104. You'll know you're almost to Roussillon when you pass a campground at 11 miles (17.7 km). At 12.3 miles (19.8 km), go left onto the D105.

5 The gateway to **old town Roussillon**, which you hike to on the Gordes–Joucas–Roussillon hike (Hike 4C), is on Rue Richard Casteau, a left at 12.6 miles (20.3

The ochre buildings of Roussillon are a photographer's delight.

km). For now, stay straight until 12.7 miles (20.4 km), when you head left at a roundabout onto the D169.

6 At 13 miles (20.9 km), take a right on Chemin de Joucas and proceed down to the floor of the valley. It's a bucolic setting and the views are wonderful—so is biking through the vineyards. At 14 miles (22.5 km), take a right on the D102. Shortly after, cross the D2 on your way to Joucas.

7 At 15.4 miles (24.8 km), just past a playground, you have a choice to make. You'll explore **Joucas** on the Gordes–Joucas–Roussillon hike (Hike 4C), so if you're happy to keep riding, go right on the D102A. If, on the other hand, you want a sneak peek of Joucas or need something, go straight. At Place des Commandeurs, there's a spot to refill your water bottle, as well as free public restrooms. Just beyond that are a couple of cafés and a small market.

The ride from Joucas to Murs is all uphill but it sure is beautiful—you'll ride past a lot of cherry trees and a large rock ridge closer to Murs. Take a left on a smaller cutoff road at 17.5 miles (28.2 km), then a left on the D4, which takes you all the way into town.

8 **Murs**, at 18.5 miles (29.8 km), is so different from the rest of the towns you'll see in the Luberon. It's almost like someone has transported you to the Alps (minus the snow-capped peaks)—you're up relatively high (2,625 feet or 800 m) in the **Vaucluse Mountains** amid big, beautiful, wildflower-strewn meadows, cherry orchards and vineyards. It's one of the prettiest spots in Provence.

There's a lot of history in town, which is dominated by a castle from the 1400s. Unfortunately the castle is closed to visitors, but there is a twelfth-century Roman church you can visit, as well as the birthplace of famous **Crillon le Brave**, a soldier who fought alongside Henry IV and whose house is now a small museum. If you want to grab a bite to eat in town, check out **Hotel Le Crillon**, which has a bar/tearoom as well as a restaurant. At 18.6 miles (29.9 km), take a left off the D4 onto the D15, which winds past rural accommodations and lavender fields. At 21.2 miles (34.1 km), take a right onto the D244.

9 The high point of the route comes at 22.4 miles (36 km). Just past that, take a left onto the D177, which runs between the Vallon (Valley) de Châteauneuf and the Vallon de Ferrière and eventually above **Abbaye Notre-Dame de Sénanque** on its way back to Gordes.

10 At 26.3 miles (42.3 km), where you emerge to great views of Gordes, take a left on the D15 and make your way back into town. At the roundabout at 26.7 miles (43 km), go right for **Place Genty Pantaly**.

4B LE VILLAGE DES BORIES AND ABBAYE NOTRE-DAME DE SÉNANQUE

Visit a village of restored stone huts from the 1600s and one of the most photographed monasteries in southern France

There's so much history in and around Gordes. This walk combines two of the best spots to visit—a village of restored huts from the 1600s and a famous monastery that dates back to 1148—into one daylong hike. Even better: You also get to experience my favorite scenic lookout of Gordes along the way, as well as get a view of the abbey from above that most people never see.

ON THE TRAIL

DURATION: 4.5 hours

DIFFICULTY: Moderate

DISTANCE: 7.5 miles (12.1 km)

ELEVATION GAIN: 1,257 feet (383 m)

ELEVATION LOSS: 1,257 feet (383 m)

START: Place Genty Pantaly in Gordes

END: Place Genty Pantaly in Gordes

EAT + DRINK: Gordes, vending machine at Le Village des Bories, café outside of Gordes, vending machine at Abbaye Notre-Dame de Sénanque

The Abbaye Notre-Dame de Sénanque is a sight to behold, especially when the lavender is in bloom. (Photo by Hans/Pixabay)

Know Before You Go

This route is a combination of two different walks, one to Le Village des Bories and another to Abbaye Notre-Dame de Sénanque, both of which are well signed. Most of the elevation gain is experienced between Le Village des Bories and the Côte de Sénancole, above the abbey.

Bring a picnic to enjoy at the peaceful grounds of the abbey as there aren't many places to eat en route.

Alternative Routes and Activities

For a shorter walk, split this route into two different days.

Tour Abbaye Notre-Dame de Sénanque while you're there. During a tour, you can visit the ancient dormitory, the cloister, the warming room, the chapter house and the church.

Navigating

This hike starts near the fountain at Place Genty Pantaly (Genty Pantaly Square) in Gordes, an easy walk from the rest of town and close to several restaurants, cafés and a grocery store.

STARTING POINT: **43.91089°, 5.20012°**

MAPS: **Available at the tourist information office in Gordes, which is conveniently located at Place Genty Pantaly.**

1 From the fountain at **Place Genty Pantaly**, head west on Rue Baptistin Picca. When you come to a roundabout in a few feet, go left to continue west on Rue de la Combe.

2 At 0.2 mile (0.3 km), take another left on Rue des Tanneurs. Stay on this as it winds out of town, becoming Rue Jean Deyrolle and Chemin de Bel Air.

3 At 0.6 mile (1 km), arrive at the best spot to capture a shot of the beautiful hilltop village of Gordes. TIP: If you think it looks amazing now, come back at sunset, when the last light touches the stone buildings and makes them glow. Shortly after the viewpoint, at 0.7 mile (1.1 km), cross the busy D15 and continue walking on Chemin des Fileuses, a quiet, narrow route that's shared with cars. Your surroundings get

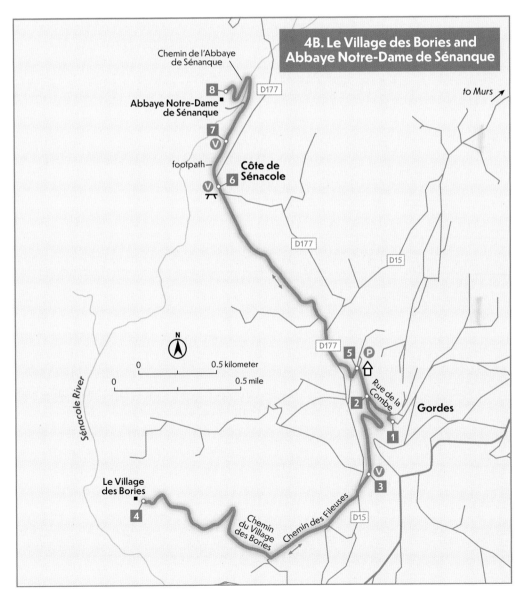

more remote as you continue walking—it's hard to believe you're less than a mile from Gordes. At 1.2 miles, take a right on Chemin du Village des Bories.

4 Come to the visitor center for **Le Village des Bories** at 2 miles (3.2 km). After purchasing a ticket, grab a free map and start your self-guided tour of the restored village of stone huts, some of which date back to the 1600s. The huts, or *bories*, are examples of dry-stone building—taking stones and creating a structure out of them without mortar or binder, using the corbelled vault technique. This type of construction was common in France during the 1600s and 1700s, and huts of this

type were often used as shelters for shepherds, as places for storing equipment or harvested crops, or as temporary and seasonal homes for farmers working on land far away from their home village.

In this area, the *bories* were used by people growing grapes, olives and cereal grains and raising livestock and silkworms. The huts were abandoned in the mid-1800s and were rediscovered—and restored—in the 1960s. In addition to wandering in and around the *bories*, you can visit a documentation center with a film and an exhibit that explains more about the huts and the building technique. When you're done exploring the village, retrace your steps to [2]. From there, take a left on Rue de la Combe.

5 There's a parking lot and a café at a curve in the road at 3.9 miles (6.3 km). This is the only non-vending-machine food on the route, so if you're hungry, it's a good opportunity to stop for a bite. Just past that, take a right on a quieter road that heads uphill past old stone walls and buildings. This cut-through takes you to a larger road, the D177/Route de Sénanque, where you take a right and walk past several high-end bed-and-breakfasts and hotels. At 4.1 miles (6.6 km), follow a sign on a telephone pole that directs you to go left onto a smaller road that eventually becomes a footpath. There's plenty to admire as you walk—olive groves, ancient stone walls and an old Roman road complete with wheel ruts. This is one of my favorite sections of the entire walk.

6 At 4.8 miles (7.7 km), go left on a paved road, the D177 again, at the **Côte de**

Several of the *bories* are open for exploring.

Sénancole. From here, the abbey is signed for 0.4 mile (0.6 km), but don't rush. There are benches near a panoramic lookout over the Sénancole Gorge and nearby mountains. This plateau is a particularly popular spot for bicyclists needing a break from the roller-coaster-like D177. At 4.9 miles (7.9 km), a footpath branches off on your left; take it as it descends relatively steeply past scurrying lizards and flitting butterflies toward the abbey. The route has small, loose rocks, so watch your footing.

7 Don't keep your eyes exclusively on your feet, though—at 5 miles (8 km), you get your first view of the impressive abbey and its beautiful lavender fields below, a view most people don't get because they drive to the abbey. This is when you want your camera!

At 5.3 miles (8.5 km), stay straight when a trail branches off on your left. Just beyond that, go left on Chemin de l'Abbaye de Sénanque. At 5.4 miles (8.7 km), take a right on a path around the abbey. Follow the path as it makes a semicircle around the front of the abbey property, until you reach the info desk and gift shop at 5.5 miles (8.9 km).

8 **Abbaye Notre-Dame de Sénanque** was founded in 1148 by Cistercian monks and took about sixty years to build. Its home is a small valley that is only 0.6 mile (1 km) long and 984 feet (300 m) wide but that perfectly fit the bill—monasteries weren't allowed in towns or villages or within rural houses, and the monks had just enough space to construct everything they needed to be self-sustaining, another rule. (Going outside of the monastery was considered bad for the soul.)

The abbey prospered until the early 1400s, when a period of discord and violence contributed to it falling into disrepair. Since then, the abbey has been inhabited on and off by monks. Changing laws about religion meant the monks were evicted several times. At one point, a local farmer lived in the abbey.

A modern group of Cistercian monks have lived at the abbey since 1988. They cultivate lavender, olives and honey, run a gift shop of local products, and arrange visits of the abbey while they continue work on restoring the property. All that, and they still manage to pray together seven times a day! TIP: There's nowhere to eat at the abbey, but there is a vending machine with water and snacks if you need to refuel.

Once you're done exploring the abbey, retrace your route to Gordes.

Bonus Hike: Gordes Self-Guided History Walks

The tourist information office in Gordes has put together several self-guided walks through town to introduce you to the extensive history of the village. You can find brochures for the walks at their office at Place Genty Pantaly.

4C GORDES–JOUCAS–ROUSSILLON

Walk to three hill towns, with stops for wine tasting and visiting a historic ochre quarry

Walking village to village is the perfect way to get off the beaten track and spend more time in the hill towns of Provence and the countryside that connects them. There's so much to discover along the way, from wineries where you can taste the very grapes you walk among to ancient remains of civilizations long past.

This route shows off the diversity of Provence in three parts. The first section, from Gordes to the tiny village of Joucas, showcases the wild beauty of the Vaucluse Mountains. From Joucas to Roussillon, the focus is on the lushness of the agriculture and vineyards that dominate the Calavon Valley, with a stop at local winery Domaine Girod. And in the village of Roussillon, the previously green landscape completely changes to hues of red and orange, colored by the ochre that has made the picturesque town so famous. End your hike with a short, easy walk through an Instagram-worthy former quarry site that stuns with riotous color.

ON THE TRAIL

DURATION: 5 hours

DIFFICULTY: Moderate

DISTANCE: 8.4 miles (13.5 km)

ELEVATION GAIN: 1,098 feet (335 m)

ELEVATION LOSS: 1,214 feet (370 m)

START: Place Genty Pantaly in Gordes

END: Viewpoint just outside the entrance to Le Sentier des Ocres (the Ochre Trail) in Roussillon

EAT + DRINK: Gordes, Joucas, Domaine Girod, Roussillon

Know Before You Go

Most of the route consists of rolling hills. There is one notable climb en route, and that's up to the hilltop village of Roussillon, but there's an opportunity partway through to stop for refreshments at Domaine Girod (see Online Resources). The winery is open Monday–Saturday but closed each day from 12 to 3 p.m. Consider making a reservation in advance for a tasting and tour, especially if you have more than six people in your group.

For the route through Gordes, carefully follow the steps outlined here or use my GPX tracks to stay on track. The hike is relatively well signed from the base of Gordes to Roussillon. Confidence markers are yellow stripes and occasionally red and white stripes.

Alternative Routes and Activities

For a shorter route, save Le Sentier des Ocres (at the end of the route) for a different day to shave a mile (1.6 km) off this hike.

Extend your outing in a couple of ways:

- With multiple villages to explore en route, this hike could easily take most of a day.
- The Ecomuseum of Ochre (see Online Resources) in Roussillon has exhibits that demonstrate in detail how ochre is processed and the pigment is extracted. It's particularly interesting for artists or others with an interest in paint.

Navigating

This hike starts near the fountain at Place Genty Pantaly (Genty Pantaly Square) in Gordes, an easy walk from the rest of town and close to several restaurants, cafés and a grocery store.

STARTING POINT: **43.91089°, 5.20012°**

RETURN: The hike ends at the viewpoint just outside the entrance to Le Sentier des Ocres in Roussillon. The best way back to Gordes is via a 15-minute taxi ride, though there is very sporadic service between the towns on Bus 917. The tourist information offices in Gordes and Roussillon can provide you with a current timetable for the bus.

MAPS: Available at the tourist information office in Gordes, which is conveniently located at Place Genty Pantaly. Maps of Le Sentier des Ocres are available at the walk's ticket booth.

 From the fountain at **Place Genty Pantaly**, cross the main road, Rue Baptistin Picca, and head south toward the large church of **Église Saint-Firmin**. Head down the small lane in front of the church. Just past the church, head right on another

From Joucas, you have sprawling views of the Calavon Valley.

stone path. TIP: If you go straight instead, there's a nice viewpoint that makes a fun detour. When you come to the curve of the larger Rue Jean Deyrolle, keep left and continue walking downhill. At 0.2 mile (0.3 km), go left on a smaller path that soon takes you to **Le Lavoir**, which looks like a raised water table but actually functioned as a washing machine in medieval times.

At 0.3 mile (0.5 km), curve left on Rue du Pavé d'Amour and take another left on Chemin de la Calade. Stay straight at 0.4 mile (0.6 km), where you see your first trail sign and the road becomes Chemin de Lourdanaud. At 0.7 mile (1.1 km), stay straight onto Chemin du Touron. There's another medieval washing machine at 0.9 mile (1.4 km), near a beautiful estate with a lot of flowers and an olive grove.

2 Just after that, head left on the main road, the D2, where Joucas is signed for 2.6 miles (4.2 km). You won't be on the road long; at 1 mile (1.6 km) from the start of the trail, take the smaller road to your left. In just a few feet, you'll continue straight on a footpath that branches off this road and leads through a vineyard and into a protected area of the **Vaucluse Mountains** that is popular with birds of prey—keep your eye out for Egyptian vultures, Bonelli's eagles, great horned owls and golden eagles.

3 At 2 miles (3.2 km), near a collection of accommodations clustered around the **Véroncle River**, stay straight. For the next 0.8 mile (1.3 km), you'll walk uphill, gaining 341 feet (104 m) in the process.

4 At 2.8 miles (4.5 km), reach the high point of **Baume Brune**, where a set of forty-three prehistoric rock shelters were found carved into a cliff, ten of which were decorated with cave paintings from the Neolithic period. (Unfortunately, they're on private land, so you can't visit them.) Joucas is signed for 0.7 mile (1.1 km) on a rocky limestone path that crosses the plateau.

5 Come to a trail sign at **Aires du Château** at 3.6 miles (5.8 km). This can be a confusing spot, because Joucas isn't on the sign, but head right; you're almost to the heart of the small hilltop village that's home to about three hundred people. Just a few feet downhill, there's a great viewpoint of the emerald vineyards that carpet the valley floor and the **Luberon mountains** beyond. Once you're done enjoying the view, head down the stairs to your right to wind your way farther into town. Photo opportunities abound here—the stone buildings and streets of Joucas, which date back to the year 960, are a photographer's delight.

6 Take a left on the D102, a main street through **Joucas**, at 3.7 miles (6 km). In a few feet, you'll pass a couple of cafés and a small *épicerie*, or market. At Place des Commandeurs, at 3.8 miles (6.1 km), there is a faucet to fill your water bottle, free public restrooms and another café across the street.

7 Just past that, take a left on the D102A. At 4 miles (6.4 km), branch off on a smaller road to your right that leads through a small enclave of houses, the

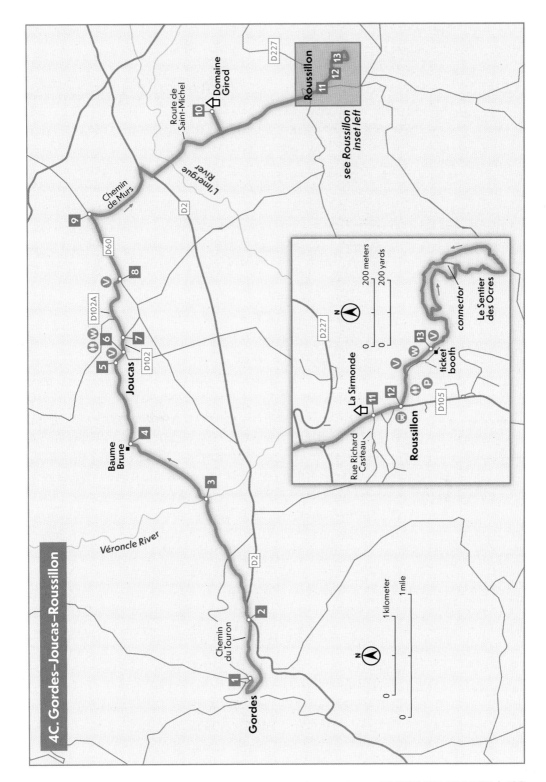

4C. Gordes–Joucas–Roussillon

Gordes

Chemin du Touron

Véroncle River

Baume Brune

Joucas

Chemin de Murs

Route de Saint-Michel

Domaine Girod

L'Imergue River

Roussillon

see Roussillon inset left

D227

D2

D60

D102A

D102

D2

N

1 kilometer
1 mile
0
0

Roussillon inset:

D227

La Sirmonde

Rue Richard Casteau

Roussillon

ticket booth

Le Sentier des Ocres

connector

D105

N

200 meters
200 yards
0
0

La Sirmonde, in Roussillon, is a terrific lunch spot with extensive views of the valley below.

lush and fertile—cherry trees, vineyards, poppies growing in wheat fields, lavender.

WINE AND THE LUBERON

People have been making wine in the Luberon for a long time—archaeological discoveries of wine-making equipment date production in the area to around AD 30. These days, local wineries (there are more than sixty of them) bottle under three different labels: AOC Luberon, AOC Ventoux and IGP Vaucluse. Want to try some local wine while you hike? Check out Domaine Girod [10].

community of Les Gardiols. This enclave marks the start of the second half of the hike, which is dominated by vineyard walking. At 4.4 miles (7.1 km), where you come to **big views of Roussillon** perched on a cliff to the south, hang a right toward the D60.

8 Take a left onto the mildly busy D60. This section won't last long—you'll only be walking alongside the road for 0.6 mile (1 km)—and French drivers are used to sharing the road with walkers and bikers; be careful all the same. Walk on the left-hand side of the road so that you can keep an eye on cars as they approach you. The land around you on the valley floor is

9 At 5 miles (8 km) from the start of the trail, take a right into the vineyards on Chemin de Murs. The quiet country lane takes you between the small communities of **Clavaillan** and **Les Bouissières**. At 5.7 miles (9.2 km), turn right onto the D2, the main route between Gordes and Roussillon. Shortly, a smaller road (Route de Saint-Michel) branches off on the left; take it. Continue past the **L'Imergue River**. At 6.2 miles (10 km), stay right when the road curves and begin to climb in earnest toward Roussillon.

10 There's an opportunity for wine tasting—and resting your legs—at the beautiful family-owned **Domaine Girod** at 6.6 miles (10.6 km). Tastings and cellar tours are free, and you can also purchase wine to take with you. Once you start walking again, the incline of the road increases. Over the next mile (1.6 km) you'll gain 381 feet (116 m) to reach the route's high point at the viewpoint outside the entrance to Le Sentier des Ocres in Roussillon. You'll know you're almost there when you see a sign welcoming you to Roussillon—and a big slab of orange-red rock above you—at 7.2 miles (11.6 km).

It is this reddish-orange rock, known as ochre, that defines Roussillon. Ochre mining was the main source of economic activity in the area from the eighteenth century to the mid-twentieth century. These days, the mine is no longer active, but the town's ochre-finished buildings show off its history in style. (Interesting fact: Ochre isn't just beautiful—it gives the buildings more sun and heat resistance.) Along with Gordes, Roussillon has been named one of the Most Beautiful Villages in France. The town is like an artist's palette, all bright contrasts—the ochre cliffs and buildings; the viridescent pine and cypress trees and the surrounding countryside; the azure sky. TIP: My favorite spot to eat lunch in Roussillon—and the one with the best views of the valley below—is La Sirmonde, which is on the main route into Roussillon (the D105), on the left just before Rue Richard Casteau (see map).

11 At 7.4 miles (11.9 km), find the entrance to the heart of **old town Roussillon** to your right, via the pedestrian-only **Rue Richard Casteau**. There's much to explore down this street: charming outdoor cafés, small shops selling wine and art, even a restored fortification. If you're ready to refuel, grab lunch before continuing on. If not, stay on the D105 through town, passing the tourist information office.

12 At 7.5 miles (12.1 km), take a left on a smaller road that's signed for Le Sentier des Ocres. This touristy little lane features a variety of shops, from souvenir stores to cafés to ice cream shops, as well as free public restrooms, a faucet for refilling your water bottle and a nice viewpoint.

13 The entrance to **Le Sentier des Ocres** is at 7.6 miles (12.2 km). This easy walk through a former ochre quarry is a great way to learn more about the ochre—clay pigmented by hematite, a reddish mineral that contains iron oxide—that gives Roussillon its reddish tint. Two routes are available: a short loop (0.5 mile or 0.8 km; 35 minutes) and a long one (0.8 mile or 1.3 km; 50 minutes), neither of which takes as long as officially signed. Free maps are available at the ticket office, which charges a small fee to access the site. My route as described includes the well-signed long route, which takes you through a beautiful ochre canyon to viewpoints, informational signage about local mining of ochre and plenty of Instagram-worthy spots for vivid photos of the landscape.

Once you're done exploring Le Sentier des Ocres, the route ends at the viewpoint outside the ticket booth, which showcases the **Vaucluse Mountains** and the **Calavon Valley** and has an orientation table to show you what's what. From there, you can easily make your way back into Roussillon or return to Gordes.

Bonus Hike: Gorges de Régalon Loop

Situated a short drive from Gordes, between the villages of Cavaillon and Mallemort, this hike passes through the Régalon gorges and the Petit Luberon Biological Reserve—with a great diversity of terrain, very pretty views and the occasional scramble over smooth boulders.

DURATION: **5 hours**
DIFFICULTY: **Moderate**
DISTANCE: **7.1 miles (11.4 km)**
ELEVATION GAIN: **1,161 feet (354 m)**
MORE INFO: **alltrails.com**

4D CALANQUES NATIONAL PARK

Discover a panoramic trail to three beautiful inlets in Calanques National Park

If you're traveling to the South of France, you can't miss the French Mediterranean. It's still Provence, but completely different from the inland hill towns. And there's no better way to experience the area than by walking in Calanques National Park, where the big highlight is a series of *calanques*, or fjords, where fingers of limestone-rimmed turquoise water reach into the land, creating incredibly scenic spots to swim and lounge. This hike takes in three of those *calanques*—those of Port-Miou, Port-Pin and d'en Vau—from the charming starting point of Cassis, a quiet seaside village that's perfect for an overnight.

ON THE TRAIL

DURATION: **5 hours**
DIFFICULTY: **Moderate to challenging**
DISTANCE: **6.4 miles (10.3 km)**
ELEVATION GAIN: **1,820 feet (555 m)**
ELEVATION LOSS: **1,820 feet (555 m)**

START: **Plage du Bestouan in Cassis**
END: **Plage du Bestouan in Cassis**
EAT + DRINK: **Plage du Bestouan, snack shack at Port-Miou**

Know Before You Go

Most of the hike is moderate, but there are two challenging sections. The first is near Plage de Port-Pin, where you need to scramble up some rocks at the beginning of what is called the blue panoramic trail. The second is on the descent to Calanque d'en Vau, where you climb down the rocks of a steep gorge wall. If you have small kids with you, the route as described will be too difficult (see Alternative Routes and Activities for tips on modifying the route). The hike is well signed and makes use of the red-and-white trail, the blue panoramic trail and the red trail.

Other notes about the route:

- Avoid this hike on a rainy day, when the rocky trail could be slippery.
- Even though this is a beach trail, don't wear flip-flops. You'll need proper hiking

It doesn't get much better than the view of Plage d'en Vau from above.

or tennis shoes, especially for the more challenging sections. And if you plan to swim, bring water shoes for the rocky beaches.

- This is an exposed and often hot trail with no water en route; pack at least 2 liters of water per person, as well as salty snacks, to help you rehydrate. Also note that in July and August, the trail is occasionally closed due to wildfire danger.

Alternative Routes and Activities

For a shorter option, walk the easy route to Plage de Port-Pin for a roundtrip hike of 3.2 miles (5.1 km). You can make the hike even shorter by taking the shuttle (see Navigating) from Parking Relais des Gorguettes to the parking lot at Calanque de Port-Miou [2]. From there, the roundtrip walk to Plage de Port-Pin is 1.8 miles (2.9 km).

Or extend your outing:

- By stopping to swim and relax at the beaches along the way, this hike can take most of a day.
- Get farther into the water of the *calanques* with a boat tour or a kayak rental, which can be arranged in the nearby Mediterranean fishing port of Cassis.
- Cassis is wonderful to explore. The harbor has charming pastel-colored

The beaches of Calanques National Park are perfect for sunning and swimming.

buildings; narrow, winding streets; sidewalk cafés and a great seaside promenade. Be sure to try the fresh local seafood and the area's wine specialty, Cassis white wine.

Navigating

This hike starts at Plage du Bestouan at the western edge of Cassis, easily walkable from the rest of town; there is also a relatively large parking lot (fee applies) across the street. Several beachside restaurants and a roadside snack shack are nearby.

STARTING POINT: 43.21304°, 5.53085°

DRIVING: Cassis is a 90-minute drive from Gordes. If you don't want to pay for parking at Plage du Bestouan, you can park in the free Parking Relais des Gorguettes park and ride (see Online Resources) on the edge of Cassis and take a shuttle to the small parking lot at Port-Miou [2]. Shuttles run every 20 minutes in high season and cost around €2

roundtrip. (I chose not to start the hike from the Port-Miou parking lot, because it's typically closed to private vehicles.) TIP: From Gorguettes, another shuttle runs to the center of Cassis, which is helpful if you stay overnight in Cassis and there's no parking at your accommodations—parking is tough to come by in town.

MAPS: Available at the tourist information office in Cassis and online at the national park website (see Online Resources).

1 From **Plage du Bestouan**, walk southwest along the sea (away from Cassis) on the main road, Avenue des Calanques. At the first curve in the road, there's a snack shack. Avenue des Calanques takes you all the way to a parking lot near the first *calanque* on your route, Calanque de Port-Miou, but it curves up and around several other streets and isn't always intuitive to follow. If you have my GPX tracks, you can use those to stay on track.

2 At 0.7 mile (1.1 km), come to the small Port-Miou parking lot that's serviced by the shuttle from Parking Relais des Gorguettes, as well as a snack shack that's often closed in the morning but opens in the afternoon to serve post-hike cold drinks and ice cream. Head left on a wide footpath that travels west along the

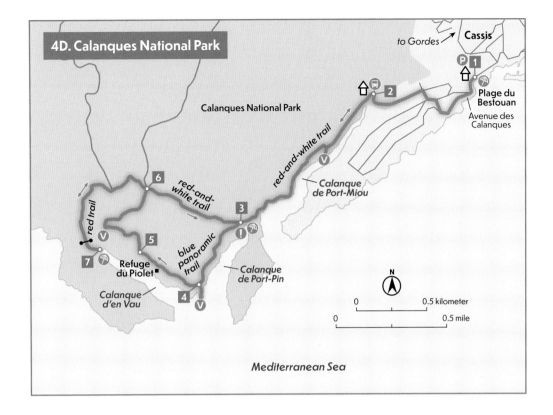

4D. Calanques National Park

shore of narrow Port-Miou, which is typically packed with boats. At 1 mile (1.6 km),
come to a national park building with an
open balcony that offers water views and
photo ops. Just past the building with the
balcony, you'll see a trail sign with Port-
Pin signed for 40 minutes on the red-and-
white-striped trail. From there, continue
walking on the wide, well-traveled and
well-signed path. At 1.4 miles (2.3 km),
admire the views of the mouth of the
calanque and the beautiful blue Mediterranean beyond.

3 Come to **Plage de Port-Pin** at 1.6
miles (2.6 km). This is a very popular destination for local families since it's easily
walkable, and you'll likely see people every-

where—sprawled out on the rocky beach
and perched in nooks and crannies on the
rocks and cliffs surrounding the beach.
Most people bring coolers and picnic supplies and stay the whole day. Just past the
beach, the trail splits. You'll come back on
the inland route to the right. For now, take
a left for the scenic blue panoramic trail.
Calanque d'en Vau is signed for 1 hour and
30 minutes on this route.

The initial part of the route is steep and
involves climbing up and over large rocks,
with cairns and the occasional blue stripe
to help mark the way. This is one of the
most challenging sections of the hike, but
the climb is worth it. From the rocky blue
panoramic trail, you have incredible views

along the *calanques* of Port-Pin and d'en Vau to the impossibly blue water beyond. You can even see back to Cassis and the mountains that surround it. It's a route that makes you want to walk slowly and soak it all in.

4 At 2 miles (3.2 km), there's an out-and-back path to a point where you can see all three *calanques*. At 2.4 miles (3.9 km), pass **Refuge du Piolet**, an empty concrete shell of a building. It is, however, a good place to get some temporary shade.

5 Some of the best views of the hike come at 2.5 miles (4 km), when you can see down to **Plage d'en Vau**. The reality of this place is just as good as the pictures—a small beach at the head of a long turquoise channel of water that's bordered by tall limestone cliffs. From above, you can see kayakers and swimmers enjoying the water, everyone as tiny as ants. Just beyond that viewpoint, there's another with a cutout through the mountains to **Pointe de l'Ilot**. And you may see rock climbers scaling the spires of the nearby *falaises* (cliffs) d'en Vau. From here, the trail flattens out, widens and turns inland on its way to meet up with the red-and-white trail at 3 miles (4.8 km).

6 At the spot where the trails intersect, Calanque d'en Vau is signed for 30 minutes, and the route immediately heads down a rocky cliff, where you'll scramble over large boulders to the bottom of a gorge. From the top, the route looks intimidating, and it isn't recommended for those who have balance issues or small chil-dren with them (even in hiking carriers). This difficult section doesn't last too long, though—it's less than 0.1 mile (0.2 km), during which you lose 144 feet (44 m) of elevation. After that, the route gets easier. At 3.2 miles (5.1 km) from the start of the trail, another trail meets up with yours; stay straight. From here, the route signage changes from the red-and-white trail to the red trail and now you're on the floor of the gorge—a lush Eden that makes you feel like you've entered another world. Hike this gently descending path to a gate at 3.6 miles (5.8 km) and **Plage d'en Vau** at 3.7 miles (6 km).

7 Given the difficult descent, fewer people visit Calanque d'en Vau than the other two *calanques* on this route, but it still has a festive atmosphere. Groups of families and friends find shade wherever they can, under trees and behind boulders. Most bring beer and baguette sandwiches with them. This is a great spot to stop for a few hours, to swim and eat and lounge in the sun on the rocky beach.

When you're done enjoying the *calanque*, retrace your steps to [6]. Be encouraged—ascending the cliff wall is easier than descending it. From there, you have options. You can retrace your route on the blue panoramic trail back to Plage de Port-Pin, or if your legs are tired or you simply want to see something new, take the easier inland route (straight) along the red-and-white trail. From Plage de Port-Pin, retrace your route to the start of the trail at **Plage du Bestouan**.

Quiet Lake Bohinj is the lesser-known cousin of popular Lake Bled. (Photo courtesy Turizem Bohinj/ Mitja Sodja)

5 LAKE BOHINJ, SLOVENIA

Exploring Slovenia's largest permanent lake and only national park

AT A GLANCE

GENERAL LOCATION: **Northwestern Slovenia**

HOME BASE: **Ribčev Laz**

LOCAL LANGUAGE: **Slovenian**

USE OF ENGLISH: **Understood and used, but typically not fluently**

FAMILY FRIENDLY: **★★★☆**

COST: **$$**

WHEN TO GO: **Mid-Jun to Sept**

SCENERY: **Slovenia's highest mountain, the Julian Alps, Lake Bohinj, waterfalls**

DON'T MISS: **Mountain huts, taking a gondola up to high-alpine routes, hiking in Triglav National Park**

I love traveling to places that haven't been completely discovered, where the culture is very different from my own and it's a little challenging to have a full conversation because not everyone speaks fluent English. This, I imagine, is how travel used to be, before the world became so interconnected. I'm a fan of Eastern European destinations like Slovenia for this reason—when I'm there, I feel like I'm in a new place.

Lake Bohinj, in the northwestern part of Slovenia, is a perfect starter destination for those who want to hike in Eastern Europe. There are great trails and all of the services you could want as a visitor, from plenty of restaurants serving up Slovenian comfort food to cheap and dependable public transportation, but without all the American and Canadian travelers—this is a spot that's popular primarily with other Eastern Europeans. And not everyone speaks much English. You'll definitely be able to get by—people can communicate the important things—but this is a spot where you can win some major points by meeting locals halfway and trying out a few Slovenian words. It's worth the extra effort.

Lake Bohinj is the largest permanent lake in Slovenia and part of Triglav National Park, the country's only national park. The quiet, protected lake (motorized boats aren't allowed) is surrounded by foothills and mountains that serve as gateways to the Julian Alps, some of the least-overrun Alps in Europe. These foothills and mountains also serve as viewpoints of the lake from above (bring your camera!) and perfect launching points for local high-alpine hikes, some of which are accessible by gondola or lift (see Hike 5B, Mount Šija

On Hike 5D, Seven Lakes Valley Loop, you'll pass traditional farm buildings and small, picturesque lakes.

and Mount Vogel Summits). Be sure to visit the traditional mountain huts, where you can order mountain cheese made from the milk of the cows in the meadows you've walked across. For the best hiking, visit mid-June through September, when the weather is nice, there's a lot of daylight each day and the higher-elevation hikes are snow-free.

It's not just the high-alpine hikes in the area that dazzle, though. The lower-elevation hikes around Lake Bohinj are great too. Several of them go to pretty waterfalls or smaller valleys that serve as perfect picnic spots, and many of them leave directly from one of the three main towns along the lake, minimizing the hassle of transportation.

While there are three towns on the shores of Lake Bohinj, the one I recommend home basing in is Ribčev Laz, the middle and largest one. Ribčev Laz has a variety of restaurants and accommodations, as well as a tourist information office. From there, it's easy to get to the hikes in the area by bus—or leave the lake entirely and explore farther afield. Lake Bohinj is only accessible from the east, so this is the quickest exit point to other nearby hot spots, such as busier and more well-known Lake Bled (see What to See and Do).

The vibe in Ribčev Laz is relaxed and happy—it's primarily a tourist town, and most everyone you'll meet is on vacation. There are plenty of places to take in local culture, though, from the Saint John the Baptist Church to the three museums in town. And I highly encourage you to talk to the Slovenians around you, especially your hosts if you stay, like I did, in family-owned accommodations—they were some of the most genuine, helpful, welcoming people I've encountered while traveling.

For world-class hikes that are relatively unknown and the opportunity to discover Eastern European culture—and make a few new friends—a stay in Lake Bohinj is worth the effort.

Getting There and Around

The closest airport to Lake Bohinj is in Ljubljana, the capital of Slovenia, a 1-hour drive away. Alternatively, you can take a bus to nearby Lake Bled, then transfer to a Lake Bohinj–bound bus.

All of the hikes I recommend in Lake Bohinj and the three largest villages in the area (which aren't very large at all) are accessible via the local bus service, which is free if you have a Bohinj Card (see Where to Stay). The buses can get very busy in the summer months, however, so get an early start to your adventures.

The Bohinj Card will also get you free parking in the area, and without it, parking is expensive. TIP: You need a vignette (toll sticker) to drive in Slovenia.

Where to Stay

While my top choice for a home base near Lake Bohinj is the village of Ribčev Laz, another great choice is nearby Stara Fužina, which is slightly smaller but is still well connected to all of the hikes and towns in the area. For a more local-feeling spot that can also be significantly cheaper

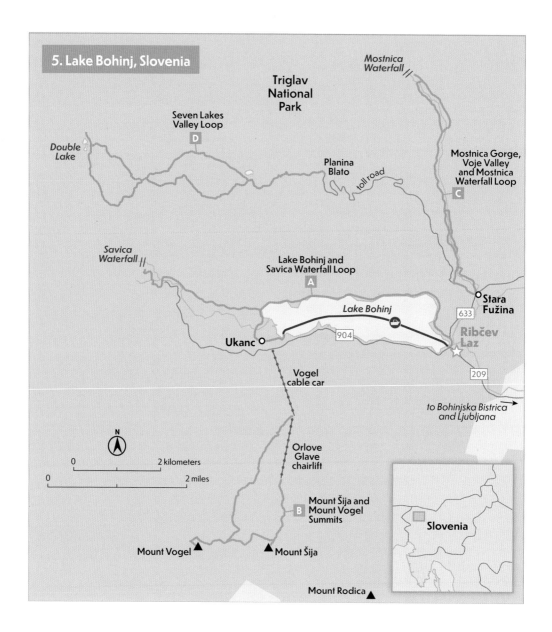

5. Lake Bohinj, Slovenia

Mostnica Waterfall

Triglav National Park

Seven Lakes Valley Loop
D

Double Lake

Planina Blato

toll road

Mostnica Gorge, Voje Valley and Mostnica Waterfall Loop
C

Savica Waterfall

Lake Bohinj and Savica Waterfall Loop
A

Lake Bohinj

Stara Fužina

633

Ukanc

904

Ribčev Laz

209

Vogel cable car

to Bohinjska Bistrica and Ljubljana

N

0   2 kilometers

0   2 miles

Orlove Glave chairlift

Mount Šija and Mount Vogel Summits
B

Slovenia

Mount Vogel

Mount Šija

Mount Rodica

than the towns closer to Lake Bohinj, I suggest Bohinjska Bistrica, a 10-minute drive from Ribčev Laz.

Those who stay in Bohinj for at least two nights and pay the tourist tax can purchase a Bohinj Card, which gets you free bus transportation in the area; free parking (as long as you buy the card with parking benefits); a free panoramic boat ride on Lake Bohinj; and free tickets to the Savica Waterfall, Mostnica Gorge, all three museums in the area and the Saint John the Baptist Church. The Bohinj Card can be purchased at local tourist information

THE ROUTES

HIKE	ROUTE NAME	DURATION	DIFFICULTY	DISTANCE	ELEV. GAIN	ELEV. LOSS
5A	Lake Bohinj and Savica Waterfall Loop	5 hours	Moderate	8.8 mi (14.2 km)	1,572 ft (479 m)	1,562 ft (476 m)
5B	Mount Šija and Mount Vogel Summits	5 hours	Moderate to challenging	5.8 mi (9.3 km)	2,025 ft (617 m)	2,448 ft (746 m)
5C	Mostnica Gorge, Voje Valley and Mostnica Waterfall Loop	4.5 hours	Moderate	7.3 mi (11.7 km)	1,183 ft (361 m)	1,183 ft (361 m)
5D	Seven Lakes Valley Loop	7 hours	Moderate to challenging	9.9 mi (15.9 km)	3,212 ft (979 m)	3,212 ft (979 m)

MAPS OF LAKE BOHINJ

While maps of the Bohinj area are available at tourist information offices in the area, you can also order them online from Sidarta (see Online Resources).

offices and from some accommodation providers. TIP: The card with parking benefits is more expensive than the standard Bohinj Card, but you only need one of those per car. Everyone else in your party can purchase the cheaper Bohinj Card.

Eat and Resupply

The town of Ribčev Laz has a grocery store. It also has several restaurants and cafés, many of them close to the lake. When you're out and about, be sure to track down the following local specialties:

- ☐ *Kranjska klobasa*: a Slovenian sausage similar to kielbasa, typically served with sauerkraut

- ☐ *Štruklji*: rolls filled with sweet or savory combinations
- ☐ *Štrudl*: a layered sweet pastry filled with apples

There's an Intersport in Bohinjska Bistrica in case you need to adjust or add to your gear.

What to See and Do

TRIGLAV NATIONAL PARK

There's so much more to see of Triglav National Park than you experience in Lake Bohinj—a wide variety of trails through the Julian Alps, traditional mountain huts where you can stay the night, and Mount Triglav, Slovenia's highest peak.

PADDLE THE LAKE

While Lake Bohinj is fun to walk around, I encourage you to spend some time on the water. The lake is typically very calm and is closed to motorized traffic, outside of the electric ferry that runs from Ribčev Laz to Ukanc—it's a great spot to kayak or stand-up paddle board. You'll find little rental spots sprinkled around the lake. A couple of local outdoor outfitters also offer canoe or kayak tours of the nearby Sava River.

LAKE BLED

Lake Bled is such a worthy day trip from Lake Bohinj, and it only takes about 30 minutes to get there. While it is another lake, the atmosphere is very different—think busier and a little more festive—and it has different attractions on tap, like a castle reminiscent of Dracula's that you can visit and a picturesque church on a small island that you can boat to.

★★★ Lake Bohinj gets three stars out of four for being family friendly. You'll see plenty of European families hanging out by the lake, and there are a lot of activities that appeal to kids, from the electric boat that runs across the lake to the lakeside campground playground in Ukanc to a beginner-friendly outdoor climbing wall in Ribčev Laz. Two of the hikes—the Lake Bohinj and Savica Waterfall Loop (Hike 5A) and the Mostnica Gorge, Voje Valley and Mostnica Waterfall Loop (Hike 5C)—are also very family friendly, especially if you shorten them to just the path around the lake and the Mostnica Gorge, respectively. TIP: My kids loved the alpine animal exhibit and the playground at the top of the Vogel cable car.

5A LAKE BOHINJ AND SAVICA WATERFALL LOOP

Walk around beautiful Lake Bohinj to the most famous waterfall in Slovenia

It would be a shame to visit Lake Bohinj and never walk its shores. A lakeside jaunt allows you to get past the popular spots of Ribčev Laz and Stara Fužina to quieter beaches and coves where you can have the lake all to yourself. This walk starts in Ribčev Laz and skirts the remote northern shore of Lake Bohinj. Near the village of Ukanc, it heads northwest to ascend to a viewpoint of the Savica Waterfall, the most famous waterfall in Slovenia thanks to its double stream of water and beautiful emerald pool. The trail then takes you to Ukanc, where you can grab lunch and ferry back to Ribčev Laz in an electric boat with commentary about the local area.

ON THE TRAIL

DURATION: 5 hours

DIFFICULTY: Moderate

DISTANCE: 8.8 miles (14.2 km)

ELEVATION GAIN: 1,572 feet (479 m)

ELEVATION LOSS: 1,562 feet (476 m)

START: Ribčev Laz ferry dock

END: Ribčev Laz ferry dock

EAT + DRINK: Ribčev Laz, Bar/Restavracija Kramar, snack shack near walking path to Stara Fužina, Planinski dom Savica, Ukanc

Know Before You Go

The first part of the route, around the lake, is flat and easy. The second part, which ascends to the Savica Waterfall, is where you'll experience the majority of your elevation gain. There are also a lot of stairs, so wear good shoes. This hike is relatively well signed. Confidence markers are yellow circles with white inside.

A Bohinj Card (see Where to Stay) gets you free transportation to the trailhead (or free parking nearby), free entrance to the Savica Waterfall and a free ferry ride from Ukanc to Ribčev Laz. The 25-minute ferry ride from Ukanc to Ribčev Laz is a great way to avoid a long, boring stretch of road-walking on the land route between Ukanc and Ribčev Laz. The boat runs every 40 minutes during high season (see Online Resources).

Alternative Routes and Activities

For a shorter route, eliminate the Savica Waterfall portion of the hike to shave off 4.4 miles (7.1 km) and 958 feet (292 m) of

Non-motorized Lake Bohinj is ideal for smaller craft, such as rowboats and stand-up paddleboards. (Photo by ivabalk/Pixabay)

elevation gain. You can also hike to the waterfall and take a shuttle back to Ribčev Laz from there; the shuttle is free if you have a Bohinj Card.

To extend your outing, consider adding one of the following activities:

- Visit the Church of Saint John the Baptist near the starting point of the hike; admission is free with a Bohinj Card.
- Paragliding is a unique way to see Lake Bohinj from above. And if you've never done it, it's pretty thrilling—something you'll always remember. See [2] in the Navigating section for more details.

Navigating

This loop hike starts and ends at the Ribčev Laz ferry dock, close to several lakeside bars and restaurants and a short walk from the center of town and local bus stops. There's also a Mercator grocery store next to the tourist information office in town.

STARTING POINT: **46.27789°, 13.88538°**

DRIVING: **All-day parking is available near the dock at a lot (46.27652°, 13.88629°) behind Hotel Jezero, where a Bohinj Card gets you free parking. From the parking lot, there's a footpath that runs to the shore of the lake and the ferry dock.**

MAPS: **Available at tourist information offices in Ribčev Laz and Stara Fužina.**

1 From the ferry dock, walk east toward the bridge over the spot where Lake Bohinj flows into the **Sava Bohinjka River**, a headwater of the Sava River. Make your way over the bridge, which is

a scenic picture spot—you can get the lake in the background from one angle and the pretty Church of Saint John the Baptist from another angle. Just past the church, see your first trail sign and take a left on a gravel path that curves along the shore of the lake, passing several little beaches that are nice for swimming and especially popular with families. At 0.2 mile (0.3 km), there's a port-a-potty up and to your right, near the paved path that you continue on. There's plenty of shade here—perfect on a warm day.

2 At 0.5 mile (0.8 km), come to a small restaurant called **Bar/Restavracija Kramar** (cash only) on the eastern shore of the lake. This out-of-the-way spot is popular with paragliders because it's near their landing zone, but it's also great for anyone who wants a quieter spot to enjoy the lake. There's a nice outdoor terrace that juts out into the lake and lawn chairs where you can sit and enjoy the views. There's also an information center for **LoopTeam Paragliding** (see Online Resources), where you can sign up to see Lake Bohinj from above. When you're ready, continue walking north along the shore of the lake; there's a nice grass area on the point that's perfect for a picnic, and you soon pass by a wildflower-strewn meadow.

3 Come to a port-a-potty and a snack shack at 0.9 mile (1.4 km), near a junction with an eastbound walking path that connects with Stara Fužina. After the snack shack, most of the walkers drop off. There's no road on this side of the lake, and the route gets a little rockier and feels more

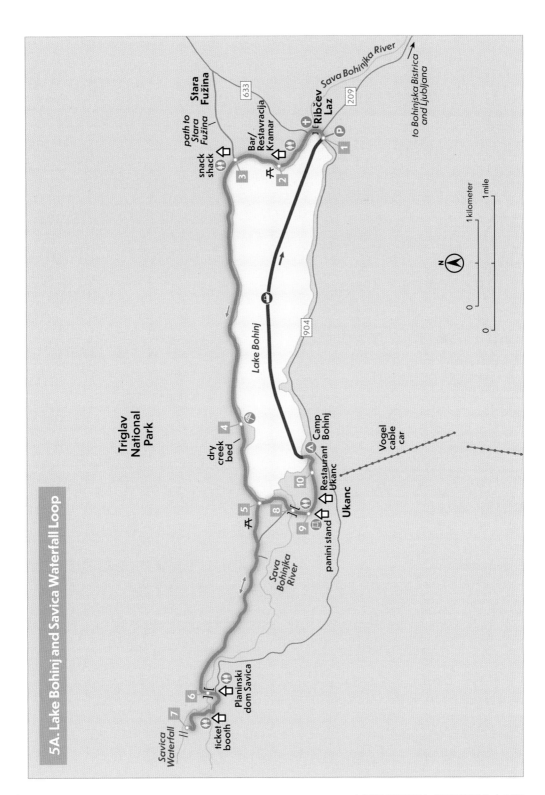

5A. Lake Bohinj and Savica Waterfall Loop

Stara
Fužina

Sava Bohinjka River

path to
Stara
Fužina

633

Ribčev
Laz

209

to Bohinjska Bistrica
and Ljubljana

Bar/
Restavracija
Kramar

snack
shack

3

2

P

1

Triglav
National
Park

N

0

0

1 kilometer

1 mile

Lake Bohinj

904

dry
creek
bed

4

Camp
Bohinj

Vogel
cable
car

Restaurant
Ukanc

5

8

10

Ukanc

9

panini stand

Sava
Bohinjka
River

Savica
Waterfall

7

6

Planinski
dom Savica

ticket
booth

The Savica Waterfall is Slovenia's most famous waterfall.

remote. There are plenty of coves along the lake to enjoy, and the area to the right of the trail is studded with boulders cleaved from the mountains above.

4 There's a nice beach at 2.9 miles (4.7 km). Just after that, pick your way across a dry creek bed. At 3.3 miles (5.3 km), you have great views across the water to the **Vogel cable car**.

5 Find the start of the trail that leads to the Savica Waterfall at 3.5 miles (5.6 km), in a grassy picnic area with views back down the lake to Ribčev Laz. Go right on the trail, which starts to gently ascend. At 3.9 miles (6.3 km), go right at the junction with a quiet paved road. You won't be on it for long. After a few feet, take another footpath that branches off on your right. The path skirts a cleared area with some

handsome rural accommodations before heading into the forest.

6 Cross over the **Sava Bohinjka River** at 5.1 miles (8.2 km) and get to the parking lot for the Savica Waterfall shortly after that. Stay to the right and wind your way up past a small tourist shop and **Planinski dom Savica**, a lodge with a restaurant and a great outdoor terrace. At 5.3 miles (8.5 km), there's an admission booth for the Savica Waterfall and a free public restroom. TIP: You can get a cold beer for takeaway from a fridge at the admission booth to enjoy at the waterfall. Bohinj Card holders get free admission to the Savica Waterfall. From the pay booth, the walk up to the Savica Waterfall is an hour roundtrip; it's a short (0.4 mile or 0.6 km each way) but steep route with a lot of stairs.

7 There's a viewpoint of the double **Savica Waterfall**, the third-most-visited attraction in Slovenia, at 5.7 miles (9.2 km). The waterfall is fed by water flowing from the Seven Lakes Valley and Mount Pršivec, which reaches the waterfall through a horizontal cave tunnel. When you're done enjoying the waterfall, retrace your route down to the shores of Lake Bohinj [5] and take a right on the footpath at the junction.

8 Cross the emerald water of the Sava Bohinjka River on a nice wooden bridge at 8.2 miles (13.2 km). Just after the bridge, there's a port-a-potty on your left.

9 Once you join the road at 8.3 miles (13.4 km), there's a great playground to your right, which is soon followed by a panini stand, where you can also order cold drinks. Lawn chairs are available, or you

can get your order to go and take it to the playground if you have littles playing. At 8.4 miles (13.5 km), there's another option for lunch—**Restaurant Ukanc**, which is open for food Friday through Sunday.

10 At 8.6 miles (13.8 km), veer left off the main road to enter **Camp Bohinj**, a camping area with a restaurant, snack shop and playground—and the ferry dock for your ride back to Ribčev Laz. The ferry ride includes some narration about the local area and offers a different perspective of the lake. The boat drops you off at your starting point in **Ribčev Laz**.

Bonus Hike: Vogar Viewpoint

Hike a short but steep trail from Stara Fužina to the Vogar Viewpoint and one of the best views of Lake Bohinj from above.

DURATION: 2.5 hours

DIFFICULTY: Challenging

DISTANCE: 3.7 miles (6 km) roundtrip

ELEVATION GAIN: 1,571 feet (479 m)

MORE INFO: alltrails.com

5B MOUNT ŠIJA AND MOUNT VOGEL SUMMITS

Get sublime views of Lake Bohinj from above, summit two peaks of the Julian Alps and walk through a working alpine meadow

Lake Bohinj is beautiful at eye level but—wow—you should see it from above. Gaining some altitude is also a great way to see the larger area from a wider angle and put everything in perspective, from the emerald green of the valley, with its small lake-adjacent villages, to the rocky mountains that rim it so perfectly—and Mount Triglav, the tallest mountain in Slovenia, reigning over everything. As if that weren't enough, this hike also takes you to two mountain summits in the Julian Alps and guides you through a lush alpine meadow with a traditional mountain hut. The hike starts from the top of the Orlove Glave chairlift, which, together with the Vogel cable car, allows you to minimize your elevation gain while maximizing your high-elevation views.

ON THE TRAIL

DURATION: 5 hours

DIFFICULTY: Moderate to challenging

DISTANCE: 5.8 miles (9.3 km)

ELEVATION GAIN: 2,025 feet (617 m)

ELEVATION LOSS: 2,448 feet (746 m)

START: Top of Orlove Glave chairlift

END: Vogel cable car mountain station

EAT + DRINK: Orlove Glave mountain hut, Sirarna Zadnji Vogel mountain hut, Vogel cable car mountain station, Merjasec mountain hut, Chalet Burja

In summer, the path to Mount Šija is full of wildflowers.

Know Before You Go

The route is relatively well signed and involves a decent amount of elevation gain and loss, including two relatively steep sections, one at 1.9 miles (3.1 km), where you'll have metal pegs to assist you in your descent, and another at 2.3 miles (3.7 km), where you'll have cables to hold on to as you climb. These sections are short—less than 0.1 mile (0.2 km) each—but they can pose a challenge for those with poor balance or a fear of heights. For everyone else, they're very doable—even fun. TIP: Put your hiking poles away for these sections so they don't get in your way. Confidence markers are red arrows with peak and meadow names next to them.

Other details to keep in mind:

- This trail is very exposed; pack extra sunscreen.
- The two mountain summits you hike to can be windy and cold, even in summer, so bring a jacket to throw on while you enjoy the 360-degree views.

Alternative Routes and Activities

Two worthy shorter hikes in the area are the hike from the top of the Orlove Glave chairlift to the summit of Šija and back (2.1 miles or 3.4 km roundtrip) or the hike from the Vogel cable car mountain station to the Sirarna Zadnji Vogel mountain hut and back (2.6 miles or 4.2 km roundtrip).

Or extend your outing in one of these ways:

- By stopping to eat and drink along the way, this hike can easily take up most of a day.
- Want to bag another peak? From the junction beneath the summit of Mount Šija, you can hike east to the summit of Mount Rodica, the tallest peak in the vicinity at 6,440 feet (1,963 m), which

adds 3.8 miles (6.1 km) and 1,455 feet (443 m) of elevation gain (and loss) to this hike.

Navigating

The trail starts at the top of the Orlove Glave chairlift and next to the Orlove Glave mountain hut, which serves food and drinks.

STARTING POINT: **46.25142°, 13.83725°**

TRANSIT: Take a seasonal bus (visit a local tourist information office for routes and schedules) from Ribčev Laz to the bus stop for the ground station of the Vogel cable car (see Online Resources).

From the ground station, ascend via the cable car to the mountain station. From the mountain station, head right, following signs to Vogel, Rodica and Šija. On your left, you'll soon see some stairs that descend to the Orlove Glave ground station. Take the lift, which is included in your cable car ticket. If the lift isn't running, you can walk to the upper station via the path below the lift, which adds 0.9 mile (1.4 km) and 516 feet (157 m) of elevation gain to your hike.

DRIVING: Free parking is available at the ground station of the Vogel cable car in Ukanc (no Bohinj Card required), a 10-minute drive from Ribčev Laz. To reach the Orlove Glave chairlift, follow the directions in the Transit section.

MAPS: Available at tourist information offices in Ribčev Laz and Stara Fužina.

1 From the top of the **Orlove Glave chairlift**, head south (uphill) on a gravel path and follow the signs toward **Mount Šija**. The hill you're initially climbing is to the top of the Šija chairlift, which is only open in the winter. Just a few feet from the Orlove Glave chairlift, there's a viewpoint on your right where you can overlook the Vogel cable car mountain station below and **Mount Triglav** across the valley to the north.

2 You get a break from the elevation gain at 0.8 mile (1.3 km), when you hit a plateau. If you're walking in wildflower season, pause here to get a photo of Mount Šija with flowers in the foreground and tiny-looking people on top of the peak. But that's not the only impressive mountain—you're surrounded by them.

3 Come to the junction with the Mount Šija summit at 1 mile (1.6 km). You'll return to this spot once you've visited the peak, but for now, continue straight for the 15-minute climb to the top on a narrow, rocky trail. When you get to the grassy 6,167-foot (1,880 m) summit, take in the incredible 360-degree panorama—you'll want your camera close at hand. When you're done enjoying the views, descend to [3] and head toward Mount Vogel (left), which is signed for 1 hour and 40 minutes on a pretty ridge trail. This is the **Slovenian Mountain Trail**, which is part of the Via Alpina (see the Via Alpina sidebar in Hike 6A).

4 There's a great viewpoint of the route up Mount Vogel at 1.5 miles (2.4 km). From here, you can also see part of the trail you'll take from Mount Vogel back to the Vogel cable car mountain station. At 1.9 miles (3.1 km), come to some wooden stairs and a steep descent. Metal pegs assist with your climb down to the flatter trail below.

Viewing Lake Bohinj from above gives you a totally different perspective of the area. (Photo by sosinda/Pixabay)

5 Just beyond that, at 2 miles (3.2 km), come to the **Vratca saddle** and a junction with trails to the Vogel summit and Planina Zadnji Vogel. For now, continue straight; Mount Vogel is signed for 50 minutes. The path is relatively steep—over the next 0.7 mile (1.1 km) to the summit, you'll gain 758 feet (231 m) of elevation.

6 There's a particularly steep section at 2.3 miles (3.7 km) from the start of the hike, where cables have been placed to assist you, but this section, like the other challenging one you encountered at 1.9 miles (3.1 km), is short—less than 0.1 mile (0.2 km)—and is followed by a gorgeous walk along a ridgeline that has amazing views back to the slanted layers of rock that make up the base of Mount Vogel. At 2.5 miles (4 km), take a left; the summit is signed for 15 minutes. Take another left at 2.6 miles (4.2 km) for the final flourish to the top.

7 The summit of 6,305-foot (1,922 m) **Mount Vogel** comes at 2.7 miles (4.3 km),

and it's a particularly gratifying one because of all of the elevation gain you tackled to reach it. This is a great place to refuel with a trail snack while you take in the vista of the **Julian Alps**, the **Karavanke Mountains** and coastal peaks. Don't forget to sign your name in the trail register before you head back down to [5].

Once you're back at the saddle junction, head left for Planina Zadnji Vogel, which is signed for 40 minutes on a trail that has you heading straight toward Mount Triglav. Watch your footing on the many small, loose rocks on this downhill. At the junction at 3.6 miles (5.8 km), continue straight.

8 At 4.1 miles (6.6 km), when you come to the beautiful alpine meadow of **Planina Zadnji Vogel**, the path levels out. This is one of my favorite sections of the route—it's so lush, the ground carpeted in small, hardy pines and brightly colored wildflowers. But it's not all beauty and no brawn—this is a working mountain pasture, one that's part of the **Bohinj Cheese Trail**. Cattle are herded here every year in late June to graze the meadow for a couple of months. You can taste the fruits of their efforts—or rather cheese and cottage cheese and sour milk made in the traditional way—at the **Sirarna Zadnji Vogel mountain hut** at 4.5 miles (7.2 km), which also serves Alpine favorites like *koruzni žganci* (cooked cornmeal served with milk or yogurt) and homemade schnapps.

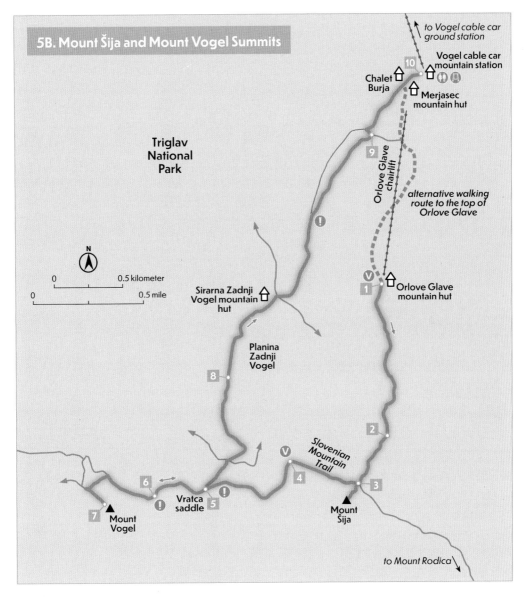

5B. Mount Šija and Mount Vogel Summits

to Vogel cable car
ground station

Vogel cable car
mountain station

Chalet
Burja

Merjasec
mountain hut

Triglav
National
Park

Orlove Glave
chairlift

alternative walking
route to the top of
Orlove Glave

N

0   0.5 kilometer

0   0.5 mile

Sirarna Zadnji
Vogel mountain
hut

Orlove Glave
mountain hut

Planina
Zadnji
Vogel

Slovenian
Mountain
Trail

Vratca
saddle

Mount
Šija

Mount
Vogel

to Mount Rodica

Just past the hut, take a soft right (but not a hard right up the hill) on a gravel path. At 4.9 miles (7.9 km), an easy-to-miss footpath branches off on your right; take it through a nice forest that provides plenty of welcome shade on a hot day.

9 At 5.4 miles (8.7 km), take a left when you come to a larger path and then an immediate right to get back to the wide gravel trail you were walking earlier on the route. There's a little more incline on your way to the mountain station of the Vogel cable car at 5.8 miles (9.3 km), but it's gentle.

10 There's plenty to do at the mountain station, which is also the **Vogel Ski**

Center, before you head back down the hill. If you're hungry, you can order a post-hike meal and a celebratory beer from the terrace (there's also a restaurant inside). The terrace has expansive views of the Julian Alps, including the peaks of Mount Šija and Mount Vogel, and a large heart frame that's perfect for snapping a photo with the mountains in the background. The real stunner, though, is the view of **Mount Triglav** and **Lake Bohinj** from the valley-facing side of the building. Kids will love the resort's alpine animals (goats and cows) and playground. There's also occasionally an outdoor bouncy house in the summer. TIP: Want to eat at a smaller spot? Merjasec mountain hut and Chalet Burja, both near the ski center, also have restaurants—the one at Chalet Burja is a pizzeria. Take the cable car back down to your starting point when you're done exploring.

5C MOSTNICA GORGE, VOJE VALLEY AND MOSTNICA WATERFALL LOOP

Travel through the famous Mostnica Gorge and the peaceful farmland of the Voje Valley on your way to the Mostnica Waterfall

One of the most popular natural attractions in the Bohinj area is the Mostnica Gorge, where the Mostnica River cuts a bold path through limestone, turning it into potholes of emerald water popular with fish, cascading waterfalls and arches that the water tucks and tumbles under. There's no better way to explore the gorge than by walking its stunning length. This walk takes you from the village of Stara Fužina into the gorge, tracing its eastern edge before nudging you up and out of the gorge to the pretty farmland of the Voje Valley, two mountain huts that serve Slovenian comfort food, and the Mostnica Waterfall. On the walk back to Stara Fužina, you'll enter the gorge once again, this time following its western path.

ON THE TRAIL

DURATION: 4.5 hours

DIFFICULTY: Moderate

DISTANCE: 7.3 miles (11.7 km)

ELEVATION GAIN: 1,183 feet (361 m)

ELEVATION LOSS: 1,183 feet (361 m)

START: Tourist information office in Stara Fužina

END: Tourist information office in Stara Fužina

EAT + DRINK: Stara Fužina, Planinska koča na Vojah (Voje mountain hut; see Online Resources), Okrepčevalnica Slap Voje (Voje Waterfall Snack Bar; see Online Resources)

Know Before You Go

The route to the Mostnica Waterfall, at the top of the Voje Valley, is gently uphill, while the walk back to Stara Fužina is gently downhill. It is relatively well signed, and confidence markers are yellow circles with white inside.

Other notes about the route:

- A Bohinj Card (see Where to Stay) gets you a free bus ride to Stara Fužina (or free parking) and free entrance to the Mostnica Gorge. Those without a Bohinj Card will need to pay the small admission fee for the gorge. Only cash is accepted.
- In the gorge, don't get too close to the river. The rocks can be slippery and dangerous. Swimming is prohibited.
- The gorge doesn't have garbage cans; be prepared to pack your trash out with you.

Alternative Routes and Activities

For a shorter option, hike both sides of the gorge but eliminate the trip to the hut and the waterfall for a roundtrip walk of 3 miles (4.8 km). Another option is to walk to Planinska koča na Vojah (the Voje mountain hut) at 1.9 miles (3.1 km) and take a shuttle back to Stara Fužina from there (visit a local tourist information office for more information on the shuttle).

To extend your outing, explore the village of Stara Fužina. It's not large, but there is the Alpine Dairy Museum in town

Over time, the Mostnica River has cut a bold path through the limestone. (Photo courtesy Turizem Bohinj/Mitja Sodja)

(see Online Resources), which is located in a former village cheese-making facility from the 1800s. You can see original cheese-making tools, objects used by the shepherds in their work in the mountain pastures and the wooden interior of a shepherd's hut from the Zajamniki settlement.

Navigating

This loop hike starts in front of the tourist information office in Stara Fužina, which is near a Mercator grocery store and several restaurants.

STARTING POINT: 46.28772°, 13.89408°

TRANSIT: There are two bus stops in the vicinity for those who would like to get to the trailhead with public transportation; visit a local tourist information office for seasonal bus routes and schedules.

DRIVING: The hike starts in town; all-day parking is available nearby in the P26 parking lot (46.28755°, 13.89468°) behind the cultural center, which is next to the tourist information office. A Bohinj Card gets you free parking.

MAPS: Available at tourist information offices in Ribčev Laz and Stara Fužina.

1 From the front of the tourist information office in Stara Fužina, walk north on the main road. In a few feet, come to an intersection. Continue straight on a smaller road that heads northwest past several accommodations. At 0.2 mile (0.3 km), the road crosses the **Mostnica River**. Just past that, the road Ts; head left. At 0.3 mile (0.5 km), take the footpath to your left, which runs close to Zois's Mansion, the Pretovka Stream and a waterfall. At 0.5 mile (0.8 km), when the footpath Ts with a larger path, go left.

2 Cross the river on **Devil's Bridge** at 0.6 mile (1 km). The single-arch stone bridge was a very challenging undertaking in the second half of the eighteenth century, when it was built. According to local lore, people worked on the bridge all day, and during the night, everything they built was demolished. Someone said,

"Let the devil build this bridge! I won't do it anymore." So the devil started building in earnest. The people asked him what he wanted for his efforts, and he said the first soul that crossed the bridge. Once the bridge was completed, a local farmer got creative and took his dog to the bridge. He threw a bone to the other side and the dog ran after it. The devil took the dog's soul, but once he figured out it wasn't a person's, he was very angry that he'd been outwitted and destroyed the walls of the bridge.

Once you've crossed the bridge (soul intact, hopefully), head right on the main footpath through the gorge. A few feet later, you'll see some gorge signage; continue right, on the path closest to the river.

3 Come to the ticket booth for the gorge at 0.8 mile (1.3 km). Once you've paid (or shown your Bohinj Card for free admission), continue across the river for the official start of the gorge trail, which heads north on a wide, well-maintained path on the east side of the river. There's so much to enjoy in the gorge as you walk— emerald pools, lush greenery, small waterfalls, fish, a potholed stream bed and rock arches—keep your eye out for the one that looks like an elephant's trunk. Near the water, the air is cool and moist (perfect for a hot day).

4 At 1.4 miles (2.3 km), come to a bridge and a picnic table. Cross the river once again and head right—from here, the path to the Voje Valley runs on the west side of the river. You start gaining elevation in earnest as you climb away from the river and out of the gorge, encountering several

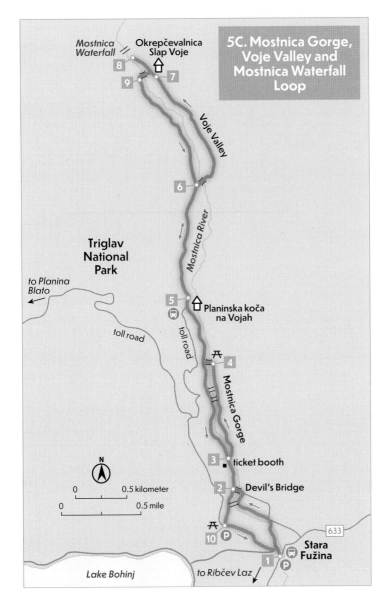

5C. Mostnica Gorge, Voje Valley and Mostnica Waterfall Loop

Mostnica Waterfall

Okrepčevalnica Slap Voje

Voje Valley

Mostnica River

Triglav National Park

to Planina Blato

toll road

toll road

Planinska koča na Vojah

Mostnica Gorge

N

0   0.5 kilometer

0   0.5 mile

ticket booth

Devil's Bridge

633

Stara Fužina

Lake Bohinj

to Ribčev Laz

playhouse for kids. You can also purchase local cheese for takeaway—perfect for a trail snack later on. The hut has a shuttle stop with service back to Stara Fužina. Just past the hut, the paved road turns to gravel. By 2.2 miles (3.5 km), you're out of the trees and into the fields, the sound of thousands of crickets all around you.

6 At 2.6 miles (4.2 km), come to a junction with the trail you'll walk back on after visiting the Mostnica Waterfall. Continue straight on the main path and cross the river. Just past that, enter the pretty meadows of the heart of the **Voje Valley**, which is speckled with small farm buildings and surrounded by wooded hillsides.

7 At 3.4 miles (5.5 km), come to the **Okrepčevalnica Slap Voje**, or Voje Waterfall Snack Bar, a mountain hut at the end of the Voje Valley that serves delicious food—much more than its name lets on—and has a nice terrace with views of the valley. The hut only takes cash.

stairs as you go. At 1.8 miles (2.9 km), go right on a paved road that continues into the valley.

5 Reach the **Planinska koča na Vojah**, or Voje mountain hut, at 1.9 miles (3.1 km), which has food and drinks and a little

From the Mostnica Gorge, it's a short walk to the peaceful Voje Valley.

You can stop in now or continue to the waterfall before you fill up. To reach the waterfall, stay straight on the gravel path.

8 The **Mostnica Waterfall**, also called the Voje Waterfall, is a 5-minute walk down the path, 3.6 miles (5.8 km) from the start of the trail. This 66-foot-high (20-meter-high) waterfall is likely not the biggest one you've ever seen, but it does give you a sense of accomplishment for having walked all the way there. Retrace your path to the hut and then take the footpath that runs west from the hut's entrance to begin the walk back to Stara Fužina on the other side of the river.

9 Cross the Mostnica River at 3.8 miles (6.1 km), then take the path to the left. At 3.9 miles (6.3 km), your smaller path joins a larger one headed south through alternating sections of forest and clearings. At 4.6 miles (7.4 km), find yourself back at [6]. Retrace your steps to [4]. Once you're back at the bridge, don't cross the river. Instead, continue straight, heading south on the gorge footpath on the west side of the river. You can look forward to similar gorge views as before, though on this side you get closer to the river. Keep an eye out for two bridges along the way that make great photo spots. At 6.4 miles (10.3 km), you're back at the ticket booth [3]. Retrace your route to Devil's Bridge [2]. Once you get there, instead of crossing the bridge like you did before, go straight.

10 At 6.8 miles (10.9 km), come to a picnic spot and parking lot. Continue to the paved road and go left, staying on it until the road Ts in **Stara Fužina** at 7.2 miles (11.6 km). Go right on the main road through town and in just a few feet, find yourself back in front of the tourist information office where you started.

Bonus Hike: Peč and Rudnica Loop

Hike from Stara Fužina to the top of Rudnica Hill for two rewarding viewpoints of Lake Bohinj. If you do this hike in late spring/early summer, you have a good chance of seeing wildflowers, including the locally famous Bohinj iris.

DURATION: **4 hours**

DIFFICULTY: **Moderate**

DISTANCE: **5 miles (8 km)**

ELEVATION GAIN: **1,365 feet (416 m)**

MORE INFO: **outdooractive.com**

Trek the picturesque Seven Lakes Valley of Triglav National Park

Seven Lakes Valley, also known as Triglav Lakes Valley, is one of the most popular hiking destinations around Bohinj for those willing to commit to a long day hike. The alpine glacial valley is located inside one of the most picturesque parts of Triglav National Park, one that is as sweet and lush as a fairy-tale world, all wildflower-strewn meadows, spruce forests, grazing cattle and—you guessed it—lakes. If there's one local hike you shouldn't miss, it's this one.

The route starts near the parking lot for Planina Blato, an alpine meadow, and ascends to several mountain pastures before climbing to the Štapce saddle, which has great views down to the valley, Double Lake and a traditional mountain hut. Continue to the hut, where you can eat lunch or stay overnight, before traversing several more working meadows on your way back to the trailhead.

ON THE TRAIL

DURATION: **7 hours**

DIFFICULTY: **Moderate to challenging**

DISTANCE: **9.9 miles (15.9 km)**

ELEVATION GAIN: **3,212 feet (979 m)**

ELEVATION LOSS: **3,212 feet (979 m)**

START: **Planina Blato trailhead**

END: **Planina Blato trailhead**

EAT + DRINK: **Koča na Planina pri Jezeru mountain hut, Koča pri Triglavskih Jezerih mountain hut, Bregarjevo Zavetišče na Planini Viševnik mountain hut (see Online Resources)**

Know Before You Go

Although it involves a significant amount of elevation gain, this trail is so long that the elevation gain doesn't feel too overwhelming—it's the length that's most challenging. The first part of the route, to the Štapce saddle, is mainly uphill. After the Štapce saddle, the route descends steeply to the Koča pri Triglavskih Jezerih mountain hut and then travels in a rolling manner back to the Planina Blato trailhead. Three short sections of the route have cables to assist you. One is at the Štapce saddle, and the other two are near Planina Viševnik. Most people don't have any trouble with these sections; just be sure to go slow. The route is well signed; confidence markers are red circles with white inside.

Other details about the route:

- This hike is best done from late June to September, when the three mountain huts along the way are open.
- To make sure you have enough daylight hours for this long hike, and to guarantee yourself a spot in the parking lot (if you drive), aim to get to the trailhead by 6:15 a.m.

- Although this route is inside Triglav National Park, you don't need a permit or pass to hike it.
- There's no swimming allowed in the lakes en route.

Alternative Routes and Activities

You can do this hike over two days by spending the night at the Koča pri Triglavskih Jezerih mountain hut (see Online Resources). Reservations should be made well in advance.

Doing the hike in one day will take up most of the day, but if you have time (especially if you're spending the night at the Koča pri Triglavskih Jezerih mountain hut), a worthy extension of this hike is the 45-minute (one-way) hike from Double Lake to Veliko Jezero, also called Jezero Ledvička (Kidney Lake), the largest lake in Triglav Lakes Valley. The roundtrip adds 3.2 miles (5.1 km) and 650 feet (198 m) of elevation gain/loss to your hike.

Navigating

This hike starts near the parking lot for Planina Blato, a popular alpine meadow. There's a port-a-potty a few feet from the trailhead.

STARTING POINT: 46.31085°, 13.84929°

TRANSIT: In summer, you can take a free shuttle most of the way to the trailhead. The shuttle runs from several villages in the area and drops you off at a stop called Vogar-Blato that's 0.4 mile (0.6 km) downhill from the trailhead. From the bus stop, be sure to head toward Blato and not Vogar. Current schedules can be obtained from local tourist information offices or the Promet bus company (see Online Resources).

DRIVING: The Planina Blato parking lot is a 25-minute drive from Ribčev Laz; the bulk of the drive is on a serpentine toll road from Stara Fužina. You pay for the toll road (about €15) on your way back down the mountain, at a machine located near town that accepts cash and card. The parking lot at Planina Blato is free but relatively small; if you don't arrive

The descent from the Štapce saddle to Double Lake is steep but affords you the best views of the hike.

early enough, you'll likely need to park on the side of the road leading to it. From the parking lot, the Planina Blato trailhead is located back down the road a few feet, on your right.

MAPS: Available at tourist information offices in Ribčev Laz and Stara Fužina.

1 From the trailhead, walk uphill through the forest on a wide gravel road. At 0.2 mile (0.3 km), take the footpath that branches off on the right. You could continue up the gravel road, but the footpath is slightly more scenic, and you'll descend via the gravel road at the end of the hike. Both routes are signed for your first alpine pasture, Planina pri Jezeru, in 50 minutes. At 0.8 mile (1.3 km), the routes meet up again; go right onto the gravel road and keep climbing. There's an animal gate to pass through in a few feet. NOTE: Don't be discouraged by this first section of the hike. It's steep and relatively boring; the scenery improves drastically at the first hut.

2 Come to your first alpine pasture, **Planina pri Jezeru**, at 1.3 miles (2.1 km). There's a hut here, **Koča na Planina pri Jezeru**, which serves food and drinks and is especially popular with hikers in the afternoon—it's on your return route as well and makes a good spot for a (nearly) post-hike beer. The hut is in the middle of the pasture and looks out at a small lake that isn't counted as one of the seven lakes of Seven Lakes Valley. From the hut, continue northwest on a grassy path that runs past the lake, following signs to your

next alpine meadow, Planina Dedno Polje, which is signed for 30 minutes. As you leave the meadow, the grassy path turns to gravel, and cows graze alongside the trail. Most of this section is through a beautiful spruce forest.

3 The alpine meadow of **Planina Dedno Polje** is at 2.2 miles (3.5 km). There aren't any services, but you'll see plenty of buildings traditionally used by herdsmen, and the lush grass is dotted with boulders—it's a charming spot that's perfect for a photo. To continue on, follow the signs toward Planina Ovčarija (signed for 1 hour and 35 minutes) and Koča pri Triglavskih Jezerih (signed for 2 hours and 15 minutes). The path out of the meadow is pretty faint, but it soon becomes an established (often rocky) footpath that's easy to follow as it travels through larch forest and smaller meadows, with pretty wildflowers decorating the sides of the trail.

4 At 3.1 miles (5 km), emerge into a clearing with superb views of the **southern Julian Alps**—Vrh nad Škrbino, Podrta Gora, Tolminski Kuk, Vrh Planje, Mahavšček and Bogatin. The alpine meadow before you is **Planina Ovčarija**. In a few feet, go straight at a junction with the trail to Planina Viševnik. There's another junction just after that where you have a decision to make. Both routes go to the Koča pri Triglavskih Jezerih mountain hut and are nearly the same length. If you have a fear of heights, follow the sign for "Prodovje" that directs you straight ahead, which is the way you'll return to Planina Ovčarija from the hut. Otherwise, head right on the

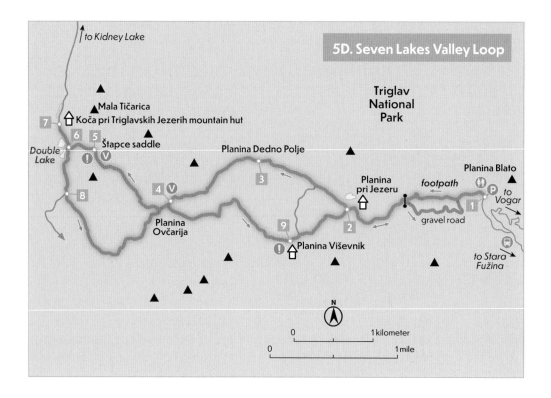

to Kidney Lake

5D. Seven Lakes Valley Loop

▲ Mala Tičarica

🏠 **Koča pri Triglavskih Jezerih mountain hut**   **7**

Triglav
National
Park

Štapce saddle   **6** **5**

Double
Lake

Planina Dedno Polje

Planina Blato

▲ to
Vogar

4 Ⓥ

Planina
pri Jezeru   footpath   **1**

8

3

🏠

9   **2**

Planina
Ovčarija

gravel road

🏠 Planina Višev nik

to Stara
Fužina

N

| 0 | | 1 kilometer |
| 0 | | 1 mile |

lush, rolling path up to the **Štapce saddle**. In midsummer, the wildflowers are incredible, and it's impossible to imagine a prettier spot.

5 Reach the saddle, tucked below **Mala Tičarica** (and **Velika Tičarica**), at 4.1 miles (6.6 km). This is where your hard work pays off—check out those views of **Dvojno Jezero** (Double Lake) and **Seven Lakes Valley** from above! The views only get better as you descend from the gap on a steep, rocky trail with the help of cables, surrounded by gorgeous flowers that grow among the rocks. TIP: Stow your hiking poles for this section so they don't get in your way. This cable-assisted section of trail is pretty short and doesn't pose too much of a challenge if you go slow. The

more difficult part of the route comes once you're on a footpath again. There are a lot of loose rocks and the descent is steep—watch your footing, not just the incredible panorama of Double Lake and the hut below.

6 At 4.4 miles (7.1 km), the trail Ts between the two lakes of **Double Lake**, which are connected in wetter months. Head right for the hut.

7 The **Koča pri Triglavskih Jezerih mountain hut** is at 4.6 miles (7.4 km). The hut serves local specialties like *jota*, a thick stew of sauerkraut and beans, and, my favorite, *Kranjska klobasa*, Carniolan sausage. There's also beer and other cold drinks, as well as a faucet in front of the hut where you can refill your water bottle.

The bathroom is on the opposite side of the building from the restaurant entrance. Just beyond the hut are a couple of smaller lakes. TIP: Get here early? In summer, the hut serves breakfast from 7 to 9 a.m.

Planina Dedno Polje is the most scenic of the alpine meadows you pass through on the Seven Lakes Valley Loop.

Once you're ready to hit the trail again, retrace your steps to [6]. From here, if you feel like you have enough gas in the tank, you can head left to retrace your route via the Štapce saddle to Planina Ovčarija. If you want a less challenging path back, and to follow my route as described, go straight through the junction, skirting the southern lake and then walking through a lush meadow.

[8] There's a junction at 5.2 miles (8.4 km), where Planina Ovčarija is signed for 45 minutes; stay straight. You'll walk a mainly flat path through the forest until you come to a ridge section with views of the mountains all around, then ascend through open forest to **Planina Ovčarija** and the junction with the trail to Štapce. Go straight, and then at the next junction, at 6.6 miles (10.6 km), take a right toward Planina Viševnik, which is signed for 45 minutes. Along the way, you'll walk through a series of smaller meadows, a couple peppered with small herdsmen's buildings, before skirting a large forest— the largest you've seen all hike. Beginning at 7.7 miles (12.4 km), descend two short sections with the help of a cable—less chal-

lenging than what you did on Štapce. After that, you walk alongside a ridge to Planina Viševnik.

[9] **Planina Viševnik**, at 7.8 miles (12.6 km), is typically the most active of the meadow settlements of the hike. You're likely to see farmers working on their buildings or land. You can also grab refreshments at **Bregarjevo Zavetišče na Planini Viševnik**, a hut that used to be a cheese factory and now offers drinks and overnight stays. Just beyond that, at 7.9 miles (12.7 km), come to a junction with two ways back to Planina pri Jezeru [2]. Take the right-hand path, which gets you there in 20 minutes rather than 30, and offers great views of the hut and lake from above. From [2], it's about an hour back to the Planina Blato trailhead via the gravel road—an easier route when your legs are tired than the footpath you initially walked.

The car-free village of Wengen clings to a ridge high above the Lauterbrunnen Valley. (Photo courtesy Jungfrau Region Tourismus AG)

6 THE JUNGFRAU, SWITZERLAND

Hiking in the shadow of Switzerland's most iconic Alps

AT A GLANCE

GENERAL LOCATION: Central Switzerland

HOME BASE: Wengen

LOCAL LANGUAGE: German

USE OF ENGLISH: Widely understood and used

FAMILY FRIENDLY: ★ ★ ★ ☆

COST: $$$$

WHEN TO GO: Mid-Jun to Sept

SCENERY: The Swiss Alps, colorful wildflowers, turquoise lakes

DON'T MISS: Mountain huts, quaint villages, Swiss comfort food, alpenhorns, *lederhosen*

I first hiked the Swiss Alpine Pass Route, a mountain lover's trail that crosses Switzerland from east to west, in 2015. My favorite part of the route passes through the Jungfrau region, the touristy heart of the larger Bernese Oberland, which also boasts some of Switzerland's best day hikes.

The larger route became the gold standard against which I now measure every other hike. And what a high bar it is. The scenery of the Bernese Oberland is almost incomparable—wildflower-strewn meadows in the shadow of snowcapped peaks, azure lakes that reflect lazy, puffy clouds, fat marmots sitting right on trail. The Alpine culture is just as enchanting. I love walking past working farms where you can buy homemade cheese, a cold beer and even a room for the night. It is heaven.

Want to learn more about the Swiss Alpine Pass Route? Check out my flagship book, *Explore Europe on Foot*.

The core Jungfrau region is no exception, dominated by a trio of 13,000-foot (4,000 m) mountains, the Eiger, Mönch and Jungfrau, that stand sentinel over two deep-cut valleys, the Lauterbrunnen and the Lütschine, and a smattering of Swiss Alpine villages—some lining the valley floors, others peering into their depths from rims high above. The geography makes for true bucket-list hiking—you feel like you're in *The Sound of Music* every minute of every day—while an incredible public transportation network makes it easy to get to those award-winning views

from a cozy village home base. For a week-long exploration of the very best of Swiss hiking, there's no better place. Trails are typically snow-free from mid-June to September. July is the busiest month for the region but generally has the best, most predictable conditions. Early September, once the kids go back to school, can mean fewer crowds and beautiful fall foliage.

Most home base hiking days in the Jungfrau start with a scenic cogwheel train, lift or cable car ride to the trailhead. This is a terrific opportunity to wake up and enjoy your morning coffee as you enter the domain of the peaks you'll soon come to know more intimately. It's also a great way to gain elevation the easy way, without all of the huffing and puffing, freeing you up to walk flat ridgelines and enjoy gentle descents to the valleys below without sacrificing the big-peak views you came for. (You can also walk up and train down if you prefer.) As you walk, there's plenty to take in, from Europe's tallest north face (see Hike 6C, the Eiger Trail) to Europe's largest subterranean waterfall (see Trümmelbach Falls in What to See and Do). You get epic views from above of the largest town in the Bernese Oberland, Interlaken, with its twin lakes of deep blue and cerulean (see Hike 6B, Schynige Platte Loop). The closer-in views are also picture-worthy: cows and sheep grazing in their high-mountain pastures, elusive ibex navigating the rocks above, and carpets of blue, white and purple wildflowers below.

The scenery is so captivating, you may never want to stop walking, at least until you come to one of the many mountain huts that dot the Swiss countryside. The rustic-looking wood structures welcome you with overflowing boxes of geraniums, tables facing the mountains and Swiss comfort food, which is hearty with a capital *H*. Family proprietors often have extensive menus that belie their simple huts. Fill up mid-hike with a melty *raclette* (an Alpine cheese) spooned over boiled potatoes and tangy pickles, served alongside an ice-cold Swiss lager. Pace yourself, because there's often more than one hut on any given trail. Better yet, make it a progressive lunch.

After a full day of fresh air and walking, you'll be ready for the comforts of town. Although the Jungfrau region has several small towns that make great home bases for hiking, I recommend Wengen, a car-free village that clings to a ridge high above the east side of the Lauterbrunnen Valley. Wengen is centrally located to the best hikes in the area and well connected to them by public transportation, which means you'll minimize the time (and money) required to get to and from your daily explorations. As a car-free village, Wengen feels more authentic and blends into its Alpine surroundings better than some of its neighbors. It's small and easily walkable, and it retains a lot of historic charm and architecture. It also has everything you need—plenty of accommodations and restaurants, a good-size grocery store and even a couple of outdoor stores.

Once you home base in Wengen and hike the Jungfrau region, it will likely become the benchmark against which you measure every other home base hiking trip—and for good reason.

Getting There and Around

The closest international airports to the Jungfrau region are in Geneva and Zürich. The main transportation hub in the Jungfrau region is Interlaken, so most people train there from the airport and then transfer to a Lauterbrunnen-bound train. From Lauterbrunnen, the main hub of the Lauterbrunnen Valley, a cogwheel train ascends the steep valley walls to the car-free village of Wengen. See Online Resources for timetables for Swiss trains.

The Jungfrau region has several car-free villages and many trailheads that are only accessible by public transportation, so if you arrive by car, the best thing to do is park it at a garage for the duration of your stay. If you're home basing in Wengen, the most convenient parking garage is Parking Lauterbrunnen (see Online Resources), which is connected to the Lauterbrunnen railway station and takes online reservations (recommended during summer).

The easiest way to get around during your home base hiking trip is the area's extensive network of trains, buses and cable cars. They run on time and often—even to small outposts—and make it possible to hike point to point, meaning that you can hike from one spot to an entirely different spot without repeating scenery or worrying about how you're going to get back to your home base.

Switzerland offers several passes to bring down the often high cost of public transportation. The best ones for the area are the Swiss half-fare card, the Berner Oberland Pass and the Jungfrau Travel Pass. The best way to decide which pass to buy is to add up the cost of each train or cable car journey you plan on taking, then compare that with what you'd pay with the Swiss half-fare card, a regional pass and a combination of the two. Passes can be purchased online or at any Swiss railway station; you must have your passport with you to purchase one. TIP: For trips of five or more days, save money by combining the Swiss half-fare card and a regional pass.

Where to Stay

While my top choice for a home base in the Jungfrau region is Wengen, another solid option is the car-free village of Mürren, which is smaller than Wengen and has good views of the Jungfrau trio.

Hotels in the area can be quite expensive, especially on Booking.com or similar hotel aggregators. You can typically find less expensive options on Airbnb, but look early because apartments go quickly. TIP: For the best deals and choice of accommodations, book your room at least six months in advance.

Location doesn't matter much in Wengen, because everything is walkable. That said, there are a few small hills in town, which can be challenging if you're carrying a lot of luggage from the train to your accommodations. To make the load lighter, you can pay for luggage storage of nonessential items at the train station in

Each year, Wengen is home to traditional celebrations when the cows are taken to their high-alpine grazing land and when they return home for the winter. (Photo courtesy Jungfrau Region Tourismus AG)

Lauterbrunnen or hire luggage transfer to your hotel; contact the Lauterbrunnen railway station for more information (see Online Resources).

Eat and Resupply

The largest grocery store in Wengen is a Coop supermarket located near the train station. The town has a nice variety of dining options. During high season, dinner

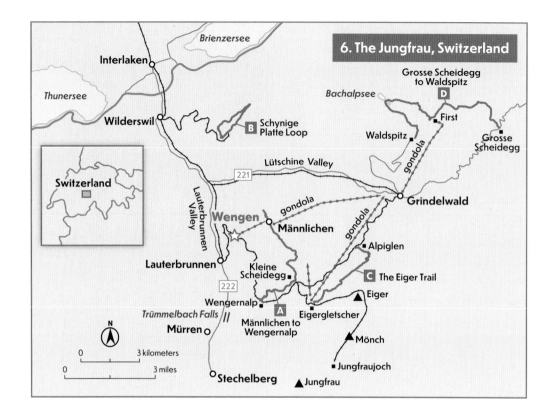

reservations are strongly recommended. Be sure to track down the following local specialties:

- *Raclette*: an Alpine cow's milk cheese that's typically melted at your table and served over boiled potatoes
- *Rösti*: a cross between hash browns and a potato pancake, often served with bacon and melted cheese
- Rivella: a Swiss soft drink produced from whey

There are a couple of outdoor stores on Dorfstrasse in Wengen in case you need to adjust or add to your gear. You'll definitely want to have these accessories for your hikes:

- A coat, hat and gloves are key for the higher-elevation hikes, especially first thing in the morning. Also make sure you have enough extra room in your day pack to store those layers once you take them off.
- If you have creaky knees, hiking poles can be helpful for this region's often steep descents.

What to See and Do
JUNGFRAUJOCH

This 11,000-foot (3,353 m) saddle between the Mönch and the Jungfrau, nicknamed the "Top of Europe," boasts the highest railway stop in Europe, as well as incredible panoramic views of the Alps on a clear

THE ROUTES

HIKE	ROUTE NAME	DURATION	DIFFICULTY	DISTANCE	ELEV. GAIN	ELEV. LOSS
6A	Männlichen to Wengernalp	3.5 hours	Moderate	6 mi (9.7 km)	798 ft (243 m)	1,961 ft (598 m)
6B	Schynige Platte Loop	2.5 hours	Moderate	4 mi (6.4 km)	1,121 ft (342 m)	1,121 ft (342 m)
6C	The Eiger Trail	2.5 hours	Easy	3.7 mi (6 km)	248 ft (76 m)	2,604 ft (794 m)
6D	Grosse Scheidegg to Waldspitz	4.5 hours	Moderate	7.5 mi (12.1 km)	1,449 ft (442 m)	1,658 ft (496 m)

day. You can explore an ice cave, play in the snow and warm up at the viewing point's restaurant. If you're feeling like a high-elevation adventure, a roundtrip hike of 2.5 miles (4 km) takes you across a snowfield to Mönchsjochhütte, the highest manned hut in the Alps (see the Mönchsjochhütte bonus hike at the end of Hike 6C). TIP: It's not worth visiting the Jungfraujoch if it's foggy. Check out the viewpoint's webcam (see Online Resources) the morning of

your intended visit and, if you're in the clear, then purchase a train ticket and seat reservation.

TRÜMMELBACH FALLS

Trümmelbach Falls is Europe's largest subterranean waterfall and the area's best rainy-day activity, with ten chutes that cascade down the inside of a mountain. The falls are viewable from a series of galleries and overlooks that are accessed via

August 1 is Swiss National Day. Each year, Wengen hosts a great celebration and welcomes visitors to take part in it. There's typically a reception with local food and drinks, activities for kids, and dance and musical performances. There's also a fun kids' lantern parade that's led by a live band that winds its way through the streets of town at dusk, followed by fireworks. TIP: Buy your lantern in advance; they don't sell them at the parade.

Swiss Alpine towns are a fascinating mix of the traditional and the modern. The buildings are rustic and some of the villages are car-free, yet there's near-perfect cell phone service everywhere and almost every establishment accepts credit cards. You can rent a room in a working farm, yet walk to a chic cocktail bar.

a network of walkways and tunnels. If you prefer not to walk the full route, there's an elevator (included in the cost of admission) that can drop you off between the sixth and seventh waterfalls. TIP: Want to see the falls as part of a longer outing? Walk there from Lauterbrunnen; it's a flat hike of 4.4 miles (7.1 km) roundtrip through a beautiful valley.

PARAGLIDING

For a bird's-eye view of the best of the Jungfrau region, paragliding around Interlaken can't be beat. The city is situated in between two beautiful lakes and has the Jungfrau range in sight, so there's plenty to admire from the air. And there's nothing like the absolute silence you experience during paragliding to put the big-money views front and center. Interlaken's tourist information website (see Online Resources) has great information on what to expect and how to book your adventure.

★★★ The Jungfrau region gets three stars out of four for being family friendly. There are plenty of parks and playgrounds; high chairs are plentiful at huts and restaurants; and kids under six travel for free on public transportation. For families with kids older than six, things can get expensive fast, considering the high cost of Swiss public transportation and food. TIP: Buy a wooden ball at Wengen's tourist information office for the many fun ball drops scattered around town. Also, a visit to the awesome playground in Männlichen (next to Berghaus Männlichen and visited on Hike 6A, Männlichen to Wengernalp) is a must.

6A MÄNNLICHEN TO WENGERNALP

Hike beyond the crowds to solitude and jaw-dropping views of the Jungfrau trio

If you want incredible views of the Jungfrau trio, this is the trail for you. The route utilizes the popular Panorama Trail from Männlichen to Kleine Scheidegg, as well as two very worthy additions that many people miss—the Männlichen viewpoint at the beginning, with its 360-degree mountain panorama, and the route from Kleine Scheidegg to Wengernalp at the end, which has the best views of the Jungfrau that you'll experience during your time in the region.

ON THE TRAIL

DURATION: 3.5 hours

DIFFICULTY: Moderate

DISTANCE: 6 miles (9.7 km)

ELEVATION GAIN: 798 feet (243 m)

ELEVATION LOSS: 1,961 feet (598 m)

START: Männlichen cable car station

END: Wengernalp train station

EAT + DRINK: Berghaus Männlichen, Berghaus Grindelwaldblick, Kleine Scheidegg, Hotel Jungfrau Wengernalp (see Online Resources)

Know Before You Go

The hike is well signed, and the route as described follows several well-maintained trails.

Other details to keep in mind:

- Several restaurants around Kleine Scheidegg serve lunch, but they tend to be crowded and busy. For more peace and quiet, and better food, eat just before the mountain pass, at Berghaus Grindelwaldblick.
- It's not worth doing the hike in the opposite direction because you'd have the best mountain views at your back.
- Check the webcam at Kleine Scheidegg the morning of your hike (see Online Resources) to make sure the mountains aren't fogged in.

Alternative Routes and Activities

For a shorter option, and to experience the predominantly flat middle section of the trail and eliminate most of the elevation gain and loss of the hike, you can walk from the Männlichen cable car station to Kleine Scheidegg, a point-to-point walk of 2.9 miles (4.7 km).

Or you can extend your outing by combining this route with a visit to the Jungfraujoch after your hike. From the end point at the Wengernalp train station, walk (see [11] in the Navigating section) or catch a train to Kleine Scheidegg, then transfer to a train that will take you the rest of the way to the Jungfraujoch.

Navigating

The hike starts at the Männlichen cable car station, which has public restrooms and beautiful views back down to Wengen. STARTING POINT: 46.61323°, 7.94115°

TRANSIT: From Wengen, it's a 6-minute cable car ride to reach Männlichen. The cable car runs every 20 minutes starting at approximately 8:10 a.m.—but confirm current schedules via the Swiss timetable (see Online Resources). TIP: For great views on a clear day, pay approximately €5 to ride on the glass-enclosed top of the car.

To get back to your starting point in Wengen from the Wengernalp train station at the end of the hike, take a Lauterbrunnen-bound train and get off in Wengen, in approximately 17 minutes. The train runs hourly.

MAPS: Available at the tourist information office in Wengen and train/cable car stations in the area.

Catch great views of Kleine Scheidegg and the Jungfrau trio from the lookout at Berghaus Grindelwaldblick.

1 From the **Männlichen cable car station**, walk through the animal gate to spot your first trail sign. Most hikers immediately head right for the Panorama Trail (the section of trail from Männlichen to Kleine Scheidegg), and you will eventually as well, but if you have time, it's worth it to first go left and walk the 20 minutes uphill on a wide gravel path to the Männlichen viewpoint.

2 Reach the crown-shaped viewpoint at 0.5 mile (0.8 km), and what a vista it offers. All around you are peaks—360 degrees worth. Pictures of the mountains and corresponding labels on the inside of the crown help you identify each one. The closest and most stunning are the Eiger, Mönch and Jungfrau, their rocky faces in stark contrast to the grassy knob of the smaller Tschuggen in the foreground, but that's just the beginning. From here, you also have a bird's-eye view of both main valleys of the Jungfrau region, the Lauterbrunnen and Lütschine, and the many alpine pastures that connect the peaks with the valleys.

When you're done at the viewpoint, head back toward the Männlichen cable car station and keep walking south, toward the Tschuggen.

3 At 1.1 miles (1.8 km) from the start of the hike, come to **Berghaus Männlichen**,

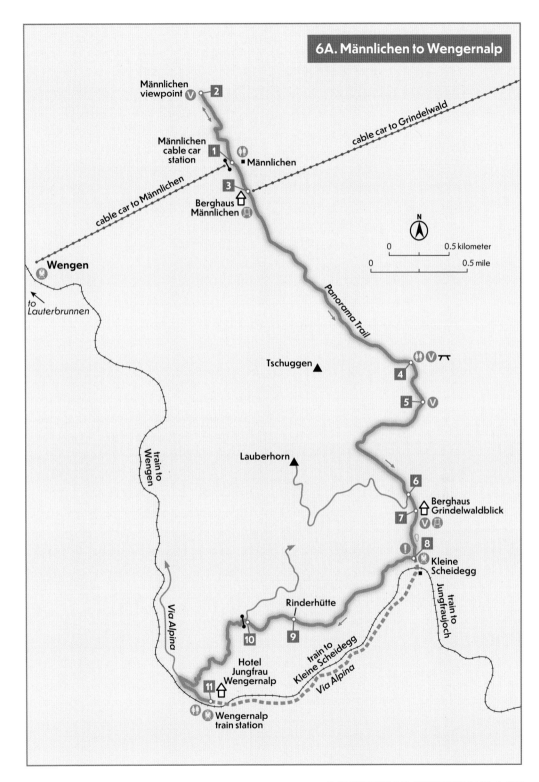

6A. Männlichen to Wengernalp

Männlichen viewpoint (V)—○—2

cable car to Grindelwald

Männlichen cable car station 1 (WC) ■ Männlichen

cable car to Männlichen

Berghaus Männlichen 3

N

0   0.5 kilometer

0   0.5 mile

Wengen

to Lauterbrunnen

Panorama Trail

(WC) (V) ⊼

Tschuggen ▲

4

5—○—(V)

train to Wengen

Lauberhorn ▲

6

Berghaus Grindelwaldblick

7

(V) ▣

8

Kleine Scheidegg

Via Alpina

Rinderhütte

10   9

train to Kleine Scheidegg

train to Jungfraujoch

Via Alpina

Hotel Jungfrau Wengernalp

11

(WC) (X) Wengernalp train station

a large mountain hut with a nice terrace restaurant and the best playground in the area. TIP: During the summer, Berghaus Männlichen regularly offers a mountain brunch on its terrace—a great way to start your hike.

Continue on the well-signed wide path to the left of the cable car station (this one with service to Grindelwald; public restrooms inside) to stay on the trail as it heads toward the eastern flank of the Tschuggen and superb views of the Lütschine Valley below. You'll likely see cows grazing on this part of the trail. They seem sweet, with their singsong bells and ambling ways, but it's best to keep your distance, especially when taking photos.

4 Wind around the green **Tschuggen**, a beautiful anomaly in this land of rocky,

The Panorama Trail winds around the eastern flank of the Tschuggen.

jagged peaks, until you get to 2.5 miles (4 km), where knockout views of the Jungfrau trio can be enjoyed from benches overlooking their north faces. If you've already hiked the Eiger Trail (Hike 6C), you'll recognize the route you took, a straight line underscoring the Eiger's massive rock walls; you can even see Berghaus Alpiglen from here. Near the benches, you'll find a port-a-potty and a simple, open structure that makes for a great break spot on a rainy day.

5 Kleine Scheidegg, both a mountain pass connecting the Lauterbrunnen and Lütschine Valleys and a main transportation hub, comes into sight at 2.7 miles (4.3 km). Just after that, enter the lush hollow between the Tschuggen and the **Lauberhorn**. This concave section of trail is more protected than the exposed sections you've been walking; wildflowers and small trees abound and birds circle above.

6 At 3.5 miles (5.6 km), come to a junction with a trail to the Lauberhorn and head left in the direction of Kleine Scheidegg.

7 **Berghaus Grindelwaldblick** is a welcome sight at 3.6 miles (5.8 km). This is the best spot for lunch on the hike. The hut has a playground, a terrace restaurant and—for overnight guests only—a sauna and hot tub that overlook the mountains. Don't miss the amazing view of the Jungfrau trio from the hut's lookout, which is accessible via a staircase off the terrace. From Berghaus Grindelwaldblick, it's about a 10-minute walk to **Kleine Scheidegg** via the downhill path between the hut and the playground.

8 At 3.8 miles (6.1 km), just before you reach the Kleine Scheidegg train station, go right onto a footpath signed for **Wengernalp**. TIP: The sign is easy to miss, so this is a good place to refer to my GPX tracks. Go up a small hill, through a cow gate and then to the left on a narrow grass footpath that climbs gently. As you start to gain elevation, you also gain solitude; most people hike only the section of trail from Männlichen to Kleine Scheidegg. They don't know what they're missing. As you wind up the grass hill on the southern slope of the **Lauberhorn**, you get your best views of the Jungfrau. Keep your camera handy as you approach the pyramid-like **Silberhorn** mountain with the massive **Jungfrau** towering above it and waterfalls cascading down the mountain's rocky slopes. This is what you came for.

9 Reach the **Rinderhütte**, a storage hut for local farmers (with no services), at 4.7 miles (7.6 km). From here, it's a 30-minute walk to Wengernalp through beautiful meadows, with more big-money views of the Jungfrau. The trail descends, first gently and then more steeply as you lose all of the elevation you've gained (plus some).

10 At 5 miles (8 km), go left at the junction, through an animal gate, and start switchbacking down the steepest part of the trail. It doesn't last too long. In 0.7 mile (1.1 km), the trail flattens out at an intersection with a wide gravel path, part of the **Via Alpina**. Head left at the junction, walking back toward the Jungfrau.

The Via Alpina is a network of five long-distance hiking paths that connect the Alps of Switzerland, Italy, France, Monaco, Slovenia, Austria, Germany and Liechtenstein.

---

11 Come to the **Wengernalp train station** at 6 miles (9.7 km), with good views of the mountains. Public restrooms are available here. Just behind the train station is **Hotel Jungfrau Wengernalp**, which serves food and is a great place to wait for your train. If you'd rather keep walking, head to Kleine Scheidegg by continuing uphill along the Via Alpina/Mendelssohnweg, for 1.4 miles (2.3 km) and get a Wengen-bound train from there.

6B SCHYNIGE PLATTE LOOP

Ascend to an exposed ridgeline high above Interlaken and its twin lakes

For a heavenly ridge walk with gorgeous views down to Interlaken and its two lakes, there's no better hike than this 4-mile loop at Schynige Platte. Gain most of your elevation the easy way, with an old-fashioned cogwheel train to the plateau. Hike through a fragrant forest before losing the trees in favor of big views of the surrounding area from the 6,800-foot (2,072 m) Daube, the 6,700-foot (2,042 km) Oberberghorn, and the true star of the hike—the ridgeline that connects them. Celebrate your hike with a visit to a traditional guesthouse that serves Swiss specialties with great views of the mountains.

ON THE TRAIL

DURATION: **2.5 hours**

DIFFICULTY: **Moderate**

DISTANCE: **4 miles (6.4 km)**

ELEVATION GAIN: **1,121 feet (342 m)**

ELEVATION LOSS: **1,121 feet (342 m)**

START: **Schynige Platte train station**

END: **Schynige Platte train station**

EAT + DRINK: **Schynige Platte train station, Berghotel Schynige Platte (see Online Resources)**

Know Before You Go

This loop hike is relatively short and mostly rolling, with two main ascents, up to the Daube and to the Oberberghorn. The route makes use of several trails, including the Panorama Trail, and is relatively well signed, although the signage is typically for the main points of interest on your route, such as the Daube, rather than the trail names or numbers. Confidence markers are two white stripes with a red stripe between them.

The train from Wilderswil to Schynige Platte is long (nearly an hour) and slow and can sometimes run behind schedule; grab a to-go coffee in Wilderswil for the ride and allow yourself extra time, especially on the return journey.

Alternative Routes and Activities

You can make this hike shorter in a few different ways, thanks to the numerous trails that branch off the described route and head back toward the train station. One such shortcut is at the Daube, another is

just before the Oberberghorn, and a third comes just after it. A trail map of the area or a GPS device will help you identify and navigate these shorter routes. To cut some of the main route's elevation gain, it's possible to skip the ascent to the viewpoint on top of the Oberberghorn at 1 mile (1.6 km).

Doing the full hike will take up most of your day, given that it takes nearly 2 hours each way to get from Wengen to Schynige Platte (don't worry—it's well worth it), but you could tack on another activity if you want to extend your outing:

- Berghotel Schynige Platte, near the Schynige Platte train station, often has traditional Swiss entertainment like alpenhorn music in the summer. It's a great place to kick back for a couple of hours post-hike. Fancy flowers? Visit the Alpine botanical garden nearby.
- Interlaken is a 5-minute train ride from Wilderswil (trains generally run every half hour), so if you're keen on exploring the biggest town in the Jungfrau region, it's a convenient post-hike destination.

From the lookout atop the Oberberghorn, the Brienzersee, the Panorama Trail and the Loucherhorn are on full display.

Navigating

The Schynige Platte train station, where this hike begins, has public restrooms and a café.

STARTING POINT: **46.65204°, 7.91091°**

TRANSIT: From Wengen, it takes nearly 2 hours and three different trains to reach Schynige Platte: a cogwheel train from Wengen to Lauterbrunnen, a regular train from Lauterbrunnen to Wilderswil, and another cogwheel train from Wilderswil to Schynige Platte. (If you have a Swiss rail pass, this is where you make some of your money back!) The train from Wilderswil to Schynige Platte is very old-fashioned and compact (think bench seating) and can be crowded in peak season, so I recommend leaving Wengen on the first train of the day (generally around 7:15 a.m., but check the Swiss train timetable for the most up-to-date information; see Online Resources) to arrive in Wilderswil before things get too busy. You'll want to queue early for the train to Schynige Platte to guarantee yourself a seat.

To get back to Wengen at the end of the hike, reverse the train journey you took to Schynige Platte.

MAPS: Available at the tourist information office in Wengen and train/cable car stations in the area.

1 From the **Schynige Platte train station**, head left (when looking at the train station) and find your first trail sign at the end of the platform. The Daube, your first viewpoint, is signed for 30 minutes, on the path straight ahead.

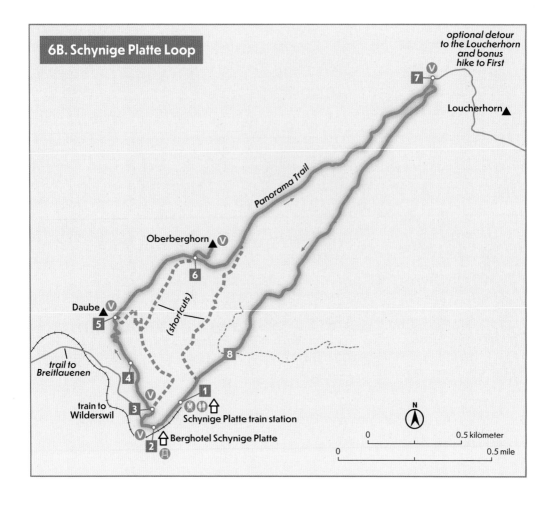

6B. Schynige Platte Loop

optional detour
to the Loucherhorn
and bonus
hike to First

7 Ⓥ

Loucherhorn ▲

Panorama Trail

Oberberghorn ▲ Ⓥ

6

Daube ▲ Ⓥ

(shortcuts)

5

trail to
Breitlauenen

4

8

train to
Wilderswil

3

1

ⓞⓞ⌂
Schynige Platte train station

Ⓥ

2

⌂ Berghotel Schynige Platte

N

0   0.5 kilometer

0   0.5 mile

2 Wind your way through the ground-level terrace of **Berghotel Schynige Platte** (see Online Resources) at 0.1 mile (0.2 km). There's typically not much going on at the hotel in the morning, but come afternoon, the air will likely be filled with the beautiful notes of the alpenhorn and enticing aromas; this is where you want to be post-hike. For now, continue past a seating area, playground and viewpoint to find the junction where you turn right and head uphill.

3 At 0.2 mile (0.3 km), take the requisite photo in the large *edelweiss*-bedecked

picture frame on trail, then head left at the Daube-signed junction. Almost immediately, you're surrounded by fragrant trees and bright wildflowers in a lush area that feels so different from what you normally experience on a Jungfrau hike. Soak it all in before the trees slowly peter out and you walk along a more exposed ridgeline with views down to the cogwheel train from Wilderswil.

4 The trail incline starts to increase at 0.4 mile (0.6 km), and it isn't long before you're switchbacking up the rocky trail to the Daube viewpoint. This is the most challenging part of the whole hike; in 0.3 mile (0.5 km) you'll gain 279 feet (85 m), but the elevation gain is worth it.

5 The highest you'll be all hike comes at 0.7 mile (1.1 km), when you finally reach the top of the **Daube**. Gaze toward **Interlaken** and its two lakes, the cerulean **Thunersee** and the emerald **Brienzersee**. In the near distance, you can see the rocky spire of the Oberberghorn, which is signed for 25 minutes. Brace yourself: Those 25 minutes are going to be some of the most beautiful of the entire hike, as you walk along an exposed ridgeline with the Brienzersee to your left and rolling meadows and big mountains to your right.

6 At 1 mile (1.6 km), come to the base of the **Oberberghorn**. The 0.2-mile (0.3 km) ascent is steep and narrow and utilizes some wooden stairs. Look for a cool cave overlook halfway up. At the top, find a flat gravel overlook with a 360-degree panorama. When you're done taking in the views, head back down the same way you came up. Once you reach the base of the peak, follow the trail as it curves around the mountain and eventually reaches another ridgeline on its path toward the grassy knob of the **Loucherhorn**, an optional extension of the hike. (Note: There's no trail to the top of the Loucherhorn but a 0.5-mile [0.8 km] walk takes you to its base.)

7 Enjoy one last look at the Brienzersee at the viewpoint at 2.4 miles (3.9 km) before taking the signed trail back toward Schynige Platte. Distance-wise, you're not that far from the route you initially walked, but the views are completely different, all rolling hills and meadows, wildflowers and grazing cows—beautiful in its own right.

8 At 3.6 miles (5.8 km), cross a gravel road and continue uphill for the last bit of the walk, which ends at the **Schynige Platte train station**.

Bonus Hike: Schynige Platte to First

Walk through flowering meadows and past pretty little lakes to the Männdlenen and Faulhorn mountain huts and incredible high-elevation panoramas of the Jungfrau range.

DURATION: **6 hours**

DIFFICULTY: **Challenging**

DISTANCE: **10 miles (16.1 km)**

ELEVATION GAIN: **2,800 feet (853 m)**

MORE INFO: **alltrails.com**

From the Schynige Platte Loop, you get a view most people don't—of Interlaken from above.

6C THE EIGER TRAIL

Discover Switzerland's most imposing north face

This lesser-traveled Alps trail gives you a lot of bang for your buck, leading you to jaw-dropping views of the Eiger, Kleine Scheidegg and the Lütschine Valley while requiring little effort in return. Starting at the Eigergletscher train station, curve your way around a rocky ledge to take in the imposing north face of the Eiger, then descend gently in the shadow of vertical rock through meadows and past a series of small waterfalls to Berghaus Alpiglen, a hut and restaurant with bucolic views down to Grindelwald.

ON THE TRAIL

DURATION: 2.5 hours

DIFFICULTY: Easy

DISTANCE: 3.7 miles (6 km)

ELEVATION GAIN: 248 feet (76 m)

ELEVATION LOSS: 2,604 feet (794 m)

START: Eigergletscher train station

END: Alpiglen train station

EAT + DRINK: Restaurant Eigergletscher, Berghaus Alpiglen (see Online Resources)

Know Before You Go

This well-signed route on the Eiger Trail/Trail 353 is neither long nor strenuous—you spend most of your time descending. You may appreciate hiking poles or other supports if you have creaky knees or ankles.

Other notes about the route:

- It's not worth doing this trail in the fog, so be sure to check out the webcam at Kleine Scheidegg the morning of your hike to be sure you're in the clear (see Online Resources). If it is foggy, wait a few hours and try again—this is a great afternoon hike.
- Even in nice weather, this high-elevation trail can be cold—you'll start at 7,610 feet (2,230 m)—so pack extra warm layers. Watch for occasional snow patches on trail in early summer or fall.

Alternative Routes and Activities

Because this hike isn't very long, it can be done on your way back from exploring the Jungfraujoch (see What to See and Do). To have enough time for both—and to avoid the worst of the crowds—it's best to be on the first Jungfraujoch-bound train of the day.

Alternatively, you could continue your walk down to Grindelwald from Berghaus Alpiglen (see [8] in the Navigating section for details) and explore the biggest town in the area before returning to your home base.

Navigating

The Eigergletscher (Eiger Glacier, literally translated) train station where you arrive is located at the foot of the Mönch and Jungfrau mountains and boasts impressive up-close views of the ice breakup on the glacier. On a clear day, you can see up to the viewpoint at the Jungfraujoch, the saddle between the two mountains, also known as the "Top of Europe," as well as across the Lauterbrunnen Valley to the picturesque village of Mürren. Amenities include public restrooms and a restaurant called Restaurant Eigergletscher. If you're not in a hurry, this is a great snack or lunch spot to take in the best views of the glacier you'll have all hike—and during your time in the Jungfrau.

STARTING POINT: 46.57500°, 7.97459°

TRANSIT: From Wengen, take the train to Kleine Scheidegg, then another train to Eigergletscher. The one-way journey takes approximately 45 minutes (including waiting time between trains) and current timetables can be found at the Swiss railway website (see Online Resources). For the best views, sit on the right-hand side of the train.

Kleine Scheidegg is a busy railway station, and the queue for the train to Eigergletscher can be chaotic as it's the first stop on the route to the popular Jungfraujoch. Bypass most of the crowd by lining up in the special Eigergletscher section of the queue; you'll be in a separate car from the mass of people continuing farther. And don't worry. Only a handful of people—mostly hikers—get out at Eigergletscher, so things will be much less busy again soon.

Once you reach the Alpiglen train station, at the end of the hike, the easiest way to get back to Wengen is to take a return train to Kleine Scheidegg and then transfer to a Wengen-bound train. In total, the return journey takes approximately an hour (including waiting time between trains).

MAPS: Available at the tourist information office in Wengen and train/cable car stations

From the Eiger Trail, the Wetterhorn towers in the distance.

in the area. You can also print your own map from the Swiss tourism bureau's website (see Online Resources).

1 At the **Eigergletscher train station**, head inside the main building and up to the second floor. A paved terrace on the west side of the building is where the trail starts. Follow the paved path as it curves up to spot your first bright yellow-orange trail sign. Continue on the path as it winds toward the Eiger and your first junction.

2 At 0.1 mile (0.2 km), take the left-hand gravel track downhill and underneath the Eigernordwand and Eiger Express cable car terminal stations. Just past the stations, the route curves left to reach the main part of the trail. You may be looking for Eiger views but hold tight; you'll soon

The largest waterfall on the Eiger Trail is a great spot to cool off on a hot day.

pass the small rocky ridge on your right that's blocking the bulk of the mountain.

3 At 0.7 mile (1.1 km), in the middle of the only real elevation gain of the hike, the trail splits at an unsigned junction. Take either trail; they meet up in just 0.1 mile (0.2 km) at [4], the junction with the **Rotstock Klettersteig** (1 mile or 1.6 km roundtrip).

A *klettersteig*, or *via ferrata*, is an assisted climbing route that typically involves clipping in to mountainside cables and ascending the occasional ladder. It's more technical and challenging than hiking but less so than full-on rock or mountain climbing.

4 From here, you have incredible views of the famed **north face of Eiger**. In the Northern Hemisphere, the north face of a mountain is typically the coldest, iciest and most formidable route to climb. This is the closest you'll be to the Eiger all hike (unless you take the short and worthy side trip to the base of the *klettersteig*). The Eiger north face is the tallest north wall, or *nordwand*, in the Alps and is an extremely technical and dangerous climb, which has earned it the nickname *mordwand*, or death wall. It has claimed the lives of more than sixty climbers since the first ascent in 1938. There is some signage showing the route of the first ascent, and you may see tents nearby for climbers who got an early start.

From here, the trail is all downhill. And although you have the imposing Eiger to your right, the focus of the trail shifts to

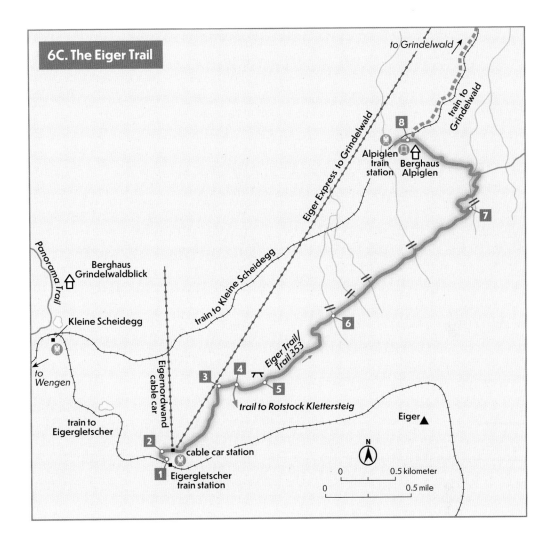

commanding views of Kleine Scheidegg to your left and Grindelwald in front of you.

5 There are benches at different points along the trail, and the pair at 1 mile (1.6 km) are especially well situated for stopping and breathing it all in for a moment: a small turquoise lake near **Kleine Scheidegg**, the gentle curve of the **Panorama Trail** as it winds from Männlichen to Kleine Scheidegg (see Hike 6A), the lush green walls of the **Lütschine Valley** and the towering peak of the **Wetterhorn** in the distance. Look for delicate wildflowers underfoot and listen for the sound of cowbells in the air. You may even have company; these are popular pastures for both cows and sheep. If you're lucky, you may spot a long-horned ibex on the rocks above you or an inky-black mountain salamander underfoot. The latter are particularly striking, with their sweet little faces and glacially slow movements.

6 At 1.7 miles (2.7 km), come to the first in a series of small waterfalls that cross the path. They will look different depending on the time of year you're hiking, but all are easily crossed by balancing on large rocks or hopping across wet areas.

7 The biggest waterfall comes at 2.7 miles (4.3 km). This is a good spot to stop for a break, especially to enjoy some cooling mist on a hot day or as a picnic alternative. A perch on a nearby boulder will let you take in the waterfall plunging into its pool, a nice slot canyon and the wild river it creates down below, not to mention the Grindelwald Grund train and cable car station and the bustling town below.

The final flourish of the hike comes after this waterfall, as over the next mile (1.6 km) you lose 931 feet (284 m) of elevation, traversing a series of switchbacks that get steeper once you go left at the signed junction at 3.1 miles (5 km). The trail gets narrow and rocky, with several deep steps, as you get closer to Berghaus Alpiglen. As you lose elevation, you gain something else—trees, which you've been too high to experience thus far.

8 At 3.6 miles (5.8 km), arrive at **Berghaus Alpiglen**, a pretty alpine hut perched on the edge of the Lütschine Valley that also takes in the splendor of the Eiger's north face and allows you to get a better perspective of the hike you just took. The hut has a small playground, as well as restrooms (they ask for a small payment if you're not a patron). Even better: You'll find a selection of local delicacies and cold beers to end your hike in style. The hut takes credit cards, and there's a train schedule for the nearby Alpiglen train station posted near the bathroom. TIP: This is a popular spot, but don't worry if the tables in the main square are full; the tables near the playground have great views of the valley and typically aren't as crowded.

It can take a while to settle up at mountain huts like Berghaus Alpiglen, and Swiss trains are famously punctual, so ask for the bill with plenty of time to spare.

Once you're done enjoying the views and refueling, find the 0.1-mile (0.2 km) path to the **Alpiglen train station** just past the playground. Catch your return train to Kleine Scheidegg and then another to Wengen. Alternatively, if you'd like to continue your walk to Grindelwald, a different path from the hut will take you there in about 90 minutes (3.4 miles or 5.5 km). You can return to Wengen from Grindelwald by train.

Bonus Hike: Mönchsjochhütte
Leave the crowds of the Jungfraujoch behind and walk on snow, with incredible peak views in all directions, to the highest manned hut in the Alps.
DURATION: 2.5 hours
DIFFICULTY: Moderate
DISTANCE: 2.5 miles (4 km) roundtrip
ELEVATION GAIN: 679 feet (207 m)
MORE INFO: alltrails.com

Catch a stunning view of the Alps across the Bachalpsee.

6D GROSSE SCHEIDEGG TO WALDSPITZ

Walk a ridge above Grindelwald to an alpine lake with unmatched mountain views

There's something for everyone on this all-star day hike. Walk among cows and along a ridge in the shadow of the imposing Wetterhorn to the ski resort of First (pronounced FEER-st), with its cliff walk and other recreation opportunities, before continuing on to one of the prettiest lakes in the Alps and its moor. End your hike at a traditional Swiss mountain hut with outstanding views across the Lütschine Valley.

ON THE TRAIL

DURATION: 4.5 hours

DIFFICULTY: Moderate

DISTANCE: 7.5 miles (12.1 km)

ELEVATION GAIN: 1,449 feet (442 m)

ELEVATION LOSS: 1,658 feet (496 m)

START: Grosse Scheidegg bus stop

END: Waldspitz bus stop

EAT + DRINK: Berghotel Grosse Scheidegg, Genepi Hütte, Berggasthaus First, Gasthaus Waldspitz (see Online Resources)

Know Before You Go

This hike is relatively long and has approximately 1,500 feet (460 m) of elevation gain and loss. There are no steep ascents or descents, however, and the walking surface of the trail is in great shape, ranging from narrow dirt footpaths to wide gravel paths. It is well signed and makes use of several trails, including the Bergwanderweg, Romantikweg and Höhenweg 2400. That said, your route will most often be signed for the places of interest you'll visit on your route, such as First and the Bachalpsee. Pack a swimsuit and towel if you want to swim in the Bachalpsee.

Alternative Routes and Activities

You can make this hike shorter in a few different ways: Walk 3.5 miles (5.6 km) from Grosse Scheidegg to First and then take the gondola back down to Grindelwald. Or take the gondola from Grindelwald up to First and walk 4 miles (6.4 km) to the Bachalpsee and Waldspitz. Or walk from First to the Bachalpsee and back, a roundtrip hike of 3.8 miles (6.1 km).

Or extend your outing with one of these options:

- There's a lot to do at First, including paragliding, zip-lining and a free cliff walk. You could easily spend a few hours there.
- Because you travel through Grindelwald for this hike, it's the perfect opportunity to explore the town on your way back to your home base.

Navigating

The hike starts near Berghotel Grosse Scheidegg, which has a restaurant and restrooms.

STARTING POINT: **46.65569°, 8.10186°**

TRANSIT: **From Wengen, it takes nearly 2 hours to reach Grosse Scheidegg. The quickest journey requires three different changes, in Lauterbrunnen, Zweilütschinen and Grindelwald. (If you're fine with a longer overall travel time, you can find journeys with only two connections.) You'll be on trains until you reach Grindelwald, where you'll transfer to a bus. There is a snack stand in the parking lot of the bus depot, and you can get coffee across the street from the snack stand if you want provisions for your bus ride. The bus ride is quite the experience; the roads**

Enjoy the breathtaking cliff walk at the ski resort of First.

up to the pass are narrow and winding and the bus has to swing wide to turn, so before every curve the driver sounds a melodic horn to warn walkers and drivers up ahead.

To return to Wengen from Waldspitz at the end of the hike, take the bus from Waldspitz to Grindelwald (be sure to check the official timetable for the latest return bus; see Online Resources), then train back to Wengen.

MAPS: Available at the tourist information office in Wengen and train/cable car stations in the area.

1 As you exit the bus in the shadow of the imposing 12,000-foot (3,658 m) Wetterhorn, your first trail sign is along the road, near the mountain hut **Berghotel Grosse Scheidegg**. The sign points you northwest, toward an uphill gravel road that's signed as the Bergwanderweg (mountain walking path), with First in 1 hour and 30 minutes. For the first 0.4 mile (0.6 km), fight the urge to look left, toward Grindelwald—you'll have plenty of time to enjoy this view later—and instead focus on the beautiful green valley to your right, which is traversed by the Via Alpina (see the Via Alpina sidebar on page 173) and will soon disappear behind a ridge.

2 At 0.8 mile (1.3 km), the trail splits three ways. Take the middle fork for the **Höhenweg 2400** trail toward the ski resort of First. Walking along the ridge, you have great views down to **Grindelwald** and the **Lütschine Valley**. This is grazing land, so you'll likely share the path with plenty of curious cows. In the morning, you may

get lucky and see the cows when they're released to pasture, a fun sight as the calves kick and frolic and get their energy out. Don't be alarmed if you see cows running toward you; their food troughs are located next to the trail.

3 Come to your first in a series of small waterfalls on trail at 1.4 miles (2.3 km).

4 At 2 miles (3.2 km), the Höhenweg 2400 trail branches off to the right; stay left for First. You're climbing now and will continue climbing until you've reached the Bachalpsee in 3.5 miles (5.6 km), but most of the elevation gain is gradual and doesn't pose too much of a challenge. Pass another stream and a sculpture of a marmot among rock piles; you may just spot one of the furry little guys as you walk.

5 Once you reach the next junction, at 3.3 miles (5.3 km), stay left for First. A few feet later, head up a series of steps and pass **Genepi Hütte** (an option for food and drinks) and the **First gondola station** on your way to the main part of the resort.

6 Curving left with the path takes you to the restaurant at **Berggasthaus First** at 3.5 miles (5.6 km), with its expansive terrace and DJ or live music on the weekends. From the terrace, you get a great view of the activities you can take part in at the resort, from paragliding to zip-lining to the free cliff walk. None of that compares to the main attraction, though: the best bird's-eye view of **Grindelwald** you'll have all trip. Crowned by the **Oberer Grindelwaldgletscher** (the Upper Grindelwald Glacier), the **Wetterhorn** and the **Eiger**, the town is especially photogenic. To continue

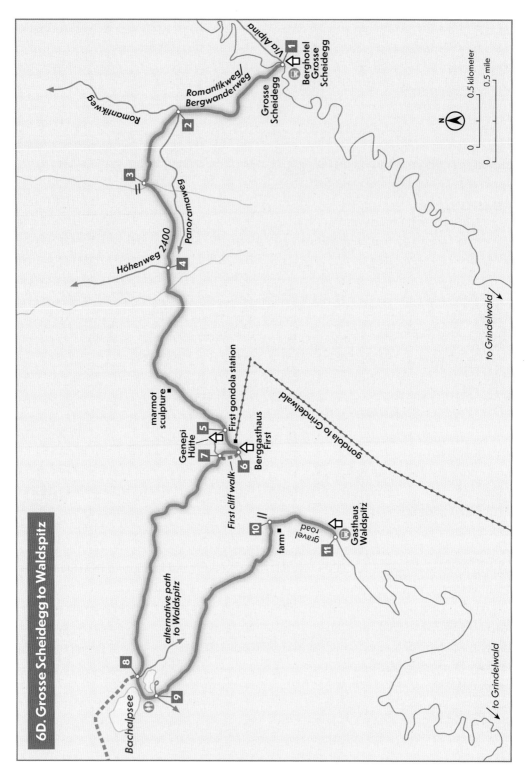

6D. Grosse Scheidegg to Waldspitz

Berghotel Grosse Scheidegg

Via Alpina

Grosse Scheidegg

1

Romantikweg/
Bergwanderweg

2

Romantikweg

Panoramaweg

3

Höhenweg 2400

4

marmot
sculpture

First gondola station

Genepi
Hütte

5

gondola to Grindelwald

7

Berggasthaus
First

6

First cliff walk

10

farm

gravel
road

Gasthaus
Waldspitz

11

alternative path
to Waldspitz

8

Bachalpsee

9

to Grindelwald

to Grindelwald

N

0   0.5 kilometer

0   0.5 mile

toward the Bachalpsee (and access the cliff walk), curve the rest of the way around Berggasthaus First, walking parallel to the cliff walk and going through an animal gate behind the resort.

7 The entrance for the First cliff walk is just past the animal gate, at 3.7 miles (6 km). It's a short, worthy detour with great views—if you don't mind heights. You'll end the cliff walk back on the terrace of the resort, so backtrack to this spot as needed. From here, the main trail to the Bachalpsee heads northwest along a relatively wide and well-signed gravel path and is signed for 50 minutes. The stretch from First to the Bachalpsee is a popular day hike, so you'll likely have company.

8 At 5.4 miles (8.7 km), go straight for Waldspitz and Bort at a signed junction just before the Bachalpsee. NOTE: Waldspitz appears twice on the signage because there are two different routes to the settlement, both of which take an hour, but the one you want is straight (not left).

From here, you start to get good views of the lake, which is split in half by a natural dam. The Bachalpsee is one of the prettiest lakes in the Alps; on a clear day, the upper lake is like an infinity pool. If you crouch down low at the back of the lake, you can get amazing views of the Alps seemingly rising out of the water. Swimming is allowed—if you want to brave the glacial water. Taking some time to wander around and enjoy both lakes (a path goes partway around the upper lake) is definitely encouraged.

When you're done exploring, continue to Waldspitz along the path between the two lakes, where there are toilets (free) and a trough to wash your hands (the water is non-potable) at 5.5 miles (8.9 km). From here, the rest of the walk is downhill.

9 Go straight at the three-way trail junction at 5.6 miles (9 km). This is where the crowds really fall away; you'll likely have plenty of solitude all the way to Waldspitz. The scenery changes as you enter a moor, and the landscape becomes more lush and flower covered. You'll see plenty of water: in the fields and cascading down cliffs across the moor. You'll also eventually get great views up to the ski resort and cliff walk at First.

10 At 7 miles (11.3 km), the trail approaches a working farm and then curves—at the last second—to the left, where you're greeted by a small, picturesque waterfall. From here, head south (to the right) on a gravel road that takes you the last 0.5 mile (0.8 km) to Waldspitz.

11 **Gasthaus Waldspitz** appears from behind a curve in the road at 7.5 miles (12.1 km), a welcome sight with its bright red-and-white umbrellas and Swiss flag. It's a great spot to enjoy homemade Swiss specialties while you wait for the return bus to Grindelwald. If it's a sunny day, a spot on the terrace can't be beat; from here, you have incredible views across the Lütschine Valley to the imposing mountains beyond. When you're ready to bus back to Grindelwald, the bus stop is located on the road just below the hut.

Some of the best views of La Morra are from Hike 7B, the La Morra Vineyard Loop.

7 THE PIEDMONT, ITALY

Into the hill towns and vineyards of one of Italy's most famous wine-producing regions

AT A GLANCE

GENERAL LOCATION: Northwestern Italy

HOME BASE: La Morra

LOCAL LANGUAGE: Italian

USE OF ENGLISH: Widely understood and used

FAMILY FRIENDLY: ★★☆☆

COST: $$$

WHEN TO GO: May to Jun; Sept to Oct

SCENERY: Vineyards, hazelnut orchards, hill towns

DON'T MISS: Local wine, community cantinas, Italian comfort food, *agriturismi*

Walking doesn't get more decadent than in the Piedmont region of Italy, where every hike is accompanied by filling Italian comfort food and some of the best wines in the world. This is the perfect spot to take it slow and have yourself an active vacation, with an emphasis on vacation. And it is an especially appealing fall destination, when the leaves of the vineyards turn bright colors as harvest approaches.

I first discovered the Piedmont region, known in Italy as the Piemonte, when I was looking for great vineyard walking with a good dose of Italian hill towns. As with all of my hikes, I wanted something relatively unknown—the experience of Tuscany, but without all of the people that now flock there.

I got exactly what I was hoping for with the Piedmont. Walking around La Morra, my favorite home base in the area, you don't see many other visitors. It's filled with locals, sometimes on their tractors, either heading back into the vineyards or taking an espresso break from work. You can tell this is a local hot spot, not an international one, by the trail signage as well—it's mostly in Italian.

The people of La Morra have it good—the quaint village is built on a hill that overlooks the local vineyards and surrounding hill towns, places you'll walk through with names you may recognize from your favorite wine bottles: Barolo, Barbaresco, Asti. But it's not just grapes that dominate the agriculture. You'll come across cherry trees and hazelnut groves, as well as small rural enclaves where you can stop for a drink or snack at an *agriturismo*—a working vineyard or farm that opens its doors to visitors and welcomes them with fragrant glasses of wine, pleasant outdoor seating areas and charcuterie platters, among other dishes. Agricola Brandini, my favorite *agriturismo* (see Hike 7A, Footpath of Sant'Anna), even has a pool. When you get to one of these spots, it's near impossible not to settle in—sometimes for an hour or two. They're that lovely and the perfect antidote to the busyness of normal life.

You can order wine by the glass (and the bottle) at most *agriturismi*, but one of the best things about the Piedmont is the prevalence of *cantine comunali*, or community cantinas, where you can taste nearly every different wine from the producers in the village where they are located, and at an affordable price. The *cantine* are great spots to not just discover new wine that you may want to ship home but also to further your understanding of how it's made. Once you see the constant buzz of activity in the vineyards, you'll understand just how time and labor intensive it is to care for the vines, and just how perfect the growing conditions need to be to create fine wine.

As you walk, eat, drink, sit in the sun and repeat, you'll understand something else—when it comes to relaxing walking vacations, no one does it quite like the Piemontese.

Getting There and Around

Most people traveling to La Morra fly into Turin, Italy, an hour's drive from La Morra.

One of the best things about hiking in Italy is the food. (Photo courtesy Turismo Torino e Provincia)

Other convenient airports are in Milan and Genoa, Italy; and Nice, France.

The best way to get around the Piedmont is by car. I always love to promote public transportation, and you can cobble together train and taxi rides to make the hikes work, but most of the hill towns don't have train stations (or frequent bus service), and taxis in the area are difficult to find unless you arrange them well in advance. Having a car will get you around quickly and easily. TIP: You need an International Driving Permit to drive in Italy.

Where to Stay

While my top choice for a home base in the Piedmont is the village of La Morra, nearby Barolo and Monforte d'Alba, both visited on the Barolo Loop (Hike 7C), are also great choices.

La Morra is built on a hill, so unless you want to climb up and down the hill each time you head to town, aim for accommodations near the center of the village.

Eat and Resupply

The town of La Morra has a small market. For more selection, you can drive 12 minutes to the large Mercatò on the way to Alba.

La Morra has quite a few restaurants and cafés, as do the surrounding hill towns, and the quality of the food is impressive. In Italy, they love big, long meals—most start with a few appetizers, followed by a pasta course and then an entrée course.

WINE AND LA MORRA

Nebbiolo is the grape of the Piedmont and the one you'll see planted all around La Morra. When it's made into wine in this region, it becomes a variety known as Barolo, named after one of the surrounding villages. Tasting rooms and wineries in the area are most often open on weekdays, though some of them are also open on weekends. When wine tasting, it's important to make a reservation and plan to be at the winery for a good amount of time—wine tastings are more formal and extensive in La Morra than they are elsewhere.

That's a lot of food! Don't feel pressured to keep up with the Italians. If all you want is one course, order it. Even better, share everything family style so you can try as many dishes as possible without ordering the menu. When you're out and about, be sure to track down the following local specialties:

- □ *Vitello tonnato*: chilled veal that's sliced and served in a creamy sauce made of tuna and capers
- □ *Bagna càuda*: a sauce made from garlic and anchovies, traditionally served hot and fondue-style with fresh raw vegetables
- □ *Tajarin*: a thin, tagliatelle-style noodle often used in pasta dishes
- □ Nutella: a spread made of ground hazelnuts and chocolate that is popular in Europe and is made from Piedmont hazelnuts

---

The white truffles from the Piedmont are some of the most prized in the world. Many locals consider *tajarin* (see Eat and Resupply) with a light dusting of grated white truffle to be the perfect dish.

The largest sporting-goods store near La Morra is the Decathlon in Santa Vittoria d'Alba. There's also an Intersport in Turin if you need to adjust or add to your hiking gear. Because you'll be in one of Italy's best wine-producing regions with so many good wines to try, bring a hydration bag to enjoy wine as you walk without the weight of the bottle (see the "Wine Bladder" sidebar in Chapter 5). And don't forget an opener!

What to See and Do
LA MORRA MARKET
Visit the small market on Monday mornings in Piazza Vittorio Emanuele II. There, you'll find everything from fish to fresh fruits and vegetables to farm tools. TIP: A bar in the piazza serves breakfast.

TRUFFLE HUNTING
In the Piedmont area, truffles are a big deal. Scientists and farmers haven't been able to crack the code on growing them, so they're harvested the old-fashioned way: by truffle hunters and their dogs taking to the local woods and searching them out. You can join a truffle hunt to see what it's all about. There are multiple entrepre-

neurs in the area offering this service. For more information, contact the tourist information office in La Morra (see Online Resources).

ALBA

The largest town near La Morra, and the capital of the Langhe (a smaller, hilly territory within the Piedmont), is Alba, a 15-minute drive from La Morra. Alba is a great spot to explore on a rest day. It has some Roman ruins, a lot of churches and a pedestrian area with the best shopping in the area. There's also a large Saturday market that's fun to walk around—bring cash. TIP: Ferrero, as in the company with the tasty toasted hazelnut chocolates and Nutella, is headquartered in Alba. While you can't tour the factory, be sure to give Alba a good sniff—at times, it smells like chocolate!

A few locals, including those at EASY-TORINO (see Online Resources) and Trekking in Langa (see Online Resources) occasionally offer free bike tours and hikes of the area. This is a great way to get to know outdoorsy locals and experience their favorite outdoor destinations!

THE CASTLE OF SERRALUNGA D'ALBA

The Castle of Serralunga d'Alba (see Online Resources), which towers dramatically over the town of the same name and is an excellent example of Gothic architecture, is widely considered the best castle in the area—and the best one to visit. You can tour the castle for up-close views of its

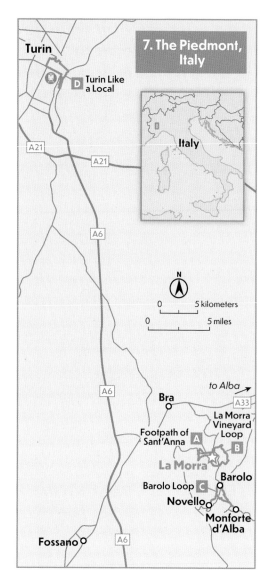

interior, including the drawbridge and a chapel with frescoes. Tours are 45 minutes long and reservations are recommended, especially on weekends and holidays.

★★ The Piedmont, specifically La Morra, gets two stars out of four for being family friendly. There's a playground in La Morra for littles to get their energy out, but most

THE ROUTES

HIKE	ROUTE NAME	DURATION	DIFFICULTY	DISTANCE	ELEV. GAIN	ELEV. LOSS
7A	Footpath of Sant'Anna	2.5 hours	Easy	4.8 mi (7.7 km)	756 ft (230 m)	756 ft (230 m)
7B	La Morra Vineyard Loop	3.5 hours	Moderate	5.1 mi (8.2 km)	1,060 ft (323 m)	1,060 ft (323 m)
7C	Barolo Loop	4.5 hours	Moderate	8 mi (12.9 km)	1,548 ft (472 m)	1,548 ft (472 m)
7D	Turin Like a Local	3.5 hours	Easy	6.6 mi (10.6 km)	645 ft (197 m)	717 ft (219 m)

kids just don't have the patience for long, drawn-out Italian meals and wine tasting. For this reason, the Piedmont works best as an adult destination.

7A FOOTPATH OF SANT'ANNA

Meander through hazelnut groves to a vineyard chapel and my favorite winery

This easy, beautiful walk through the hazelnut groves to the west of La Morra is as peaceful as they come. It's a perfect invitation to slow down and enjoy everything around you—the hazelnut trees, a seventeenth-century country chapel set in the vineyards, and nice views of the Tanaro Valley and Monviso, the highest mountain in the Cottian Alps. The real gem of the walk is a stop at Agricola Brandini, a wonderful winery where you can relax for an hour—or five.

ON THE TRAIL

DURATION: 2.5 hours

DIFFICULTY: Easy

DISTANCE: 4.8 miles (7.7 km)

ELEVATION GAIN: 756 feet (230 m)

ELEVATION LOSS: 756 feet (230 m)

START: Tourist information office in La Morra

END: Tourist information office in La Morra

EAT + DRINK: La Morra, Agricola Brandini, Azienda Agricola Voerzio Alberto (see Online Resources)

My favorite *agriturismo* in La Morra, Agricola Brandini, is set in a beautiful vineyard.

Know Before You Go

For being on the side of a giant hill, this route doesn't have a lot of elevation gain—most of what you experience is pretty gentle. Though the route is an established local walk (Sentiero di Sant'Anna, Trail 4), the trail isn't always well signed. I have modified the starting point of the walk from [2] to the tourist information office to make the route easier to navigate. Follow the walking directions outlined here, or use my GPX tracks to stay on track. Confidence markers are pink.

Alternative Routes and Activities

I recommend a good, long stay at Agricola Brandini that includes lunch and some pool time. You'll need to make a reserva-tion in advance if you want to swim. Typically, you'll also need to have lunch there.

If you're up for a short road trip (15 minutes) after your hike, check out Le Bancarelle di Elisa (see Online Resources) in Monforte d'Alba, which sells local hazelnut products; you can taste everything you've walked past. (Or save your visit for Hike 7C, when you'll already be in Monforte.)

Navigating

This hike starts in front of the tourist information office in La Morra, which is easily walkable from the rest of town and close to many cafés and restaurants.

STARTING POINT: **44.63887°, 7.93427°**
MAPS: **Available at the tourist information office in La Morra.**

[1] From the tourist information office, head toward the main road, **Via Roma**. Cross it and continue straight on Via Vittorio Emanuele II, which descends past homes and the occasional shop on its way out of town. Go straight through the roundabout at 0.4 mile (0.6 km).

[2] Take a left onto a gravel road, Strada Vecchia per Cherasco, at 0.6 mile (1 km), where a pink trail sign points the way. In short order, the view opens up and you can see the **Tanaro Valley** and the town of **Cherasco**. In the distance, you can see a chain of Alps, which are dominated by the pyramid-like peak of **Monviso**, the highest mountain in the Cottian Alps. The path continues between hazelnut groves and cultivated fields to the enclave of **Mascarelli**.

[3] At 1.2 miles (1.9 km), take a right on the SP58. You're only on this road for a few feet before you take a double track that branches off on your right and you're walking downhill through hazelnut groves once again. Take in the pretty view at 1.5 miles (2.4 km) of the area's extensive vineyards and small hamlets dotting the green hillsides. This is an active growing area, and you'll likely see people working in the fields, their bags and jackets hung on fence posts as they care for the vines and grapes.

[4] Just past that, come to the country **chapel of Sant'Anna** (Saint Anne), which is set in the vineyards. The chapel was built in 1625 and features an altar painting by local artist Pietro Paolo Operti of the Virgin Mary and her parents, Saints Anne and Joachim. Although the church doesn't have a chaplain, regular services are held here by parishioners, including on July 26, the Feast of Saint Anne. The church is typically unlocked, so you can pop in and look around.

[5] At 1.7 miles (2.7 km), take a left. At 1.9 miles (3.1 km), where you see a traditional farmhouse, the route begins to gently climb back toward La Morra. At 2.4 miles (3.9 km), take a right on the SP58 and then a left on a footpath through an extensive hazelnut grove set among vineyards and orchards. From this path in the fields, you have great views of the Tanaro Valley on your right. The footpath ends at a quiet paved road at 3.1 miles (5 km). Take a left.

[6] Come to **Agricola Brandini** at 3.4 miles (5.5 km). This winery is a little slice of heaven in the vineyards, with

LA MORRA HAZELNUTS

Hazelnuts are an important part of the economy in La Morra. The famous subspecies that is produced locally, the Tonda Gentile, is widely recognized as the best in the world, and the nuts are sold to the Ferrero company to make Nutella. As you walk, you'll notice that the hazelnut groves are very clean; there's no random brush or grass on the ground. That's because the farmers want to find every hazelnut possible when they shake the trees for harvest in September. Another interesting fact about hazelnuts: They contain oleic acid, which is also in olive oil and can help keep cholesterol in check and lower blood pressure.

There's nothing like stopping mid-hike for a long, lingering Italian lunch.

lawn chairs to soak up the sun, good food and refreshing wine (try the Alta Langa brut), a panoramic view of the vineyards and even a pool that you can pay to use if it's not booked up by people staying overnight. This is a spot you'll want to keep coming back to during your time in La Morra—I did. When you're ready to head back to La Morra, keep walking uphill on the paved road.

7 At 3.9 miles (6.3 km), when you come to the winery **Azienda Agricola Voerzio Alberto** (open by reservation only) and good views of La Morra, head right on a smaller path. NOTE: It can be easy to miss this junction because the sign for the walk is close to the ground and hard to see. Walk downhill on a grass track toward a small forest. You won't

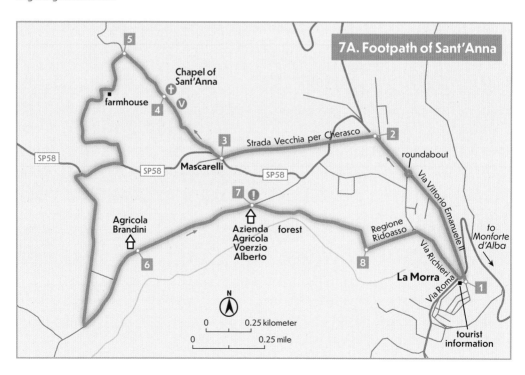

actually enter the forest, you'll just skirt it, but the beautiful trill of the many birds within is loud enough to reach your ears and makes a good soundtrack to this part of the walk. When you reach the base of the hill at 4 miles (6.4 km), near the forest and a small river, a trail sign directs you left on a small path that will skirt the fields and an industrial area on the outskirts of town.

8 At 4.3 miles (6.9 km), take a left on the paved **Regione Ridoasso** and then a right on **Via Richieri**, which curves up through a residential section of La Morra on its way into town. At 4.7 miles (7.6 km), take a left on Via Roma, followed by a quick right, which gets you back to the tourist information office where you started.

Bonus Hike: La Morra Self-Guided Walks
The tourism office in La Morra has cultivated seven different walks in the area, three of which you visit in whole or part with my recommended hikes (see Hike 7A, Footpath of Sant'Anna, which follows Trail 4 in the La Morra trail network; and Hike 7B, La Morra Vineyard Loop, which contains part of both Trail 6 and Trail 7 in the La Morra trail network). That means there are plenty more to explore. For more information on these walks, contact the local tourist information office.

7B LA MORRA VINEYARD LOOP

Hike the vineyards of La Morra and taste local wine at a traditional osteria

Whereas the Footpath of Sant'Anna (Hike 7A) showcases the western slopes of La Morra and local hazelnut production, the focus of this walk is on local wine. Walk through the vineyards on the eastern slope of La Morra and into small hamlets populated by local wineries where you can taste the very grapes you've walked amongst. The route also passes by a couple of traditional *osterias*, wine bars that serve local comfort food, where you can rest your legs and take in the scenery.

ON THE TRAIL

DURATION: 3.5 hours

DIFFICULTY: Moderate

DISTANCE: 5.1 miles (8.2 km)

ELEVATION GAIN: 1,060 feet (323 m)

ELEVATION LOSS: 1,060 feet (323 m)

START: Tourist information office in La Morra

END: Tourist information office in La Morra

EAT + DRINK: La Morra, Osteria Veglio, Cantina Fratelli Ferrero, L'Osteria del Vignaiolo (see Online Resources)

The La Morra Vineyard Loop makes use of two local trails; one of them is yellow-signed Trail 6.

Know Before You Go

Although the first half of the hike is pretty much all downhill, what goes down must come up, and the second half is a gradual climb back up to La Morra. Though the route is an established local walk on Trail 6 (Sentiero delle Grandi Vigne, or Footpath of the Grand Vineyards) and Trail 7 (Sentiero del Barolo, or Footpath of the Barolo), it is not always well signed. Follow the detailed walking directions here, or use my GPX tracks to stay on track. Confidence markers are yellow signs for Trail 6 and red signs for Trail 7.

You can get lunch at Osteria Veglio Tuesday–Saturday and at L'Osteria del Vignaiolo Friday–Tuesday. The two restaurants have limited lunch hours, so it's hard to hit both on the same hike. Note that tastings and tours of Cantina Fratelli Ferrero need to be booked in advance.

Alternative Routes and Activities

Check out the small farmers' market on Monday mornings in La Morra's Piazza Vittorio Emanuele II, which is a short detour from the start of this hike.

Visit the Cantina Comunale di La Morra (see Online Resources) after your walk, which showcases wine from La Morra.

Navigating

This hike starts in front of the tourist information office in La Morra, which is easily walkable from the rest of town and close to many cafés and restaurants.

STARTING POINT: **44.63887°, 7.93427°**

MAPS: **Available at the tourist information office in La Morra.**

1 From the tourist information office, head west on Via Venti Settembre and through the center of town to Via Giuseppe Garibaldi. Along the way, stop in for a morning coffee at one of the many cafés. When you get to Via Giuseppe Garibaldi, turn left. At 0.2 mile (0.3 km), arrive at an intersection of several roads near the ramparts of town, which date back to the 1300s. Take a hard right to head west, in the direction of the main road, Via Roma, where you'll take a left.

2 Take your next left onto the smaller Strada Fontanazza at 0.4 mile (0.6 km). At the intersection of these two paths, there's a terrific bakery where you can get pastries and breads to go—perfect for eating as you walk. A yellow trail sign here marks **Trail 6**, Sentiero delle Grandi Vigne, or Footpath of the Grand Vineyards. At 0.6 mile (1 km), take a left off the paved road onto a footpath that descends through the vineyards and past the enclave of **Boiolo** to a thicket. This section has great views of La Morra if you turn around, so don't forget to look back.

3 Once you enter the thicket, it's like being in another world. There aren't many forests to walk through around La Morra, so the trees and the birdsong are a treat—and the shade, on a hot day.

It only lasts 0.3 mile (0.5 km) before you come to a small paved road near the homes and agricultural buildings of **Torriglione**. Head left on the road, which in short order curves right. You'll likely see people working in the vineyards around you, trimming the vines and driving tractors.

4 At 1.5 miles (2.4 km), take a right onto a dirt/grass path that runs about as close to the vines as you can get. The views ahead of you are stunning—extensive vines, hill towns, a castle. At 1.7 miles (2.7 km), a table and bench underneath a tree offer a great spot to rest your legs. At 1.8 miles (2.9 km), near the village of Annunziata, spot a sign for **Trail 7**, Sentiero del Barolo, or Footpath of the Barolo, which you are also now on.

5 **Annunziata** is small, but it has several interesting sights on tap, including a Romanesque bell tower with eighteenth-century frescoes inside and an inscribed Roman headstone embedded in the

The extensive vineyards around La Morra make for an especially scenic walk.

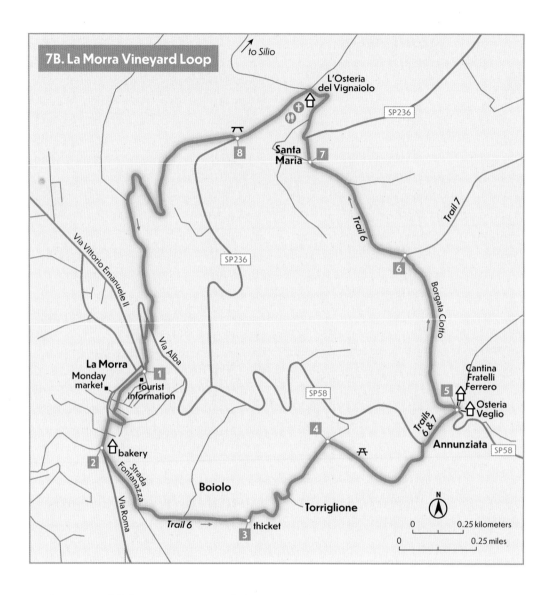

paving. In addition, **Museo Ratti** (see Online Resources) showcases the history of Alba wines and several wineries.

The best part of Annunziata is the restaurant **Osteria Veglio** at a curve in the SP58 at 2.1 miles (3.4 km). In summer, this traditional *osteria* serves up specialties from the Langhe region on a terrace overlooking the hills and surrounding vine-yards—it makes a great lunch stop. Once you're done, find the smaller road, Borgata Ciotto, that initially heads west from the curve in the SP58—this is your path. It's across from **Cantina Fratelli Ferrero**, where you can taste local wine and get a cellar tour. Borgata Ciotto takes you out of town and into rural land—fields, apple orchards and hazelnut groves.

6 At 2.7 miles (4.3 km), the route Ys and Trail 6 and Trail 7 deviate. Head left on Trail 6, which leads past an apple orchard toward Santa Maria, which has an impressive church of the same name perched on the highest point of the hill.

7 Arrive at the houses of **Santa Maria** at 3.1 miles (5 km). In addition to the church on the hill, **Chiesa di Santa Maria in Plaustra**, the town features several wineries and a popular restaurant, **L'Osteria del Vignaiolo**, which serves local dishes (and wine, of course) in a rustic setting. If you need a restroom, you can find one located along the northern side of Chiesa di Santa Maria in Plaustra. From the church, keep walking up the SP236.

8 Take a right at the gigantic red bench at 3.8 miles (6.1 km), which has views over the vineyards of nebbiolo. As you ascend through the vineyards, the views get better and better, which is great because it's a bit of a trek to the top—667 feet (203 m) and 1.3 miles (2.1 km). At 4.5 miles (7.2 km) from the start of the trail, come out onto a quiet road and go left. Take it to the larger Via Alba at 4.9 miles (7.9 km) and go right. After only a few feet, you'll see a footpath on your left that climbs the hill. Take it until you're on the serpentine Via Alba once more. Keep walking uphill until you're back at the tourist information office where you started.

THE BIG BENCH TREND

You'll see many giant benches scattered around the Langhe. The trend was started in 2010 by American designer Chris Bangle, who constructed the first one in Clavesana with the help of a few friends. The idea was to help people see the landscape through the wonder-struck eyes of a child, and it has become known as the Big Bench Community Project. You can get a passport and stamps to track your bench visits at the project's website (see Online Resources).

Bonus Hike: Bar to Bar

If you're interested in a village-to-village hike in the area, the Bar to Bar, a circular route from Barbaresco to Barolo and back, is a great option. Although the trail is typically biked, it can also be walked. For more information, check out the trail's official website (see below), which has a free large downloadable trail guide—in English! Trekking in Langa (see What to See and Do) can arrange luggage transfer and accommodations for the route.

DURATION: **Varies**

DIFFICULTY: **Moderate**

DISTANCE: **77.1 miles (124 km)**

ELEVATION GAIN: **11,109 feet (3,386 m)**

MORE INFO: **piemontescape.com/en/ hiking/btb-bar-to-bar/d400cffc6aa103c ba9c075f023910151/**

Monforte d'Alba is the second hill town you visit on the Barolo Loop.

7C BAROLO LOOP

Walk the rolling hills of Barolo wine country to three pretty hill towns

This countryside walk in Barolo wine country showcases some of the most beautiful natural features of the area, from a peaceful ridgetop forest to big views of the Alps to gently rolling hills that birth some of the most famous wines in the world. One of the best things about this walk is that it visits three different hill towns—Barolo, Monforte d'Alba (often referred to as Monforte) and Novello—all with charming shops and restaurants and opportunities to taste local wine. This is one hike that shouldn't be missed.

ON THE TRAIL

DURATION: 4.5 hours

DIFFICULTY: Moderate

DISTANCE: 8 miles (12.9 km)

ELEVATION GAIN: 1,548 feet (472 m)

ELEVATION LOSS: 1,548 feet (472 m)

START: Parcheggio Piazza Colbert parking lot in Barolo

END: Parcheggio Piazza Colbert parking lot in Barolo

EAT + DRINK: Barolo, Monforte d'Alba, Novello

Know Before You Go

This hike is relatively long and has a decent amount of elevation gain (especially up to the town of Novello), but there are plenty of places to rest and refuel along the way. The route is relatively well signed for the towns along the way.

If you want to taste local wine along the route, you can do so at *enotecas* (wine shops) and *cantine comunali* (community cantinas), which don't require reservations. If you want to do a tasting at a winery, you'll need to arrange it in advance.

Alternative Routes and Activities

You can easily spend all day on this hike if you stop to explore the three towns on the route.

On the way back to La Morra, consider stopping by the Cappella delle Brunate (see Online Resources), a boldly colored chapel/art installation that honors the Barolo wines and is one of the most modern symbols of the area. The road to the chapel is closed to cars on Sundays, but you can always walk the final stretch—it takes about 20 minutes.

Navigating

This hike starts at the Parcheggio Piazza Colbert parking lot in Barolo, which is a short walk from the cafés and restaurants of town.

STARTING POINT: **44.61098°, 7.94268°**

TRANSIT: **There's no easy public transportation between La Morra and Barolo, so if you don't have a car, call a taxi.**

DRIVING: **Barolo is a 10-minute drive from La Morra. Parking is free but fills up later in the morning, so arrive early to guarantee yourself a spot.**

MAPS: **Available at the tourist information offices in La Morra and Barolo.**

1 From the **Parcheggio Piazza Colbert parking lot**, head into town via a staircase on the south side of the parking lot. At the top of the staircase, take a right on Via Roma, which has several cafés and restaurants if you'd like to sit and enjoy a morning coffee before continuing. At 0.1 mile (0.2 km), where you see your first trail sign directing you to Monforte d'Alba, take a left on Vicolo del Pozzo. When the road Ts at the bottom of the street, take a left. TIP: There's not much going on in Barolo in the morning, so save your exploration of town until after your walk.

2 Wind your way to a campground and playground in a curve of the road at 0.3 mile (0.5 km). Your route, which changes from the road to a trail here, is signed for Monforte in 2.8 miles (4.5 km) or 1 hour and 5 minutes. Ascend through a wooded ravine and emerge into vineyards with beautiful views of La Morra on the hills behind you. At 0.8 mile (1.3 km), come to a confusing junction; stay straight on the main path (don't go left into the vineyards). At 1.2 miles (1.9 km), you start to get nice views of the **Alps**, **Monforte** and **Novello**.

3 Come to a rural farm complex at 1.3 miles (2.1 km). Just past that, at 1.4 miles (2.3 km), take a left on a footpath through a forest. The trail gently climbs along a ridge with great peek-a-boo views of the mountains and nearby hill towns. Sun filters through the leaves, creating a glow; this is a very peaceful section of trail, one of my favorites on the route. Keep an eye out for lizards.

4 At 2.2 miles (3.5 km), come to a junction that you'll return to after visiting Monforte. For now, continue straight to walk on the pavement toward town. It's a pretty walk in a quiet residential district on the outskirts of Monforte, and many of the houses have beautiful gardens to admire. At 2.7 miles (4.3 km), take a left on the busier main road, the SP57, for the final flourish to town.

5 **Monforte d'Alba**, at 3 miles (4.8 km), is a village of romantic, winding lanes built on a slope and the perfect spot to stop for a while and explore. At the base of the hill, the *piazza* has a couple of cafés with nice terraces. A tourist information office and a small market are nearby as well. Make the trek up the hill through old, narrow roads for a beautiful open-air auditorium,

The open-air auditorium in Monforte hosts many musical performances and is perfect for a night out.

charming little shops and lovely views of the surrounding countryside. TIP: The auditorium often hosts jazz and other musical performances; this is a terrific spot to return to for an evening out. If you want to taste the hazelnuts you walked past on the Footpath of Sant'Anna (Hike 7A), check out local Monforte shop Le Bancarelle di Elisa (see Online Resources).

When you're ready to keep walking, retrace your route to [4] at 3.8 miles (6.1 km), where Novello is signed for 55 minutes. Go left onto a dirt path that winds through vineyards with big vistas of the surrounding countryside. (And no, your camera just won't do the wide-open views justice!)

6 At 4.1 miles (6.6 km), the trail ends at the SP163. Go right. Across the street, there's a picnic table with signage for **Bar to Bar**, a circular bike route from Barbaresco to Barolo and back that's divided into seven stages (see Bonus Hike in Hike 7B). Just past the picnic table, take a left on a smaller road and then an immediate right, which takes you to a footpath that runs parallel to the SP163 until 4.5 miles (7.2 km), when the trail takes a sharp left and soon heads uphill for the climb to Novello. When the trail starts to climb at 4.6 miles (7.4 km), you'll know you're just 1.4 miles (2.3 km) and 417 feet (127 m) of elevation gain from the top. This part of the hike showcases the alluring rolling hills of the area. At 5 miles (8 km), go left on a paved road.

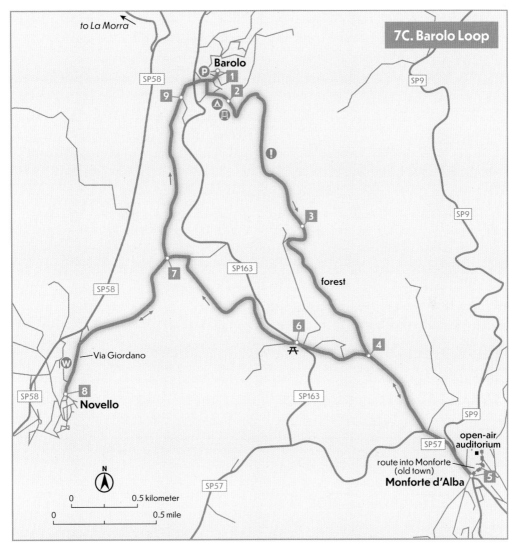

to La Morra

Barolo

SP58

SP9

SP9

SP163

forest

SP58

SP58

Via Giordano

Novello

SP163

SP9

open-air auditorium

SP57

route into Monforte (old town)

Monforte d'Alba

SP57

N

0   0.5 kilometer

0   0.5 mile

7 Just a few feet uphill, at 5.1 miles (8.2 km), is a junction with a path you'll return to after visiting Novello. For now, keep walking uphill on the road. Novello is signed for 25 minutes. At 5.8 miles (9.3 km), head left on Via Giordano, which takes you into town. You can refill your water bottle at the water fountain at 5.9 miles (9.5 km).

8 Get to the heart of hilltop **Novello** at 6 miles (9.7 km), where you can wander

quiet, narrow roads that are populated with small shops, wineries and quaint *piazzas* where you can get food. There is even a *cantina comunale* (see Online Resources) where you can taste wine from the picturesque rolling hills you just walked through. When you're done exploring Novello, head back to [7] and take a left on the small footpath that soon becomes a grass track through the vineyards. Walk along a ridge of sorts, above the SP163 and worlds away. At 7.3 miles (11.7 km), you start to get views of the village of Barolo ahead of you.

[9] Come out to a paved road, Via Vittorio Veneto, at 7.7 miles (12.4 km). Continue straight. Soon after, cross the SP163 and head into **Barolo**.

As you walk Via Roma back to your starting point, there are a lot of places to stop and explore, from *enotecas* (wine shops) that run events where you can meet local winemakers to bakeries perfuming the streets with the smell of fresh bread. The **Faletti Castle**, in the northeast corner of town, houses the **Wine Museum of Barolo** and the **Enoteca Regional del Barolo** (see Online Resources), where you can taste many of the local wines from automated tasting machines. When you are at the Faletti Castle, don't miss a visit to the small, sweet **Church of San Donato**, which is located in a *piazza* next to the castle that's a favorite of local musicians—a great place to people watch.

When you're done exploring, head back to the staircase on Via Roma that takes you down to the **Parcheggio Piazza Colbert parking lot**. TIP: If you have littles with you that need to burn some energy, there's a playground at the eastern end of the parking lot.

Bonus Hike: Monforte–Cissone

Leave the Barolo wine region behind for totally different scenery—hazelnut groves, wild forests and rich meadows—as well as the quiet towns of Roddino and Cissone.

DURATION: **4 hours**
DIFFICULTY: **Moderate**
DISTANCE: **7.2 miles (11.6 km)**
ELEVATION GAIN: **1,686 feet (514 m)**
MORE INFO: **outdooractive.com**

7D TURIN LIKE A LOCAL

Meander the historic city streets and extensive parks of Turin, the Paris of Italy

Turin (or Torino in Italian), the capital of the Piedmont and Italy's first capital, is well worth a day trip. The city is gorgeous, all wide boulevards, stately Baroque buildings and grand squares—you'll think you're in Paris. There's no better way to discover the town than to wander like a local, stopping at a large open-air market, drinking a *bicerin* (a magical mix of coffee, hot chocolate and cream), relaxing in beloved parks like the Giardini Reali and Parco del Valentino and walking alongside the Po River. This walk gets you those local favorites, as well as several historical points of interest along the way, including an original Roman gate and a replica of a medieval village from the fifteenth century.

ON THE TRAIL

DURATION: 3.5 hours

DIFFICULTY: Easy

DISTANCE: 6.6 miles (10.6 km)

ELEVATION GAIN: 645 feet (197 m)

ELEVATION LOSS: 717 feet (219 m)

START: Porta Susa train station in Turin

END: Porta Susa train station in Turin

EAT + DRINK: Caffè Al Bicerin, Imbarchino del Valentino (see Online Resources), various other cafés and restaurants in Turin

Know Before You Go

This route is on the city streets and park paths of Turin, without much elevation gain or loss. The route is not signed, so follow the detailed walking directions provided here, or use my GPX tracks, which cover the main part of the route, from the Porta Susa train station to the tram stop outside of Parco del Valentino.

Other notes about the route:

- This walk is best done Monday through Friday from 7 a.m. to 3 p.m. or on Sat-

urday from 7 a.m. to 7 p.m., when you can visit the open-air market on Corso Palestro.

- Guided tours of the Borgo Medievale, including the fortress and the garden, must be arranged in advance and are available by contacting the Società Cooperativa Theatrum Sabaudiae Torino (see Online Resources). However, you don't need a tour to wander the streets of the medieval village since it's considered an open-air museum.

Parco del Valentino is home to many historical buildings, including the Castello del Valentino. (Photo courtesy Città di Torino/Bruna Biamino)

- Bring cash to pay for the tram at the end; on most trams, you must buy a ticket before you board.

Alternative Routes and Activities

Pair this hike with a museum visit or two—or a historical walking tour of town—for a deeper overview of Turin.

Navigating

This walk starts at the Porta Susa train station in Turin. The station has a bar and a McDonald's and is located near many restaurants, cafés and shops.

STARTING POINT: **45.07133°, 7.66643°**

TRANSIT: **You can reach the Porta Susa train station by train from Alba, the largest town near La Morra. Several direct trains run throughout the day and take approximately 1 hour and 20 minutes.**

DRIVING: **Turin is a 1-hour drive from La Morra. The Porta Susa train station has a public parking garage (fee applies).**

MAPS: **Available at Turin's several tourist information offices, including the one in Piazza Castello (on the corner of Via Garibaldi), which is open every day. You can also use Google Maps for navigating around town.**

1 From the **Porta Susa train station**, head northeast under the porticos of Piazza XVIII Dicembre, which becomes Corso San Martino after the roundabout, to **Piazza Statuto** at 0.4 mile (0.6 km). TIP: Cross from the west side of the road to the east side of the road at 0.2 mile (0.3 km), at the intersection of Corso San Martino and Via Antonio Bertola—it's much easier than at the busy Piazza Statuto. This large square has a fountain dedicated to the workers who built the Fréjus rail tunnel through the Alps and is the meeting point for many Turin tours. In the past, it was a Roman necropolis, or ancient burial ground. Head southeast through Piazza Statuto and onto Via Garibaldi, one of the major pedestrian thoroughfares of town.

2 At 0.6 mile (1 km), come to a meeting point of two streets—Corso Valdocco on your left and Corso Palestro on your right. If you've timed your walk right, you'll see a large open-air market spread out before you in double rows on the street. This is one of the best markets in Turin and it specializes in clothing, accessories, perfumes and makeup. Once you're done exploring the market, head northeast on Corso Valdocco. Take your first right onto Via del Carmine. When you come to the obelisk marking **Piazza Savoia**, the joining point between the old city and the eighteenth-century western expansion, head left. At 1.3 miles (2.1 km), just before the large church of **Santuario della Consolata,** take a right into **Piazza della Consolata**.

3 The marquee café of the *piazza,* **Caffè Al Bicerin**, which dates back to the 1800s, is a great place to try *bicerin,* a famous local drink made by pouring a shot of espresso into a tall glass, then adding a layer of thick hot chocolate and a layer of cream. From the outside of the glass, you can see the different layers, and you're not supposed to stir them up. The drink gets stronger the more you drink and will give you a good coffee buzz for the rest of your walk.

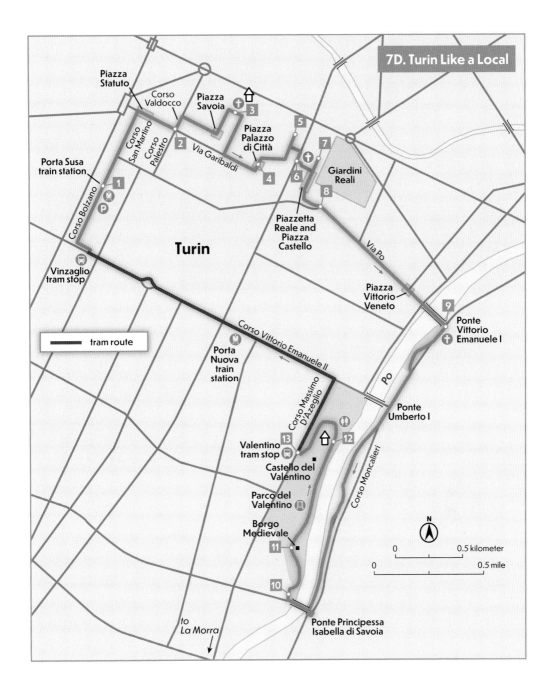

Piazza
Statuto

Corso
Valdocco

Piazza
Savoia

3

Corso San Martino

Corso Palestro

2

Via Garibaldi

Piazza
Palazzo
di Città

5

7

Porta Susa
train station

1

Corso Bolzano

4

6

Giardini
Reali

8

Turin

Piazzetta
Reale and
Piazza
Castello

Vinzaglio
tram stop

Via Po

Piazza
Vittorio
Veneto

9

Ponte
Vittorio
Emanuele I

━━━━ tram route

Corso Vittorio Emanuele II

Porta
Nuova
train
station

Po

Ponte
Umberto I

Corso Massimo
D'Azeglio

Valentino
tram stop

13

12

Castello del
Valentino

Parco del
Valentino

Corso Moncalieri

Borgo
Medievale

11

N

0   0.5 kilometer

0   0.5 mile

10

*to
La Morra*

Ponte Principessa
Isabella di Savoia

From Caffè Al Bicerin, continue heading southeast through the *piazza*. Take a right onto the larger Via delle Orfane, which you follow back to retail-heavy Via Garibaldi at 1.5 miles (2.4 km); take a left. At 1.7 miles (2.7 km), take a left on Via Milano.

4 In a few feet, pass the statue of the **Green Count** in the middle of **Piazza**

Via Po is one of the most significant thoroughfares in Turin and is home to many interesting shops and cafés. (Photo courtesy Turismo Torino e Provincia)

Palazzo di Città. The statue is dedicated to Amadeus VI, Count of Savoy, also known as the Green Count because of his predilection for wearing green, who during the fourteenth century fought against the Turks. Just beyond the square, take a right on Via IV Marzo. At 1.9 miles (3.1 km), just before Piazza San Giovanni, take a left on Via Porta Palatina, which runs alongside a green space to the Palatine Gate.

5 The **Palatine Gate**, at 2 miles (3.2 km), is a Roman-age city gate that provided access from the north to Julia Augusta Taurinorum, now known as Turin. It's one of the best-preserved Roman gateways in the world. Together with the remains of a nearby Roman theater, it's part of the city's open-air archaeological park.

6 When you're done exploring, head to Piazza San Giovanni for a look inside the fifteenth-century **Turin Cathedral**,

which was built on the site of three medieval churches dedicated to the Savior, Saint John the Baptist and Saint Mary. Afterward, walk along the south side of the cathedral to find the Palazzo Reale and the entrance to the Giardini Reali.

7 The **Giardini Reali**, at 2.3 miles (3.7 km), is a quiet park enclosed by the old city walls, where locals admire art installations, read books on benches in the sun and take a break from the hustle and bustle of the city, and it's the perfect place to feel like a local yourself. When you're done at the park, exit where you entered and continue walking straight through the Piazzetta Reale and Piazza Castello.

8 Curve around the south side of Palazzo Madama to find Via Po at 2.6 miles (4.2 km), which connects Piazza Castello with Piazza Vittorio Veneto and ends at the banks of the Po River. This is one of the most significant thoroughfares in the city. You'll walk the broad path in the cover of arched porticos from buildings that house all manner of interesting shops, cafés and restaurants—perfect for popping into. When you reach **Piazza Vittorio Veneto**, cross **Ponte Vittorio Emanuele I**, a bridge over the Po river, and head toward the imposing church of **Gran Madre di Dio**, which is rumored to be a secret repository for the Holy Grail.

9 Once you're across the bridge, head southwest along the Po. Although you can walk alongside Corso Moncalieri, the smaller paths get you closer to the river and wind through green spaces. Pass another bridge, Ponte Umberto I, as you walk. When you come to **Ponte Principessa Isabella di Savoia**, at 4.8 miles (7.7 km), head up to the bridge and cross it.

PARCO DEL VALENTINO

Turin's Parco del Valentino opened in 1856 and was Italy's first public garden. Although these days the park is a quiet, peaceful place, between 1935 and 1955 several major auto races were held on the paved streets of the park, reflecting the character of Turin—Italy's motor city. Among the park's many attractions is a bench dedicated to Enzo Ferrari, the country's best-known race-car driver.

10 At 5 miles (8 km), take a footpath on your right into **Parco del Valentino**, Turin's version of Central Park and the second-largest park in the city, one that's full of wandering paths, riverside cafés and fun things to explore, from a botanical garden to a Baroque castle that now serves as academic offices. The footpath takes you to a junction with a couple of paved roads. Continue straight on Viale Stefano Turr, one of the main routes through the park.

11 Come to the **Borgo Medievale** (see Online Resources), a life-size replica of a medieval village that was built for the 1884 World's Fair, at 5.3 miles (8.5 km). This open-air museum is free to explore and includes a drawbridge, several artisan workshops and a pilgrims' hotel (just for show). With a paid guided tour, you can also access the fortress and the garden. If you want to experience what life was like in medieval times in the Piedmont, this is a great stop.

12 At 5.7 miles (9.2 km), come to a couple of riverside cafés. I like **Imbarchino del Valentino**, the one at 5.8 miles (9.3 km), which has a nice deck overlooking the river. Just past Imbarchino is a stand where you can rent bikes to pedal around the park. After the bike stand, come to a roundabout and go left on Viale Mattioli, which curves around a green space before heading southwest.

13 Exit the park at 6.1 miles (9.8 km) by taking a right on a small entrance/exit road that leads to Corso Massimo d'Azeglio, which runs parallel to the length of the park. Take a right on this main road and in a few feet, come to the **Valentino tram stop** for Tram 9, which runs every 12 minutes and gets you most of the way back to the Porta Susa train station. (Verify current times with Google Maps.) Take the tram for eight stops, to **Vinzaglio**. When you disembark at the Vinzaglio tram stop, head northwest on Corso Vittorio Emanuele II for nearly 0.1 mile (0.2 km). Take a right on Corso Bolzano and stay on that until you're back at the **Porta Susa train station**, 6.6 walking miles (10.6 km) from the start of the route.

Split is my top pick for a home base in Dalmatia. (Photo courtesy the Tourist Board of Split)

8 DALMATIA, CROATIA

Exploring the Adriatic and the sunny coast of Dalmatia

AT A GLANCE

GENERAL LOCATION: **Southwestern Croatia**

HOME BASE: **Split**

LOCAL LANGUAGE: **Croatian**

USE OF ENGLISH: **Widely understood and used**

FAMILY FRIENDLY: **★★★☆**

COST: **$$**

WHEN TO GO: **Jun; Sept**

SCENERY: **Rocky Dalmatian coastline and mountains, Adriatic Sea and islands, incredible waterfalls**

DON'T MISS: **Secluded beaches, catamaran rides, coastal walking, warm climate**

When it comes to beautiful coastline that's also really affordable to vacation at, it's hard to beat Dalmatia, in southern Croatia. This is the land of beautiful beaches, picturesque towns and multitudes of small Adriatic islands that are perfect for exploring. What's more: Because of the chain of mountains just inland from the coast, you can also be in the mountains in less than half an hour. With an hour of driving, you can be at a stunning national park that features Europe's largest travertine waterfall. If you want a bit of everything for your home base hiking trip—and good weather to boot—this is the spot for you. June and September are great months to visit, when it's warm but not prohibitively so. In September, there are fewer crowds because the kids are back in school, and the sea is warmer and thus more swimmable than it is in June.

With so many different hiking experiences available in Dalmatia, no two days look exactly alike. But you can count on a chill Mediterranean vibe, a lot of opportunities for swimming and relaxing on the beach, and as much fresh seafood as you can eat: fish, mussels, shrimp, squid. You could try a different type of seafood at every meal and not run out of new dishes. My favorite spots to enjoy these meals aren't traditional restaurants, they're the little beach bars you can find as you hike, remote places on secluded pebble beaches where you can take your time and dip your feet into the water as you eat.

My top pick for a home base in Dalmatia is Split, a gorgeous city that's the largest in Dalmatia but manages to feel small and accessible. It's a port town, built on the water, with a sprawling old town filled with ancient history. It was originally founded as a colony by the Greeks in the third or second century BC.

The largest historical wonder that defines Split is actually from Roman times—Diocletian's Palace, which was built in AD 305. Inside its walls, you'll find little markets to browse for souvenirs—jewelry, hats, treasure boxes; in its squares you can often find local musicians serenading the crowds, especially around sunset. I love

listening to that music, ice cream in hand. As the sun goes down and the buildings take on an ethereal glow, the music helps transport you to another time.

Split is ideal because it has character and is well connected to many of the best hikes in the area. The port and the local bus station are very helpful for getting where you need to go, whether it's to the islands, the mountains or the incredible Krka National Park (see Hike 8D, Skradinski Buk) and beyond. There's even a great hike you can walk to—Split's version of Central Park, complete with viewpoints of the islands and sea, secluded beaches to swim at and tiny churches that are centuries old. From history to hikes, Dalmatia has it all.

Getting There and Around

Split is the second-largest travel hub in Croatia after Zagreb. The Split airport is located only 12 miles (20 km) from downtown, and it's easy to get to old town via rental car, shuttle, taxi or bus. If you're headed to Split from another European destination, it's worth checking out flights to the Zadar airport, which is serviced by budget airline Ryanair and is only 93 miles (150 km) away.

Split itself is a very walkable town, but if you're headed to a farther-out hike, the easiest way to get there is by bus or, in the case of the Hvar Island Coastal Walk (Hike 8B), by catamaran. The relatively large bus station in Split is a good place to go for information on bus timetables, which can sometimes be difficult to navigate online.

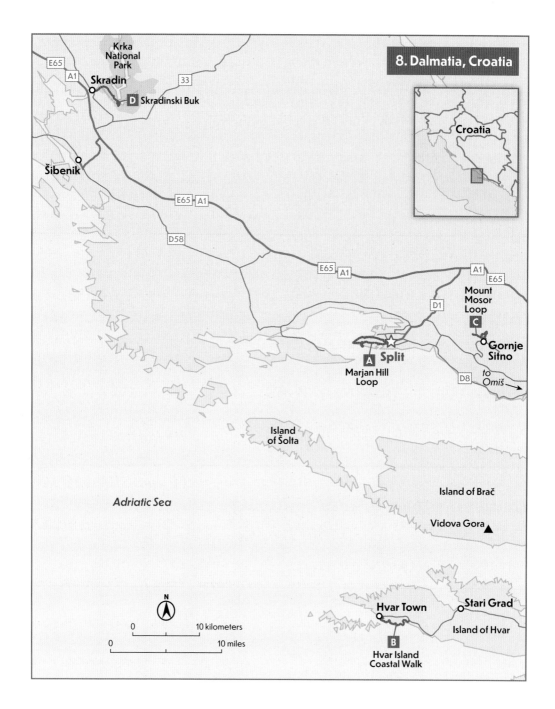

Krka National Park

E65
A1
Skradin

33

D Skradinski Buk

Croatia

Šibenik

E65 A1

D58

E65 A1

A1
E65

Mount Mosor Loop

D1

C

Gornje Sitno

A Split

Marjan Hill Loop

D8

to Omiš

Island of Šolta

Island of Brač

Adriatic Sea

Vidova Gora

N

0   10 kilometers
0   10 miles

Hvar Town

Stari Grad

Island of Hvar

B

Hvar Island Coastal Walk

Visit the station on the first day of your trip to get all of the information you need for the length of your stay.

Driving is also possible in and around Split, as long as your accommodations offer parking, which is difficult to come by

THE ROUTES

HIKE	ROUTE NAME	DURATION	DIFFICULTY	DISTANCE	ELEV. GAIN	ELEV. LOSS
8A	Marjan Hill Loop	4.5 hours	Moderate	7 mi (11.3 km)	1,023 ft (312 m)	1,023 ft (312 m)
8B	Hvar Island Coastal Walk	2 hours	Easy	4.3 mi (6.9 km)	389 ft (119 m)	519 ft (158 m)
8C	Mount Mosor Loop	2.5 hours	Moderate	2.6 mi (4.2 km)	820 ft (250 m)	820 ft (250 m)
8D	Skradinski Buk	2.5 hours	Easy	4.4 mi (7.1 km)	440 ft (134 m)	446 ft (136 m)

in town. Having a car can give you more flexibility with your trip plans.

Where to Stay

While my top choice for a home base in Dalmatia is Split, another great option in the area is Omiš, a smaller seaside town that's a popular adventure hub because of its proximity to the Cetina River and the mountains. Omiš is a 30-minute drive from Split.

Accommodations on the east side of Split are close to the city's main beaches, Bacvice and Firule, while accommodations on the west side of Split are close to Marjan Hill (see Hike 8A, Marjan Hill Loop). TIP: If you want to maximize your beach time in Split, aim for a spot close to Firule Beach, which is much more low-key (especially for families) and local than Bacvice.

Eat and Resupply

Split is a relatively large town with plenty of grocery stores and dining options. Dalmatian cooking involves a lot of seafood, which is served fresh from the Adriatic,

LOCAL GUIDE SPOTLIGHT

If you want a walking guide for Split or a hiking guide for Marjan Hill or the other hikes I suggest, I recommend Ivica Profaca, an expert on local history and an avid hiker (see Online Resources).

typically with a bit of an Italian influence. When you're out and about, be sure to track down the following local specialties:

- Paški sir and pršut: a starter of famous cheese from the island of Pag and thin-sliced smoked Dalmatian ham
- Pašticada: a traditional Dalmatian beef stew
- Brodet: a fish stew made from several different kinds of fish, including the scorpion fish, and typically served with risotto

Iglu Sport, one of the most well known of the Croatian outdoor retailers, has a location on the west side of Split in case you need to adjust or add to your gear. Be sure to pack plenty of sunscreen and water, especially if you're doing the hikes in warm weather. Most of the recommended hikes give you an opportunity to swim, so bring a swimsuit and towel as well.

What to See and Do

PICIGIN

If you're on the beach in Dalmatia, you'll likely see people playing this game, also called "water ball," that was invented in Split. It's played in shallow water and involves several players trying to keep a small ball from touching the water. Locals call it a sport of vanity, since more attention is paid to the fantastic leaps and dives the players make to save the ball than to anything else. It's very fun to watch, and if you're lucky, you can even join a pickup game to try it for yourself.

WALKING TOUR OF SPLIT'S OLD TOWN

Split has such a fascinating history, it would be a shame to miss out on learning more about it. A walking tour of old town will take you past Diocletian's Palace and other can't-miss spots while teaching you about life in Dalmatia during the reign of the Romans. For more information on tours, visit one of the city's tourist information offices. TIP: You'll visit a tourist information office at the start of Hike 8A, Marjan Hill Loop.

DUBROVNIK

The historic city of Dubrovnik, known as the "Pearl of the Adriatic," is located south of Split and is well worth a couple of days if you're in Dalmatia. The old town is a UNESCO World Heritage site and a pretty one at that—think red-tiled roofs, stone ramparts and an imposing fortress that looks toward Venice, the city's historic rival. A must-do: Walk on the ramparts at sunset, when the setting sun makes the buildings glow and the sea sparkle.

★★★ Dalmatia gets three stars out of four for being family friendly. It's rela-

The Riva in Split is a lively place to wander or grab a drink. (Photo courtesy the Tourist Board of Split)

tively inexpensive compared to many other places in Europe, especially when you get away from touristy spots and dine in more local restaurants. Kids will love the beaches and the boats, and the recommended national parks (Krka and Plitvice Lakes) feature short (but also stunning) hikes that are very accessible for littles.

8A MARJAN HILL LOOP

Walk the Central Park of Split to centuries-old churches, secluded beaches and incredible views

The one spot where locals love to hike and play more than any other is Marjan Forest Park, also called Marjan Hill or just Marjan, the heavily forested western tip of the peninsula that also houses Split. Although these days the park is best known for its trails and recreation opportunities, it has a fascinating—and long—history, dating back to at least the third century. At one point it was the home of a Roman temple to the goddess Diana. Later on, the temple was replaced with churches, many of which were protected by hermits; twelve of the churches still stand. A walk around the peninsula is the perfect way to experience this history—and the many features that make the park so beloved today.

This loop walk starts on the Riva promenade near Diocletian's Palace, which was at one point connected to Marjan Hill so its many residents could walk and picnic there. It winds along the sea to the Marjan Forest Park information center and up the Marjan stairs to a beautiful café with stunning views of the city and then makes its way through the gates of the park. There's plenty to discover as you continue your ascent to the top of the hill, from an ancient church to a zoo and several viewpoints of Split, the Adriatic and surrounding islands. Descend through pine forests and olive groves to more churches— one with fascinating cliff dwellings—and sunny Kašjuni Beach on the southern shore of the peninsula before walking to the western cape, curving northeast toward quiet and shaded Bene Beach and then walking the northern shore of the peninsula back to Split.

ON THE TRAIL

DURATION: 4.5 hours

DIFFICULTY: Moderate

DISTANCE: 7 miles (11.3 km)

ELEVATION GAIN: 1,023 feet (312 m)

ELEVATION LOSS: 1,023 feet (312 m)

START: The Riva tourist information office of the Tourist Board of Split

END: The Riva tourist information office of the Tourist Board of Split

EAT + DRINK: Riva, Teraca Vidilica, Kašjuni Beach, Bene Beach

Marjan Forest Park is easily walkable from old town Split and gives you some of the best views of the city.

Know Before You Go

Although the trail surface is great—paved paths and dirt footpaths—there's a decent amount of elevation gain in the first third of the hike (this is, after all, a hill hike) and a lot of stairs. The route is moderately well signed. The walk from the Riva to the entrance of the park, however, doesn't have signage. Once you're in the park, you'll see signs for different points of interest, but these are mainly directional and don't include time or distance.

Other notes about the route:

- This trail is mainly exposed; pack plenty of water and sunscreen.
- Marjan Forest Park is free and open 24/7.
- There are two main beaches and a couple of more isolated spots to swim on this route; pack a swimsuit and towel if you want to swim.

Alternative Routes and Activities

You could easily choose a shorter route from the many walking paths on Marjan Hill, perhaps one that doesn't take in so many sights. A "land train" and an electric bus also travel within the park; contact the Tourist Board of Split (see Online Resources) for more information, including current timetables.

Alternatively, you could extend your outing by stopping to swim, eat and drink, and easily spend a full day at Marjan Hill.

Navigating

This walk starts in front of the tourist information office of the Tourist Board of Split, located on the Riva, a seaside pedestrian path that has many restaurants and shops and is a short walk from the rest of old town Split. Though it is possible to get closer to Marjan Forest Park with a bus or by parking on the street near the entrance to the park (if you can find parking), walking from the Riva is a lot less stressful and takes about the same amount of time.

STARTING POINT: 43.50809°, 16.43787°

MAPS: Available at the tourist information office where the walk starts, as well as at the Info Center Park Šuma Marjan (Marjan Forest Park information center), which is on the route.

1 From the tourist information office, head northwest on the **Riva**. When you get to the end of the promenade and see a large fountain ahead of you, turn left and walk beside the main road, Trumbićeva Obala, past a fishermen's port with small boats. At 0.3 mile (0.5 km), come to the Info Center Park Šuma Marjan, where you can get maps and information for the park. Just behind the info center is a long set of stairs that will take you up to the park.

2 At 0.5 mile (0.8 km), a beautiful little café called **Teraca Vidilica** is situated at the informal entrance to Marjan Forest Park. This is a great spot to grab a morning coffee and then enjoy big views of the city below from the viewpoint next to the café—the best views of Split that you'll have all hike. The city looks magnificent with its burnt-orange rooftops in striking contrast to the turquoise of the bay—and the dry, rocky mountains beyond a perfect backdrop. An old Jewish cemetery lies to the right of the café. You're welcome to explore it if the gates are open; if they aren't, you can get the keys from the café.

Opposite the viewpoint, there's some signage about the park and a paved path with a pedestrian gate. Take this path, which is one of the main routes through the park. There are several benches to sit on and viewpoints to enjoy as you climb the hill. You'll likely see plenty of locals running, pushing baby strollers and walking with friends.

3 At 0.7 mile (1.1 km), come to the first of several tiny churches on your route and one of the most important for spiritual life in old Split, the stone **church of Saint Nicholas**, which dates back to the thirteenth century and was named for one of the most revered saints in the Mediterranean, the patron saint of sailors. The location of the church allowed those sailing by to see it and hear its bells. In the past, the church

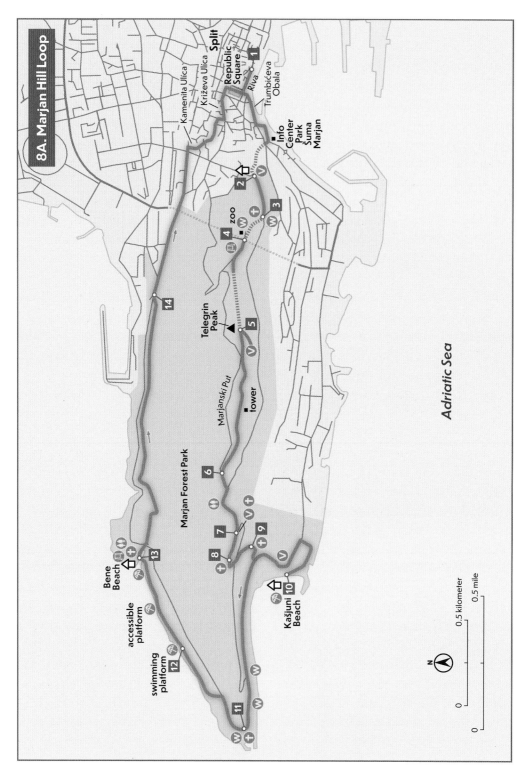

8A. Marjan Hill Loop

Split
Republic Square
Riva
Kamenita Ulica
Križeva Ulica
Trumbićeva Obala
Info
Center
Park
Šuma Marjan
zoo
Telegrin Peak
Marjanski Put
tower
Marjan Forest Park
Bene Beach
accessible platform
swimming platform
Kašjuni Beach
Adriatic Sea

N

0   0.5 kilometer
0   0.5 mile

was cared for by Benedictine monks and hermits—next to the church, you can see the remains of a house where the monks lived. Nowadays, it's looked after by the Marjan Society, which restored it in 1990. The church is open on select church holidays, like Saint Nicholas Day on December 6.

There's a spot to refill your water bottle and a long staircase that you'll take up to the zoo. At the top of the stairs, there's an additional faucet to refill your water bottle.

4 The **small zoo** (see Online Resources) at the top of the stairs features traditional Croatian animals like donkeys. This is a quirky spot that's worth a visit, especially if you have kids along. You can purchase a small bag of food to feed the animals, and the zookeepers will often let you into the enclosures to get even closer to some of the small creatures, like the tortoises and the rabbits.

From the zoo, continue northwest on the road until you see a smaller footpath on your left at 0.9 mile (1.4 km), just past the playground. Take this footpath, which soon turns into stairs—314 of them if you're counting—on its way to 584-foot (178 m) **Telegrin Peak**, the top of Marjan Hill. A Croatian flag marks the spot.

5 A large stone terrace acts as a viewing platform when you get to the top at 1.2 miles (1.9 km). From here, you can enjoy 360-degree views of Marjan Hill and views back to Split, as well as take a break at one of the many benches that line the terrace. When you're done enjoying the views, head west to another set of stairs that take you to a parking lot and two smaller lookouts in the southeast corner of the parking lot. The views here are all about the sea and islands.

To continue your walk, find a dirt footpath in the southwest corner of the parking lot, which will take you through olive groves and pine trees and past WWII bunkers from the Italian Fascists' occupation of 1941–1943. You'll also pass a **memorial to Umberto Girometta**, a Croatian naturalist and the father of local mountaineering, on your way to the saddle of Marjan Hill. NOTE: Several small footpaths run through the forest here. As long as you keep the paved road on your right and walk west, you'll end up in the right spot.

6 At 1.9 miles (3 km), the footpath heads down a few stone steps and ends at **Marjanski Put**, one of the main roads of the park. Head left on the road to a curve and the saddle, which has views to the north and south. After going around the curve, the road continues west, past a port-a-potty in a parking lot. The road splits at 2 miles (3.2 km); continue on the main road to the left.

7 Come to the small **Our Lady of Bethlehem church** at 2.1 miles (3.4 km). This simple single-nave building was built sometime in the 1400s and has a beautifully preserved stone altar that depicts Christ's birth, Christ's crucifixion, Saint Jerome and Saint Anthony the Hermit. Unfortunately, most travelers never see it, because the doors to the church are usually locked, except for on Christmas Eve, when it hosts a midnight mass that's popular with locals.

The church of Saint Jerome is well known for the nearby remnants of ancient cliff dwellings.

(It's popular, in large part, because this traditional "midnight mass" is held untraditionally at 4 p.m. so those who attend can make it home early enough to celebrate Christmas Eve.)

Just west of the church is a balcony viewpoint with good views of Kašjuni Beach below. At 2.2 miles (3.5 km), where the road curves, continue onto a footpath that heads west.

8 Come to the most well known of the small Marjan churches, **Saint Jerome**, at 2.3 miles (3.7 km). This small stone structure dates back to the end of the fourteenth century and was named for the patron saint of Dalmatia. What makes it so well known is the cliff dwellings you

can see in the vicinity, which were used by hermit monks who protected the church. TIP: The church is open September 30 for Saint Jerome Day. Descend the small set of stairs just to the west of the church to reach a paved road beneath it. Cross the road and continue on a dirt footpath that leads through the forest and down some stairs to the next church.

9 Reach **Our Lady of Seven Sorrows** at 2.4 miles (3.9 km). This little church is interesting because on its walls are prayers, mostly from people asking for health and peace. From the church, continue on the dirt path to a paved road, where you'll take a left. At 2.6 miles (4.2 km), there's a viewpoint for Kašjuni Beach. Take a right at 2.7 miles (4.3 km) on a road that leads to the low-key beach.

10 **Kašjuni Beach**, at 3 miles (4.8 km), is a great spot to swim, and there are a couple of beach bars with food and drinks. Renting beach chairs can be quite expensive, but you can pack a towel and sit on the pebble beach for free. The beach is a dead end, so when you're ready to keep walking, backtrack to the entrance, then walk the main paved road past the junction with the dirt path to Our Lady of Seven Sorrows. The road curves west, following the tip of the peninsula. Find faucets to refill your water bottle at 3.8 miles (6.1 km) and 4 miles (6.4 km).

11 Reach the westernmost point of the peninsula at 4.1 miles (6.6 km), where in Roman times there was a temple to the goddess Diana, patroness of hunting. The temple isn't here anymore but there is a pre-Romanesque church, the **church of Saint George**, which was built in the eighth or ninth century.

Continue on the road until 4.3 miles (6.9 km), where you see a footpath on your left that heads toward the water and skirts the road for the next 0.6 mile (1 km). Walk past several concrete and stone tables and benches as well as wild, stone-covered beaches where you can swim. The water here is clean and clear and there aren't many people.

12 At 4.6 miles (7.4 km), there's a small paved terrace for swimming, as well as a shower and changing rooms. Just 0.1 mile (0.2 km) past that is another paved platform, this one for people with disabilities.

13 At 4.9 miles (7.9 km), you'll reach secluded and rocky **Bene Beach**, which is far more well known to locals than travelers. It also features tennis courts (you can rent not only a court but also equipment), a playground, a bathroom and a café. Near the main road are the remains of the small **church of Saint Benedict**. At the roundabout in front of the church, head east (straight) on Šetalište Bene, which soon turns into a footpath that travels above the main road on the north side of the peninsula.

14 Leave the footpath and head east (right) on the main road at 6 miles (9.7 km), where you soon enter **Split** proper once more. At 6.6 miles (10.6 km), just past Prilaz Vladimira Nazora, take a right on smaller Kamenita Ulíca as it winds its way through the historic **Varoš** neighborhood of Split. This is Split's oldest neighborhood,

MARJAN BEACHES

There is a clear distinction between the beaches on the south side of Marjan Forest Park and those on the north side. The ones on the south side get more sun, are accessible by car and are relatively large, so they tend to attract more people. The beaches on the north side are heavily shaded, inaccessible by car and smaller—perfect for when you're seeking solitude.

founded by poor fishermen, farmers and peasants who built small stone houses for their families, and it's heavy on the charm.

When the road Ts at 6.7 miles (10.8 km), take a right on Bilanova and then an immediate left on Križeva Ulíca. The road eventually turns into a small alley that enters arched, pink **Republic Square**, which has several outdoor cafés and restaurants. Once you're in the square, head right, toward the bay and a large fountain. Once you reach the bay entrance of Republic Square, turn left and find yourself on the **Riva** once more.

Bonus Hike: Vidova Gora

Explore Brač, the largest island in Dalmatia and one that's only 7 nautical miles (13 km) from Split, while hiking to the summit of its tallest peak, Vidova Gora.

DURATION: **4 hours**

DIFFICULTY: **Moderate**

DISTANCE: **6.7 miles (10.8 km) roundtrip**

ELEVATION GAIN: **2,335 feet (712 m)**

MORE INFO: alltrails.com

8B HVAR ISLAND COASTAL WALK

Take a catamaran to an island with beautiful coastal walking, isolated beaches and chill beach bars

This hike is a terrific opportunity to get out on the water in a catamaran and explore one of the beautiful islands around Split. The path meanders along the rocky southern coast of Hvar Island, from the tiny seaside village of Milna, Hvar, to the bustling port of Hvar Town. Along the way, find several gorgeous remote beaches where you can swim, sunbathe and enjoy the turquoise Adriatic in solitude, and walk-in beach bars where you can relax with a drink in your hand. At the end, there's a great optional hike to the imposing fortress high above Hvar Town, where you can enjoy amazing views of the city.

ON THE TRAIL

DURATION: **2 hours**

DIFFICULTY: **Easy**

DISTANCE: **4.3 miles (6.9 km)**

ELEVATION GAIN: **389 feet (119 m)**

ELEVATION LOSS: **519 feet (158 m)**

START: **Milna, Hvar, bus stop**

END: **Port of Hvar**

EAT + DRINK: **Milna, Hvar; three beaches with beach bars; Hvar Town**

Know Before You Go

This is a mostly flat hike on hard-packed dirt. Occasionally the trail is rocky. It is relatively well signed; confidence markers are red and white circles, as well as red and white stripes. The route is mainly exposed.

Other details to know:

- The name of the island and the port town you boat to are both Hvar. I use Hvar Island and Hvar Town to make things clear.
- The beach town of Milna, where you start the walk, is referred to as Milna, Hvar, to avoid confusion with another Milna on the neighboring island of Brač.
- Bring cash; several places on this hike don't take cards.

Alternative Routes and Activities

For a shorter option, take the path from Milna, Hvar, to Hvar Town that's only an hour long (see [3] in the Navigating section for more details). That path stays high—no beaches or beach bars.

Or you can extend your outing in a couple of ways:

- The walk-in beach bars on this route make it perfect for a bar crawl of sorts. You could easily spend all day stopping at different ones, swimming at remote spots and taking full advantage of the least-crowded beaches you'll have all trip.
- Hvar Town is a great place to grab food and drinks by the water. You can also explore the shops and walk up to a for-

The first of the remote beach bars you come to on the Hvar Island Coastal Walk is my favorite.

tress (see the "Hike to the Hvar Fortress" sidebar) for the best views of the town. Hvar Town also makes a good overnight if you don't want to be hemmed in by the catamaran schedule.

Navigating

This hike begins from the Milna, Hvar, bus stop on the side of the main curvy road out of Hvar Town, the D116. When you get dropped off, you'll feel like you're in the middle of nowhere because you can't see the town, but Milna, Hvar—and its shops and restaurants—is only 0.3 mile (0.5 km) downhill.

STARTING POINT: 43.16595°, 16.48897°

TRANSIT: From Split, Hvar Town (on Hvar Island) is approximately an hour by catamaran. Several companies travel the Split–Hvar

Town route, including TP Line, Jadrolinija and Krilo; get an overview of all of the catamarans to Hvar Town on the Hvar Tourist Board's website (see Online Resources) and find current timetables and tickets on the individual company websites (see Online Resources). Tickets should be purchased at least a couple of days in advance. Try to get to the ferry area of the Split port at least 20 minutes before your catamaran ride. There are several docks, and it can be confusing to find the right one.

From your drop-off point on the Riva, it's a 5-minute walk to the Hvar Town bus station: walk north until you get to the main pedestrian street heading east, Trg Svetog Stjepana. You'll know you're in the right spot because the tourist information office will be on the corner. Walk down Trg Svetog

The Hvar Island Coastal Walk skirts the coastline and is mostly flat.

Stjepana past the cathedral and take a left on Dolac. There, on the corner, you'll see a taxi stand and the bus station. Several buses run to Stari Grad each day; get the current timetable at the Hvar Tourist Board's website or by emailing the bus company directly (see Online Resources). Ask the driver to let you out at Milna, approximately a 10-minute drive from Hvar Town.

MAPS: Available at the tourist information office in Hvar Town.

1 From the bus stop, head downhill and toward the water on the paved, olive-grove-lined road to Milna, Hvar. At 0.2 mile (0.3 km), stay straight (downhill) when a smaller road branches off to the right.

2 At 0.3 mile (0.5 km), the road Ts at a plaza in front of the main rocky beach of **Milna, Hvar**. This is a great little village to explore. Before heading right to continue the hike, go left to see more of the restaurants and shops of town. TIP: Don't miss the bakery, which has delicious pastries you can nosh on as you walk. When you're done looking around, continue west from the plaza toward the campground. Rather than walk through the private campground, follow the trail signs that direct you to descend toward the beach to skirt it; the trail rejoins the road on the other side of the private land, then quickly becomes a dirt footpath. This route gets rocky and gains elevation as you ascend above the beaches and past gnarled old olive trees, big cacti and fragrant pines.

3 Reach a junction at 0.8 mile (1.3 km) with an alternative route to your destination. The path straight ahead is signed for Hvar Town in 50 minutes; this trail stays high and doesn't skirt the water or beaches. You want the trail to the left, which is signed for Hvar Town in approximately 1 hour and 30 minutes. Initially, the trail descends past more fields, olive groves and even private gardens.

4 At 1 mile (1.6 km), come to another junction. The path on the left takes you to a small, secluded beach. The main path continues to the right to good views of the cove and Milna, Hvar, then gets close to the coast. It's beautiful here, and the colors are vivid: the bright blue of the sea, the bleached white of the rocks, the red clay of the path. Wild rosemary grows alongside the trail; its warm smell mixes with the tang of the salt water. The occasional boat

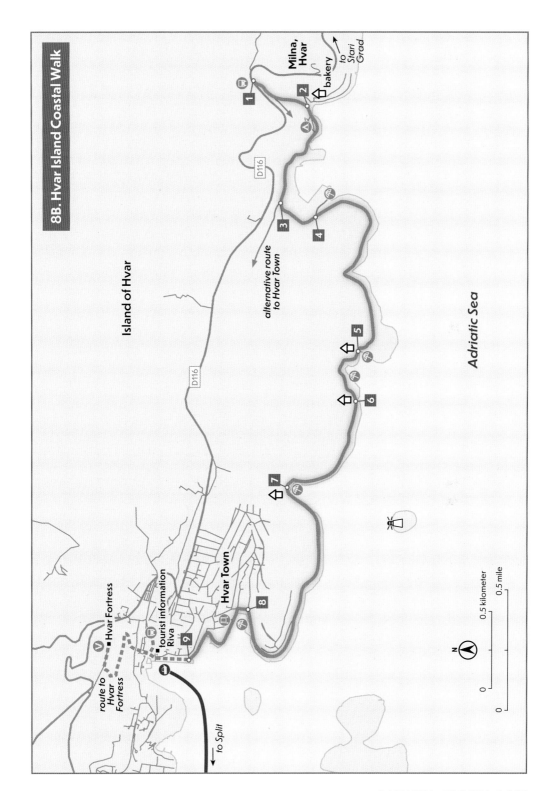

8B. Hvar Island Coastal Walk

Milna, Hvar

to Stari Grad

bakery

1

2

Island of Hvar

D116

3

4

alternative route
to Hvar Town

D116

5

6

Adriatic Sea

7

Hvar Town

8

Hvar Fortress

route to
Hvar
Fortress

tourist information

Riva

9

1

to Split

N

0   0.5 kilometer

0   0.5 mile

From the tourist information office on the corner of the Riva and Trg Svetog Stjepana, walk east (toward the bus station) and take your first left on Kroz Grodu, a small road that soon turns into a staircase. Ascend the stairs until you get to a road, then cross the road and continue walking up the footpath. A couple of paths branch off the main one; don't take them. Follow the main path as it continues past a water and ice cream stand, climbing the whole time. At 0.5 mile (0.8 km) and 264 feet (80 m) of elevation gain from the start of the trail, come to benches and the best free views down to Hvar Town. To enter the fortress, continue to the ticket booth at its rear. There's a small restaurant inside, a souvenir stand and ramparts from which you can enjoy more views of the city.

TIP: The fortress is expensive, especially by Croatian standards, so if all you want is a great photo of Hvar Town, skip the fortress itself and take your photo at the benches outside.

glides by, but beyond that, you have complete solitude.

5 My favorite beach bar is at 1.9 miles (3.1 km). It serves food and rents beach chairs in a relaxed environment that will have you itching to stay for a couple of hours. (You can sit on the private beach for free if you don't want to rent a chair.) From here, you have nice views of a tiny island with a lighthouse. TIP: Check out the tide pools for interesting fish and lobster-looking creatures. If you'd rather relax in solitude, head to the small beach at 2 miles (3.2 km).

6 At 2.2 miles (3.5 km), you'll reach a hip spot to rent cabanas that have been built on the boulders of the shoreline (there's no beach here). The associated

food stand sells salads, seafood and drinks, and you can even book a massage. As you leave the beach bar behind, you'll walk close to the shore with great views of the small island across the water and pass through a nice grove of trees that offers plenty of welcome shade.

7 The busiest beach on this trail is at 2.7 miles (4.3 km), on the outskirts of Hvar Town, where you'll find busy waterside bars plying beachgoers with pop music and umbrella drinks. There's an ice cream stand as well. Curve along the path in front of the bars and continue walking toward town by passing through the parking lot and following the paved road west. You'll find several benches alongside the road for enjoying the views of the water and, soon, Hvar Town and its imposing fortress. You'll also pass several spots to swim, from swim ladders to concrete docks to pocket beaches.

8 At 3.8 miles (6.1 km), just past the **INA gas station**, take a left on an unnamed road that skirts a small beach, and then take another left when the road splits on the other side of the beach. You'll pass a playground at 4 miles (6.4 km) and many restaurants, bars, snack shacks and stands selling towels and snorkels on your way back into the center of Hvar Town.

9 You're back on the **Riva** at 4.3 miles (6.9 km). This is where you can find your catamaran back to Split or launch out on a more extensive exploration of **Hvar Town**. I highly suggest walking up to the fortress (see the "Hike to the Hvar Fortress" sidebar) for great views of the city from above.

8C MOUNT MOSOR LOOP

Hike the locals' favorite mountain trail to a mountain hut and big views of Split and the Adriatic

If there's one hike that those from Split love more than any other, it's the hike up nearby Mount Mosor to the Umberto Girometta mountain hut. It's more than a local favorite— it's a tradition for groups of friends and coworkers to go there on the weekend. They go for the expansive views of their city and the Adriatic and for the chance to sit and visit at the hut's picnic tables while enjoying the caretaker's famous *pašta fažol*. The hike starts outside the town of Gornje Sitno, which is easily reachable from Split by bus or car. It winds up a rocky path through boulder fields, meadows and forests to the mountain hut before descending on a different path through similar scenery. The many viewpoints along the way offer outstanding views of Split, Omiš and the coastline between the two towns.

ON THE TRAIL

DURATION: 2.5 hours

DIFFICULTY: Moderate

DISTANCE: 2.6 miles (4.2 km)

ELEVATION GAIN: 820 feet (250 m)

ELEVATION LOSS: 820 feet (250 m)

START: Hikers Parking Vrk Mosor

END: Hikers Parking Vrk Mosor

EAT + DRINK: Gornje Sitno, Umberto Girometta mountain hut (see Online Resources)

Know Before You Go

Although the route isn't very long, it has nearly 1,000 feet of elevation gain—much of it earned while threading your way up a very rocky, boulder-strewn path. Be sure to wear good shoes. It's a moderately well-signed route, though it can be confusing to figure out which of the many paths to the top is the right one; my GPX tracks can help. Confidence markers are red circles filled with white, as well as red and white stripes. The name of the mountain hut that's your destination is often written on signs as "PL. Dom."

Other notes about the route:

- This hike is best done on a weekend, when the Umberto Girometta mountain hut is open. And the early bird gets the worm; the hut sometimes runs out of popular dishes on busy afternoons.
- Bring cash for the hut.
- The trail is mostly exposed, so sunscreen up and pack plenty of water.

Alternative Routes and Activities

There is a shorter, steeper trail to/from the Umberto Girometta mountain hut that can be found where the trail to the Gornje Sitno bus stop intersects with the main gravel path (see the hike map and [2] in the Navigating section).

Or extend your outing with one of these options:

- Several trails continue from the mountain hut to various peaks in the area, including 4,393-foot (1,339 m) Veliki Kabal, the highest peak of Mount Mosor.
- If you'd like the experience of staying in a mountain hut, you can hike to the Umberto Girometta mountain hut on a Saturday and stay the night (make a reservation in advance), then hike out on Sunday. Kids stay free.
- Explore a couple of small villages on the drive to Gornje Sitno (see Driving in the Navigating section).
- Drive back to Split via the cool coastal town of Omiš, a local adventure hub and

From the Mount Mosor Loop, you can admire Split, Omiš and the coastline between the two towns.

takeoff point for boat excursions up the Cetina River.

Navigating

This hike begins from Hikers Parking Vrk Mosor (searchable on Google Maps), just beyond the town of Gornje Sitno, which has a couple of small restaurants.

STARTING POINT: 43.52004°, 16.60314°

TRANSIT: Take Bus 28 from Split to Gornje Sitno, where the trail to Mount Mosor begins. The bus takes approximately 40 minutes and runs several times each day. Get tickets and more information at the Split Bus Terminal or from the Promet bus company (see Online Resources). Once you get off the bus, head uphill on Ulíca Svetog Kuzme. It's a 5-minute walk to Hikers Parking Vrk Mosor, where the trail starts; you can also take a shortcut at 0.1 mile (0.2 km) via a staircase and footpath that intersect with the main trail above.

DRIVING: Hikers Parking Vrk Mosor (free) is in Gornje Sitno, a 30-minute drive from Split,

The middle section of the path up to the Umberto Girometta mountain hut is very rocky.

on a route that passes by the town of Stobreč and through a few small enclaves, including Žminjača and Žrnovnica. For a scenic loop, drive another 30 minutes southeast after the hike to the adventure hub of Omiš, then return to Split via a pretty route that hugs the coast.

MAPS: Available at Iglu Sport in Split, as well as online (see Online Resources).

Don't be too surprised if you're asked to deliver something to the Umberto Girometta mountain hut. When I hiked Mount Mosor, a local woman appeared in the parking lot and handed my family a bottle of cooking oil, asking us to take it to the hut because they'd run out. There aren't any roads to the hut and most supplies are hiked in weekly by donkey, so last-minute deliveries often require helpful hikers. When we showed up at the hut and presented the bottle of oil to the proprietor, we were given a huge grin and a high-five.

---

1 From **Hikers Parking Vrk Mosor**, look for the sign for Mount Mosor; it'll direct you east on a wide gravel path that's above the road. You'll be on this path for 0.8 mile (1.3 km), walking uphill with expansive views of the Adriatic and the coastline from Split to Omiš, as well as a planetarium on a nearby hill. As you ascend the gravel road, the views just get better and better,

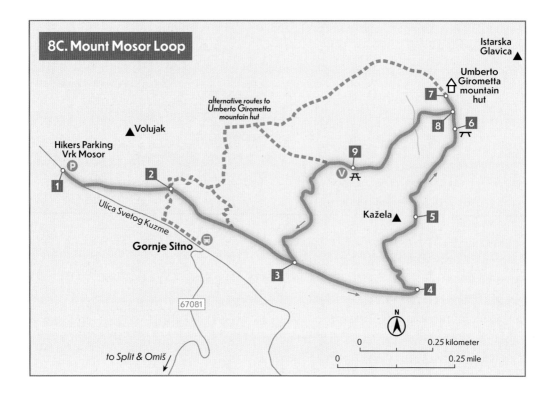

especially of the lush green valley to your right. TIP: Get your photos on the way back down, when you're walking toward, instead of away from, the coast.

2 At 0.2 mile (0.3 km) from the start of the route, to your right, the shortcut trail from the bus stop meets up with the main trail. To your left is the shorter trail to/from the mountain hut (see Alternative Routes and Activities).

3 At 0.6 mile (1 km), you'll see another trail on your left; this is the one you'll descend to create a loop. For now, go straight.

4 The wide gravel trail ends at 0.8 mile (1.3 km); look for the rocky trail to your left marked with red circles filled with white. The path is narrow and climbs up, over

and around boulders. The painted circles are your best chance of staying on the right path. When you reach one, look for the next set, walk to it, and repeat. TIP: Keep an eye out for snakes sunning themselves on the rocks. It's rare to see one, but venomous snakes do live in this area.

5 At 1.1 miles (1.8 km), you're through the boulder field and the path flattens out some. The trail becomes more lush than it has been thus far, with grass and occasional trees that soon come together in a peaceful forest. Butterflies flit and lizards scamper across the path. You may even run into grazing goats or wandering donkeys.

6 Arrive at a stone building and a bench at 1.3 miles (2.1 km), but it isn't the mountain hut, so continue on. In just a few

UMBERTO GIROMETTA

The Umberto Girometta mountain hut is named for Umberto Girometta (1883–1939), a high school science teacher and one of the most influential naturalists in Dalmatia. He founded two branches of the Croatian Mountaineering Association and co-founded the Split Museum of Natural History. He even discovered a new species of sightless cave spider in the Vranjača Cave near Split, and it was named after him. Girometta published travelogues in several magazines to extol the natural beauty of Dalmatia and educate people on the flora and fauna of the local mountains. Thanks to his efforts, mountain lodges and shelters were built on Kamešnica, Vaganj, Cincar, Vošac and Vidova Gora.

feet, you'll pass a trail on your left [8]. This is the one you'll descend on after you visit the hut; for now, stay straight.

7 The **Umberto Girometta mountain hut** is in a clearing at 1.4 miles (2.3 km). Picnic tables are available for sitting outside and enjoying the fresh mountain air, along with tables inside. Simple menus are posted inside on the wall near the kitchen. Everything is good (think sauerkraut, cured meats and bread), but the hut is best known for its traditional *pašta fažol*, a kind of soup made with pasta and beans, usually served with a sausage. (You can also order drinks, including beer.) The man who takes your order and

prepares it is likely Špiro Gruica, a local legend and mountain rescue volunteer who has been opening the hut for hikers every weekend since 1975. He inherited the job from his parents; his daughter and grandson plan on taking over some day. Špiro is proud of the hut and will let you tour it if you'd like, even if you're not staying the night.

8 Once you're done at the hut, head back the way you came and take a right at the first junction you come to. You'll descend through trees until the path opens up in a pretty meadow and crosses a small stream.

9 There's a table and viewpoint of Split and the Adriatic at 1.7 miles (2.7 km), and just beyond that a junction where you head left toward a steep and boulder-strewn section of trail that's very similar to what you hiked earlier. It doesn't last long, though. In 0.3 mile (0.5 km), you're back on the wide gravel path you started on. Head downhill to return to the parking lot, which is in 0.6 mile (1 km).

Bonus Hike: Omiš to the Starigrad Fortress

Get great views of Omiš, the coast and the Cetina River canyon by hiking up to this fifteenth-century fortress that was built to defend against Ottoman invaders.

DURATION: **2 hours**

DIFFICULTY: **Moderate**

DISTANCE: **2.6 miles (4.2 km) roundtrip**

ELEVATION GAIN: **1,017 feet (310 m)**

MORE INFO: **alltrails.com**

The main viewing area at Skradinski Buk takes in one level of this half-mile-long waterfall; there are sixteen more levels to discover on your walk.

8D SKRADINSKI BUK

Explore Europe's largest travertine waterfall

When it comes to impressive sights in Dalmatia that just can't be missed, Krka National Park tops the list. The Skradin entrance to the park is only an hour's drive from Split and well worth a day trip—or a couple of days. Krka is smaller than its more famous counterpart, Plitvice Lakes National Park, but no less impressive. Visitors go for views of the park's seven majestic waterfalls, especially the crown jewel of Skradinski Buk (*buk* means "cascade"), Europe's largest travertine cascade. The best way to discover the waterfall is on foot, on the national park's loop trail that shows off the seventeen levels of the 0.5-mile-long (0.8 km) waterfall and its lush surroundings from countless viewpoints. Start your adventure with a peaceful boat ride up the Krka River (included in the cost of park admission) and hike the loop trail, then return to your starting point in Skradin by foot, which gives you a chance to enjoy the park in solitude along its quiet riverside access trail (most people enter and exit the park by boat).

ON THE TRAIL

DURATION: 2.5 hours

DIFFICULTY: Easy

DISTANCE: 4.4 miles (7.1 km)

ELEVATION GAIN: 440 feet (134 m)

ELEVATION LOSS: 446 feet (136 m)

START: Parking Skradin

END: Parking Skradin

EAT + DRINK: Skradin, Skradinski Buk main service hub, beach bar on the way back to Skradin

Know Before You Go

This mostly flat hike is on hard-packed dirt, boardwalks and one stretch of paved road. Several paths wind around Skradinski Buk, including a wheelchair- and stroller-friendly one that makes a wider circle. It's not always necessary to be on exactly the path I describe, as long as you're moving in the same direction. The trails through the park aren't always signed, but it's relatively difficult to get lost.

The boat ride to/from the park is included in your admission. It's best to buy your tickets well in advance, especially if you want a seat on the first boat of the day (between 8:00 a.m. and 9:30 a.m. depending on the month). Tickets can be purchased on the national park's website (see Online Resources). Swimming is prohibited in the waterfalls of the national park, but you can swim in the river on the walk back to Skradin, so pack a swimsuit and towel.

Alternative Routes and Activities

For a shorter route, you could boat to and from the national park, then just walk the trails around the waterfalls.

You could also do the hike in the opposite direction, by walking from Skradin to Skradinski Buk and taking the boat back, but the line for the boat back to Skradin can be very long and is shadeless—tough on a hot day. It's not uncommon to wait 45 minutes or more for a seat. TIP: Although you can buy a timed boat ticket online for the ride from Skradinski Buk to Skradin, there's no separate queue and no priority given to those tickets—you'll be competing for a boat seat with everyone else who's waiting—so don't bother.

Extend your outing with any of the following activities:

- The waterfalls and boardwalks of Krka National Park are so beautiful, you could easily spend multiple hours in the park taking them in, snapping pictures and getting something to eat.
- There are several other hikes, boat excursions and even an old monastery in the national park—multiple days' worth of things to do. If you have more time to explore, check out the attractions around the other main park entrance at Lozovac.
- Skradin is often overlooked as a place travelers pass through to get somewhere else (Krka National Park), but the small riverside port town with its own fortress is worthy of a real visit. In fact, it's Bill

Gates's favorite place in the world, as reported by *Forbes* magazine. The town is surrounded by vineyards and wineries. Bibich Winery (see Online Resources) is a popular spot for people who want to taste the local wine and food that pairs well with it.

- Only about 15 minutes away from Skradin is Šibenik, a medieval coastal town with a lot of history that's located where the Krka River flows into the Adriatic.

If you want to see more enchanting waterfall chains like the ones at Krka, check out Plitvice Lakes National Park, a 1-hour-and-45-minute drive north.

Navigating

The hike begins at the Skradinski Buk main dock, which you'll reach via the Skradin–Krka National Park boat. The ride to Skradinski Buk takes approximately 25 minutes. Pay toilets and restaurants are available within 0.2 mile (0.3 km) of the dock.

STARTING POINT: 43.80759°, 15.96167°

TRANSIT: Several buses run each day from Split to Skradin. The bus takes around 1 hour and 15 minutes and drops off near Parking Skradin. Get tickets and more information at the Split Bus Terminal.

To reach the national park boat dock from the bus stop, walk south (toward the water) on a small street with market stands along it. A pay toilet and the national park office will be on your right. Just around the bend in the road, you'll see signs for the boat.

DRIVING: From Split, the drive to Skradin takes approximately an hour, mainly along the E65. As you approach Skradin, you'll see many parking lots and people trying to wave you into their lot, as if there's not enough parking to go around. Don't panic and choose one of these faraway lots. Continue into town to Parking Skradin, the lot closest to the national park office and boat dock. This is a large parking lot with plenty of room, and you shouldn't have any problem finding a space as long as you arrive in the morning, before the park gets busy. (You can always backtrack to one of those other lots if needed.) Parking Skradin is a pay lot; you pay on your way out.

To reach the national park boat dock, walk through the playground to the west of the parking lot, then take a left on the small market street beyond. Just around the bend in the road, you'll see signs for the boat.

MAPS: Available online at the Krka National Park website (see Online Resources) or at the national park office in Skradin. There's also a trail map near the base of the waterfall that you can take a picture of before you embark on the loop portion of the hike.

1 From the Skradinski Buk main dock, head toward the main path and take a right. At 0.1 mile (0.2 km), there is a pay toilet. At 0.2 mile (0.3 km), come to the main service hub of Skradinski Buk, where you'll find a series of small food stands and sit-down restaurants.

2 It doesn't take long to get to Krka's main attraction—**Skradinski Buk**, the base of which is on full display at 0.3 mile

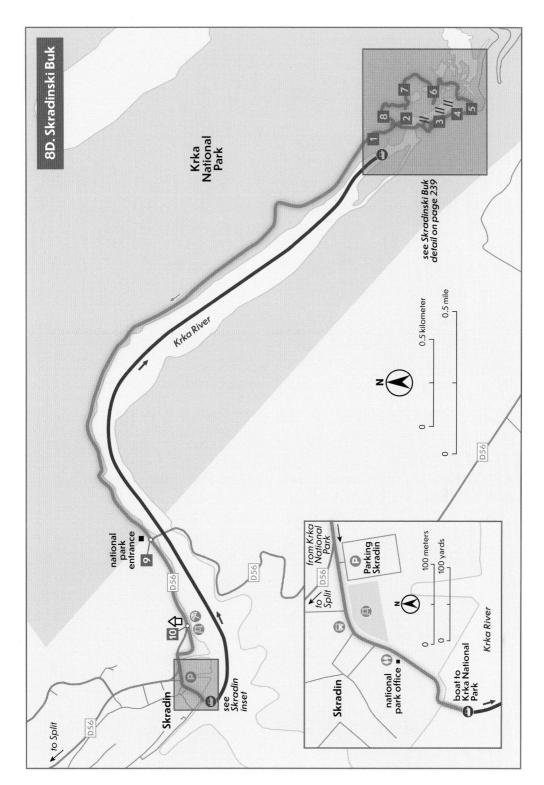

8D. Skradinski Buk

Krka National Park

Krka River

see Skradinski Buk detail on page 239

N

0.5 kilometer
0.5 mile

0

0

D56

national park entrance

9

D56

10

D56

D56

Skradin

P

see Skradin inset

to Split

D56

from Krka National Park

to Split

D56

Parking Skradin
P

N

100 meters
100 yards

0

0

Skradin

national park office

boat to Krka National Park

Krka River

The water in Krka National Park is an enchanting green.

(0.5 km). There are several viewing spots along the shore, each with a slightly different view. The full waterfall is much bigger than what you can see here—it's actually seventeen steps over 0.5 mile (0.8 km), making it the longest waterfall on the Krka River. (The vertical drop is 164 feet or 50 m.) Beautiful terraces, ponds and islands chain the steps together.

The counterclockwise loop path to admire the upper part of the waterfall is to the right of the base and starts with a wooden bridge with some of the best views of the cascade. After the bridge, the trail starts to climb and offers many viewpoints to admire the water. As you walk, you'll see remnants of and signage about hydro-electric dams, which are an important part of the history of the river. The Krka Dam produced Croatia's first hydroelectric alternating current and was the work of famous Croatian Nikola Tesla.

3 There are free public toilets, followed by a water fountain, at 0.5 mile (0.8 km). Along this stretch of trail, you will also see several stands with vendors selling dried fruit, nuts and olive oil. There's also the occasional restaurant and ice cream stand.

4 At the top of the falls, you'll find an **old village with water mills**, where you can see a mill and blacksmith still in action. The water mill complex is at the base of a wide spot in the river that's

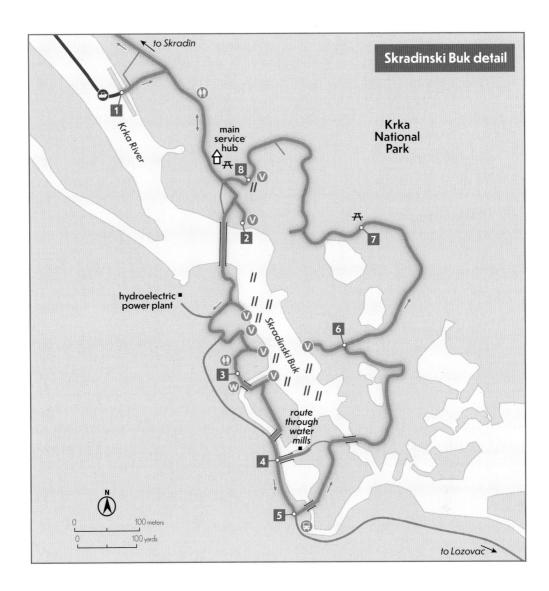

filled with fish. After walking through the mill, backtrack to the original path.

5 At 0.7 mile (1.1 km), come to a shuttle bus drop-off point for people who have entered the national park via the Lozovac entrance. A left takes you on a beautiful boardwalk path at the head of the wide section of the river. This starts my favorite part of the hike, which is all about the little details. Small streams run under the boardwalk; there's water trickling everywhere. The streams and ponds you walk past are filled with fish; the plants are an iridescent green. It's the definition of lush. Keep your eye out for frogs; you'll spot them everywhere once you start looking for them. This section of trail is shaded, which is especially welcome on a hot day.

6 Come to a turnoff for one of the only waterfall viewpoints on the east side of the loop at 1.1 miles (1.8 km). Just be prepared to wait—people tend to queue here for photos.

7 If you brought food, you can enjoy it at a small, shaded picnic area at 1.3 miles (2.1 km). This is also a good spot to learn about the flora and fauna of the park from the surrounding signage.

8 At 1.6 miles (2.6 km), close the national park loop by entering a clearing that has several picnic tables and is close to the food options. Don't miss the smaller waterfall by the entrance to the clearing; it's one of the best picture spots of the whole hike (we took our family Christmas card photo there, in fact). When you're done enjoying this part of the park, head down the main path back toward the restaurants and in the direction of the boat dock; this turns into the path back to Skradin.

As you pass the boat dock, you leave the crowds behind. This is an experience that most people don't get because they take the boat in both directions. The wide path follows the river, sometimes next to it and sometimes above it. The path is fragrant with pines. Watch for butterflies and listen for birdsong; the birds love the marshland alongside the river.

9 Exit Krka National Park via the pedestrian entrance at 3.8 miles (6.1 km). Stay straight on what is now a paved road, the D56. There is a pedestrian path on the river side of the road for most of the walk back to Parking Skradin.

10 At 4.2 miles (6.8 km) there's a playground and a public beach that's perfect for swimming in the Krka River, or at least soaking your feet. In the summer, you can also grab a drink from the little beach bar—the perfect end to your Skradinski Buk hike. Make your way back to **Parking Skradin** when you're ready.

The Bavarian village of Berchtesgaden makes an excellent home base for exploring Berchtesgaden National Park. (Photo courtesy Berchtesgadener Land Tourismus)

9 BERCHTESGADEN NATIONAL PARK, GERMANY

Hiking one of Bavaria's best national parks

AT A GLANCE

GENERAL LOCATION: Southeastern Germany

HOME BASE: Berchtesgaden

LOCAL LANGUAGE: German

USE OF ENGLISH: Widely understood and used

FAMILY FRIENDLY: ★ ★ ★ ★

COST: $$$

WHEN TO GO: Mid-Jun to Sept

SCENERY: Berchtesgaden Alps, alpine meadows and wildflowers, Bavaria's deepest lake

DON'T MISS: Mountain huts, swimming in an alpine lake, taking a gondola up and hiking down, visiting a salt mine

Hitler's Eagle's Nest is a short drive from Berchtesgaden—perfect for a rest day adventure. (Photo courtesy Berchtesgadener Land Tourismus)

When I travel, I like to visit spots that locals recommend. So when I was looking for great hiking in the Alps, I made sure to ask my Bavarian hiking friends, and their recommendation was quick and enthusiastic: the area in and around Berchtesgaden National Park.

It didn't take long for me to discover the things they loved about it, and to love those things myself. Berchtesgaden National Park is the complete package for those looking for a home base hiking destination. The national park is just south of the town of Berchtesgaden, a Bavarian village near the border with Austria that's popular with outdoors lovers. You can tell at a glance: Most people—the majority of whom are German and Austrian—amble around town, before or after their adventures, with their hiking clothes and hiking boots still on. One of the most-visited spots in town is the Haus der Berge, or Mountain House, where national park staff distribute free maps, brochures and guidance for the extensive array of hikes in the area. There are so many hikes—some of which are guided adventures the national park staff put on—that you could spend weeks trying to do them all. The variety is incredible—alpine hikes that take in the peaks of the Berchtesgaden Alps, lake hikes that loop and provide excellent opportunities to swim, flat ridge hikes that put the surrounding valleys on full display. Even better: Almost every hike passes by at least one mountain hut, if not several, where you can get cold German beer and warm specialties like *schweinshaxn* and *kaiserschmarrn* (see Eat and Resupply)—perfect for refueling. And with the high-elevation hikes, there's usually the opportunity to take a gondola or lift up and hike down. The mountains are snow-free, and all of the hiking in the area is open and accessible, mid-June through September. In spring and late fall, many routes are still open, but they're lower-elevation ones.

I love hiking in Bavaria. While the hikes are world-class, it's the locals and the culture that keep me coming back for more. People are happy to chat on trail and share a table at a mountain hut. Walking is a big part of local culture, and it's common to see whole families or friend groups making the trek to a mountaintop hut for a meal on a weekend day. This is also when many huts host traditional Bavarian performances. There's nothing better than being out in nature, taking in incredible mountain scenery and enjoying belly-filling Bavarian food while listening to folks in *lederhosen* play traditional tunes. Hiking in Bavaria is my idea of heaven.

While the local hiking is wonderful, town life near Berchtesgaden National Park is also great. The village of Berchtesgaden makes an excellent home base, and not just because it's the heartbeat of the national park. Berchtesgaden has a lot of shops and restaurants to explore in your time off, as well as its own brewery, Hofbrauhaus Berchtesgaden. It's also surrounded by places of historical importance, such as Hitler's Eagle's Nest and a

salt mine that shaped the history of the area, which are interesting spots to explore on a rest day (see What to See and Do). What's more, you can reach these attractions, as well as the hikes and other villages in the area, by public transportation—you can bus almost everywhere.

From incredible hikes to one of the best home bases I've encountered, the area in and around Berchtesgaden National Park has it all.

Because Berchtesgaden National Park has organized hikes and the trails are extremely well signed and maintained, it's a slam dunk for solo travelers.

Getting There and Around

The largest airports around Berchtesgaden are in Salzburg, Austria (19 miles or 30 km away), and Munich, Germany (124 miles or 200 km away). From either of those airports, you can easily train to the town of Berchtesgaden.

Bus is the best way to get around the Berchtesgaden area, including to most trailheads. The buses run frequently and are free with a Guest Card (see Where to Stay). More information on bus transportation in the area is available in Online Resources.

If you have a car with you, note that some parking lots require a parking disk, a cardboard or plastic card with an adjustable time dial, which you can purchase at gas stations. And if you drive in nearby Austria, you will need a vignette, which

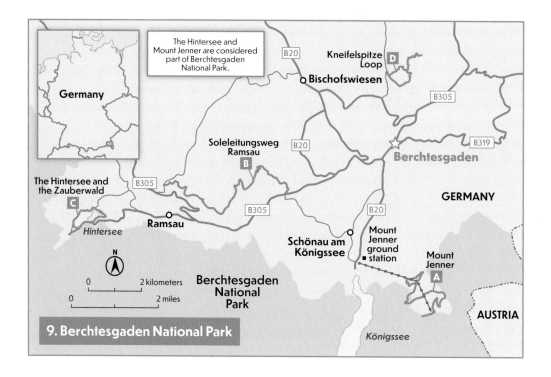

9. Berchtesgaden National Park

is a toll sticker or digital permit. These are available at gas stations, post offices, or tobacconists in Austria or online (see Online Resources for Destination 10).

Where to Stay

While my top choice for a home base is the town of Berchtesgaden, another, more rural home base option is the nearby town of Schönau am Königssee, which is still well connected by bus to all of the hikes in the area, has quite a few apartments for rent and can be a little cheaper than Berchtesgaden. It's also a good choice for those who have a rental car since parking is more available in the country.

Once you check in to your accommodations in the area (including Berchtesgaden, Schönau am Königssee, Bischofswiesen,

Marktschellenberg and Ramsau), you'll get a Guest Card for the duration of your stay (see Online Resources), which entitles you to various discounts, including free bus rides and a 25 percent discount on participating parking lots in the area.

Eat and Resupply

The town of Berchtesgaden has multiple grocery stores. The best area for stocking up is across the main road from the Berchtesgaden train station. There, you'll find two grocery stores and other useful retail stores, including a drugstore and an Intersport.

Berchtesgaden has many dining options. When you're out and about, be sure to track down the following local specialties:

THE ROUTES

HIKE	ROUTE NAME	DURATION	DIFFICULTY	DISTANCE	ELEV. GAIN	ELEV. LOSS
9A	**Mount Jenner**	2.5 hours	Easy to moderate	4.4 mi (7.1 km)	551 ft (168 m)	2,530 ft (771 m)
9B	**Soleleitungsweg Ramsau**	2.5 hours	Easy	5.2 mi (8.4 km)	636 ft (194 m)	1,732 ft (528 m)
9C	**The Hintersee and the Zauberwald**	1.5 hours	Easy	1.9 mi (3.1 km)	215 ft (66 m)	215 ft (66 m)
9D	**Kneifelspitze Loop**	3.5 hours	Moderate	3.8 mi (6.1 km)	1,480 ft (451 m)	1,480 ft (451 m)

□ *Schweinshaxn*: a slow-roasted ham hock served with the skin still on and typically accompanied by sauerkraut and potato dumplings

□ *Kaiserschmarrn*: a mildly sweet pancake that's scrambled and cut as it's cooked and is served with powdered sugar and jam

□ Hofbrauhaus Berchtesgaden: a local beer from Berchtesgaden

What to See and Do

SALZBERGWERK BERCHTESGADEN

This salt mine is an important part of local history and is a fun place to visit, especially with kids. Things to look forward to include riding a roller-coaster-esque train into the belly of the mountain, sliding down a giant slide, and taking a boat across a salt brine lake while watching a light show. Reservations should be made in advance. Get more information from the Salzbergwerk Berchtesgaden website (see Online Resources).

WATZMANN THERMAL BATHS

This very local spot is a great place to relax on a rest day or be inside on a rainy day. You can soak in a variety of warm pools, some inside and some outside, and there are plenty of lawn chairs to sprawl out on next to the pools. There's also a sauna and a salt room, and you can book spa treatments like massages. You don't even have to leave for lunch, since there's a restaurant in the building (see Online Resources).

HITLER'S EAGLE'S NEST

Hitler's Eagle's Nest (see Online Resources), known in German as the Kehlsteinhaus, is a mountaintop retreat that was built by the Nazis for Hitler's fiftieth birthday and was primarily used for government and social meetings. These days, it operates seasonally as a restaurant and beer garden with fabulous views. You can walk up to the Eagle's Nest on a winding road used by the tourist buses that are included in the price of admission (the only

The Berchtesgaden area has a lot of live music in the summer, much of it traditional Bavarian folk music. Most of it is free too, offered by various accommodations and mountain huts as a way to entice people to stay for a drink or a meal. Find a calendar of events on the national park's website (see Online Resources). If you're in Berchtesgaden on a Friday night, be sure to check out Hofbrauhaus Berchtesgaden's Hometown Night.

motorized transportation allowed on the approach) or launch out from above on a walk to surrounding peaks. Tickets should be purchased well in advance; go first thing in the morning to avoid the crowds.

★★★★ Berchtesgaden gets four stars out of four for being family friendly. There are many parks and playgrounds in the area, including at most mountain huts. A lot of other activities also appeal to kids: gondolas, trains, a variety of easy walks and, of course, Salzbergwerk Berchtesgaden, which is suitable for kids of all ages (see What to See and Do). My kids especially loved the traditional music we came across in Berchtesgaden—at one Hometown Night at Hofbrauhaus Berchtesgaden, they were even taught a traditional dance by children from the area. Berchtesgaden National Park's website has helpful information on family-friendly places and events in the area, including guided hikes that are specifically for families.

9A MOUNT JENNER

Ride a gondola to a high-mountain viewpoint and descend past traditional mountain huts to a pretty little lake

For a high-elevation hike in Berchtesgaden National Park that you can access by gondola, Mount Jenner can't be beat. Reach the summit station at 5,906 feet (1,800 m) without breaking a sweat, then ascend a short trail to great viewpoints of the Königssee, the Watzmann and the Bavarian Alps. Descend a wide gravel path past launch points for paragliders and hang gliders and through mountain pastures alive with the sound of cowbells. Stop at a scenic mountain hut—or a couple—for refreshments, then relax at a lovely lake before taking the gondola back down the mountain.

ON THE TRAIL

DURATION: 2.5 hours

DIFFICULTY: Easy to moderate

DISTANCE: 4.4 miles (7.1 km)

ELEVATION GAIN: 551 feet (168 m)

ELEVATION LOSS: 2,530 feet (771 m)

START: Mount Jenner summit station

END: Mount Jenner middle station

EAT + DRINK: Mount Jenner summit station, Mitterkaseralm mountain hut, Dr. Hugo Beck Haus, Mount Jenner middle station (see Online Resources)

Know Before You Go

There's really only one uphill section on this route, and that's from the Mount Jenner summit station to the actual summit. The rest of the hike is all downhill, which can present its own challenges. With 2,530 feet (771 m) of elevation loss over only 4.4 miles (7.1 km) of trail, the pitch is relatively steep. Watch your footing on small, loose rocks and bring your hiking poles if you have creaky knees. The route is well signed.

Other details to keep in mind:

- The last gondola down typically leaves the summit station at 5 p.m., but on Thursdays in the summer, the lift is usually open later. See the Jennerbahn (Jenner gondola) website for more

The small lake below the Mount Jenner middle station is the perfect place to take in the Berchtesgaden Alps—and catch some rays.

information (see Online Resources); it's also a good source of information on the mountain's extensive trail network.

- Of all the places to eat on the route, I suggest the Dr. Hugo Beck Haus, which is a bit off the beaten path and thus quieter and more authentic.
- Swimming is prohibited at the small lake just below the middle station.
- The path is mainly exposed; wear sunscreen and bring plenty of water.

Alternative Routes and Activities

For the main views of this hike but a shorter walk, take the gondola to the summit station and do the 15-minute walk to the summit lookout point, then take the gondola to the middle station and walk around the little lake.

Or extend your outing with one of these options:

- From the Mount Jenner middle station, you can walk to the ground station, which adds 2 hours—and a lot more elevation loss—to your hike.
- Since the Mount Jenner parking lot is the same as the one for the Königssee, this is a great opportunity to explore the lake—Bavaria's deepest—before your hike (or swim, after your hike). A vintage electric boat excursion takes you down the crystal-clear 5-mile (8 km) lake and back in 2 hours, if you don't get off the boat. Among the things you'll experience on your cruise: the lake's echo chamber (your boat captain will play a trumpet to demonstrate the echo) and the quaint white church of Saint Bar-

tholomä, which dates back to 1134. TIP: Buy timed admission tickets for the boat in advance (see Online Resources) so you don't have to wait in line at the pier. For two hikes that take in the best of the Königssee, see the Bonus Hike (Saint Bartholomä to the Ice Chapel) in this section and the Bonus Hike (Malerwinkel Loop) in Hike 9D.

Navigating

This hike begins at the Mount Jenner summit station, which has several restaurants and bars as well as free public restrooms. There's also a small play area for kids, a free exhibition on local wildlife and a lot of lawn chairs to enjoy the mountain views.

STARTING POINT: 47.57609°, 13.02439°

TRANSIT: Reach the Mount Jenner ground station via a 12-minute bus ride from Berchtesgaden on Bus 841 (direction Jennerbahn). The bus stop is called "Jennerbahn, Schönau am Königssee." Current timetables can be found on the German railway website (see Online Resources). TIP: Show your Guest Card to ride the bus for free.

At the Mount Jenner ground station, buy a ticket for the summit station with a return from the middle station. Your Guest Card gets you a discount on the gondola. You will pass through the middle station on your way to the summit station. There's no need to get out and board another gondola; remain in your seat and the gondola will keep going after slowing down momentarily.

DRIVING: The Mount Jenner ground station is 6 minutes from Berchtesgaden. There is a large parking lot (Parkplatz Königssee) at the station, but get there early; it can get very full in the summer since the parking lot is shared with those recreating on the Königssee. The parking meters only take coins; you can make change from the change machine near the restrooms. TIP: Parking is cheaper with a Guest Card. To reach the summit station, follow the directions in the Transit section.

MAPS: Available at Haus der Berge, the national park office in Berchtesgaden.

1 From the gondola exit at the **Mount Jenner summit station**, head to the paved pavilion between the two main buildings of the station (the one across from you is a restaurant). Go right for the signed uphill trail to the true summit.

2 There's a nice terrace lookout over the **Königssee** at 0.2 mile (0.3 km), then the trail continues up to a rocky area with a summit marker and 360-degree views. Retrace your route back to the summit station when you're done. Just be sure not to miss the equally incredible views over the valley between Mounts Jenner and Schneibstein, all lush meadow, pretty wildflowers and winding trails. Continue through the paved pavilion between the summit buildings to find your first trail sign, with the Mitterkaseralm mountain hut signed for 30 minutes—all downhill. You descend on a wide gravel path.

3 At 0.9 mile (1.4 km) from the start of the hike, come to a launch point for paragliders and hang gliders. Next to their prep area, a small footpath leads to a large rock with a summit cross on it—a fun optional detour.

4 At 1.4 miles (2.3 km), come to the turnoff for the **Mitterkaseralm mountain hut**, nestled in a fold of the mountains. There's a full menu and a small play area for kids. Just past the turnoff, the *mittelstation*, or middle station, is signed for 1 hour. Your route down is the same wide gravel path, which in winter is a ski run. As you walk, you may see cows—you'll certainly hear the melodious jingle of their bells—grazing in their summer pasture; the cows are sent to high-mountain pastures in the summer to preserve the grass near their home farm for hay production for the winter.

5 At 2.8 miles (4.5 km), take the footpath to your right for the **Dr. Hugo Beck Haus**.

From the lookout below the summit of Mount Jenner, you can admire the Königssee, Bavaria's deepest lake.

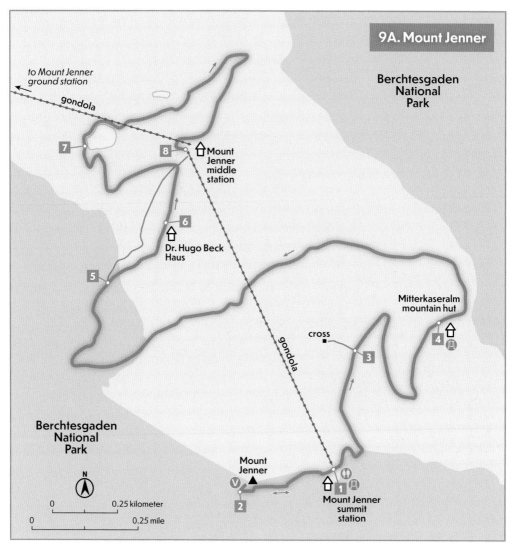

Berchtesgaden
National
Park

to Mount Jenner
ground station

gondola

7

8

Mount
Jenner
middle
station

6

Dr. Hugo Beck
Haus

5

Mitterkaseralm
mountain hut

cross

3

4

gondola

Berchtesgaden
National
Park

N

0   0.25 kilometer

0   0.25 mile

Mount
Jenner

V

2

1

Mount Jenner
summit
station

6 The cozy mountain hut, at 3 miles (4.8 km), is a scenic and authentic-feeling spot to refuel. After you're done eating, continue walking downhill to the middle station. At 3.2 miles (5.1 km), at a junction with several trails just above the middle station, head left on a wide gravel path toward the lake.

7 The lake, at 3.5 miles (5.6 km), is one of the best spots on the hike and offers lawn chairs for soaking up the rays and the huge views. After you're done relaxing, continue walking clockwise around the lake. On the other side of it is a path back up to the middle station.

8 Just like the summit, the **middle station** at 4.4 miles (7.1 km) isn't just a gondola station—it's also a spot to relax and enjoy the views of the **Watzmann** and the valley below from the station's lawn chairs and its restaurant. When you're done exploring here, take the gondola back to the Mount Jenner ground station.

Bonus Hike: Saint Bartholomä to the Ice Chapel

This out-and-back hike leads from the church of Saint Bartholomä (at the end of the Königssee, accessible only by boat) to the lowest-lying permanent icefield in the German Alps—and a cavernous space known as the Ice Chapel.

DURATION: **3 hours**

DIFFICULTY: **Moderate**

DISTANCE: **4.3 miles (6.9 km) roundtrip**

ELEVATION GAIN: **1,033 feet (315 m)**

MORE INFO: **Berchtesgaden National Park hiking guide**

9B SOLELEITUNGSWEG RAMSAU

Walk a historic trail high above the Wimbach Valley to three scenic mountain huts

The Soleleitungsweg Ramsau walking path travels along a sunny high-elevation hillside above Ramsau from Berggasthaus Zipfhäusl to Berggasthof Gerstreit and Berggaststätte Söldenköpfl before dropping down to the Wimbach Valley floor at Engedey. Along the way, the path alternates between forest walking and wide-open views of lush meadows and the Berchtesgaden Alps, including the impressive Watzmann and Hochkalter massifs.

This flat, easy trail has great significance in local history. It follows the path of the salt brine pipeline that was commissioned in 1816 to bring salt brine from Salzbergwerk Berchtesgaden to Bad Reichenhall, where it was processed into salt. It was a major feat of engineering at the time. With the help of its famous Reichenbach Pump, designed by Georg von Reichenbach, it pumped the brine 18 miles (29 km)—and 1,168 feet (356 m) uphill at Ilsank—and operated continuously until 1927. You can still see vestiges of the old wooden pipeline and stone tunnels along what is now very similar to a rail trail.

ON THE TRAIL

DURATION: **2.5 hours**

DIFFICULTY: **Easy**

DISTANCE: **5.2 miles (8.4 km)**

ELEVATION GAIN: **636 feet (194 m)**

ELEVATION LOSS: **1,732 feet (528 m)**

START: **Zipfhäusl parking lot above Ramsau**

END: **Ilsank bus stop in Engedey, Bischofswiesen**

EAT + DRINK: **Berggasthaus Zipfhäusl, Berggasthof Gerstreit, Berggaststätte Söldenköpfl (see Online Resources)**

The Soleleitungsweg Ramsau is mainly flat and is similar to a rail trail.

Know Before You Go

This hike has minimal elevation gain. That said, there is a significant amount of elevation loss (1,234 feet or 376 m) from Berggaststätte Söldenköpfl to the Ilsank bus stop, which may be challenging for those with creaky knees. The route is well signed.

Other notes about the route:

- There are multiple salt brine trails, or *soleleitungswegs*, in the area, including the one known as the Soleleitungsweg Berchtesgaden, which runs for 2.5 miles (4 km) from Salzbergwerk Berchtesgaden to Haus der Berge in Berchtesgaden. This walk is on part of the Soleleitungsweg Ramsau, to the west of Berchtesgaden. Although at one time they were part of the same pipeline, the two Berchtesgaden-area salt brine trails don't connect anymore.

- Berggasthof Gerstreit occasionally has live Bavarian music on the weekend.
- There's nothing except a smattering of homes and apartments near the Ilsank bus stop in Engedey, so bring a book in case you have some time to kill before your return bus.

Alternative Routes and Activities

Many people walk a shorter out-and-back section from Zipfhäusl to Berggasthof Gerstreit, which is 3.8 miles (6.1 km) roundtrip.

Or you can extend your outing:

- Tour Salzbergwerk Berchtesgaden before you hike. The guided tour will give you a lot more perspective on the salt brine pipeline and is one of the best things to do in the area (see What to See and Do).
- You could easily walk both of the Berchtesgaden-area salt brine trails in a day. To do so, start at Salzbergwerk Berchtesgaden and walk to Haus der Berge in Berchtesgaden, then walk over to Berchtesgaden Hauptbahnhof (the main train station) and take the bus to Zipfhäusl for the Zipfhäusl–Engedey stretch, which has more charming options for an afternoon meal.
- This is a great opportunity to explore the nearby town of Ramsau.

Navigating

This hike begins from the Zipfhäusl parking lot next to Berggasthaus Zipfhäusl (see Online Resources), which has a full menu and restrooms for customers.

STARTING POINT: **47.61733°, 12.89456°**

TRANSIT: **The 35-minute bus journey from Berchtesgaden takes two different buses, Bus 846 from Berchtesgaden Hauptbahnhof** (direction Hintersee, Ramsau) to Hochkalter, then Bus 845 (direction Hochschwarzeck, Ramsau) from Hochkalter to Zipfhäusl. Current timetables can be found on the German railway website (see Online Resources). TIP: **Show your Guest Card to ride the bus for free.**

The walk ends at the Ilsank bus stop in Engedey, a neighborhood of Bischofswiesen, just east of Ramsau. To return to Berchtesgaden directly from the end of the hike, take Bus 846 (direction Berchtesgaden Hauptbahnhof) for the 10-minute trip back to Berchtesgaden. There is also an on-demand bus called the RufBus (see Online Resources) that you can schedule at least 2 hours in advance of when you want to be picked up—good for in between regular bus times. It's a few euros per person, plus a small fee per zone that you cross with the bus. When you call, indicate your departure stop, your desired departure time and your end destination. The phone number is +49 8652 964822. For more information, see Online Resources or contact the Berchtesgaden National Park office.

DRIVING: **The Zipfhäusl parking lot (free) is a 15-minute drive from Berchtesgaden.** TIP: **The west side of the Zipfhäusl parking lot is where the bus drops off and the parking is free—the east side is reserved for guests of Berggasthaus Zipfhäusl.**

To retrieve your car after the hike, take a bus from the Ilsank bus stop, where the walk ends, for the 30-minute journey back to your starting point at Zipfhäusl. Take Bus 846 (direction Hintersee, Ramsau) to Hochkalter, then transfer to Bus 845 (direction Hochschwarzeck, Ramsau) to Zipfhäusl. There's also an on-demand bus in the area; see the Transit section for more information.

MAPS: Available at Haus der Berge, the national park office in Berchtesgaden.

1 From the west side of the Zipfhäusl parking lot, walk east to Schwarzecker Weg. To the right, you'll see Berggasthaus Zipfhäusl. To the left you'll find your first trail sign, with Berggasthof Gerstreit signed for 45 minutes on a wide gravel path through the forest. There's a waterfall and a small wooden bridge at 0.2 mile (0.3 km) and occasional benches along the trail. In summer, you can often find wild straw-

On the Soleleitungsweg Ramsau you can see—and walk through—part of an original stone tunnel for the salt brine pipeline.

berries and vibrant wildflowers growing alongside the path.

2 You can see—and walk through—part of an original stone tunnel for the salt brine pipeline at 0.4 mile (0.6 km). As you walk, you'll see more remnants of the pipeline, including old wooden pipes. At 0.5 mile (0.8 km), come out of the trees and into views down to the country houses of **Ramsau**, the **Wimbach Valley** and the **Berchtesgaden Alps** beyond. There's a bench to enjoy the panorama.

3 There are a couple of well-signed junctions at 0.7 mile (1.1 km). Continue on the main path as it curves right and crosses a bridge over another waterfall.

4 Reach **Berggasthof Gerstreit** at 1.9 miles (3.1 km), which has tables with nice views of the valley below and the **Watzmann** and **Hochkalter** massifs beyond, as well as plenty of German comfort food—and beer—on tap. This is where many people stop for a meal and turn around. Because Berggasthof Gerstreit can be busy (even in the morning you'll see people toasting their hike with a beer), wait to eat until the quieter Berggaststätte Söldenköpfl in 1.6 miles (2.6 km), especially if you have kids along—Söldenköpfl has a fun playground. As you continue walking, you'll gain some solitude—perfect for enjoying those viewpoints of the lush valley and towering mountains.

5 At 2.5 miles (4 km), your big views disappear for 0.8 mile (1.3 km) as you hike around a wooded hill that obstructs them. Once you start getting the views back and have a touch of elevation gain (the only

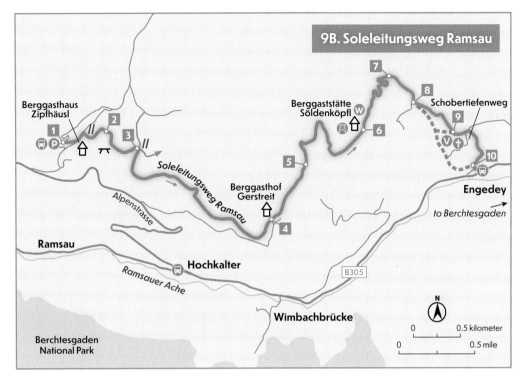

Berggasthaus
Zipfhäusl

Berggaststätte
Söldenköpfl

Schobertiefenweg

Soleleitungsweg Ramsau

Alpenstrasse

Berggasthof
Gerstreit

Engedey

to Berchtesgaden

Ramsau

Ramsauer Ache

Hochkalter

B305

Wimbachbrücke

N

Berchtesgaden
National Park

| 0 | 0.5 kilometer |
| 0 | 0.5 mile |

uphill section of the hike), you'll know you're close to Berggaststätte Söldenköpfl.

6 **Berggaststätte Söldenköpfl** is a welcome sight at 3.5 miles (5.6 km). There's a large playground with some charming wooden buildings for kids, made even better by the fact that you can keep an eye on your littles from the tables below. This is the perfect spot to enjoy lunch with great views. Don't miss the *kaiserschmarrn*, a warm, fluffy pancake made with rum-soaked raisins that's sprinkled with powdered sugar and served with jam. TIP: You can refill your water bottle from the faucet near the playground. After the hut, it's all downhill—literally. Continuing on, you'll lose 1,234 feet (376 m) of elevation over the last 1.7 miles (2.7 km) of the hike, much of which is in the woods.

7 At 3.9 miles (6.3 km), the footpath meets up with a quiet paved road that descends alongside a pretty little stream; you'll see more evidence of the salt brine pipeline.

8 There's a trail sign at 4.3 miles (6.9 km) for Engedey-Ilsank in 30 minutes. Just past that is a junction. You could continue downhill on the paved road and reach the town and bus stop in 25 minutes, but the more scenic dirt footpath on your left will get you to the same spot in 30 minutes.

9 At 4.6 miles (7.4 km), the footpath comes to a paved road. Cross the road for the **Bachmannkapelle**, a little countryside chapel with a beautiful panorama. Once you're done enjoying the views from the chapel, continue east (right, when looking at the paved road from the chapel). Just past Schobertiefenweg, you'll find a gravel double track that skirts a cow pasture—take it.

10 Come out onto the quiet paved roads of **Engedey** at 5.1 miles (8.2 km). Head left, then take another left on Bachmannweg.

The **Ilsank bus stop** (with a shelter for rainy days) is where Bachmannweg meets the busier B305. Take the bus back to Berchtesgaden, or to Zipfhäusl to retrieve your car.

9C THE HINTERSEE AND THE ZAUBERWALD

Circumnavigate a picturesque alpine lake and visit the nearby forest

This hike around the Hintersee, a pretty alpine lake near Ramsau, is perfect for a day when you want to walk but you also want to do other things too—like explore town or take it easy. Most people walk only around the lake, but swinging the hike a little wider, to encompass part of the Zauberwald ("magic forest"), adds not only a nice wooded section but also the opportunity for some scenic river walking on the way back to the lake. Paired with lunch and some time on the water, this makes for a chill Berchtesgaden day.

ON THE TRAIL

DURATION: 1.5 hours

DIFFICULTY: Easy

DISTANCE: 1.9 miles (3.1 km)

ELEVATION GAIN: 215 feet (66 m)

ELEVATION LOSS: 215 feet (66 m)

START: Parking lot on the southwestern shore of the Hintersee

END: Parking lot on the southwestern shore of the Hintersee

EAT + DRINK: Various restaurants on the western shore of the Hintersee

Know Before You Go

The hike has minimal elevation gain and is on well-maintained, well-signed paths. Pack a bathing suit and a towel if you want to swim in the Hintersee.

Alternative Routes and Activities

For a shorter option, you can walk around just the lake, which is 1.7 miles (2.7 km) roundtrip and can be done in 45 minutes.

A passenger ferry also crosses the lake, so you could feasibly walk to the other side of the lake and boat back.

Or you can extend your outing with one of these options:

- The Hintersee has a few restaurants. One of the only ones that's open for lunch is the Alpenhof am Hintersee (see Online Resources), which is located across the road from the parking lot I recommend.

The Hintersee has captured many an artist's imagination thanks to its alluring shades of green.

- On the northwestern shore of the lake is a spot where you can rent paddle and pedal boats to explore more of the lake from the water.
- This is a great opportunity to explore nearby Ramsau.

Navigating

The hike starts at the Hintersee parking lot, which is close to several restaurants and next to free public restrooms.

STARTING POINT: 47.60431°, 12.84949°

TRANSIT: The Hintersee is a 30-minute bus ride on Bus 846 from Berchtesgaden Hauptbahnhof (direction Hintersee, Ramsau). Current timetables can be found on the German railway website (see Online Resources). There are a couple of bus stops in the area; you want the one on the western shore of the lake, near the shops and restaurants. To return to Berchtesgaden by bus after the hike, take Bus 846 (direction Berchtesgaden Hauptbahnhof). TIP: Show your Guest Card to ride the bus for free.

DRIVING: You can also get to the Hintersee with a 15-minute drive. The lake has several parking lots. The best one for this hike is a paid lot on the southwestern shore of the lake, which is near the recommended bus stop and is where this hike begins. TIP: Parking is cheaper with a Guest Card.

MAPS: Available at Haus der Berge, the national park office in Berchtesgaden.

1 From the parking lot, head north on the gravel path around the **Hintersee**. For

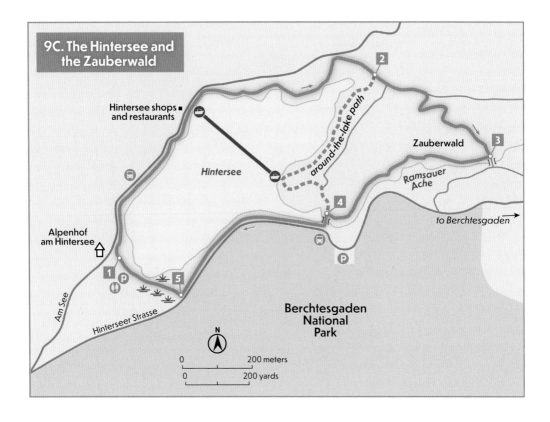

9C. The Hintersee and the Zauberwald

Hintersee shops and restaurants

Hintersee

Zauberwald

around-the-lake path

Ramsauer Ache

to Berchtesgaden

Alpenhof am Hintersee

Am See

Hinterseer Strasse

Berchtesgaden National Park

N

0   200 meters

0   200 yards

the first 0.4 mile (0.6 km), as you walk along the western shore of the lake, you'll pass by restaurants, small shops and places to rent small boats once you're done hiking. Your first trail sign is at the end of the populated part of the western shore, just before the trail dips into a more forested area with quieter views of the little coves of the lake and signage about painters who used this landscape as inspiration. It's not hard to imagine why—the lake has so many shades of green (especially on a sunny day), it nearly begs to be painted.

2 Come to a junction with the around-the-lake trail at 0.7 mile (1.1 km). A path to the right circumnavigates the lake; stay straight to continue the hike as described,

which heads into the **Zauberwald**. At another junction at 0.8 mile (1.3 km), go right on a downhill gravel footpath through the trees. You'll lose 171 feet (52 m) of elevation over the next 0.3 mile (0.5 km), until you bottom out alongside the pretty **Ramsauer Ache river**.

3 Reach the river and a bridge over it at 1.1 miles (1.8 km), where you'll see a trail sign for the Hintersee in 15 minutes—if you can tear your eyes away from the greenish-blue, mineral-heavy water of the river. Don't cross the bridge—just before it, take a footpath to the right. The route back to the lake runs alongside the river, and it's nice and shady—perfect on a hot day—with plenty of benches. You'll likely see walkers with their feet in the cold water. This stretch of trail is popular with families; kids love the numerous little caves made by the big mountain rocks that have been swept down the river.

4 Come to another junction with the lake trail at 1.4 miles (2.3 km), where the lake and river meet. A small building with a large overhang makes for great shelter on a rainy day. At the junction, go left. NOTE: To reach the ferry landing for the boat across the lake (in 0.1 mile or 0.2 km), go right at the junction and then left at a Y junction. Almost immediately, the main path takes you to the road that travels around the Hintersee (there's another parking lot and a bus

The route around the Hintersee and Zauberwald is lush and green thanks to an abundance of water.

stop here); you'll walk alongside this road as you make your way along the southern shore of the lake.

5 At 1.8 miles (2.9 km), the path leaves the road, cuts right and crosses a wetland area on its way back to the parking lot where you started.

9D KNEIFELSPITZE LOOP

Hike to a mountain hut with incredible views of Berchtesgaden from above

This short but steep hike is worth the effort, taking you through pretty forests and lush meadows to gorgeous views of Berchtesgaden and the surrounding mountains from the 3,900-foot (1,189 m) peak of the Kneifelspitze. Enjoy the views from the multilevel terrace of Berggaststätte Kneifelspitze, a traditional mountain hut perched at the top of the mountain that offers a sumptuous mountain breakfast and plenty of German comfort food—a good reward for all your hard work getting there.

ON THE TRAIL

DURATION: 3.5 hours

DIFFICULTY: Moderate

DISTANCE: 3.8 miles (6.1 km)

ELEVATION GAIN: 1,480 feet (451 m)

ELEVATION LOSS: 1,480 feet (451 m)

START: Wallfahrtskirche Maria Gern

END: Wallfahrtskirche Maria Gern

EAT + DRINK: Gasthaus-Hotel Maria Gern, Berggaststätte Kneifelspitze (see Online Resources)

Know Before You Go

Distance-wise, this hike isn't that long, but it packs a punch with 1,480 feet (451 m) of elevation gain as you ascend to Berggaststätte Kneifelspitze. While the way there is up, up, up, that means your return hike is all downhill. Though the Kneifelspitze hiking path is well signed at junctions, there's an extensive network of trails in this area and the signage can be confusing, with multiple directions signed for the same destination. I've hiked several of the routes and recommend this one specifically.

A couple of other things to bear in mind:

- Several electric fences along the route keep animals in their pastures.
- Berggaststätte Kneifelspitze only takes cash. It also has a delicious mountain breakfast (with mimosas!) that you can pre-order. Contact the hut for more details (see Online Resources).

Alternative Routes and Activities

Extend your outing with one or both of these options:

- Pop into Wallfahrtskirche Maria Gern for a look at its beautiful Baroque architecture; it's widely considered one of the most beautiful churches in Bavaria.

- Gasthaus-Hotel Maria Gern often has live Bavarian music in the evenings, which can pair nicely with dinner. Contact them in advance for the schedule (see Online Resources).

Navigating

The hike starts at Wallfahrtskirche Maria Gern (the Pilgrimage Church of Maria Gern). It's a short walk from Gasthaus-Hotel Maria Gern, which has a full menu and restrooms for customers.

STARTING POINT: 47.65262°, 13.00234°

TRANSIT: Wallfahrtskirche Maria Gern is a 25-minute bus ride from Berchtesgaden. The Maria Gern bus stop is just north of the church, which is serviced several times a day by Bus 837 (direction Hintergern) from Berchtesgaden. Current timetables can be found on the German railway website (see Online Resources). TIP: Show your Guest Card to ride the bus for free.

To get back to Berchtesgaden by bus after the hike, take Bus 837 in the opposite direction (direction ZOB/Hauptbahnhof, Berchtesgaden).

DRIVING: Maria Gern is a 10-minute drive from Berchtesgaden. Park in the small parking area in front of the church on Gerner

At Berggaststätte Kneifelspitze, you can dine on German comfort food high above Berchtesgaden and surrounded by the peaks of the Berchtesgaden Alps.

Strasse, or just south of the church on the street if needed.

MAPS: Available at Haus der Berge, the national park office in Berchtesgaden.

1 From Wallfahrtskirche Maria Gern, walk up Kirchplatz to **Gasthaus-Hotel Maria Gern**, then take a right on the steep **Kneifelspitzweg**.

2 At 0.2 mile (0.3 km), come to signage in German for the Kneifelspitzweg, with the Kneifelspitze signed for 1 hour and 30 minutes. Note that the area is a protected plant zone, and picking flowers is forbidden and punishable with a hefty fine. This sign marks the beginning of the loop part of the walk. You'll come back down the mountain via the road on your left; for now, take a right on the gravel path through the forest.

3 Go straight and through an animal gate at the junction at 0.5 mile (0.8 km). Once inside the pasture, you'll likely see cows and goats grazing—they're used to walkers, but give them space all the same. There's some signage about wildflowers in the area midway through the pasture. You're likely to spot many pretty ones on this route, from dainty gentians to vivid oxeyes. TIP: Snap a photo of the sign so

The Kneifelspitze Loop starts and ends at the historic Pilgrimage Church of Maria Gern.

the Kneifelspitze is on the dirt footpath to the left, so take that. Just uphill, you'll see a road on your right; stay on the footpath.

5 Come to another junction at 1.1 miles (1.8 km). This is where the out-and-back to the Kneifelspitze starts. Stay to the right. At 1.4 miles (2.3 km), the route starts to switchback up through the forest. It feels steep but the switchbacks only last 0.4 mile (0.6 km). Head left at the junction at 1.8 miles (2.9 km) from the start of the hike; you're almost there.

6 Reach **Berggaststätte Kneifelspitze** at 2 miles (3.2 km). There's a small playground to your left; the multilevel terrace of the hut is reached via a short path to your right. This is a great spot to enjoy some food before heading back down the mountain. The hut has hot dishes and cold appetizers, pastries and cakes and beer and wine. While the food is fantastic, the real stunner of the hut is the view over Berchtesgaden, the surrounding mountains and emerald meadows, and the extensive local trail system that connects everything.

More views await once you finish your food. Head back to the main trail and take a right. The trail here is relatively flat (thank goodness, right?) and leads to a viewpoint called the **Salzburgblick** at 2.1 miles (3.4

you can refer to it as you walk. At 0.7 mile (1.1 km), exit the pasture via another gate, and you're walking in the forest again.

4 At the junction at 0.8 mile (1.3 km), the signage is confusing because it says both ways go to the Kneifelspitze—this area has an extensive network of trails, more than the simple maps on the trails' placards let on. The most scenic way to get to

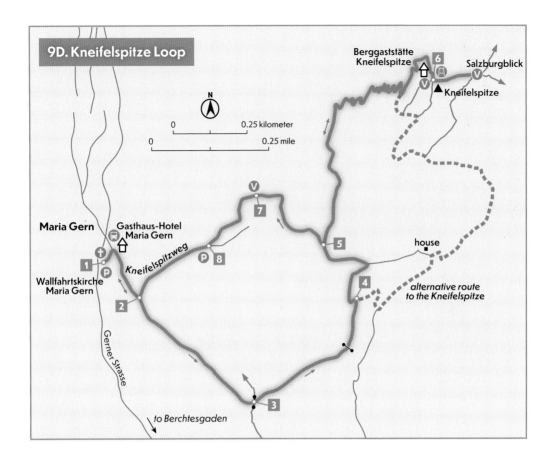

9D. Kneifelspitze Loop

Berggaststätte Kneifelspitze

Salzburgblick

Kneifelspitze

Maria Gern

Gasthaus-Hotel Maria Gern

Kneifelspitzweg

Wallfahrtskirche Maria Gern

house

alternative route to the Kneifelspitze

Gerner Strasse

to Berchtesgaden

0   0.25 kilometer

0   0.25 mile

N

km), where you can get views to the other side of the Kneifelspitze and north toward Salzburg. Once you're done enjoying the viewpoint, retrace your route to [5] and take a right.

7 At 3.2 miles (5.1 km), find yourself in a lush meadow with an idyllic mountain background—a good photo opportunity.

8 Come to a small parking lot at 3.4 miles (5.5 km) and take a right on the paved road that heads back to the main trail signage and will complete the loop when you return to [2]. Staying on this paved road, the Kneifelspitzweg, will take you all the way back down to Gasthaus-Hotel Maria Gern.

Bonus Hike: Malerwinkel Loop

Get great views of the Königssee, with the pretty church of Saint Bartholomä in the distance, from this easy hike on mostly gently rolling terrain.

DURATION: **1.5 hours**

DIFFICULTY: **Easy**

DISTANCE: **2.4 miles (3.9 km)**

ELEVATION GAIN: **420 feet (128 m)**

MORE INFO: **Berchtesgaden National Park hiking guide**

The village of Dürnstein, on the banks of the Danube River, is the perfect home base for exploring the Wachau Valley. (Photo courtesy Donau Niederösterreich, extremfotos.com)

10 THE WACHAU VALLEY, AUSTRIA

Vineyard walking on the banks of the beautiful blue Danube

AT A GLANCE

GENERAL LOCATION: Northeastern Austria

HOME BASE: Dürnstein

LOCAL LANGUAGE: German

USE OF ENGLISH: Widely understood and used

FAMILY FRIENDLY: ★★★☆

COST: $$$

WHEN TO GO: Mar to Oct

SCENERY: Extensive vineyards, the Danube River, bucolic farmland

DON'T MISS: Abbeys, castles, local wine, tiny wine-producing villages

When I was in college, I was lucky enough to study abroad in Vienna, Austria. I spent three months discovering this gorgeous city—Austria's cultural hot spot—but some of my favorite explorations were the ones we took to experience the surrounding countryside. We hiked and biked to country chapels, famous abbeys and family-run wine taverns, and that's when I first fell in love with the Wachau Valley, the stretch of the Danube (Donau, in German) River valley between the towns of Melk and Krems, about an hour outside of Vienna.

The Wachau is one of Austria's most famous wine-growing regions—and one of its oldest. Wine production in the area goes back to the Roman emperor Probus, who had vineyards planted on both banks of the Danube in about AD 280. In the Middle Ages, local monasteries took over wine production for use in communion, but in the eighteenth century local families began growing their own grapes and focusing on producing quality wines, specifically white wines. These days, the region produces some of Austria's most well-known grüner veltliner and riesling.

The mild climate and landscape of the Wachau—tall valley walls rising majestically from the beautiful blue Danube and a multitude of dry-stone walls to hold the soil in place—aren't just good for wine production. The valley is also a walker's paradise, with 242 miles (390 km) of walking paths in the area. They're some of the most beautiful—and cultural—you can find, which is why the area is a UNESCO World Heritage site. The trails weave through family-owned vineyards to romantic viewpoints of the river and lead you to abbeys, castles, ruins and charming wine-growing villages where tasting rooms abound.

The area looks very different depending on when you visit. Hiking in the valley is ideal anytime from March to October. In late March and early April, the nearly one hundred thousand apricot trees in the valley flower. Starting in May, the vineyards are green with new growth, and toward fall, when harvest approaches and the leaves change colors, they become a riotous mix of red and gold. TIP: Want to visit the area in summer? Aim for mid-July, when local apricots are being harvested and sold at local fruit stands.

One of my favorite features of trails in the area is that they typically pass by several *heurige*, seasonal family-run wine taverns where you can taste the wine produced by that family. *Heurige* are only allowed to operate for two weeks at a time, a few times a year, and you can identify open ones by the bundle of pine twigs on the door. (A calendar is also available at local tourist information offices and on the local tourism bureau's website; see Online Resources.) There's nothing better mid-hike than stopping for a refreshing glass of cold grüner veltliner and a warm apricot dumpling made from local fruit.

The best of the Wachau Valley can be experienced during a weeklong home base trip centered in the town of Dürnstein, a delightful riverside town full of quaint restaurants and small shops. You can stay at a family-owned winery, a wonderfully local experience, and the town is located in the shadow of one of the top ruins in the area, the Dürnstein Castle—a perfect sunset excursion. Another thing that's great about Dürnstein is that it's well connected to the rest of the valley by frequent public transportation, so it's easy to hike—and bike—the area without a car.

With Dürnstein as your home base, you can hike village to village through local vineyards, experience a traditional working farm, cruise the beautiful blue Danube, visit one of the most famous abbeys in Austria and bike along the banks of the Danube—all while experiencing the alluring Austrian countryside I fell so hard for all those years ago.

Getting There and Around

The closest major airport to the Wachau Valley is in Vienna, Austria. From there, you can easily train to Krems, the largest town in the Wachau Valley, and then hop on a bus to Dürnstein or one of the other small towns in the valley. You can also drive from Vienna to Dürnstein in just over an hour.

The easiest way to get around during your home base hiking trip is the Wachau Valley's extensive network of buses. (There are more buses in the valley than trains.) Although a car can be helpful for visiting farther-out abbeys and ruins, you won't need one for the hikes and bike ride I recommend—they're all accessible with public transportation, which is cheap and reliable and runs often.

If you rent a car, make sure it has a vignette or that you buy one—they're required in Austria. Vignettes can be purchased from local gas stations based on the duration of your stay. You can also purchase vignettes online (see Online Resources).

Where to Stay

If you book early, you can often find accommodations at local family-owned wineries, giving you a chance to meet locals and buy discounted wine. When I was in Dürnstein, the family who owned the winery where I stayed gave me a key to the tasting room so I could grab a bottle or two of wine—on the honor system—day or night. At the end of my stay, they just tallied everything up and let me know how much I owed.

While my top choice for a home base in the Wachau Valley is Dürnstein, another great option is Krems, a college town that's larger, has decent nightlife and is well connected to the other villages in the valley by bus.

Eat and Resupply

The largest grocery store in Dürnstein is a Nah und Frisch on the east side of town. The grocery store has limited hours and a somewhat limited selection; larger supermarkets are located in Krems if you want to stock up for your stay. You can also get produce from local farmers' markets. There's a good one on the river between Dürnstein and Krems that's open daily.

Dürnstein has a variety of restaurants. They're busiest during the middle of the

Even from afar, the Melk Abbey is an impressive sight.

day, when the town is inundated by travelers from the big boats that cruise the Danube, and calmer at dinnertime. Be sure to track down the following local specialties:

- *Wienerschnitzel*: a thin breaded, panfried pork cutlet
- *Wachauer marillenknödel*: an apricot dumpling rolled in bread crumbs that have been fried in butter
- Grüner veltliner: a white wine that's Austria's most significant wine variety

There are a couple of outdoor stores in Krems in case you need to adjust or add to your gear.

TIP: Because you'll be in one of Austria's best wine-producing regions with so many good wines to try, bring a hydration bag to enjoy wine as you walk without the weight of the bottle (see the "Wine Bladder" sidebar in Chapter 5). And don't forget an opener!

What to See and Do

MELK ABBEY

Melk Abbey (see Online Resources) is one of Austria's most famous and most picturesque abbeys. The stately yellow-and-white building overlooks the Danube River and the town of Melk and catches your eye from miles around. Although the abbey was founded in 1089, the current structure dates back to the early 1700s, and it's an incredible example of the Baroque style. The interior of the abbey, which you can

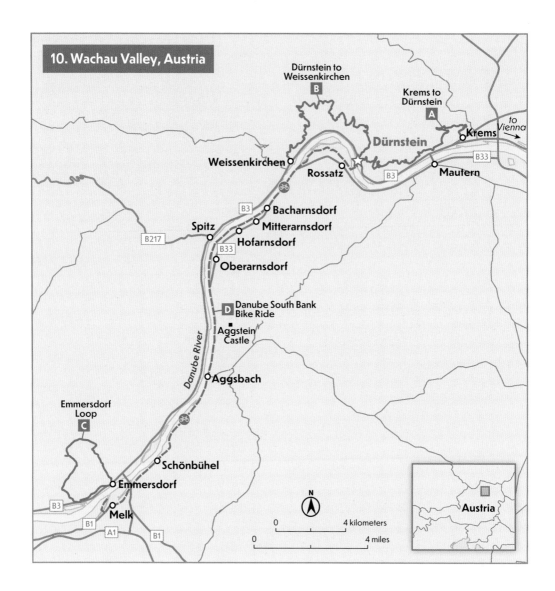

10. Wachau Valley, Austria

Dürnstein to
Weissenkirchen
B

Krems to
Dürnstein
A

to
Vienna →

Dürnstein

o**Krems**

B33

Weissenkirchen o

Rossatz

B3

Mautern

o
B3

Bacharnsdorf

Spitz

Mitterarnsdorf

B217

B33

Hofarnsdorf

Oberarnsdorf

D Danube South Bank
Bike Ride

Aggstein
Castle

Danube River

o**Aggsbach**

Emmersdorf
Loop
C

o Schönbühel

o **Emmersdorf**

B3

o
Melk

B1

A1   B1

N

0   4 kilometers

0   4 miles

Austria

---

visit at certain times of the year only with a guided tour, is stunning—especially the frescoes. In addition to visiting the abbey and walking the grounds (there's a park that makes for a nice walk), you can also take part in Sunday worship services and daily noontime prayers. In the summer, the abbey hosts a concert series.

Want to visit a lesser-known abbey? Check out Göttweig Abbey (see Online Resources) outside of the town of Mautern, which offers a "Stay in the Monastery" program that allows you to try out simple monastic overnight accommodations.

THE ROUTES

HIKE	ROUTE NAME	DURATION	DIFFICULTY	DISTANCE	ELEV. GAIN	ELEV. LOSS
10A	**Krems to Dürnstein**	4.5 hours	Moderate	8.3 mi (13.4 km)	1,541 ft (470 m)	1,511 ft (461 m)
10B	**Dürnstein to Weissenkirchen**	6 hours	Challenging	10.7 mi (17.2 km)	2,664 ft (812 m)	2,707 ft (825 m)
10C	**Emmersdorf Loop**	4 hours	Moderate	7.3 mi (11.7 km)	1,105 ft (337 m)	1,105 ft (337 m)
10D	**Danube South Bank Bike Ride**	2.5 hours	Easy	17.9 mi (28.8 km)	1,010 ft (308 m)	1,050 ft (320 m)

AGGSTEIN CASTLE

The Aggstein Castle (see Online Resources), near the town of Aggsbach, is accessible by car. You can tour the entire premises and even get an audio guide to learn about the life of medieval knights. Explore hidden stairways, courtyards and towers, as well as a dungeon, a chapel, a knight's hall and a tavern. Don't forget to peek over the side of the ramparts for amazing views of the Danube, which the castle was originally built to control. The castle hosts regular events, such as a medieval festival each May and a storyteller the second Sunday of each month.

DANUBE BEACHES

There are several beaches on the Danube, including one in Dürnstein, next to where the passenger ferry drops off (see Bike Ride 10D, Danube South Bank Bike Ride). This is a great spot to post up when it's sunny and hot; you can swim and watch the riverboats go by. The beach is especially ideal for kids, who will dig in the sand and wade in the shallow water for hours.

★★★ The Wachau Valley gets three stars out of four for being family friendly. There are plenty of parks and playgrounds for littles to get their energy out, buses are

DAY TRIP TO VIENNA

It would be a shame to come this close to Vienna and not visit the incredible city—one of my favorites in the world. There's a lot to love about Vienna's old town, from the local coffeehouse culture (you can expect your coffee and pastries to be brought to you by a tuxedoed waiter) to the history all around (this was the seat of the Hapsburg Empire and home to some of the most admired minds in history, such as Sigmund Freud). A walking tour is an interesting way to learn about the city and visit its most important spots, from Schönbrunn Palace to Saint Stephen's Cathedral. If you have time, the quirky Prater amusement park is a must.

free for kids six and under, and *heurige* are very family friendly—many have outdoor seating built around a playground so you can drink wine while watching the kids play. Pick up a brochure from local tourist information offices about all of the family-friendly things to do in the valley.

10A KREMS TO DÜRNSTEIN

Walk through extensive vineyards from Krems, the largest town in the Wachau Valley, back to charming Dürnstein

✦ **Stage one of the Wachau World Heritage Trail**

This hike along the first stage of the Wachau World Heritage Trail combines city and countryside for a good look at what makes the Wachau Valley so appealing. The path starts in Krems, the largest town in the valley, where a bustling pedestrian zone, weekly farmers' market and plenty of historical attractions offer the perfect place to spend a morning. After you're done exploring town, head into the hills for a peaceful walk on paved and gravel paths that run parallel to the beautiful blue Danube. Along the way, take in local art installations set in the vineyards alongside the trail and rest your legs at numerous wooden benches set among the vines. The route ends in Dürnstein, where you have an opportunity to visit the most famous ruins of the area.

ON THE TRAIL

DURATION: **4.5 hours**

DIFFICULTY: **Moderate**

DISTANCE: **8.3 miles (13.4 km)**

ELEVATION GAIN: **1,541 feet (470 m)**

ELEVATION LOSS: **1,511 feet (461 m)**

START: **"Krems Stadtpark" bus stop in Krems**

END: **Kremser Tor trailhead in Dürnstein**

EAT + DRINK: **Krems, Dürnstein**

Know Before You Go

This route is relatively long and has more than 1,500 feet (460 m) of elevation gain and loss, including a long series of steps on the route out of Krems. The walking surface is great, though, on quiet paved country roads for the most part. This route mainly follows the first stage of the Wachau World Heritage Trail and is moderately well signed in the countryside. My described route starts from the "Krems Stadtpark"

Get a better understanding of the landscape and the Wachau wine region with the help of panoramic signage on the route from Krems to Dürnstein.

bus stop, while the official route starts in the Hoher Markt part of Krems. Follow the walking directions here, or use my GPX tracks to stay on track in town. Once you're out on trail, the confidence marker is a wavy letter *W*. The trail is also signed for the Welterbesteig (World Heritage Trail).

Other notes about the route:

- This walk is best done on a Saturday so you can take in the Krems farmers' market in Pfarrplatz and gather provisions before your hike (see [3] on the map and in the Navigating section). The farmers' market is typically open from 7 a.m. to 12 p.m.; verify current open times at the tourist information office in Krems.
- You can walk this trail in the opposite direction (from Dürnstein to Krems) but

it's more beautiful and fitting to walk from the city to the countryside.
- In the countryside between Krems and Dürnstein, there aren't any places en route to stop for food or drinks, so plan accordingly.

Alternative Routes and Activities

For a shorter route, walk just the first 3.4 miles (5.5 km) in and around the towns of Krems and Stein; from there, walk farther into Stein and taxi back to Dürnstein. If you want a completely flat hike, walk along the water on the Danube Cycle Path from Krems to Dürnstein.

Or you can extend your outing:

- Krems is the largest town in the Danube Valley, so there's plenty to see and explore, including several museums,

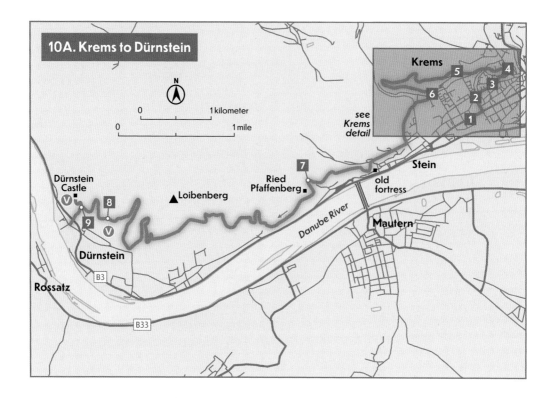

10A. Krems to Dürnstein

N

0   1 kilometer

0   1 mile

Krems

see Krems detail

Stein

old fortress

Dürnstein Castle

Loibenberg

Ried Pfaffenberg

Danube River

Mautern

Dürnstein

Rossatz

B3

B33

historic churches and a bustling pedestrian zone with great shopping.

- The ruins of the Dürnstein Castle are an excellent place to visit at the end of the hike, especially if you bring a bottle of wine with you. Just don't forget your headlamp if you plan to head back down the trail after sunset.

Navigating

The hike begins from the "Krems Stadtpark" bus stop in a peaceful city park, a short walk from several restaurants and cafés.

STARTING POINT: 48.40749°, 15.59641°

TRANSIT: From Dürnstein, Bus 715 (direction Krems) runs at least hourly, if not more, for the approximately 20-minute trip to the "Krems Stadtpark" bus stop. You can find the timetable for Bus 715 at local tourist information offices. Times are also available on Google Maps.

The hike finishes at Dürnstein's Kremser Tor trailhead on Hauptstrasse, at the southeast end of the Dürnstein town center.

MAPS: Available at tourist information offices in Krems, Weissenkirchen and Melk. A booklet called *Hikers' Guide: Wachau World Heritage Trail*, which contains simplified maps of each stage of the trail, can also be downloaded for free from the trail's website (see Online Resources).

1 From the "**Krems Stadtpark**" bus stop, walk east on Ringstrasse toward Utzstrasse. Take a left on Utzstrasse and a right

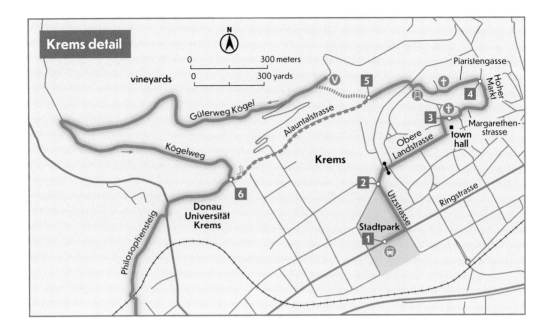

Krems detail

vineyards

0   300 meters
0   300 yards

Güterweg Kögel

Kögelweg

Philosophensteig

Alauntalstrasse

Krems

Donau
Universität
Krems

Obere
Landstrasse

Stadtpark

Ulzstrasse

town
hall

Margarethen-
strasse

Piaristengasse

Hoher
Markt

Ringstrasse

on Südtirolerplatz, which will turn into Obere Landstrasse once you go through the medieval town gate.

2 From the medieval gate at 0.3 mile (0.5 km), walk Obere Landstrasse, a pedestrian boulevard with retail, pharmacies and grocery stores, for 0.2 mile (0.3 km). Take a left just before the *rathaus*, or town hall, on a small walkway that leads to **Stadtpfarrkirche Krems St. Veit** (a church) and **Pfarrplatz** (a public square). TIP: Most Austrian village churches are unlocked during the day, so feel free to pop in as you pass. The beautiful Baroque Stadtpfarrkirche Krems St. Veit is well worth a look.

3 The farmers' market at 0.5 mile (0.8 km), open Saturday mornings (see Know Before You Go), is a great place to grab local snacks for your walk. When you're done shopping, curve east around the church and take a right on Margarethenstrasse, then a left on **Hoher Markt**, which is where the World Heritage Trail officially starts, near the Hercules Fountain in the middle of the square.

The first mention of Krems is from 995, making it one of the oldest cities—if not the oldest—in Lower Austria. For centuries, Krems and the neighboring villages of Stein and Mautern, which share the second bridge ever built on the Danube, were incredibly important for shipping and transportation—even more so than Vienna. A wealthy merchant class sprung up that demanded the best art, architecture and education, all of which you can still see evidence of today. Thanks to its rich cultural heritage, Krems has been protected as a UNESCO World Heritage site since 2000.

You pass by the old village of Stein on stage one of the Wachau World Heritage Trail.

4 At 0.7 mile (1.1 km), the road splits; head left on Piaristengasse and walk past **Piaristenkirche** (a church). Just after the church and the covered staircase, take the footpath on the left, which leads you past a playground and back onto Piaristengasse (go left) before coming to a big intersection of streets at 0.9 mile (1.4 km). Go right to curve northwest on Alauntalstrasse.

5 At 1 mile (1.6 km), take the long staircase, called the **Kreuzbergstiege**, on your right. This staircase is a gateway to the vineyards and takes you effectively up and out of Krems and to a nice hillside viewpoint over the town. TIP: If you prefer to skip the elevation gain of the stairs and the viewpoint, continue straight on Alauntalstrasse and rendezvous with the main trail in 0.4 mile (0.6 km), near the university. At the top of the stairs, initially go right for the viewpoint, which is just a few feet down the street, then backtrack to the stairs and continue west on Kreuzbergstrasse for 0.1 mile (0.2 km). Take a right on Güterweg Kögel, which meanders past wildflowers and vineyards, then a left at the hairpin turn at 1.9 miles (3.1 km). Shortly after, the road becomes Kögelweg and drops you back down to Alauntalstrasse.

6 At 2.3 miles (3.7 km), head right on Alauntalstrasse, walking past the campus of **Donau Universität Krems**. At 2.5 miles (4 km), when the road Ts, take a left and then an almost immediate right on Philosophensteig. At 2.9 miles (4.7 km), head right on Steiner Kellergasse. At 3.2 miles (5.1 km), go down the staircase on your left. Cross Reisperbachtalstrasse, then walk up another staircase and onto a path

Most of the stone walls that separate the vineyards of the Wachau and support its extensive terraces are considered dry-stone walls, which means they're composed of special stones fit together in a way that doesn't require mortar or cement. Wine growers gather rocks throughout the year from caved-in structures, abandoned vineyards and local quarries, then rebuild their walls in winter. Even with the right kind of stone, it takes special masons who are specifically trained in the art of dry-stone walls to build or repair these beautiful structures.

that follows a fence past houses and an old fortress on the outskirts of town as you trek into the countryside.

7 Come to a trail sign at 3.9 miles (6.3 km) and go right on Pfaffenbergweg. Just past the famous vineyard of **Ried Pfaffenberg**, the route diverges from Pfaffenbergweg, heading left to closer views of the water. From here, you can look forward to vineyards, countryside and the occasional art installation all the way to Dürnstein. This is the most beautiful part of the walk. The route is gently rolling, leading you up and down and along a ridge. Occasionally you'll find trees and a spot of shade, but for the most part the path is exposed. Look closely at the low stone walls alongside the trail; if you're lucky, you'll spot one of the shy, bright emerald lizards that call them home.

8 As you walk, you'll take in sweeping views of the Danube and the vineyards that line its shores. Get a better understanding of the landscape and the Wachau wine region at 7.6 miles (12.2 km), where panoramic signage explains what you're looking at.

9 At 8.1 miles (13 km), just above Dürnstein, come to a junction with a trail to the ruins of the **Dürnstein Castle**. Right takes you to the castle in 0.3 mile (0.5 km); left takes you down to Dürnstein and the end of the trail on Hauptstrasse in 0.2 mile (0.3 km). TIP: You'll visit the ruins of the Dürnstein Castle on the walk from Dürnstein to Weissenkirchen, so if your legs are tired, by all means head into Dürnstein. The most beautiful time of day to experience (and photograph) the ruins, however, is golden hour, so if it's edging toward that time and you'd like somewhere to watch the sun sink lower on the horizon, this is an excellent spot. You could also hike back up here after breaking for dinner.

10B DÜRNSTEIN TO WEISSENKIRCHEN

Ascend to ruins high above Dürnstein, then walk a ridgetop to vineyards and the town of Weissenkirchen

+ **Stage two of the Wachau World Heritage Trail**

This hike is your best opportunity to get high above the Danube and walk the forests that crown the terraced valley. On the way, you'll get to explore the most famous ruins in the region—a castle that once held Richard the Lionheart—visit a mountain hut that serves local comfort food; wander through working vineyards; and visit Weissenkirchen, a charming wine village on the shores of the Danube that's a little larger than Dürnstein and home to many *heurige*.

The cliff next to the Dürnstein Castle is the perfect place to watch the sunset.

ON THE TRAIL

DURATION: 6 hours

DIFFICULTY: Challenging

DISTANCE: 10.7 miles (17.2 km)

ELEVATION GAIN: 2,664 feet (812 m)

ELEVATION LOSS: 2,707 feet (825 m)

START: Dürnstein Altstadt trailhead

END: "Weissenkirchen/Wachau Fähre" bus stop

EAT + DRINK: Dürnstein, Fesslhütte, Weingut Pomassl (see Online Resources), Weissenkirchen

Know Before You Go

The hike is long and has quite a bit of elevation gain. The most challenging part of the route is the initial 1.1 miles (1.8 km), as you ascend the first big ridge and gain more than 1,100 feet (335 m) in the process. After that, the elevation gain is more gradual. The route follows stage two of the Wachau World Heritage Trail and is well signed to the Dürnstein Castle ruins, then less so in the forest and through Weissenkirchen. The confidence marker on trail is a wavy letter *W*. The trail is also signed for the Welterbesteig (World Heritage Trail).

Other notes about the route:

- This hike is best done after 9:30 a.m. Thursday through Sunday, as well as on holidays, when the hut on the top of the ridge, Fesslhütte, is open (see Online Resources).
- You can walk this trail in the opposite direction (from Weissenkirchen to Dürnstein), but it's more beautiful to walk toward Weissenkirchen. Walking in this direction also allows you to tackle most of the elevation gain while your legs are still fresh.
- The forested sections of this hike can be buggy depending on the time of year and how much rain there's been; bring bug spray.

Alternative Routes and Activities

For a shorter option, at 2.8 miles (4.5 km), in the forested section of the hike, there is a turnoff for Gartenhotel und Weingut Pfeffel (see Online Resources). The boot path takes you down to the shores of the Danube in 20 minutes on a path that isn't on most maps. From the hotel-winery, you can walk back to Dürnstein along the river.

Or extend your outing by exploring Weissenkirchen, a slightly larger town than Dürnstein that boasts many wineries, *heurige* and tasting rooms.

Navigating

The hike starts at the Dürnstein Altstadt trailhead on Hauptstrasse, at the south-east end of the Dürnstein town center and next to the cemetery, with many restaurants and cafés nearby on Hauptstrasse where you can provision before your hike. (For a favorite, check out nearby Bäckerei Schmidl.) The trailhead sign is bright yellow, and it's easiest to spot from the northwest.

STARTING POINT: **48.39467°, 15.52095°**

TRANSIT: **The hike ends in Weissenkirchen, where Bus 715 (direction Krems) runs hourly from the intersection of Untere Bachgasse and the B3 for the approximately 5-minute trip back to Dürnstein. You can find the timetable for Bus 715 at local tourist information offices. Times are also available on Google Maps.**

MAPS: **Available at tourist information offices in Krems, Weissenkirchen and Melk. A booklet called *Hikers' Guide: Wachau World Heritage Trail*, which contains simplified maps of each stage of the trail, can also be downloaded for free from the trail's website (see Online Resources).**

1 Head up the footpath, also called the Ruinenweg, from the **Dürnstein Altstadt trailhead**. From here, the ruins are signed for 20 minutes and the end of the hike in Weissenkirchen's Marktplatz for 6 hours. Straight out of the gate, the path leads up, up, up, with many stairs along the way. As you gain elevation, you start to rise above the buildings of town, affording you some pretty great views of the village with the river in the background.

2 Catch your breath at a bench with a beautiful panorama at 0.3 mile (0.5 km).

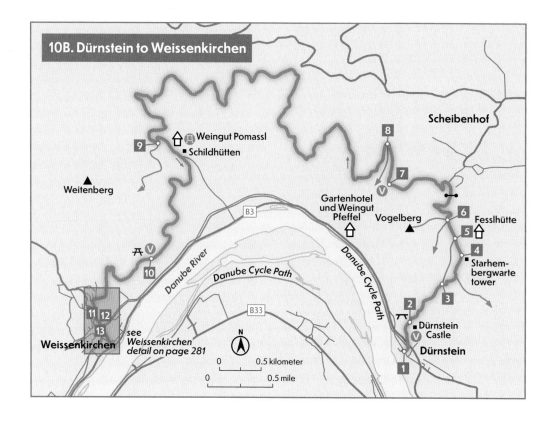

Scheibenhof

Weingut Pomassl

Schildhütten

Weitenberg

Gartenhotel
und Weingut
Pfeffel   Vogelberg

Fesslhütte

Starhem-
bergwarte
tower

Danube River

Danube Cycle Path

Danube Cycle Path

Weissenkirchen

see
Weissenkirchen
detail on page 281

Dürnstein
Castle

Dürnstein

N

0   0.5 kilometer

0   0.5 mile

Just past the bench on the main trail is the entrance to the **Dürnstein Castle** (open 24/7, free). It's worth the short detour to walk in and around the jutting rocks, all that's left of the castle that once famously held Richard the Lionheart for several months from 1192 to 1193, when he was imprisoned on his way back from the Third Crusade after dishonoring the Austrian flag. Although the imprisonment of Richard the Lionheart inspired tales such as Robin Hood, Austrians love to talk instead about the king's troubadour, Blondel, who traveled through the Holy Roman Empire from castle to castle singing Lionheart's favorite song in order to find him. Legend has it that when he sang the song beneath a high

barred window of the Dürnstein Castle, the king answered by singing the second verse.

TIP: The view of Dürnstein and the Wachau Valley from the castle is the most stunning one you'll have of the area all trip, so pack your camera and take your time. Photos from the ruins are particularly majestic as the sun is rising and setting. When you're done exploring the ruins, continue uphill with great peek-a-boo views of the Danube.

3 At 0.8 mile (1.3 km), the trail splits. Go right; on a rock step you'll see some signage, as well as a green sign nearby for Fesslhütte in 30 minutes. The path becomes less rocky as the trail splits again at 0.9 mile (1.4 km); this time head left.

4 Reach the **Starhembergwarte tower**, which dates back to 1882, at 1.1 miles (1.8 km). You can enter the tower and climb the staircase, but the openings at the top of the staircase are locked. The tower marks the top of your first climb; from here, the elevation gain on trail is more gradual.

5 If you're ready for coffee and a snack, you'll be happy to see **Fesslhütte** at 1.3 miles (2.1 km). The mountain hut has seating both inside and out and is a cozy place to take a load off before continuing. From here, the next opportunity for refreshments, Weingut Pomassl, is signed for 3 hours, Weissenkirchen for 4.5 hours.

6 At 1.4 miles (2.3 km), several routes converge in the forest around the **Vogelberg**, a pyramid-like rock that juts into the air. At the first junction, go straight. Almost immediately, come to another junction and head right. Your route becomes a wide road through the forest. Walking through the trees allows you to focus not on the views but on the sounds—you're surrounded by birds. Walk around a gate at 1.9 miles (3.1 km), then veer onto a footpath at the junction just beyond, one that's clearly signed for the **Welterbesteig** (World Heritage Trail).

7 As your route takes you through the forest, it's easy to feel worlds away from the Danube and its vineyards. You'll finally catch a glimpse of the **Danube** and **Rossatz** across the water at 2.5 miles (4 km). This is what you have to look forward to as you follow the topography of the ridge for the next 5 miles (8 km) or so, a peaceful alternation of forest and peek-a-boo views.

NOTE: In this forested section, there is a network of unsigned paths; follow these directions carefully. It also helps to follow my GPX tracks.

8 At 2.8 miles (4.5 km), come to a turnoff for **Pfaffental**. If you're interested in shortening the hike, you could be at **Gartenhotel und Weingut Pfeffel**, near the shores of the Danube, in 20 minutes. NOTE: This boot path isn't on most maps of the area, and thus isn't shown on the hike map included here. To return to Dürnstein proper from the hotel-winery, head east on the Danube Cycle Path. If you're not taking this shortcut back, head straight and follow the trail as it makes a sharp turn left.

9 At 7.7 miles (12.4 km), go left and leave the main track behind as you come to the buildings of **Schildhütten** and **Weingut Pomassl**, a family-owned winery that operates a *heuriger*, or wine tavern, several weeks a year. *Heurige* (the plural form of the word) are an Austrian tradition; they're an opportunity for winemakers to serve new wine in a family-friendly atmosphere (many have playgrounds outside, including Weingut Pomassl). They operate under a special license that only allows them to be open during alternating months during the growing season, so check the winery's website (see Online Resources) to verify if and when Weingut Pomassl is open.

Just past the winery, at 8 miles (12.9 km), take the footpath on the right to head into the vineyards above Weissenkirchen. Your path is not just a walking path; it's also an access route for those working in the

From the vineyards, you get the best views of the wine-producing village of Weissenkirchen.

vineyards—and the equipment they bring with them. Step aside as needed. There are multiple benches along this stretch from which to enjoy the vineyards.

10 The most beautiful rest spot comes at 9.3 miles (15 km), where a table has been placed among the vines to take in the views of Weissenkirchen and the Danube. A sign on an ornate metal cross reads, "Dear walker, rest here, where your eyes capture the most beautiful valley." This is indeed one of the most enchanting views of the valley that you'll have during your time in the Wachau. As you continue your walk to Weissenkirchen, you'll pass several family wineries like the one that placed this table in the vineyards. Be on the lookout for ones that are open for *heuriger* service or self-service—some sell wine on the honor system or via a vending machine.

11 At 10.3 miles (16.6 km), go left and climb the *kirchensteig*, or church stairs, to **Pfarrkirche Mariä Himmelfahrt**.

12 Built into the walls of the outside church gate are free public restrooms. Walk past the main church entrance to find another set of stairs that descend to **Weissenkirchen's Marktplatz**, the official end of stage two of the Wachau World Heritage Trail.

TIP: Thirsty? There's a wine vending machine in an alcove across from the covered staircase. If you'd rather find a *heuriger* or restaurant for a post-hike snack, two good options are Kremser

---

Weingut Pomassl is also signed as Weingut Pomaβl; the German character β is roughly equivalent to ss.

Strasse (to the left as you descend the stairs) and Obere Bachgasse (head right after you descend the stairs and then take another right on Obere Bachgasse).

13 To reach the bus stop with return service to Dürnstein, take a left at 10.5 miles (16.9 km) on Untere Bachgasse and walk to the intersection with the B3; the bus stop is on the left, next to **Weissenkirchen Tourist Information**.

TIP: My favorite *heuriger* in Weissenkirchen is Weingut-Heuriger Hermenegild Mang (see Online Resources), which has a large playground and extensive outdoor seating and is located very close to the bus stop, along the B3.

Bonus Hike: Wachau World Heritage Trail

There are twelve more stages of the 112-mile (180 km) Wachau World Heritage Trail to enjoy, several of which are accessible by bus from Dürnstein. There's also a 56-mile (90 km) Jauerling loop, which can be broken up into seven stages. For more

information, check out tourism information for the Wauchau in Online Resources.

10C EMMERSDORF LOOP

Explore the fields and forests of the Austrian Danube's only nature park

The Emmersdorf Loop is a terrific way to get beyond the vineyards that dominate the Wachau Valley and experience the local farmland that's just as beautiful. Starting near the Danube River in the town of Emmersdorf (or more formally, Emmersdorf an der Donau), curve through the town and head out into fields with amazing views of the famous Melk Abbey. Pass through two small agricultural hamlets before making your way through oak, pine and spruce forests to a traditional working farm with animals and a delicious restaurant. Enjoy more field and forest walking on your way to gorgeous elevated views of Emmersdorf and the surrounding area.

ON THE TRAIL

DURATION: **4 hours**

DIFFICULTY: **Moderate**

DISTANCE: **7.3 miles (11.7 km)**

ELEVATION GAIN: **1,105 feet (337 m)**

ELEVATION LOSS: **1,105 feet (337 m)**

START: **"Emmersdorf/Donau Bundesstrasse"** eastbound bus stop in Emmersdorf

END: **"Emmersdorf/Donau Bundesstrasse"** eastbound bus stop in Emmersdorf

EAT + DRINK: **Gasthaus Langthaler (see Online Resources), Emmersdorf**

Know Before You Go

The trail is relatively long and has just over 1,100 feet (335 m) of elevation gain. The walking surface is easy, though, and makes use of paved roads, country roads and dirt footpaths. A couple of different routes loop around Emmersdorf, and this walk is mainly on the shorter loop trail, which is sometimes signed as such but sometimes signed more generally as the Emmersdorfer Rundwanderweg, or Emmersdorf Loop. Since signage is sometimes spotty, navigate using the walking directions here, or use my GPX tracks, especially in the last third of the hike, if you have them.

This hike is best done on a weekend or holiday from April to October, when Gasthaus Langthaler, the charming guesthouse located at the halfway point, is open. (They're also open select weekdays; verify current hours of operation on their website, which you can find in Online Resources.)

Alternative Routes and Activities

You could extend your outing in a couple of ways if you have a car:

- Because Melk Abbey is only a short drive away, it's perfect to pair with this hike if you don't explore it as part of the Danube South Bank Bike Ride (see Bike Ride 10D).
- After your hike, check out the Naturpark Gasthaus am Jauerling hut (see Online Resources; it's a 20-minute drive followed by a 10-minute walk) for beautiful views of the Jauerling mountain range and a higher-elevation taste of the Jauerling-Wachau Nature Park. TIP: The *käsespätzle*, a salty and cheesy pasta typically served with chunks of bacon, is the best around; the hut is closed on Wednesdays. For even more views of the nature park, don't miss the nearby Aussichtswarte Jauerling observation tower. For more information on attractions in the nature park, check out the park's website (see Online Resources).

My favorite view of Emmersdorf comes near the end of the Emmersdorf Loop, just before you cross a meadow and into the village.

Navigating

This hike begins at the "Emmersdorf/ Donau Bundesstrasse" eastbound bus stop in Emmersdorf, which is very close to the entrance to town. If you need any supplies, there is a Nah und Frisch supermarket nearby.

STARTING POINT: 48.24070°, 15.33700°

TRANSIT: From Dürnstein, take Bus 715 (direction Melk Bahnhof) to the start of the trail. The bus runs hourly for the approximately 30-minute trip to the "Emmersdorf/ Donau Bundesstrasse" westbound bus stop. The bus back to Dürnstein (direction Krems/ Donau Bahnhof) leaves from the eastbound island bus stop just a few feet away. You can find the timetable for Bus 715 at local tourist information offices. Times are also available on Google Maps.

DRIVING: From Dürnstein, it's a 30-minute drive along the B3 to reach Emmersdorf. The easiest parking for the hike is at the Emmersdorf dock (48.24201°, 15.33913°), across the B3 from Hotel Donauhof. Parking here is free. To find the start of the trail, double back through the parking lot to the eastbound island bus stop on the B3.

MAPS: Available at the tourist information office in Emmersdorf.

1 From the eastbound island bus stop, head into the town of **Emmersdorf** on the main street in front of you. More shops and restaurants are open later in the day, so save your exploration of the town until after your hike. Walk toward the large viaduct, and when the road splits just before it, take the road on the left,

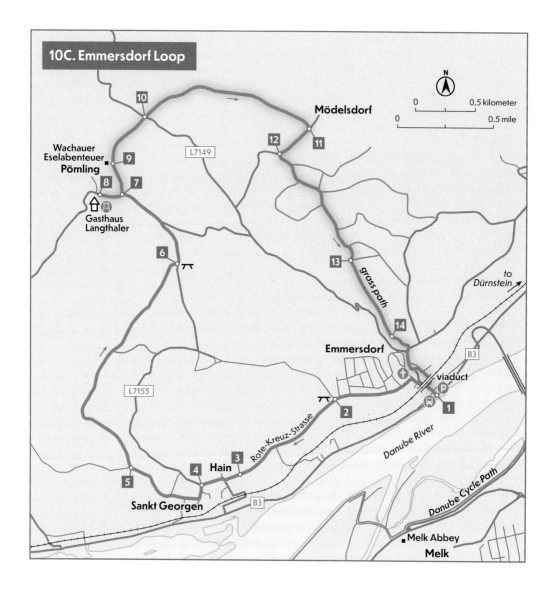

Mödelsdorf

0   0.5 kilometer

0   0.5 mile

Wachauer
Eselabenteuer
Pömling

L7149

Gasthaus
Langthaler

to
Dürnstein

grass path

Emmersdorf

viaduct

B3

L7155

Rote-Kreuz-Strasse

Danube River

Hain

Danube Cycle Path

Sankt Georgen

B3

Melk Abbey

Melk

Rote-Kreuz-Strasse. Almost immediately, the road curves left; stay on it as it heads into the fields on the outskirts of town—and soon, to views across the water to the famous **Melk Abbey**.

2 Arrive at a bench under a chestnut tree to enjoy the views at 0.6 mile (1 km). You'll also find your first trail sign for the Emmersdorfer Rundwanderweg, or Emmersdorf Loop. As you continue, the land becomes more agricultural until you're surrounded by wheat, corn and wildflowers growing alongside the road and the hum of grasshoppers everywhere. Occasional benches underneath large trees help you take it all in.

3 Enter **Hain**, the first of two small farming communities, at 1.2 miles (1.9

km). Keep your eye out for free-ranging chickens, the sign advertising fresh eggs and the corresponding self-service stand. There's not much else in quiet Hain, save a few houses, and the same holds true of the next town, Sankt Georgen.

4 At 1.4 miles (2.3 km), when you enter **Sankt Georgen**, two routes diverge. Drivers stay straight for the more direct (and busier) road to Pömling and Gasthaus Langthaler. Hikers should go left to stay on more walking-friendly roads. Take a right at the next street before heading back into the fields and starting a gradual climb that will continue for the next 3.4 miles (5.5 km).

5 At 1.9 miles (3.1 km) from the start of the hike, take a right onto a gravel track and into a tunnel of foliage that leads to more fields and the first wooded section of your hike. Walk past pine and spruce trees, a Christmas tree farm and deer stands (hunting blinds). If you're lucky, you'll also find patches of ripe wild raspberries along the trail. At 2.8 miles (4.5 km), veer left when the route splits.

6 Leave the forest for a paved country road once again at 3.3 miles (5.3 km). Head left and find a bench that's perfect for a short break. Continue to walk uphill, staying on the main road when another road joins it from the east.

7 The road Ts at 3.7 miles (6 km) at the entrance to the hamlet of **Pömling**. Although the main route continues right (you'll backtrack to this junction), first head left for the short walk to Gasthaus Langthaler, which is well worth the detour.

8 **Gasthaus Langthaler**, at 3.9 miles (6.3 km), is a working farm that has plenty to offer visitors, especially families. There is a field full of deer that you can feed, as well as rabbits to pet and pigs to peek in on. TIP: Bring coins if you want to purchase little packets of food for the animals. There's also a sizable playground for kids to get their energy out. Once you've taken in all of the farm attractions, you can enjoy traditional German food in the restaurant's

Kids love the many animals at Gasthaus Langthaler.

pretty little courtyard. When you're done at Gasthaus Langthaler, backtrack to [7] and head uphill.

9 You'll pass **Wachauer Eselaben-teuer**, a donkey farm that offers pre-arranged guided donkey excursions, at 4.2 miles (6.8 km). TIP: To schedule an excursion, email Anita, the owner (see Online Resources).

10 At 4.5 miles (7.2 km), cross the main road and head into the forest on a shaded walking path that's alive with the sound of birdsong. Partway through this forest track, the trail starts to head downhill. Wind through the trees until you join the paved road to Mödelsdorf.

11 Reach the tiny enclave of **Mödelsdorf** at 5.4 miles (8.7 km). There aren't any services in town—it's just a smattering of houses—so take a right when the road Ts and head into the countryside once again. You won't be on the paved road for long.

12 In just 0.2 mile (0.3 km), at 5.6 miles (9 km), veer off on the Emmersdorf Loop–signed footpath to your left. Almost immediately, as you approach the forest, the trail splits. NOTE: This is where things can get a little tricky. Several logging roads and boot paths wind through this last forest that stands between you and Emmersdorf, and the quickest way back to town utilizes both the secondary and main loop trails, which aren't consistently signed here. Take the path on the right, then stay straight when the trail splits again. Just past that, reach another junction, this one of three different trails. Head right, then

stay straight (there will be several trails meeting up with yours at right angles) until you reach a grass path down into the fields at 6.4 miles (10.3 km).

13 The grass path that leads back to Emmersdorf is beautiful and provides wonderful views of **Schönbühel Castle** to the left and Emmersdorf, the Romanesque-Gothic parish church of **Sankt Nikolaus**, and **Rothenhof Castle** straight ahead. This is one of the very best, and most peaceful, sections of the whole trail, and it ties the hike up nicely.

14 At 6.8 miles (10.9 km), the grassy footpath ends at a paved road. Stay straight, weaving your way through farm buildings on the outskirts of town. When you reach a T-intersection, head right and follow the main road around a curve, then go left when the road splits around the church of Sankt Nikolaus. Stay straight until you reach a set of stairs that descend to the lower part of **Emmersdorf** and trail signs marking the official start of the loop, near where you began. To reach the bus stops and parking along the B3, take a right at the bottom of the stairs and an immediate left. The B3 is a block away.

TIP: There is more to explore in Emmersdorf than you saw on your walk. To take in the majority of the shops and restaurants, stroll down Marktstrasse, or Market Street, which is at the base of the stairs at the end of the hike. The street is bisected by Georg Prunner Platz, so be sure to check out both sections.

10D DANUBE SOUTH BANK BIKE RIDE

Take a 2.5-hour boat cruise on the Danube to the famous Melk Abbey, then bike back to Dürnstein along the south bank of the river

This bike ride is an excellent opportunity to experience not only the beautiful Danube, as you cruise its blue waters, but also the south bank of the river. Start your adventure with a 2.5-hour boat cruise from Dürnstein to Melk, during which you can watch the scenery of the Wachau Valley pass by as you enjoy local food and drink specialties from the ship's sundeck. For an optional side trip, explore the town of Melk and the famous Melk Abbey, which dates back to 1089. Then hop on the Danube Cycle Path, a paved and mainly flat route that follows the south bank of the river past orchards growing cherries and apricots, vineyards that produce some of the world's best white wine and a chain of small villages. Along the way, there are many places to eat and drink, from *imbiss* stands to *heurige*—and even a wine vending machine or two.

ON THE TRAIL

DURATION: **2.5 hours**

DIFFICULTY: **Easy**

DISTANCE: **17.9 miles (28.8 km)**

ELEVATION GAIN: **1,010 feet (308 m)**

ELEVATION LOSS: **1,050 feet (320 m)**

START: **Boat dock in Melk**

END: **Rossatz–Dürnstein ferry dock in Dürnstein**

EAT + DRINK: **Melk, Schönbühel, Aggsbach, Aggstein, Oberarnsdorf, Sankt Lorenz, Rossatz**

Know Before You Go

The elevation gain on this route is spread out over nearly 18 miles, so this is a mostly flat bike ride. To make it even easier, you can rent an e-bike. The route as described follows the Donauradweg, or Danube Cycle Path (part of EuroVelo Route 6), on the south side of the Danube River. The bike path is relatively well signed. Follow the signs for Krems and Mautern.

Other notes about the route:

- Take the boat from Dürnstein to Melk and tour Melk Abbey before starting the

bike ride so that you get everything that is scheduled out of the way first and can take your time stopping wherever you want to on the bike ride back to your home base. But if you prefer to bike to Melk and return to Dürnstein via the boat, I still recommend biking on the south bank of the river, which has the nicest views and the most places to stop.

- You can also bike both directions, rather than taking a boat one-way. If you bike to and from Melk, ride the Danube Cycle

Path on both sides of the river to vary your scenery.

- There are a couple of good options for renting bikes. Regiothek Wachau (see Online Resources) rents a variety of bikes and will deliver them to your accommodations. You could also rent a bike from nextbike (see Online Resources), which has self-service bike stands throughout the Wachau Valley, including in Melk (near the bridge into town) and Dürnstein (near the dock for the boat to Melk). Pack a bike lock so you can confidently leave your bike as you explore. If you're using my GPX tracks, bring a handlebar-mounted cell-phone holder.

Alternative Routes and Activities

For a shorter outing, take a bus back to Dürnstein from the north side of the river; you can cross to the north bank to catch a bus from multiple places on the south bank.

Extend your outing with one of these activities:

- This is the perfect opportunity to explore the town of Melk and its famous abbey. Buy tickets for Melk Abbey in advance; you can count on spending about 2.5 hours there (see What to See and Do).
- Stretch the bike ride to several hours by stopping to explore the many towns and restaurants along it. You can also swim in the Danube.

Navigating

This bike ride begins from Melk's main boat dock, which is on a little peninsula just outside of town. There aren't any services until you cross the bridge to town at 0.6 mile (1 km).

From the Danube Cycle Path, you can see the Hinterhaus ruins (on the hill to the left).

STARTING POINT: 48.23456°, 15.33114°

TRANSIT: There are several boat docks in Dürnstein. The correct one for the boat to Melk is at the base of the Grübelgasse stairs, which connect Dürnstein's Hauptstrasse (Main Street) with the Danube Cycle Path on the north shore of the river.

Several boat companies cruise the river to Melk, but I suggest DDSG Blue Danube (see Online Resources), which runs up to three boats a day in peak season for the 2.5-hour ride to Melk. Tickets can be purchased online and you need to pay extra if you bring a bike on board. There's a bar on the top deck of the boat. (Head up there imme-diately for a seat—they fill up fast. If you miss out at first, try again when the boat docks in Spitz and a lot of people disembark.) You can also pay to eat lunch in the ship's dining room, which is windowed so you can enjoy the views. You can order à la carte or there is a buffet filled with regional specialties. TIP: Make a table reservation in advance as tables can fill up fast. Also, the food in the buffet dwindles as you get close to Melk, so eat early if you want the best selection. The boat will drop you off at the main boat dock in Melk.

At the end of the bike ride, there is a small private passenger ferry (see Online Resources) to get you from Rossatz, on the south shore of the river, back to Dürnstein on the north shore. From May to September, the ferry runs daily. There's no real schedule; the boat crosses whenever it has enough people, and it takes around 15 minutes to transit the river. Bikes are allowed on board for a small surcharge. In Dürnstein, the boat drops off at a dock on the Danube Cycle Path, 0.2 mile (0.3 km) southeast of the boat dock where you started the day.

MAPS: Available at tourist information offices in Krems, Weissenkirchen and Melk.

1 From the dock in Melk, pedal through the parking lot to the main road leaving the peninsula. Pass a campground, an event arena and, just before the bridge into Melk, a nextbike stand with rental bikes.

2 After crossing the bridge at 0.6 mile (1 km), you'll see **Melk Abbey** towering above you. To explore Melk and/or the abbey, cross the main road and head into town on the road straight ahead, Kremser Strasse, which will take you to the town center at Hauptplatz and onto Haupt-strasse. From there, you will see signage for Melk Abbey. There is a staircase short-cut up to the abbey for walkers, but for bike access, continue on Hauptstrasse, which will turn into Wiener Strasse. Just after Café Teufner, take a left; the road leads to a small parking lot in front of the abbey that has bike stands. NOTE: This optional side trip is not included in the mileage and ele-vation gain of the bike ride.

When you're done exploring, backtrack to the bridge (cross the B1 again) and head northeast on the wide bike and pedestrian path (to the right, when you're looking at the bridge from the direction of town). Your first trail sign for the **Donaurad-weg** (Danube Cycle Path) comes in just a few feet, where you veer left on a smaller path to follow the trail in the direction of Mautern and Krems.

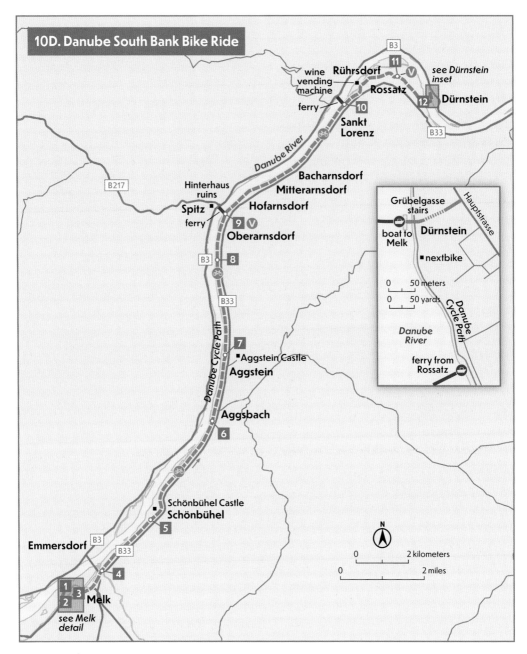

10D. Danube South Bank Bike Ride

B3

11
wine
vending—
machine
Rührsdorf
V
see Dürnstein
inset

Rossatz
12
Dürnstein
ferry
10

Sankt
Lorenz
B33

Danube River

Bacharnsdorf
Mitterarnsdorf

B217
Hinterhaus
ruins
Hofarnsdorf

Spitz
ferry
9 V
Oberarnsdorf

B3
8

B33

Danube Cycle Path

7
▪Aggstein Castle
Aggstein

Aggsbach
6

Schönbühel Castle
Schönbühel
5

Emmersdorf
B3
B33
4

1 3
2 Melk
see Melk
detail

Dürnstein inset:
Grübelgasse
stairs
Hauptstrasse
boat to
Melk
Dürnstein
▪nextbike

0   50 meters
0   50 yards

Danube
River

Danube Cycle Path

ferry from
Rossatz

N

0   2 kilometers
0   2 miles

3 At 0.9 mile (1.4 km), when you come to an intersection with a road that bridges the water, go right toward the main road. When you reach that main road, the B1, head left on the signed bike path, which initially runs alongside the B1 and then the B33.

4 At 2.1 miles (3.4 km), the bike path leaves the main road behind and begins what will be its normal route alongside the water. It's a lovely path, with the river on your left and the countryside, vineyards and towns on your right. As you pedal, you'll get good views of everything, from people launching kayaks and sunbathing along the calm side channels of the Danube to farmers working their fields. There are many places to stop and enjoy the views—shady sections in the trees (a good respite from the sun on a hot day) and pretty little beaches.

5 Reach the small town of **Schönbühel** at 3.6 miles (5.8 km), where you'll cycle past several restaurants down by the water. Just after that, at 3.7 miles (6 km), there's an optional detour; if you take a left on Schlossstrasse, you can admire the **Schön-bühel Castle**, which is closed to visitors but makes a pretty picture alongside the river.

6 At 6.6 miles (10.6 km), pedal into the outskirts of another small town, **Aggs-bach**, where you'll find a traditional *imbiss*, or fast-food, stand near the ferry landing. In Austria, *imbiss* stands are a great choice when you want something quick to eat and don't need sit-down service. Don't let the term "fast food" fool you, though. These aren't chains and they don't necessarily serve burgers and fries, although some do. Rather, here you'll find sausages and pretzels on the go. TIP: If you'd like to explore more of Aggsbach, you can get to the center of the village by taking a right on Hauptstrasse in 0.3 mile (0.5 km).

7 At 8.1 miles (13 km), just beyond the town of Aggstein, there's another spot on trail to stop and eat. This one is very

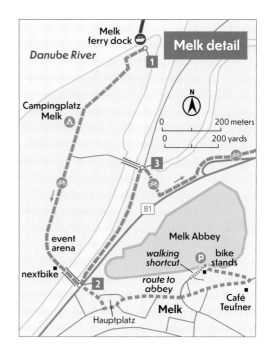

popular with bikers and is in the shadow of the hillside ruins of the twelfth-century **Aggstein Castle**, a great destination for another day (see What to See and Do).

8 At 10.4 miles (16.7 km), you'll start to pedal past beautiful orchards and then vineyards. This is such a peaceful part of the trail. Keep your eye out for farm stands selling fruit like cherries and apricots on the honor system—and have cash on hand.

9 Also not to be missed—the best on-trail castle view you'll have all bike ride at 11.4 miles (18.3 km), of the **Hinterhaus ruins** (see Online Resources; free and open to the public) across the water, perched above the town of **Spitz**. Around this same mile marker, you'll enter the village of **Oberarnsdorf**, which is followed in relatively quick succession by **Hofarnsdorf**,

The pedestrian ferry from Rossatz to Dürnstein allows bikes for a small surcharge.

Mitterarnsdorf and **Bacharnsdorf**. There are occasional food stands and restaurants alongside the trail in these spots.

10 At 15.3 miles (24.6 km), enter my favorite part of the ride, the section that runs through tiny **Sankt Lorenz**, small **Rührsdorf** and not-quite-as-small **Rossatz**. It feels very idyllic as you pedal along a lazy side channel of the Danube, where the communities are small and quaint, the houses have lovely gardens and you pass several *heurige*, or wine taverns. At

15.9 miles (25.6 km), there's even a wine vending machine along the trail.

11 At 17.2 miles (27.7 km), you'll get your first views of **Dürnstein** across the water. Just 0.1 mile (0.2 km) later, you can take an optional detour into Rossatz by taking a right on In der Tölling, across from the Rossatz playground. The town has several shops and *heurige*. To return to Dürnstein, you must take a ferry across the Danube. The turnoff for the **Rossatz–Dürnstein ferry** is on your left at 17.8 miles (28.6 km).

12 Reach the ferry landing at 17.9 miles (28.8 km). It runs on demand (see the Transit section of Navigating), and in the summer there can be a queue, but you'll find plenty to do here while you wait. The beach is good for swimming and enjoying the views across the water to Dürnstein, and you can even get a cold beer from a beach bar. You may find yourself giving up your place in the ferry line, like I did, to stay a little longer before heading back to Dürnstein.

Bonus Bike Ride: Danube Cycle Path

The Danube South Bank Bike Ride is part of the larger Danube Cycle Path, which runs for 1,200 miles from Donaueschingen in Germany to the Hungarian capital of Budapest. There are several stages in Lower Austria, and the path runs on both sides of the Danube. For more information, check out tourism information for the Wachau in Online Resources.

PART

2

PLAN AND PACK

CHAPTER

3

PRIME YOUR BODY

One of the best places to start when it comes to preparing for the home base hiking trip of a lifetime is with your body. You don't need to be a superathlete to walk Europe but you should still train for the trails you'll be hiking to ensure you're as healthy and prepared as possible for your trip. Training helps you prevent injuries that can make it difficult or painful to move, or can even cut your walk short entirely. It also guarantees that you'll enjoy your trip as much as possible. After all, it's hard to take in everything around you, from the wildflowers to the birds to the incredible views, when you're having a hard time making it up the trail. Training also gives you time to get to know your body and figure out where you might have issues—and then come up with solutions in advance.

TRAIN FOR THE TRAIL

You can't start optimizing your body for the trail unless you're already relatively fit, so your initial challenge is to get to that point. What does that mean? For the purposes of home base hiking Europe, it means you can walk 6 miles (9.7 km) with 500 feet (150 m) of elevation gain in 3 hours, no problem. If you're not able to do that yet, check out the "Build Your Base Level of Fitness" sidebar. If you're already there, great! Keep reading.

Now for the fine print: I'm not a doctor or a personal trainer. The information in this chapter is based on what I've discovered over years of researching for and experimenting with optimizing my own body for walking—and on my travel companions' experiences too. It should be a good starting point for you as well. Let the training commence!

BUILD YOUR BASE LEVEL OF FITNESS

If you're not already relatively fit, don't despair. Depending on where you're starting from, you can improve your fitness in as little as three to six months if you do a couple of workouts each of cardio and strength training every week. If you're not sure where to start, talk to your doctor or a professional trainer. They can design a training program for you based on your age, health and current fitness level. Most gym memberships come with a complimentary consultation. You could also check out the variety of free couch-to-5K training programs available online, which can help you increase your base level of fitness slowly and safely. Remember, getting fit doesn't need to be expensive or complicated. At the most basic level, all you need are some comfortable clothes, a pair of tennis shoes and the determination to keep yourself on track.

Training for your home base hiking trip is worth the effort; it can drastically improve your experience on trail.

Create a Training Plan

Start with a training calendar that assigns one of the four types of trail-fit workouts (cardiovascular training, strength training, flexibility and balance training, and walk training) to each day. Then adjust the time and intensity of your workout depending on what you're training for and how soon your trip is coming up. Here are the goals and guidelines for each type of training:

Cardiovascular training: Aim for a variety of aerobic activities for 30 minutes two times per week. Your goal is to fatigue your body but not exhaust it. This will strengthen your lungs and heart to make it easier to walk uphill.

There are plenty of books and online videos that offer detailed advice and specific exercises for training for hiking, including my own previous book *Explore Europe on Foot*.

Strength training: Do a variety of upper- and lower-body exercises two times per week. Always give yourself 48 hours between strength training sessions to recover and build more muscle. Strength training will strengthen your muscles so you can more easily walk uphill and down-hill and wear a backpack.

Flexibility and balance training: Work on stretching, yoga and balance twice a week. This goes a long way toward com-batting any achiness on trail and can help you walk on uneven terrain.

Walking: Get outside for a long walk at least once a week. Once you've mastered long walks, do them several days in a row to simulate the distance and elevation gain you'll tackle in Europe. Not only will this get you ready for walking several days a week, it will grow your confidence that you can do it comfortably.

In calendar format, your training plan could look like this:

TRAINING PLAN

DAY OF WEEK	TYPE OF WORKOUT
Sunday	Flexibility and balance training
Monday	Cardiovascular training
Tuesday	Strength training
Wednesday	Cardiovascular training
Thursday	Flexibility and balance training
Friday	Strength training
Saturday	Walking

You'll notice that I assign a workout for every day of the week. Some people suggest taking at least one day off each week, but I find it's a lot easier to do something every single day than sporadically. It seems to take less willpower to get yourself to work out when it becomes part of your daily rou-tine—a habit. I don't recommend working out hard every day, however, and that's the beauty of the flexibility and balance train-ing days; they are perfect for sitting on the grass in the park as you stretch and take the opportunity to physically and mentally recover.

Even if you're gung ho about starting your training program, ease into things. You don't need to jump into working out for an hour a day, especially if your body isn't at all used to it—you can do more harm than good that way, injuring yourself and burning out. So if you haven't worked out in a while, warm up for the first week by aiming for only 15 minutes of activity each day. If you're in great shape and active as can be, 30–45 minutes is probably your sweet spot.

Want to make your workouts more fun? Set a training goal with your travel companion and either work out together or hold each other accountable. And don't forget to give yourself some variety; if your workouts look the same week in and week out, you're likely to get bored and give up. Also, your muscles could get used to the exercises, and the workouts could lose their effectiveness. Increase your chances of sticking with your training goals by mixing things up a bit.

If you work out consistently, you should start to see results within six weeks, although your base level of fitness will start to increase long before that. If you're any-

The best thing you can do when something small is bothering you is to stop and fix it so it doesn't create a big problem.

thing like me, you'll love how healthy and toned your body starts to feel—and how much farther you can walk.

Address Any Aches and Pains

Once you start training for the trail, you may encounter some aches and pains. In a way, that's great, because it gives you time to evaluate and treat them now, before your trip. If you suspect you are injured, suspend your training and make an appointment with your doctor or see a sports medicine specialist. Your body may need professional attention.

Here are the most common aches and pains people experience when training for the trail—and some remedies that can help.

BLISTERS

Blisters are a walker's worst fear. The best thing you can do for blisters is to prevent them. In the months leading up to your trip, I recommend forgoing pedicures—and definitely don't remove any calluses. As unsightly as they are, you need those calluses to protect your delicate skin from friction and blisters.

Two foot-care tasks to keep in your routine: clipping your toenails short and filing down any nails that could snag your socks or impact your other toes. If you're blister prone, try walking in toe socks like the ones made by Injinji. If you have a hot spot, treat it as soon as you feel any pain or notice any rubbing.

One of the unique challenges of hiking in Europe is walking on uneven cobblestones. It helps to have strong ankles.

the general area. I like to aim for a margin of at least a half inch (1.25 cm) around the blister, if not more. Take the moleskin off at night while you sleep—airing your feet out (try sleeping with your feet out of the covers) will help everything dry out and heal.

IT (ILIOTIBIAL) BAND PAIN

What it feels like: Pain and sometimes inflammation on the outside of your upper leg.

How to make it better:
- Wear an IT band strap while you walk.
- Massage the tissue by rolling on your side on a firm foam roller.
- Do stretches that target the IT band.

KNEE PAIN

What it feels like: Pain and sometimes swelling in and around the kneecap.

How to make it better:
- Strengthen your legs, especially your inner thighs and hamstrings.
- Wear an elastic knee brace while you walk.

If it's too late for prevention and you already have a blister, drain it by piercing it with a clean needle—don't remove the skin, just deflate the bubble—and stick enough moleskin on top to cover and pad

TREAT TRAVELER'S DIARRHEA

The most common ailment you'll likely face in Europe is traveler's diarrhea. It usually strikes about the third day after you arrive; it can be caused by a number of things (including too much rich food or caffeine) and is usually more annoying than serious. Drink a lot of fluids (but avoid alcohol, sugar and dairy), rest and eat bland and starchy foods. If there's any blood in your stool, or if your diarrhea lasts for more than a couple of days, get an appointment with a local doctor (see the "I Think I Need a Doctor" sidebar for how to find one).

I THINK I NEED A DOCTOR

If you need medical attention in Europe for a minor ailment (for example, a fever) and you're in a town, it can save you quite a bit of time and money to head to the pharmacy before the doctor. European pharmacies have greater latitude on what they can prescribe than North American pharmacies, and oftentimes they'll have some medications available over the counter that you'd need a prescription for back home. If the pharmacy can't help you, they can refer you to a doctor or clinic.

If you need to see a doctor for a more serious health issue, the following resources can refer you to the right kind of physician—even one who speaks English:

- The local tourist information office
- Your guesthouse proprietor or hotel concierge
- Your travel health insurance company, via their 24-hour assistance number

- Search out flatter walks with less elevation gain and loss for your training walks and European adventure.
- Tackle softer trails—dirt paths rather than pavement.
- Use trekking poles.
- Take shorter steps and walk in a zigzag pattern (switchbacks) when going downhill.

GENERAL MUSCLE ACHES AND PAINS

How to make them better:

- Have an arsenal of stretches you do after you work out or walk.
- Make sure you drink enough water and consume enough electrolytes.
- Take a nonsteroidal anti-inflammatory such as ibuprofen for pain and inflammation (acetaminophen doesn't have an anti-inflammatory effect).
- Use an ice pack for 15–20 minutes on the affected area, especially if there's swelling.
- Don't rely on topical muscle-rub creams or gels: according to Mayo Clinic Sports Medicine, there's no conclusive evidence that they work.

CHAPTER

4

BUILD YOUR SKILLS

When it comes to preparing yourself for the walking component of home base hiking Europe, priming your body is only half of the battle. The other half is mastering a few key outdoor skills that will keep you safe, confident and happy on trail.

Ultimately, the number and type of outdoor skills you should add to your tool belt will be determined by how technical and remote the walks are that you're attempting. TIP: The hikes in this book aren't particularly remote and don't require any technical skills, but if you select your own hikes, check the trail guidebook or online description; any technical skills or special considerations that a trail requires should be spelled out. But there are five basics that you should learn no matter how challenging—or downright easy—your chosen trail is. They include learning how to hike with the help of GPS data, getting familiar with European measurements, planning for inclement weather, knowing how to get help and minding your trail manners.

LEARN HOW TO HIKE WITH THE HELP OF GPS DATA

One of the best advances in hiking has come in the form of navigating on trail with the help of GPS data. It's a game changer. I still bring along a paper map when I hike—you should always carry one as a backup—but mine now

European trails are typically well signed—much more so than trails in North America.

normally stays tucked in my pack. Here's a tutorial on the top things you need to know about GPS data and how you can use it to more easily navigate on trail in Europe.

What Are GPS Coordinates?

GPS coordinates are a unique identifier of a precise geographic location on the earth. They're typically made up of two parts, latitude and longitude, and in simplified form often look like this: 46.606285°, 7.921530°.

WHY THEY'RE HELPFUL

As long as you have active cell service, you can use Google Maps to navigate to the GPS coordinates of your choosing. This can come in very handy, for example, if you arrive at a hike by bus, train or car and

need help finding the exact right place to start the hike.

WHERE TO FIND THEM

If you open up Google Maps and navigate to a specific point you're interested in, clicking on that point will bring up a little box with the GPS coordinates. The GPS coordinates for each of the trailheads in this book are listed just before the walking directions in each hike write-up.

HOW TO USE THEM

To navigate to a set of GPS coordinates, open up Google Maps and type the numbers in the search bar, separated by a comma and without the degree symbol (e.g., 46.606285, 7.921530). Then hit "Directions." Google Maps will give you turn-by-turn directions to that specific location.

What Are GPX Tracks?

GPX tracks are a GPS route similar to what Google Maps gives you for driving directions, but for walking on trails. GPX files look like gobbledygook if you try to open them on your computer and typically have file extensions like .klm or .gpx.

Although GPX tracks can be helpful for navigating on trail, it's important to always have a paper map backup with you in case your GPS device breaks or dies.

WHY THEY'RE HELPFUL

If you download the GPX tracks for a route you're hiking, you can see exactly the path you should be on as well as the path you have been walking—the two lines are shown with different colors on your device. Keeping the two sets of lines one over the other means you're walking exactly where you want to be: on the route. There's something very reassuring about knowing where, exactly, you are on the map and which direction you're traveling in. More than once, I've missed an important junction that was poorly signed and needed the GPX tracks to get back on route.

WHERE TO FIND THEM

You can download GPX tracks from websites like AllTrails and Outdooractive. You can also create your own GPX tracks with

a program like Gaia GPS (see the next section). My GPX tracks for nearly all of the trails in this book are available for free (see the "Home Base GPX Tracks" sidebar in the Online Resources section at the back of the book).

THE MOST HELPFUL GPX TRACKS FOR THIS GUIDE

While I always prefer to navigate with GPX tracks, there are several trails in this book where they are especially helpful:

- 2A: Thiepval Memorial Loop
- 2C: Newfoundland Memorial Loop
- 2D: Saint-Valery-sur-Somme Coastal Loop
- 3A: Palamós to Calella de Palafrugell
- 3C: Pals to La Bisbal d'Empordà
- 4A: Luberon Countryside Bike Loop
- 6A: Männlichen to Wengernalp
- 7A: Footpath of Sant'Anna
- 7D: Turin Like a Local
- 8A: Marjan Hill Loop
- 8C: Mount Mosor Loop
- 9D: Kneifelspitze Loop
- 10A: Krems to Dürnstein
- 10B: Dürnstein to Weissenkirchen
- 10C: Emmersdorf Loop

HOW TO USE THEM

1 Pick a device: You can use GPX tracks on a variety of devices, and it can be a little overwhelming to choose which device you'll use for creating and following them. If you were planning to walk a remote trail through mostly wilderness and rely heavily on your device—and its dependability—for navigation, I'd recommend a stand-alone GPS unit. But for walking anywhere else (and for all of the trails in this book), use the Gaia GPS app on your smartphone, which will be significantly cheaper, lighter (you won't need a separate device, batteries or charger) and easier to use. TIP: The Gaia GPS app can navigate off-line but is at its most dependable when you have cell service so you can regularly refresh the maps. Sign up for an account on the Gaia GPS website, then download the free app and log in with your credentials. The following tips apply to Gaia GPS specifically.

2 Upload your GPX tracks: It's easiest to upload GPX tracks to your Gaia GPS account using their website. As long as you have used the same login information online and in the app, the information will automatically sync to the app.

3 Pull up the route: Go into the Gaia GPS app and find the routes you uploaded in the Saved tab. Click on the one you want to view.

4 Get directions to the trailhead: Once you're in your saved route, click "Directions" and Google Maps will open with transit, driving or walking directions to the trailhead.

5 See the route on a map: Pull up the route you want to hike and click on the map of the track. Select "Show on Main Map" and it will bring the route up as the main view. Oftentimes, I use this view when I hike, rather than "Guide Me" (see step 7).

6 See where you are on the map: Click the arrow icon in the bottom left of your route's map (when it's in the main view) and you'll automatically be centered on the map, with an arrow pointing in the direction you're traveling. Click the arrow until the icon turns into two arrows pointing toward each other and then the base layer map will keep you centered as you walk. (I have this view on when I walk and ride my bike because it eliminates the guesswork of where I am and which direction the map should be pointed in.)

7 Have Gaia guide you on trail (optional): Pull up the route you want to hike and click on "More," then "Guide Me."

8 Practice at home: Go to AllTrails or Outdooractive, or even use the search function in the Gaia GPS app, to find GPX tracks of trails near you. Download them and then upload them to Gaia GPS (or from the Gaia GPS app, simply save them to your account), then practice the steps above (over and over, if needed) until you're comfortable navigating on trail with GPX tracks. The more you practice at home, the more confident you'll be navigating on trail in Europe.

When you hike with a GPS device, even one that functions as an app on your phone, always pack a power bank and a cord to charge up on trail—having your screen on and following GPX tracks drains your device a lot faster than normal.

GET FAMILIAR WITH EUROPEAN MEASUREMENTS

It only takes looking at a trail sign, your guesthouse's weather report or the train station clock to know that Europe expresses distance, temperature and time differently from what you may be used to. Here are some tips for decoding those foreign measurements:

Distance

Most European countries use the metric system, which means that most of the distances you'll see—from walking directions to trail signs—will be in kilometers. If that's not the standard measurement at home (that's you, Americans), practice converting kilometers to miles. Multiply the number of kilometers by six and then move the decimal point one spot to the left. For example, 10 kilometers is approximately 6 miles (10 × 6 = 60, then move the decimal one spot to the left to yield 6.0).

Temperature

To know what to wear for your walk, it helps to know what the temperature forecast is. In Europe, that's measured in Celsius, not Fahrenheit. But don't despair, fellow Americans. It's not that hard to figure out what temperature to expect: Multiply the number in Celsius by two and add thirty. For example, 10 degrees Celsius is approximately 50 degrees Fahrenheit (10 × 2 = 20, 20 + 30 = 50). Or just remember this cute rhyme: "Zero's freezing, ten is not; twenty is warm and thirty hot."

Time

In Europe, the 24-hour clock, rather than the 12-hour clock, is the standard (as it is for military time). Midnight is 0:00 on the 24-hour clock, and the times between that and 12:59 p.m. are the same on both clocks. To figure out what time you're looking at on the 24-hour clock for any time between 1:00 p.m. and 11:59 p.m., subtract twelve. For example, to convert 19:30 to the 12-hour clock, subtract twelve, which means it's 7:30 p.m.

PLAN FOR INCLEMENT WEATHER

If weather conditions change suddenly when you're on trail, you need to be able to handle anything that nature throws at you. Here's how to cope with the most common weather situations that can sneak up on you while you're walking:

Intense Sun

Make sure to stay hydrated—drink at least 1 liter of water an hour in warm climates—reapply your sunscreen at least once every 2 hours, and limit your exposure to the sun as much as possible; for example, take your breaks in the shade.

Intense Rain

Put on your raingear and pack cover as soon as possible and seek shelter even if it's just under a big tree, until the worst of the storm has passed. Watch your footing on rocks and other surfaces that could be slick. If you're in a canyon or another place that could be in danger of flash flooding, head for higher ground.

> What should you do if your walking shoes get soaked on trail? As soon as you get to your accommodations for the night, stick as much newspaper in your shoes as will fit. It'll absorb the water better than pretty much anything else. Make sure to swap in dry paper every hour or so until you go to bed (or you run out of newsprint), and leave it in your shoes overnight. By morning, your shoes should be only damp, if not completely dry.

Lightning

Stay away from exposed ridges, rock faces, meadows and marshy areas. Whenever possible, seek shelter in uniform forests, where the trees are all roughly the same height. Stay low to the ground while bringing your arms and legs in to give your body the smallest footprint possible; a crouching position is best—don't lie down.

Fog

Slow down and take care to stay on the trail; if you get lost, stop and wait until visibility improves before trying to find your way. If you get chilled, do jumping jacks or squats to stay warm while you wait for the fog to lift.

Snow

Fight the cold by putting on extra layers. Watch your footing; trails can be very slick, especially if there's ice in addition to snow. If you have traction devices (such

Wear or bring layers when you hike to keep yourself comfortable no matter the weather. (Photo by Caroline Calaway)

as Yaktrax) with you, put them on. Don't proceed if the trail is unsafe to walk.

KNOW HOW TO GET HELP

You should always know how to call for help from the trail if you need it. If you have cell phone service, this can be as simple as dialing the local emergency number or **the international emergency number: 112**. This international emergency number works for most of the countries in the European Union, as well as for many other countries around the world. Before you travel, verify that it's valid in the country you're traveling to.

Things get a little trickier when you're walking in an area with no cell phone service. If it's important to you to have the peace of mind that comes with being able to send an emergency signal no matter what, consider carrying a SPOT device, a satellite communicator or a personal locator beacon.

If you're confident that there will be a decent number of other walkers on your route and that civilization, even a mildly popular road, is somewhat nearby (as with the recommended trails in this book), you could ask a passerby to help you by walking out to the road or to a nearby town and alerting the proper authorities for you. Depending on how popular your route is, you may have to wait a while for someone who might help you to come by. Because of this, it can be helpful to let a friend or family member know where you're hiking, when you should be back and what to do if you don't check in as scheduled. That way, if you're in distress on trail and can't call for help, you don't have to wait for someone to come by to help you.

GET HELP IMPROVING YOUR OUTDOOR SKILLS

Falling in love with exploring on foot means having a lifelong love affair with walking. Get familiar with the resources that can help you improve your skills. Here are a few of my favorites:

- Some of the best online walking and hiking tutorials you can find are through *Backpacker* magazine, which offers self-paced classes in things like navigation and wilderness first aid and publishes a lot of free online articles that can help you do everything from get in shape to build an emergency shelter.
- Local outdoor stores typically have a variety of free classes on things like map reading that are good for beginners.
- Joining a local hiking group, like the ones available on Meetup.com or through your local outdoor organization, can help you learn on trail and in the real world from people who are more experienced hikers than you.

MIND YOUR TRAIL MANNERS

The more you walk, the more you'll come to revere the land you're walking through. And that's a good thing, because walkers can leave quite an impact on a landscape. En masse, we're like a continuous drop of water that eventually creates a canyon, except our impact isn't nearly that scenic. Instead, it's quite ugly: erosion, trash (toilet paper on trail is the worst!), aggressive wildlife that learns to prefer human food—the list goes on.

Be a better kind of walker—this is a point of pride for most experienced walkers—by reducing your impact on the environment with the help of Leave No Trace (LNT) principles, a collection of best practices that was developed by the US Forest Service in the 1960s and has since become the worldwide standard for how to behave when you're in nature. The LNT principles can be summed up pretty easily: minimize your impact and leave things the same as (or better than) you found them.

MIND YOUR TRAIL MANNERS IN TOWN TOO

You'll get a much warmer reception from guesthouse owners, restaurateurs and shopkeepers if you're considerate with your walking gear when you're in town. Here are some things to remember:

- If requested, leave your day pack outside. (But be smart about where you leave it and keep an eye on it the whole time.)
- Be careful with your raingear—don't let it drip all over the floor. Instead, look for a coat hook and hang it up.
- Don't take your boots and socks off in establishments, especially bars or restaurants. It's a definite no-no to subject other people to your stinky feet, and in some cultures it's considered insulting.
- Don't track mud all over your accommodations' common areas or your room—remove your dirty shoes as soon as possible. Some places will make you leave them at the door.
- Don't dry wet clothes by draping them over wooden furniture—it can discolor the wood. Instead, use a laundry line and/or dry your clothes in the bathroom.
- When using public transportation, don't take up an extra seat with your day pack unless there is an abundance of open seats (and never make someone stand just so your bag can have a seat beside you). Instead, keep your pack on your lap.
- When you're in a store or restaurant, be conscientious of your day pack and its size, especially when you turn around or are in a tight space—you could easily knock something over. Have more control over your pack by wearing it on the front of your body.

My take on the list (below) includes the most important points.

Leave No Trace
- Know and obey the rules where you're going.
- Whenever possible, travel in small groups.
- Be considerate of others.
- Stick to the trail.
- Don't cut switchbacks.
- Close all gates behind you.
- Pack out all trash, including leftover food.
- If you have to go to the bathroom while you're on trail, walk off trail to where no one can see you, bury your waste in a cathole that's 6–8 inches (15–20 cm) deep and pack out your toilet paper (yes, you must) and any feminine hygiene products.
- Don't take elements of the natural world (for example, pretty rocks) with you.
- Watch wildlife from a distance—don't try to get close.
- Don't feed wild animals, including birds and squirrels.

5

PACK YOUR BAGS

It's time to embark on one of the most exciting parts of your preparations: figuring out what to take with you. While you won't need to worry about your pack weight and contents as much as if you were walking a village-to-village or hut-to-hut route, you'll be happiest if you put some real time and effort into this part of the process. In turn, we'll cover the packing elements that are most essential to a successful home base hiking trip: your trail clothes, trail shoes, day pack and day pack essentials.

TRAIL CLOTHES

When it comes to home base hiking, one of the best things you can do for yourself is pack good clothing—the right items, and high-quality ones at that. This isn't just important—it's essential if you want to enjoy your trip. After all, it's hard to have a good time on trail if you get caught in an intense rain shower without a rain jacket—or with a low-quality one that soaks you to the bone. But if you're properly attired for walking on trail, you'll pay no mind to challenging situations such as unexpectedly frosty mornings or muddy paths. The following sections describe the individual items you'll need for three-season walking in continental Europe, as well as provide suggestions for choosing the best options possible.

Socks: If you're trekking in low-top hiking shoes, ankle-height socks, such as quarter-height crew socks that hit just above the anklebone, save weight and space in your pack. Regardless of the height of your socks, merino wool socks that sport at least a medium cushion are your best bet. (I love Darn Tough socks, which have a lifetime guarantee.)

If you're blister prone, try wool toe socks like the ones offered by Injinji. Because the fabric goes in between each of your toes, kind of like gloves for your toes, they're a little awkward to put on and they look goofy, but they do their job extremely well—they completely eliminated all of my problems with toe blisters.

Underwear: Merino wool undies (trust me, they're way less scratchy than they sound) with flat-lock seams are the way to go—they're really comfortable, they resist odors and they dry more quickly than anything else on the market. They're expensive but worth it—you'll launder your undies more than any other piece of clothing, and low-quality ones tend to fall apart when you scrub them. If you can't wrap your mind around wool undies, ExOfficio also has some good synthetic travel underwear options. For women, I also recommend a quick-dry sports bra.

Walking pants: If you'll be walking on a brushy trail, long pants are a better option than shorts or capris because they guard your ankles and calves against scratches. Choose pants (or shorts or capris if weather and trail conditions permit) that are large and stretchy enough not to hinder your movement on trail—you should be able to easily climb onto a bench or rock. (Convertible long pants that zip off into shorts are a great single-item option for leg coverage in a wide range of weather conditions.) Choose a quick-dry fabric that's comfortable and has a durable water-repellent (DWR) coating—if there's a sprinkle, your pants are less likely to soak through.

My favorite trail base layer for cool weather is a black, merino wool, short-sleeve shirt and matching long underwear bottoms. (Photo by Carol Veach)

Short-sleeve shirt: The best base layer on trail is a short-sleeve shirt because, unlike a tank top, the fabric in the shoulders is wide enough to prevent chafing from backpack straps. And unlike a long-sleeve shirt, it's the layer you'll want to strip down to if it gets hot. I suggest merino wool because it's equally comfortable in the cold and in the heat. It's also odor resistant, so you can wear your shirt for multiple days without having to wash it because it's gotten stinky.

Long-sleeve full-zip shirt: For those chilly mornings or windy days, you'll need something to wear over your base layer; a

When it comes to clothing, fabric choice is incredibly important. It is the key determinant in guaranteeing that your clothes are lightweight, compact and functional. So what is the best fabric choice for a trail wardrobe?

Do: Use merino wool as your base fabric. As noted for many of the items listed in the Trail Clothes section, merino wool is generally light and thin, but it also keeps you warm even when it's wet, which is important if you sweat a lot or a surprise rain shower soaks you before you can put on your rain jacket. It also rolls easily for compact packability and doesn't wrinkle.

But the best property of wool is that it's antimicrobial. That means it resists bacteria, which is the culprit behind stinky clothes. Because of this, you can walk in your wool clothes for days on end without smelling like you've been on trail for a month. I use wool as my main fabric for traveling. Some good brands to choose from for outdoor-recreation-weight wool include Smartwool and Ibex.

Don't: Rely on performance fabrics. Modern-day performance fabrics like polyester blends start to smell almost as soon as you put them on—and they need to be washed thoroughly in a washing machine for the odors to go away. Even though they're marketed to runners and outdoor enthusiasts, they're practical only if you have a washing machine nearby. I use performance fabrics only for layers that don't get exposed to many body odors, such as walking pants rather than shirts.

merino wool long-sleeve top that zips up is perfect—it will give you a little more control over your temperature than a normal long-sleeve shirt because you can zip or unzip the shirt to your liking. Also, it's highly breathable and will keep you warm even if you're damp with rain or sweat.

Puffy vest: A vest is an amazing layer. It's versatile—you can wear it over everything from a short-sleeve shirt to a long-sleeve full-zip shirt. It'll give you some extra warmth (in your core, where you need it), and it'll add pockets to any outfit. Just make sure that the pockets secure with a zip or button (you can add these yourself) so you don't lose something. For the most warmth for the weight, choose a down vest; if the area you'll be visiting gets a lot of rain, choose a synthetic fill. And for the most outfit options, choose a relatively plain design and a neutral color that matches the rest of your trail wardrobe.

Puffy jacket: If you're traveling in summer, a light puffy jacket—sometimes marketed as a down or synthetic "sweater" because it's so lightweight—is your best bet for your warmest layer. If you're traveling in the shoulder seasons, look for something a little heavier; you might also consider a puffy with a hood for a built-in hat. Keep your eye out for a puffy that compresses into its own stuff sack or pocket, making it easy to pack.

Long-underwear bottoms: A good pair of long-underwear bottoms aren't just for wearing under your walking pants on cold days; they're also great as pajama pants, and women can wear them as leggings under a travel skirt or dress in town. Merino wool works best because it resists odors and will keep you warm even when it's wet; choose a versatile, neutral color like black that works well for layering and as part of a larger trail wardrobe.

Rain shell: If you're traveling in summer, a basic lightweight rain shell or waterproof windbreaker will be just fine; make sure it has a hood. If you're traveling in the shoulder seasons, look for something that can withstand more rain and wind. Good features for any season include armpit zippers, helpful for when you need some venting and rain protection at the same time, and adjustable elastic cord in the hood, wrists and waist, perfect for when the wind kicks up and you don't want excess fabric blowing in the breeze. If you bring a rain shell that you've used a lot at home, make sure to rewaterproof it—DWR coatings are only dependable for seven to ten rains before they need to be refreshed.

Thin gloves: It can get cold at higher elevations, and sprinkles happen even in summer, so keep a pair of lightweight gloves in your pack regardless of the season. Look for a pair with a DWR coating; merino wool will keep your fingers warm even if the gloves are wet.

Lightweight hat: For the same reason that lightweight gloves are a good idea, bring a thin hat for chilly mornings and evenings. Choose a fabric like merino wool that will let your skin breathe, and wash your hat often to avoid scalp breakouts.

TRAIL SHOES

Your shoes can make or break your walking trip. If you've ever suffered through ill-fitting shoes or blisters, you

---

DRESS FOR THE WEATHER

Stay warm: It's an old wives' tale that we lose a disproportionate amount of heat through our heads. We lose heat through any exposed skin, so if you're cold, cover everything up that you can, including fingers, neck and head—and layer up too.

Stay dry: If you're walking during the rainy season—or if you're going someplace where the weather could be dicey—pack rain pants and a heavier raincoat.

Stay cool: One of the ways your body gets hot is by absorbing heat from your environment, so if you're in a hot climate, reduce that absorption by covering up (as counterintuitive as it seems); to maximize coverage and minimize sun exposure, pack an ultralightweight long-sleeve base layer that has additional SPF applied to the fabric. Other ways to stay cool include wearing clothes that are light in color, loose-fitting and made of breathable fabrics: you should be able to hold your mouth up to the fabric and breathe through it. If you're walking when it's hot and sunny out, pack a sun hat.

know what I'm talking about. In my experience, the best shoes for home base hiking Europe, when you don't have the space and weight restrictions of thru-hiking a longer route, are lightweight, low-top hiking boots. If you have weak ankles or other body issues or plan to walk a more strenuous trail in adverse weather conditions, high-top hiking boots might work better for you because they offer more stability and support. Narrow down your choices and find what you like best at your local outdoor store.

What to Look for in Walking Shoes

When selecting walking shoes for home base hiking, keep these features in mind:

- Look for shoes that have a definite raised rubber pattern on the sole for the best grip. You don't want uniform and flat soles (like Keds).
- Choose only waterproof shoes to avoid wet feet on trail.
- Make sure the main material isn't porous or matte, like suede, otherwise you'll have a difficult time cleaning and/or waterproofing your shoes (leather works well, for shoes that are easy to wipe down on the go).
- Choose shoes that are as light as possible, to keep your load light and reduce strain on your knees.
- Select a high-quality brand for shoes that will last a long time; I like The North Face and Merrell.

If you plan on taking your time-tested and well-loved walking shoes or hiking boots to Europe, make sure to refresh the DWR coating before you leave for maximum protection against rain and puddles on trail.

If there's a chance you could encounter ice or snow on your walk (think shoulder seasons, alpine adventures or winter), be sure to pack traction devices such as Yaktrax.

EUROPEAN-STYLE WALKING SHOES

As an alternative to low-top hiking boots, I love European-style walking shoes, which have the traction, padding and waterproof qualities that you need for the trail without the very athletic look of hiking boots— or the weight: most walking shoes are incredibly light. My favorite thing about European-style walking shoes, though, is that they're not one-trick ponies, good only for the trail. They can also blend in with clothes you'd wear around town. European-style walking shoes can be found at stores like WalkingCo; brands that make them include Naturalizer, Aravon and Geox.

How to Get the Best Fit

When shopping for walking shoes, follow these tips to get a good fit:

- Try them on with the socks you'll wear on trail so you don't have any last-minute surprises such as extra room or too-tight shoes (both of which can cause blisters).
- Shop for shoes at the end of the day, when your feet are slightly swollen from standing and walking, to simulate how your shoes will fit on trail.
- Make sure there's plenty of room in the toe box to prevent your toes from hitting the front of your shoes when you walk downhill (this is a recipe for losing a toenail—or several).
- Make sure that your heels don't slip inside the shoes; friction causes blisters.

Give yourself plenty of time to break in your trail shoes and identify any hot spots. I like to wear mine every day in the month leading up to my trip; that way when I get to Europe, there are no shoe surprises.

DAY PACK

Of everything you pack for home base hiking Europe, one of the most important items is your day pack. It will contain all your necessities and be with you every mile you walk, so it needs to be comfortable. To maximize the functionality of your pack and its comfort, look for a day pack with the following features:

- A size of 20–35 liters

- A padded waistbelt to keep the weight of the pack on your hips instead of your shoulders
- Wide and comfortable shoulder straps
- A sternum strap to keep your shoulder straps from slipping down your shoulders while you walk
- Mesh next to your back to vent heat while you're walking, especially on challenging sections
- A lot of pockets and compartments to organize your gear, including a variety of external pockets for items you'll need to access frequently on trail
- Two side compartments to hold your water bottles
- A large waistbelt pocket to store your cell phone or camera
- A pack cover

Surprise sprinkles happen even in summer, so make sure you have a pack cover to keep your belongings dry. Some day packs come with a pack cover (check for a zippered compartment on the underside of the pack); for others, you'll need to buy a separate one. You can find a selection of generic pack covers at your favorite outdoor store.

DAY PACK ESSENTIALS

What you pack in your day pack is nearly as important as the pack you choose. When you home base hike Europe, you'll typically be relatively close to your village (or other ones in the region) and pass by multiple huts and cafés, so you can pack more lightly than you would on a day hike in North America. Here are the essentials to stow in your pack:

Trail navigation tools: Even if you use a GPS app on your phone to navigate on trail like I do (see Learn How to Hike with the Help of GPS Data in Chapter 4), always bring a paper map as a backup. You'll also need walking directions and a small compass. Other things to remember: Bring a power bank and an extra charging cord if you pack a stand-alone GPS unit or rely on a GPS app on your phone—following GPX tracks takes a lot of battery, and you'll likely go through more than one charge a day.

THE TEN ESSENTIALS

This section's packing list is based on The Mountaineers' Ten Essentials, although I've modified it to be more relevant to home base hiking Europe. Here's the original list of the Ten Essentials, for reference:

1. Navigation
2. Headlamp
3. Sun protection
4. First aid
5. Knife
6. Fire
7. Shelter
8. Extra food
9. Extra water
10. Extra clothes

Headlamp: A headlamp is a great addition to your trail gear, and not just as a survival tool. It's essential for sunrise or sunset hikes and can even allow you to read in bed without disturbing your partner. Start your trip with fresh batteries, or opt for a rechargeable model.

Sunglasses and sunscreen: Especially if you're walking in bright sunlight or on snow or a glacier, it's important to have sunglasses that block ultraviolet (UV) light. Don't forget to also bring a hard case for them so they don't break when tossed around in your day pack. Sunscreen is also vital; an SPF of at least 30 is the standard recommendation.

First-aid kit: Pack a small medical kit in case you cut your knee, turn your ankle, have an upset stomach, et cetera. The most common thing you'll probably need it for? Blister care. (See the "Treat Blisters" sidebar in Chapter 3.) In addition to carrying a first-aid kit, you should also know how to use its contents. Here are the specific items I recommend:

- Bandages
- Packaged cleanser such as alcohol wipes
- Blister-care items such as moleskin, collapsible scissors and a needle
- Ibuprofen (anti-inflammatory)
- Acetaminophen (analgesic)
- Anti-diarrheal pills
- Antacid pills
- Antibacterial cream
- Cortisone cream

Picnic tools: There are a lot of farm stands and wine vending machines on trail in Europe, so pack these basic picnic tools:

THE BEST WAY TO PACK A BACKPACK

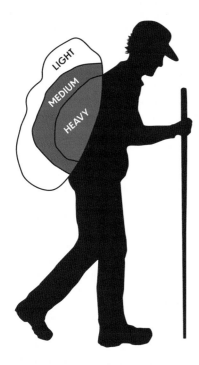

LIGHT

MEDIUM

HEAVY

- Pack heavy things next to your back and in the middle (core zone) of your backpack; place light things on top and down below.
- Pack big things first, then small things.
- Attach your trekking poles to the tool loops or lash-on points on the outside of your pack when you're not using them.
- If you're walking with someone else, store your trail essentials in the outside pockets of their pack—and have them do the same with yours— so it's easier to get to your things without taking off your pack.

- A small pocketknife (see the "Getting through Airport Security: Picnic Tools" sidebar in this section)
- Small travel flatware
- A small bottle of hand sanitizer
- 1-liter hydration bag to use as a wine bladder (see the "Wine Bladder" sidebar in this section)
- TSA-approved wine opener

Matches: In case of an emergency in which you get stuck sleeping outside, it's helpful to have a way to make a fire and stay warm. Your best option is to pack a normal book of safety matches (not "strike any-where" ones—they won't make it through airport security) or a lighter in your back-pack—this has to be in a carry-on, not in a

When you home base hike Europe, you can leave most of your essentials at your accommodations and hike with only a light day pack.

Make sure the travel flatware you pack is sturdy plastic instead of metal, and avoid anything that looks too much like a knife—sporks work great. Interestingly, pocketknives with blades shorter than 2 inches (5 cm) are typically allowed through security, but larger, duller knives you would use for eating are not. If you'd rather purchase an eating knife or pocketknife in Europe, you can buy them at most supermarkets or *tabacs* (tobacco stands that also carry incidentals like stamps and mobile phone rechargers). If you bring a wine opener on the plane, make sure it's TSA-approved (it should be called out in the product description) or it will likely be confiscated.

checked bag. If you'd rather purchase your matches or a lighter in Europe, you can do so at any *tabac* (tobacco stand).

Space blanket: In case you need to spend the night outside or you need to warm up—say you're extremely cold after getting drenched in a thunderstorm—you should carry an emergency space blanket in your pack.

Extra food: It's always smart to have some extra food on hand when you're walking. Since there are typically places to stop for lunch on trail, you should only need to pack snacks such as dried fruit, nuts and jerky, but check what's available on your specific routes to be sure.

Extra water: Whether you're walking in the heat or not, you'll need plenty of water (1–2 liters of water per person, depending on the heat) and something to put it in. The majority of trails in Europe have potable water, so you likely won't need to bring a water purification device.

Extra clothing: Always carry extra layers with you in case there's a sudden change in the weather.

Repair kit: A few simple tools can come in handy in case you need to repair something on trail, from a tear in your jacket to a broken strap on your backpack. Below are the specific items I recommend for a fix-it kit—you can fix pretty much anything with this lineup (plus the small pocketknife in your picnic tools):

- A few strips of duct tape
- A small sewing kit

Unless you're on an urban trail or you have a bladder of steel, you'll probably have to go to the bathroom while you're out on the trail. Please don't try to avoid it by drinking less water than your body needs! (I see this all the time with my female walking companions.) Instead, get comfortable with the idea of going to the bathroom while you're on trail (see Mind Your Trail Manners in Chapter 4 for tips). Once you do, you may find that it's kind of freeing and certainly much quicker (and more convenient) than finding an actual restroom.

- Safety pins
- Rubber bands
- Twist ties
- Superglue

Bug protection: Even if you're not anticipating a lot of bugs where you're going, pack a few insect repellent wipes just in case.

Bathroom kit: While many trails pass through towns and/or places like mountain huts that have restrooms, occasionally the timing won't line up and you may need to go to the bathroom on trail. To be prepared for that, pack a small amount of toilet paper, several quart-size bags to pack out your trash and a small plastic trowel in case you need to dig a cathole.

Trail comfort items: If you need braces or bands to support aching muscles and joints, or trekking poles for navigating

GETTING THROUGH AIRPORT SECURITY: TREKKING POLES

You can't fly with trekking poles in your carry-on because of their sharp tips. Either check them, buy them in Europe (and check them on the way home) or rent them in Europe, a service that's available at many outdoor retailers.

intense inclines and declines, make sure they're in your pack and that you know how to use them.

Cash: While many restaurants, wine bars and mountain huts accept credit cards, some don't, so always carry some cash with you, along with a card. Cash will also come in handy if you want to buy something from a farm stand.

WINE BLADDER

My favorite trail accessory of all time is a 1-liter hydration bag dedicated to carrying wine. Especially when I'm traveling in Italy or France (but honestly, wherever I go in Europe), I love finding local wine and carrying it with me for impromptu wine hours. Yes, it's extra weight, but it's totally worth it!

With a soft wine container, it's a lot easier to enjoy wine on the go because you don't have the weight (or breakability) of a glass bottle, and when you're not using the container, it folds up very compactly and weighs almost nothing. Look for a hydration bag with a screw-off top, not a drinking tube. You can drink the wine straight out of the hydration bag or pour it into cheap paper or plastic cups.

CHECKLISTS

Download and print your own checklists at exploreonfoot.com.

Trail Clothes

THE BASICS

- ☐ 2 pairs trail socks
- ☐ 4 pairs trail underwear
- ☐ 2 pairs walking pants, shorts or capris
- ☐ 2 short-sleeve trail shirts
- ☐ 1 long-sleeve full-zip trail shirt
- ☐ 1 puffy vest
- ☐ 1 puffy jacket
- ☐ 1 pair long-underwear bottoms
- ☐ 1 lightweight rain shell
- ☐ 1 pair thin gloves
- ☐ 1 lightweight hat

OPTIONS

- ☐ Sports bra
- ☐ Heavier puffy jacket
- ☐ Thicker socks
- ☐ Warmer hat
- ☐ Warmer gloves
- ☐ Long-sleeve long-underwear top
- ☐ Rain pants
- ☐ Heavier rain jacket
- ☐ Long-sleeve sun shirt
- ☐ Sun hat
- ☐ Swimsuit (and towel)

Trail Shoes

- ☐ Trail shoes
- ☐ Traction devices (optional)

Day Pack

- ☐ Day pack
- ☐ Pack cover

Day Pack Essentials

THE TEN ESSENTIALS

- ☐ Trail navigation tools (see separate list)
- ☐ Headlamp
- ☐ Sunglasses (and case) and sunscreen
- ☐ First-aid kit (see separate list)
- ☐ Small pocketknife (see Picnic Tools)
- ☐ Matches
- ☐ Space blanket
- ☐ Food—trail snacks
- ☐ Water (in water bottles or bladders)
- ☐ Extra clothing

TRAIL NAVIGATION TOOLS

- ☐ GPS app or stand-alone unit (optional) with power bank and charging cord
- ☐ Paper map
- ☐ Walking directions
- ☐ Small compass

FIRST-AID KIT

- ☐ Bandages
- ☐ Packaged cleanser such as alcohol wipes
- ☐ Blister-care items such as moleskin, collapsible scissors and a needle
- ☐ Ibuprofen (anti-inflammatory)
- ☐ Acetaminophen (analgesic)
- ☐ Anti-diarrheal pills
- ☐ Antacid pills
- ☐ Antibacterial cream
- ☐ Cortisone cream

PICNIC TOOLS

- ☐ Small pocketknife
- ☐ Small travel flatware
- ☐ Small bottle of hand sanitizer
- ☐ 1-liter hydration bag
- ☐ TSA-approved wine opener

REPAIR KIT

- ☐ Strips of duct tape
- ☐ Small sewing kit
- ☐ Safety pins
- ☐ Rubber bands
- ☐ Twist ties
- ☐ Superglue

BATHROOM KIT

- ☐ Toilet paper
- ☐ Quart-size bags
- ☐ Small plastic trowel

OTHER ITEMS

- ☐ Bug protection
- ☐ Trail comfort items (braces, bands, trekking poles)
- ☐ Cash

One of the highlights of my time researching for this book was a sunrise *via ferrata* at Grand Cir in the Dolomites (Destination 1).

MY FINAL WORDS OF WISDOM

This is the moment you've been looking forward to and preparing for. It's time for you to lace up your walking shoes, heft your day pack onto your shoulders and start your journey. It's finally time to home base hike Europe! I have some final tips for you on doing it well.

Take Breaks

When it comes to walking for several hours, the old adage usually applies: the tortoise is faster than the hare. So don't get caught up in walking as fast as you can and never take a break. You need to stop at regular intervals—at least once every 2 hours for 10 to 15 minutes at a minimum—to rest your body, stretch out any sore muscles, fuel up (even if you're not hungry), hydrate (even if you're not thirsty) and reapply sunscreen. And you should always stop if something hurts—this is the number one way to make sure that something small, like a hot spot on your foot, doesn't turn into something

big, like a blister that's so painful you can't keep walking. Put a warmer layer on when you take a break, especially in a windy spot or when you start down a big descent—it'll keep you from getting chilled.

Give Yourself Some Downtime Each Day

You'll have the best chance of making the most of the amazing opportunities you have on your trip if you give yourself some downtime each day. If you're anything like me, that's a hard task. When I travel, I tend to go, go, go because I don't want to miss out on anything. But traveling at that pace can catch up with you, and ultimately you crash—or you go home more exhausted than when you left.

The solution is to build some downtime into your travel routine. I take an hour or two of downtime each day post-hike. I have a little routine that includes showering, changing into clean clothes and then

---

Avoid running out of energy while you walk by consuming enough calories. How much is enough? Probably more than you think. According to *Backpacker* magazine, a 160-pound (72 kg) person walking for several hours with a backpack can burn more than 4,000 calories per day.

diving into some light reading while enjoying a glass of wine and a predinner snack. It's the perfect time for me to relax.

I highly recommend stretching during your downtime—it will help your body transition to a resting state and decrease any soreness you're feeling. You can also help your body recover by eating a snack well balanced with protein within 30 to 45 minutes of finishing your walk. Also drink 16 ounces (half a liter) of water per hour for the next 2 or 3 hours.

Your downtime is also perfect for something else: taking a break from your adventure companion. No matter how much you love this person and being around them, it's smart to take some time apart each day, even if you don't think you need it. Take it from someone who's been there—your chances of a drama-free trip are much higher if you're proactive, rather than reactive, about your time apart.

One of the best ways to combat soreness and muscle fatigue is to get a good night's sleep. If you want to feel your best, don't settle for your normal 7 hours of sleep—give yourself at least 8 or 9 hours to recharge. Trust me, you'll feel much better in the morning.

Be a Visitor Rather Than a Tourist

Even with downtime and a good night's sleep, you'll still have hours and hours each day to explore Europe on foot, both on trail and in town. Not only do you have time, you also have sheer opportunity: you're off the beaten path, deep in the heart of a place where you'll find real locals, not hordes of tourists. Don't pass this by. Make the most of this opportunity by approaching your travels not as a tourist—someone who comes into a community, looks around, takes a few pictures and then moves on—but, rather, as a visitor, someone who's there to actively learn about and participate in a different way of life. Don't just admire local cuisine—learn how to make it. Rather than just sit in a pub as people blow off steam after work, join in the conversation with your fledgling language skills. These are the moments you'll always remember.

I like to take classes when I travel, and one of the best classes I've ever taken was a half-day language, cooking and culture class in Marrakesh, Morocco. In the span of only a few hours, I learned a handful of Arabic words and nonverbal gestures, cooked my own *tajine* (the most famous of Moroccan dishes) and had tea with a local. This class also gave me the opportunity to ask all of the questions I had about Morocco. It was a great experience, one that deepened my understanding of the local culture. You can find these kinds of experiences in Europe as well.

Allow Your Travels to Change You

Even if you take in those memorable times and truly savor them, you still won't get the most out of your travels until you allow them to change you. And for that change to happen, you need to be prepared to ask some big questions about the culture you're experiencing and how it applies to your own life.

Exploring on foot is perfectly suited to this exercise because there's no better time to ponder than when you're walking for hours at a time. As your feet methodically hit the trail, something magical happens to your brain. Even things you've been wrestling with for a while can suddenly become clear. It's no surprise to me that some of the greatest thinkers of all time were walkers. Put your walking mind to work by letting it chew on questions like these:

- *What do these people do better than me?* For instance, cook, make time for their family, et cetera.
- *What do they have that I want?* Maybe it's more time off or a stronger sense of community.
- *What can our differences teach me?* Perhaps to be slower to judge, to be more accepting of other people, and so on.
- *What steps could I take to bring that value, skill, trait or lesson into my own life?* Don't forget to ask yourself this perhaps most important question of all.

Don't Get Sad, Get Planning

Eventually the day arrives when thoughts will come crashing into your consciousness about your flight home, what's going on at work and how much you'll need to catch up on. That's when you'll know your trip is almost over.

The prospect of heading home to real life after such a memorable travel experience—the highs, the lows, the crazy adventures, the magic of it all—can be daunting, especially if your world was rocked by falling in love with home base hiking Europe. It was certainly daunting for me—until I learned a secret: the best cure for post-trip sadness is to start dreaming about another trip.

And don't wait until you're home to start planning, because the perfect time to set yourself up for future travels is while you're still in Europe. You're surrounded by Europeans and well-traveled fellow walkers who can help you build your bucket list. Ask them where they've walked and what trails they recommend. This is a great way to get insider information on trails that you might otherwise never hear about in North America. Write these ideas down.

While you're at it, jot down notes on things you want to remember for next time. I debrief after every trip, which is why my method, my gear and my experience get better every time I explore on

---

One of my very favorite souvenirs is a new custom or attitude. From Italy, I brought home a love of long, lingering meals. From France, it was a greater reverence for history. And from Germany, it was a whole new appreciation for being on time. Wherever you travel, think about something the local culture does well that you'd like to bring home—it will probably be your longest-lasting souvenir of all.

There are many moments for contemplation—and seeing your life from a different perspective—when you're hiking.

foot. It can be the same for you—ask yourself these questions:

- *What was I super happy about on this trip?*
- *What would I do differently next time?*
- *Are there any gear changes I want to make in the future?*

As you head home, take heart: If you're anything like me, you'll find a way to make the next trip happen—and the next. There are so many amazing spots in Europe that are just waiting to be hiked. I hope you keep lacing up your boots—and that you continue to find inspiration and discover new tools in this book as your European hiking explorations evolve. Thank you for inviting me to be part of your journey; it is an honor, and I can't wait until we connect again, whether we meet in person at an author event or virtually in another of my books. Until then, happy trails!

ACKNOWLEDGMENTS

If I would have known how difficult it would be to find the time to research and write this book at this stage in my life—being the primary caregiver of two active toddlers—I'm not sure I would have been brave enough to attempt it. As it was, I was so excited about the concept and finally being able to travel again after being cooped up during the pandemic that I ignored all of the funny looks and side-eyes from people who *could* very well imagine what traveling for three months with kids—while working—would look like, and I blazed ahead making *Home Base Hiking Europe* a reality.

More than anyone else, my husband, Mac, and my girls, June and Ginger, deserve a huge thank you for joining me on the crazy ride that was our three-month research trip. It was the best of times and the worst of times for our family. Mac and I carried the girls on our backs for nearly every hike in this book. And after our adventure was done each day, exhausted Mac would log on to his work and be on client calls until the early hours of the morning. It was hard, but there were such sweet moments to remember too: watching the girls play with kids from all over the world at the playgrounds we visited, seeing June try—and love—my own favorite food, *wienerschnitzel*, and watching Ginger discover gondolas and ask for them over and over again. Thank you, family, for helping me make my dreams come true.

We had several friends and family members who joined us during our travels: Peter and Meredith Wright (and kids); Rich and Carol Veach; Linda Mendoza; Meghan, Emmit and Eulabee French; Caroline Calaway and Graham Golbuff; Eli and Gwen Langi. Your presence made the trip so much more fun, and your help with the girls was beyond appreciated.

Thank you to my team at Mountaineers Books for being a great partner in producing this book: Kate Rogers, Mary Metz, Janet Kimball, Erin Cusick, Amelia von Wolffersdorff, Bart Wright, Laura Case Larson and Susan Elderkin. From catching spelling errors to reorganizing sections, your mark is on this book, and it's so much better because of you.

Finally, to my friend and mentor Rick Steves—you have been such an encouragement to me. I'm so grateful for the platform you've given me to teach people about hiking in Europe, from lecturing at your travel center to doing radio interviews together to filming our *Rick Steves' Europe* episode in the French Alps. When I told you this book was becoming a reality, you even offered to write the foreword for it. Thank you for believing in me and the concept of exploring Europe on foot, and I can't wait for our next hike.

ONLINE RESOURCES

1 THE DOLOMITES, ITALY

Tourism information: www.valgardena.it/en
Val Gardena Active program; partner accommodations: www.valgardena-active.com/en
Lift timetables: www.valgardena.it/en/summer-holidays-dolomites/lifts/

1A: Sassolungo Loop

Rifugio Emilio Comici: www.rifugiocomici.com/en/
Passo Sella Dolomiti Mountain Resort: www.passosella-resort.com/en/
Rifugio Toni Demetz: https://tonidemetz.it/en/index.php
Rifugio Vicenza: www.rifugiovicenza.com/en/

1B: Sëurasas Loop

Baita Sëurasas: https://seurasas.it/en/welcome/
Moon & Honey Travel hike extension to Monte Pic and the Seceda Ridgeline: www.moonhoneytravel.com/monte-pic-hike-val-gardena-dolomites/

1C: Alpe di Siusi Loop

Almgasthof Mont Sëuc: www.montseuc.it/en/
Contrin hut: www.malgacontrin.it/en/
Malga Sanon hut: https://sanon.it
Sporthotel Sonne: www.sporthotelsonne.com/en/
Schgaguler Schwaige hut: www.schgagulerschwaige.com/en/

1D: Croda da Lago Loop

Transportation from Santa Cristina to Cortina: www.sad.it
Taxi Cortina: www.taxicortina.com/en/jeep-service-for-dinners-at-mountain-refuges-2/
Grand Hotel Cristallo: www.dolomiti.org/en/cortina/accommodation/hotel/cristallo-hotel-spa-e-golf-eng/
Ristorante Al Camin: www.ristorantealcamin.it
Museo all'aperto delle 5 Torri: https://cortinadelicious.it/EN/p56-Open-air-Museum-of-the-5-Torri
Tourism information for Cortina: www.dolomiti.org/en/cortina/

DolomitiBus: https://dolomitibus.it
Overview hiking map of the Cortina area: www.dolomiti.org/en/cortina/downloads
Berghotel Passo Giau: www.passogiau.it/en/
Rifugio Croda da Lago / Gianni Palmieri: www.crodadalago.it/en/

2 THE SOMME, FRANCE

Tourism information for the Somme: www.visit-somme.com
The Battle of the Somme and the memorials: www.calameo.com/books/000111526c22ab051d2a3
Brigitte De Cuyper, Somme battlefield guide: gitou63@gmail.com and www.visit-somme.com/guide-brigitte-de-cuyper/mailly-maillet/ascpic080v50o5dp
Carl Ooghe, Somme battlefield bike guide: https://cyclingthewesternfront.co.uk/tours.html
The Tiny Train of the Upper Somme: www.petittrainhautesomme.fr/all-you-need-to-know-about-us/

2A: Thiepval Memorial Loop

Reservations for Auberge de la Vallée d'Ancre: bourgognedenis@gmail.com and www.visit-somme.com/auberge-de-la-vallee-dancre/authuille/respic0800040027
Thiepval Memorial: www.cwgc.org/visit-us/find-cemeteries-memorials/cemetery-details/80800/thiepval-memorial/
Le Cottage Geneviève et Auguste tearoom: www.le-cottage-thiepval.com

2C: Newfoundland Memorial Loop

Avril Williams "Ocean Villas" Guesthouse and Tea Room: www.avrilwilliams.eu
Beaumont-Hamel Newfoundland Memorial: www.veterans.gc.ca/eng/remembrance/memorials/Beaumont-Hamel

2D: Saint-Valery-sur-Somme Coastal Loop

Tourism information for Saint-Valery-sur-Somme: www.tourisme-baiedesomme.fr/en/

For all but two of my recommended routes, I give you access to my personal GPX tracks, which can be downloaded for free from the Resources section of my website, exploreonfoot.com (password: Love2HomeBaseHike!). (The GPX tracks for those other two routes, in Costa Brava, are protected by the Camí de Ronda® company, which sells them on their website. See the Costa Brava entry here in the Online Resources section.)

These free GPX tracks are one of the most valuable parts of this book, and they'll greatly increase your confidence in navigating each route. I have made every attempt to share accurate, up-to-date GPX tracks and walking directions with you. That said, trail closures and reroutes occasionally happen. Always carry a paper map of the area as a backup, which can help you troubleshoot the route if needed. Each hike write-up includes information on where to find a local map, whether that's online or at a local shop or tourist information office.

See also the Learn How to Hike with the Help of GPS Data section in Chapter 4 for more information on how to navigate with GPX tracks and specific GPS coordinates.

Crossing the Bay of the Somme with a guide:
www.visit-somme.com/somme-bay/crossing-bay-fascinating-guides

Herbarium Fruticetum Baie de Somme:
www.facebook.com/people/Herbarium-Fruticetum-Baie-de-Somme/100057112105213/

3 COSTA BRAVA, SPAIN

Tourism information for Calella de Palafrugell:
https://visitpalafrugell.cat/en/calella/

Sarfa bus from Barcelona to Palafrugell:
www.compras.moventis.es/online/

Corredor Mató Villas: www.corredormato.com/en/

Gran Fondo bike shop: www.granfondocommunity.com/en/

Cycle Tours Catalonia: www.cycletourscatalonia.com/touring-bike-tours/

Tourist Service kayak tours and rentals:
www.touristservice.es/en

Camí de Ronda® company: www.camideronda.com/en/home.html

3A: Palamós to Calella de Palafrugell

Cap Roig Botanical Gardens:
https://fundacionlacaixa.org/es/jardines-cap-roig-reservas

Tourist bus from Cap Roig Botanical Gardens to Calella: https://visitpalafrugell.cat/en/julivia-tourist-bus/

Museu de la Pesca (the Fishing Museum):
http://museudelapesca.org

Hotel Sant Roc: www.santroc.com/en

3B: Calella de Palafrugell to Tamariu

Far NOMO Japanese restaurant: https://gruponomo.com/en/restaurantes/far-nomo/

El Far Hotel-Restaurant: www.hotelelfar.com/en/

3C: Pals to La Bisbal d'Empordà

Restaurant Bonay: www.restaurantbonay.com

3D: Portlligat to the Cap de Creus Lighthouse

Conditions report for Cap de Creus Natural Park:
https://interior.gencat.cat/ca/arees_dactuacio/agents-rurals/pla-alfa/

Salvador Dalí House: www.salvador-dali.org/en/

Trails in Cap de Creus Natural Park:
https://parcsnaturals.gencat.cat/ca/xarxa-de-parcs/cap-creus/el-parc/mapa-del-parc/

Restaurant Bar Sa Freu: restaurantbarsafreu.com

Restaurant Cap de Creus: restaurantcapdecreus.com

4 PROVENCE, FRANCE

Tourism information for Gordes and the surrounding villages: https://uk.destinationluberon.com

Les Caves du Palais Saint-Firmin: caves-saint-firmin.com

Les Oreilles du Luberon donkey tours:
www.oreilles-luberon.fr

4A: Luberon Countryside Bike Loop

Electric Move bike rentals: https://electricmove.fr

4B: Le Village des Bories and Abbaye Notre-Dame de Sénanque

Le Village des Bories:
https://en.levillagedesbories.com

Abbaye Notre-Dame de Sénanque:
www.senanque.fr/en/

4C: Gordes–Joucas–Roussillon

Domaine Girod: https://domainegirod.com/en/

Ecomuseum of Ochre: https://okhra.com/en/
accueil-english/

Le Sentier des Ocres: https://en.luberon-apt.fr/
the-ochre-trail-roussillon

4D: Calanques National Park

Parking Relais des Gorguettes park and ride:
www.ot-cassis.com/en/relais-des-gorguettes
-car-park.html

Trail map of Calanques National Park:
https://calanques-parcnational.fr/en/
getting-here-cassis

5 LAKE BOHINJ, SLOVENIA

Tourism information for Lake Bohinj:
www.bohinj.si/en/

Public transportation information for Lake Bohinj:
www.bohinj.si/en/information/how-to-get
-around/

Sidarta hiking maps of Bohinj: www.sidarta.si/en/
product/bohinj-125-000_en/

5A: Lake Bohinj and Savica Waterfall Loop

Ferry from Ukanc to Ribčev Laz: www.bohinj.si/en/
panoramic-boat/

LoopTeam Paragliding: www.looptandem
-paragliding.com/en/

Restaurant Ukanc: www.restavracija-ukanc.com/en/
restaurant/

5B: Mount Šija and Mount Vogel Summits

Vogel Ski Center and cable car:
www.vogel.si/summer

5C: Mostnica Gorge, Voje Valley and Mostnica Waterfall Loop

Alpine Dairy Museum: www.bohinj.si/en/museums/
alpine-dairy-museum/

Planinska koča na Vojah (Voje mountain hut):
www.pzs.si/koce.php?pid=194

Okrepčevalnica Slap Voje (Voje Waterfall Snack Bar): www.facebook.com/SlapVoje/

5D: Seven Lakes Valley Loop

Koča pri Triglavskih Jezerih mountain hut:
www.pd-ljmatica.si/koce/sedmera/

Information on the bus to Planina Blato (updated seasonally): https://promet.bohinj.si/en/
organised-transport/

Koča na Planina pri Jezeru mountain hut:
www.pdlpp.si/en/

Bregarjevo Zavetišče na Planini Viševnik mountain hut: www.pzs.si/koce.php?pid=216

6 THE JUNGFRAU, SWITZERLAND

Tourism information for Wengen: https://wengen
.swiss/en/summer/

Timetable for Swiss trains, buses and cable cars:
www.sbb.ch/en/timetable.html

Parking Lauterbrunnen rates and reservations:
www.jungfrau.ch/en-gb/parking/

Lauterbrunnen railway station: www.jungfrau.ch/
en-gb/arrival-at-station-car-parks/lauterbrunnen
-railway-station/

Webcams for the Jungfrau region: www.jungfrau
.ch/de-ch/live/webcams/

Paragliding in Interlaken: www.interlaken.ch/
en/experiences/sport-adventure/
experiences-in-the-air/paragliding

6A: Männlichen to Wengernalp

Berghaus Männlichen: www.berghaus
-maennlichen.ch/en/

Berghaus Grindelwaldblick:
www.grindelwaldblick.ch

Hotel Jungfrau Wengernalp:
https://wengernalp.ch

6B: Schynige Platte Loop

Berghotel Schynige Platte:
https://en.hotelschynigeplatte.ch

6C: The Eiger Trail

Printable map of the Eiger Trail:
www.myswitzerland.com/en-us/experiences/
route/eiger-trail-the-swiss-alpine-experience
-trail/
Berghaus Alpiglen: https://alpiglen.ch

6D: Grosse Scheidegg to Waldspitz

Berghotel Grosse Scheidegg:
www.grosse-scheidegg.ch/150
Genepi Hütte: https://berggasthausfirst.ch/en/
genepi-ski-hut/
Berggasthaus First: https://berggasthausfirst.ch/en/
Gasthaus Waldspitz: https://gasthaus-waldspitz.ch/
index.php/Home_en

7 THE PIEDMONT, ITALY

Tourism information for La Morra:
www.lamorraturismo.it/en/
EASYTORINO: www.easytorino.com
Trekking in Langa: www.trekkinginlanga.com
Castle of Serralunga d'Alba:
www.castellodiserralunga.it/en/visite.php

7A: Footpath of Sant'Anna

Le Bancarelle di Elisa: https://lebancarelledielisa.it
Agricola Brandini: www.agricolabrandini.it/en/
Azienda Agricola Voerzio Alberto: voerzioalberto
.com

7B: La Morra Vineyard Loop

Cantina Comunale di La Morra:
www.cantinadilamorra.com
Museo Ratti: www.ratti.com/en/museum-and
-culture/visits-to-the-museum/
Osteria Veglio: www.osteriaveglio.it
Cantina Fratelli Ferrero: www.baroloferrero.com
L'Osteria del Vignaiolo: osteriadelvignaiolo.it
Big Bench Community Project passport:
https://bigbenchcommunityproject.org/
en/bbcp-passports-stamps

7C: Barolo Loop

Cappella delle Brunate: www.atlasobscura.com/
places/cappella-del-brunate-barolo-chapel
Le Bancarelle di Elisa: https://lebancarelledielisa.it
Novello Cantina Comunale:
www.nascettadinovello.com/en/

Wine Museum of Barolo: www.wimubarolo.it/en/
Enoteca Regional del Barolo:
www.enotecadelbarolo.it

7D: Turin Like a Local

Tourism information for Turin:
www.turismotorino.org/en
Società Cooperativa Theatrum Sabaudiae Torino:
www.arteintorino.com/english-version.html
Caffè Al Bicerin: https://bicerin.it/en/home-english/
Borgo Medievale: www.borgomedievaletorino.it/en/
home-en/
Imbarchino del Valentino:
www.imbarchino.space/eng

8 DALMATIA, CROATIA

Tourism information for Split: https://visitsplit.
com/en
Split guide Ivica Profaca: https://split-guide.com

8A: Marjan Hill Loop

Split Zoo: www.facebook.com/ZooloskiSplit

8B: Hvar Island Coastal Walk

**Overview of the catamarans to Hvar Island and
Hvar Town bus timetables:** https://visithvar.hr/
visit-hvar/how-to-reach-hvar/
TP Line: www.tp-line.hr
Jadrolinija: www.jadrolinija.hr/en
Krilo Shipping Company: https://krilo.hr
Bus company servicing Hvar (email inquiries):
cazmatrans.otok.hvar@st.t-com.hr

8C: Mount Mosor Loop

Umberto Girometta mountain hut: www.hpd
-mosor.hr/index.php?option=com_
content&view=article&id=48&Itemid=59
Promet bus company: https://promet-split.hr/en/
Map of Mount Mosor: www.iglusport.hr/
katalog/63GSS%20MOSOR/HGSS-MOSOR

8D: Skradinski Buk

Krka National Park: www.npkrka.hr/en_US/
Bibich Winery:
https://bibich.superbexperience.com
Maps of the trails in Krka National Park:
www.npkrka.hr/en_US/posjeti/karte-i-brosure/

9 BERCHTESGADEN NATIONAL PARK, GERMANY

Tourism information for Berchtesgaden National Park: https://nationalpark-berchtesgaden.de/english/index.htm

Tourism information for the town of Berchtesgaden, including music and events: www.berchtesgaden.de/en/home

Berchtesgaden Guest Card, RufBus and local transportation information: www.berchtesgaden.de/en/general-information/guest-card

Train and bus timetables for the Berchtesgaden area: www.bahn.de

Salzbergwerk Berchtesgaden: www.salzbergwerk.de/en

Watzmann Thermal Baths: www.berchtesgaden.de/en/top-experiences/watzmann-therme

Hitler's Eagle's Nest: www.kehlsteinhaus.de/english/

9A: Mount Jenner

Jennerbahn (Jenner gondola): www.jennerbahn.de

Tickets for the Lake Königssee boat: www.seenschifffahrt.de/en/koenigssee/

Mitterkaseralm mountain hut: www.mitterkaser.de

Dr. Hugo Beck Haus: https://hugobeckhaus.jimdosite.com

9B: Soleleitungsweg Ramsau

Berggasthaus Zipfhäusl: https://zipfhausl.de

Berggasthof Gerstreit: https://berggasthof-gerstreit.de

Berggaststätte Söldenköpfl: www.berggaststaette-soeldenkoepfl.de

9C: The Hintersee and the Zauberwald

Alpenhof am Hintersee: www.alpenhof-hintersee.de

9D: Kneifelspitze Loop

Berggaststätte Kneifelspitze: https://kneifelspitze-berchtesgaden.de

Gasthaus-Hotel Maria Gern: mariagern.de

10 THE WACHAU VALLEY, AUSTRIA

Tourism information for the Wachau: www.donau.com/en

Tourism information for Dürnstein: www.duernstein.at/en/

Seasonal *heuriger* calendar: www.donau.com/en/the-danube-in-lower-austria/eating-drinking/enjoying-experiencing-wine/online-heuriger-calendar/

Digital vignettes for driving in Austria: www.asfinag.at/en/toll/vignette/digital-vignette/

Melk Abbey: www.stiftmelk.at/en/

Göttweig Abbey: www.stiftgoettweig.at

Aggstein Castle: ruineaggstein.at/en/

10A: Krems to Dürnstein

Wachau World Heritage Trail information: www.donau.com/en/wachau-nibelungengau-kremstal/outings-activities/exercise/wachau-world-heritage-trail/

10B: Dürnstein to Weissenkirchen

Fesslhütte: www.fesslhuette.at

Gartenhotel und Weingut Pfeffel: www.pfeffel.at/en/home/

Wachau World Heritage Trail information: www.donau.com/en/wachau-nibelungengau-kremstal/outings-activities/exercise/wachau-world-heritage-trail/

Weingut Pomassl: www.herbstzauber.at

Weingut-Heuriger Hermenegild Mang: www.weingut-hermenegild-mang.at

10C: Emmersdorf Loop

Gasthaus Langthaler: gasthaus-langthaler.at/de/index.php

Naturpark Gasthaus am Jauerling hut: www.naturpark-gasthaus.at

Jauerling-Wachau Nature Park: www.naturpark-jauerling.at/en

Wachauer Eselabenteuer: esel.anita@gmail.com or www.eselabenteuer.com

10D: Danube South Bank Bike Ride

Regiothek Wachau bike rentals: wachaubike.at/rent-a-wachau-bike/

nextbike bike rentals: www.nextbike.at/en/niederoesterreich/

DDSG Blue Danube tickets and information: https://ddsg-blue-danube.at/?lang=en

Ferry from Rossatz to Dürnstein: https://faehre-wachau.at/ferry-boat/

Hinterhaus ruins: www.ruinehinterhaus.at

INDEX

About the Author

Cassandra Overby grew up hiking and camping in the beautiful Pacific Northwest. She started adventuring internationally in college, when study abroad programs in Germany and Austria got her firmly hooked on travel. Her adventures have taken her all over the world, from Central America to Southeast Asia, but she loves exploring Europe more than anywhere else.

Both hiking and traveling continue to shape her life—and her career. As part of her travel company, Explore on Foot, Cassandra regularly gives talks and teaches classes on how to explore Europe on foot. She also offers travel consultations for people who'd like some help putting together their dream trip. Learn more about Explore on Foot at exploreonfoot.com.

Other books by Cassandra include:

- *Explore Europe on Foot: Your Complete Guide to Planning a Cultural Hiking Adventure*
- *Explore France's Alsace Wine Route on Foot*
- *Explore Germany's King Ludwig's Way on Foot*
- *Explore France's GR 34 on Foot*

 exploreonfoot.com   facebook.com/exploreonfoot

YOU MAY ALSO LIKE:

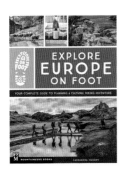

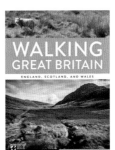
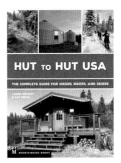

What are you waiting for? Your European hiking adventure awaits.